Geoff Tibballs is the author of the bestselling *The Mammoth Book of Jokes* and *The Mammoth Book of Dirty Jokes* as well as many other books, including *Business' Blunders* and *Legal Blunders*. A former journalist and press officer, he is now a full-time writer who lists his hobbies as sport, eating, drinking and avoiding housework. He lives in Nottingham, England.

The Mammoth Book of

More Dirty, Sick, X-Rated and Politically Incorrect Jokes

Geoff Tibballs

RUNNING PRESS
PHILADELPHIA · LONDON

Constable & Robinson Ltd.
55–56 Russell Square
London WC1B 4HP
www.constablerobinson.com

First published in the UK by Robinson,
an imprint of Constable & Robinson Ltd, 2013

A copy of the British Library Cataloguing in Publication
Data is available from the British Library

UK ISBN: 978-1-78033-801-9 (paperback)
UK ISBN: 978-1-78033-802-6 (ebook)

1 3 5 7 9 10 8 6 4 2

First published in the United States in 2013 by Running Press Book Publishers,
A Member of the Perseus Books Group

Books published by Running Press are available at special discounts for bulk purchases in the United
States by corporations, institutions, and other organizations. For more information, please contact the
Special Markets Department at the Perseus Books Group, 2300 Chestnut Street, Suite 200, Philadelphia,
PA 19103, or call (800) 810-4145, ext. 5000, or e-mail special.markets@perseusbooks.com.

US ISBN: 978-0-7624-4945-3
US Library of Congress Control Number: 2013939942

9 8 7 6 5 4 3 2 1
Digit on the right indicates the number of this printing

Running Press Book Publishers
2300 Chestnut Street
Philadelphia, PA 19103-4371

Visit us on the web!
www.runningpress.com

Printed and bound by CPI Group (UK) Ltd, Croydon, CR0 4YY

CONTENTS

INTRODUCTION

Welcome to the second volume of *The Mammoth Book of Dirty, Sick, X-Rated and Politically Incorrect Jokes*, and if you happen to be offended by any of the material in this book can I just say: why the hell did you buy/borrow/steal it? After all, when it comes to the content surely the clue is in the title!

Since the first volume was published in 2005, the thought police have become more active than ever, seemingly intent on creating a joyless world where every prospective joke has to be vetted by a committee composed of Jehovah's Witnesses, social workers and direct descendants of Oliver Cromwell. Some topics are rightly taboo but often the best way to deal with adversity is to laugh at it. I bet there were some cracking Black Death jokes doing the rounds in the fourteenth century, and would Hitler have been able to wreak such havoc in the Western world if the crowds at the Nuremberg Rally had simply burst out laughing at everything he said? The trouble with today's self-appointed moral guardians is that they see offence everywhere. Soon the only joke permitted for public consumption will be the one about the chicken crossing the road – provided, of course, that it does not imply criminal neglect by the National Farmers' Union for allowing domestic fowl to wander unsupervised on the highway or, indeed, that the repeated interrogation of the bird regarding its motive for crossing the aforementioned road does not amount to an infringement of its statutory rights.

So my advice is: enjoy this book while it is still legal.

In the hope that my mentioning their names will not result in their receiving abusive mail from gingers, nuns, nymphomaniacs, Mexicans, lepers, necrophiliacs, sailors, dwarfs, virgins, bankers, wankers, inflatable dolls or any of the other "victims" of jokes in this book, I would like to thank Duncan Proudfoot, my editor at Constable & Robinson, and Howard Watson, copy editor.

Geoff Tibballs

Accidents

Two police officers knocked on the door of a man's house. "Is this your wife?" they asked, holding up a photo.

"Yes," replied the man.

"I'm afraid it looks like she's been hit by a bus," they said.

"Well, yes," said the man, "but she's got a lovely personality."

A young man was showing off his new car to his girlfriend. As he put it through its paces on country roads, he turned to her and said: "If I do 100 mph, will you take all your clothes off?" She said it sounded like fun and so he stepped on the gas. When the speedo touched 100, she began to strip off, but, distracted by her state of undress, he took his eyes off the road for a second and crashed the car into a hedge. The girl was thrown clear, unhurt, but all her clothes were trapped in the car along with her boyfriend.

"Go and fetch help," he yelled.

"I can't," she replied. "I'm stark naked."

Noticing that one of his shoes had also been thrown clear, he pointed to it and said: "Cover your crotch with that and go and fetch help. Please!"

So she picked up the shoe, covered herself with it and ran half a mile to the nearest gas station. "Help me, please!" she cried to the elderly attendant. "My boyfriend's stuck!"

The attendant glanced down at the shoe covering her crotch and said: "I'm sorry, miss. He's too far in."

Did you hear about the man who accidentally swallowed some Lego? – The doctors aren't too worried, but he's shitting bricks.

Two guys were sitting at a bar. One said: "My girlfriend's really upset because the day before her birthday she lost her legs in a car crash."

"That's terrible," said his friend.

"But what about me?" asked the first guy. "I've bought her a pair of jeans and I can't find the receipt!"

We taunt our next-door neighbour by calling him Mr Burns, not because he's old and looks like *The Simpsons* character, but because he was involved in a horrific house fire.

One day a farmer's son was out ploughing the field when a terrible accident happened and he lost his right eye. The old farmer was too poor to buy his son a glass eye, so instead he made one out of finely polished oak wood, and hand-painted it.

It was many months before the son was brave enough to venture out in public with his false eye, but eventually he felt sufficiently confident to buy a ticket for a square dance that the farmers had organized for their sons and daughters. That night the boy got dressed up in his best clothes and headed off to the dance, but once there all the girls steered well clear of him and he ended up spending the entire evening alone in a corner.

Then, just as the DJ announced the last dance of the evening, the farmer's son spotted a girl in another corner who had a harelip. He thought to himself: "There's a girl who would understand me." So, throwing caution to the wind, he walked over to her.

"Would you like to dance?" he asked.

The girl replied: "Would I!"

The boy shouted: "Hey, I didn't call you cuntface, did I?"

A man was walking along the street when he bumped into his old friend Larry.

"Hi, Larry," he said.

"Don't ever call me Larry again. From now on you call me Lucky Larry!"

"Why? What happened?"

"Well, I was walking past this house the other day when a piano that was being hoisted up to the third floor came loose from its rope and came crashing down right behind me. A split second earlier, and I"d have been mashed to hamburger. So you call me Lucky Larry."

The following week, the man bumped into him again and called out: "Hi, Lucky Larry."

"Don't ever call me Lucky Larry again. From now on you call me Lucky Lucky Larry!"

"How come?"

"Well, I was crossing the street yesterday when this jerk in a truck came screeching round the corner through a red light and shot right in front of me. A split second later, and I"d have been mashed to hamburger. So you call me Lucky Lucky Larry."

The next week, the man saw him again and greeted him: "Hi, Lucky Lucky Larry."

"Don't ever call me Lucky Lucky Larry again. From now on you call me Lucky Lucky Lucky Larry!"

"Tell me about it."

"Well, last night I was getting it on with this woman in her apartment. We were on the sofa in her living room when suddenly this huge glass chandelier fell down from the ceiling and hit me right in the butt. I had to go to hospital to have half a dozen stitches."

"Hang on, you want me to call you Lucky Lucky Lucky Larry because you had to have half a dozen stitches in your butt?"

"Yeah, because if that chandelier had fallen a couple of minutes earlier, it would have busted my head!"

Did you hear about the man who ended up in hospital after getting a vacuum-cleaner hose stuck up his ass? – Doctors say he's now picking up nicely.

A police officer was called to the scene of a road accident where a driver had run over a morbidly obese American. The officer told the driver: "I have a witness who says the victim stepped slowly out into the road giving you plenty of time to avoid him, yet you ran him straight over."

"I suppose I could have gone round him," confessed the driver, "but I wasn't sure if I had enough petrol."

When I finished school, I wanted to take all my savings and buy myself a motor-cycle, but my mum said no. She had a brother who died in a horrible motorcycle accident when he was eighteen. So she said I could just have his.

A man called his wife from hospital and told her that his finger had been cut off on the building site where he worked.

"Oh my God!" cried the wife. "The whole finger?"

"No," he said, "the one next to it."

I read a story about a man who lost a leg after ignoring a shark warning. I bet he's kicking himself now.

Looking out of his window, a guy saw a group of people gathering around a young man who had come off his motorbike. So he frantically rushed over.

"Out of the way!" he shouted, as he pushed through the crowd.

"Are you a doctor?" one woman screamed.

"No," he replied. "The idiot was delivering my pizza."

A trucker staggered into a country pub, looking a bit shaken, ordered a double Scotch, and then downed it in a single gulp. He turned to some of the regulars and said: "I just hit a pig with my truck. Went right through the radiator!"

The old timers had seen it all before and one of them said: "Yep. Same thing happened to me back in '96. What'cha do is get a hacksaw, saw the legs off, 'n' pull it out backwards."

The trucker gulped, said he would give it a go and then went back outside. Half an hour later, looking a bit pale and covered with blood, he returned and said: "Yeah, your idea worked. Now how do I get his motorcycle out?"

My friend stepped on a landmine. I'm helping him find his feet again.

A man was knocked down by a mobile library van. As he lay in the road, screaming in agony, the driver ran up to him and went: "Sssssssshhh!"

A woman was asked to give a talk on the power of prayer to her local women's group. With her husband sitting in the audience, she recounted how they had turned to God when her husband suffered an unfortunate accident.

"Three months ago," she began, "my husband Kevin was knocked off his bicycle and his scrotum was smashed. The pain was excruciating and the doctors didn't know if they could help him. They warned that our lives might never be the same again. Kevin was unable to get close to either me or the children and every move caused him enormous discomfort. It meant we could no longer touch him around the scrotum.

"So we prayed that the doctors would be able to repair him. Fortunately, our prayers were answered and they were able to piece together the crushed remnants of Kevin's scrotum and wrap wire around it to hold it in place. They said he should make a complete recovery and regain full use of his scrotum."

As the audience burst into spontaneous applause, a lone man walked up to the stage. He announced: "Good afternoon. My name is Kevin, and I just want to tell my wife once again that the word is 'sternum'."

I saved a man who was badly burned in a car crash . . . as a JPEG.

A man walked into a bar with his arm in a plaster cast. "What happened to you?" asked the bartender.

"I got in a fight with O'Reilly."

"O'Reilly? But he's only a little guy. He must have had something in his hand."

"He did – a shovel."

"Didn't you have anything in your hand?"

"I did – Mrs O'Reilly's left tit. And a beautiful thing it was, too, but not much use in a fight!"

I often give my wife flowers and my children teddy bears. Living near an accident blackspot has its advantages.

Accountants

Accountancy: Every Parent's Worst Nightmare

Dear Sir,

I am writing to you as the parent of a child who became an accountant, in the hope that my story may provide solace and advice to others who find themselves in the same terrible predicament.

At school, Henry (not his real name) was a perfectly normal kid who loved football and had an active dope habit. He hung around with the neighbourhood gangs but never gave us any real cause for concern until one day he suddenly announced that he was kicking dope and mugging old ladies in order to take up accountancy.

Now I'd read that smoking dope can lead to irrational behaviour and crazy experimentation but I'd never dreamed that it would lead Henry into accountancy. Like all parents, I never thought it would happen to me.

We tried everything. We invited his dealer round for tea, we talked to his college principal, we tried forbidding Henry from taking the accountancy course. But nothing worked. We even offered to buy him bags of cocaine for his birthday, but instead he insisted he wanted a briefcase, an umbrella and a ledger book.

We had started to notice marked changes in his personality. He threw out all his ripped jeans, leather jackets and T-shirts and replaced them with three-piece suits. His Nirvana and Metallica CDs were consigned to the garbage bin, replaced by – and my God, it pains me to write these words – easy listening. He had become an accountancy addict. When his mother died three years ago, all he could talk about was the estate duty and whether her coffin might be tax-deductible because she was self-employed and had died at her place of work.

To support his habit, he started auditing during his holidays and staying up all night playing with his calculator. I knew then that it was too late to save him. Soon Henry passed his exam and became a partner in a firm of chartered accountants. He was thereby effectively lost to humanity forever.

It was then that I started Accountants Anonymous, an organization dedicated to helping parents spot early signs of accountancy in their children, because if you are able to nip it in the bud, there is still every chance that your child will go on to lead a normal, productive life.

Watch out for these tell-tale signs:

Personality change. Children who were once dynamic, witty and adventurous suddenly become dull and boring.

They drink copious amounts of tea.

They start stockpiling pens and other items of office equipment.

The only bands they're interested in are tax bands.

They replace their bedroom poster of J-Lo with one of economist J. K. Galbraith.

They celebrate New Year not on 1 January but at the start of a new tax year.

They become sexually aroused on Budget Day.

If you are worried that your child is on the way to a career in accountancy, there are a number of steps that you can take:

Listen to your child's explanation about why he wants to become an accountant – and try not to fall asleep while he is talking.

Take him along to a firm of auditors to see for himself the devastating effects that accountancy can have on the human brain.

Encourage him to skip school and get bad marks. If he asks for help with his maths homework, tell him the wrong answers. With most parents, this should come naturally.

Engage him in conversation about non-accountancy topics – such as the advantages of having unprotected sex.

If, even after these measures, you are still unable to prevent your child becoming an accountant, set aside all feelings of shame and disappointment. Don't be embarrassed to tell your friends and relatives about it. You'll be surprised how many people will eventually admit under intense interrogation to knowing someone who is an accountant.

Above all, remember: accountancy doesn't just happen.

What's the wildest thing a group of young accountants can do? – Go into town and gang-audit someone.

An accountant unexpectedly decided to leave his wife. He left her a note which read: "Dear Marie, I am fifty-seven years old and have never done anything wild in my life. But now I'm leaving you for a stunning nineteen-year-old glamour model. We'll be staying at the Ritz."

When he arrived at the hotel, a message was waiting from his wife. It read: "Dear Adam, I, too, am fifty-seven years old. I have followed your example and am staying at the Royal Palace with a nineteen-year-old stud. And I'm sure that as an accountant you will appreciate that nineteen goes into fifty-seven many more times than fifty-seven goes into nineteen . . ."

Adultery

John and Jim were just about to start their regular weekly round of golf when they were approached by a third player whom they had never met before.

"Do you mind if I join you?" asked the stranger.

"Sure," said John, introducing himself. "I'm John, and I work in HR. And this is Jim – he's an auditor. What do you do for a living?"

"Actually," said the stranger, "you'll probably find this hard to believe, but I'm a hitman."

"You mean you're paid to kill people?!" gasped John. "I don't believe you. You're having us on!"

"Take a look in my golf bag," said the stranger.

So John looked in the golf bag and found a powerful rifle with a huge scope attached.

"My God!" exclaimed John to Jim. "It's true: this guy really is a hitman. This scope is truly awesome. I bet I can see my house through it. Yeah, there's my wife naked . . . and there's our next-door neighbour. Wait! He's naked, too. The cheating bitch and that lying bastard!"

John angrily handed the rifle back to the stranger and asked: "How much do you charge for a hit?"

"It's £1,000 for every time I pull the trigger."

"Right," said John, "I want two hits. I want you to shoot my wife in the mouth to pay her back for all her nagging over the past fifteen years. And I want you to shoot my neighbour in the dick to pay him back for screwing around with my wife."

The hitman pointed the rifle at the house and carefully lined up his shot through the scope. He continued taking aim for five minutes, by which time John was growing impatient.

"What are you waiting for?" he demanded.

"Hold on a second," said the hitman, squeezing the trigger. "I'm about to save you £1,000."

"That wife of mine is a goddamn liar," said an angry husband to the bartender.

"How do you know?" asked the bartender.

"She didn't come home last night, and when I asked her where she'd been she said that she'd spent the night with her sister Jenny."

"What makes you think she's not telling the truth?"

"Because I spent the night with her sister Jenny!"

Dale came into the pub one evening and saw his best buddy Matt slumped over the bar.

"What's up?" asked Dale. "I've never seen you looking so rough."

"Woman trouble," Matt replied.

"Woman trouble?" said Dale. "Anyone in particular?"

"I'd rather not say."

"Come on, buddy, you can tell me."

"Okay, Dale, if you must know, it's your wife."

"My wife?" said Dale, surprised. "What about her?"

"I think she's cheating on both of us."

A husband was late home from work one evening. "I'm sure he's having an affair," said his wife to her mother.

"Why do you always think the worst?" said the mother. "Maybe he's just been in a car crash."

Sent by his wife to buy cigarettes from the store one evening, the husband found it closed. So instead he went to a local bar to use the vending machine there. Having got the cigarettes, he decided to stay for a quick drink before returning home. As he sat down at the bar, he noticed a beautiful brunette perched on the next stool and began chatting to her. He bought her a few drinks and when the bar closed, she invited him back to her apartment.

Back at her apartment they wasted no time in jumping into bed. After great sex, he looked at his watch and saw to his horror that it was one o'clock in the morning.

"Jesus Christ!" he exclaimed, leaping out of bed. "I had no idea it was so late. My wife's going to kill me. Do you have any talcum powder?"

The woman looked puzzled but gave him some talcum powder, which he rubbed into his hands. And without further ado he left.

Back home, his wife was waiting for him. "Where have you been?" she demanded. "Do you know what time it is? I only sent you out for a packet of cigarettes but you've been gone over four hours!"

"Listen, I'm really sorry, honey," he said. "I went to the store for your cigarettes but it was closed. So I tried the vending machine at Joe's Bar and while I was there I met this hot chick and we ended up in bed together."

"Let me see your hands!" she yelled, and he showed her his hands covered in talcum powder. "You goddamn liar!" she boomed. "You went bowling again!"

A man walked into the pub sporting a black eye.

"How did you get that?" asked his friend.

The man explained: "I was having sex with this woman in her kitchen when we heard a key in the front door. 'That's my husband,' she said. 'Quick, try the back door.'"

"I know I should have left before her husband caught us, but there was no way I was going to refuse an offer like that!"

A little boy asked his dad: "What's between Mum's legs?"

His father answered: "Paradise, my son."

The son then asked: "What's between your legs?"

His father replied: "The key to paradise."

The son said: "A piece of advice, Dad: change the lock. That bastard next door has a spare key!"

A husband arrived home from work to find his wife in bed with his friend. Angered by the betrayal, the husband produced a gun and shot him dead. His wife shook her head in despair and said: "If you keep behaving like this, you'll lose all of your friends."

Mrs Fortescue-Smythe was unhappy with the way that the maid cleaned the house. Finding a layer of dust on the dining-room table, she decided to reprimand the girl.

The maid responded angrily: "I clean the house better than you and I'm a better cook than you."

"Who told you that?"

"Mr Fortescue-Smythe. And I'm better in bed than you!"

"I suppose my husband told you that, too?"

"No, the gardener!"

I think my wife is cheating on me. Her nickname for me is "Next".

A woman picked up a cowboy in a bar and took him back to her place. After they had finished having sex, he told her about his days on the range. "It's the only life for me," he said. "In fact, I wanna die with my boots on."

Hearing a car pull into the driveway, the woman said: "Well, you'd better pull 'em on fast. That's my husband – the sheriff."

A man came home with some hot gossip. "You know our janitor?" he told his wife. "The word is that he's slept with every woman in this apartment block except for one."

The wife said: "That'll be that stuck-up bitch at number twenty-seven. Nobody likes her."

A woman was at home one afternoon when she heard a knock at the door. She answered it and a man asked her: "Do you have a vagina?" She immediately screamed and slammed the door in his face.

The next afternoon, there was another knock at the door and she answered it to find the same man standing there. Again he asked her: "Do you have a vagina?" So she slammed the door in his face.

That evening, she told her husband about the sinister caller. The husband came up with an idea. "I'm going to take tomorrow off work," he said, "and when this guy calls, you keep him talking so that I can confront him."

"Okay," agreed the wife.

Sure enough, the following afternoon there was a knock on the door and the wife answered it.

The same man was standing there. "Do you have a vagina?" he asked.

"Yes, I do," replied the wife.

"Good," said the man. "Then tell your husband to stop shagging my wife."

A man arrived home and found his wife in bed with his best friend. He shouted at his wife: "You whore, you've cheated on me! Pack your things and get out. I never want to set eyes on you again!"

Then the man turned to his best friend and said: "And as for you . . . bad dog!"

Ken complained to his friend Jerry that all the excitement had gone out of his marriage.

"That often happens when people have been married for ten years, like you," said Jerry. "Have you ever considered having an affair? That might put a bit of life back into your relationship."

"No, I couldn't possibly do that," said Ken. "It's immoral."

"Get real," said Jerry. "This is the twenty-first century. These things happen all the time."

"But what if my wife found out?"

"No problem. Be upfront. Tell her about it in advance."

Overcoming his initial misgivings, Ken plucked up the courage to break the news to his wife the next morning while she was reading a magazine over breakfast. "Honey," he began hesitantly, "I don't want you to take this the wrong way . . . and please remember that I'm only doing this because I truly, truly love you, otherwise I would never dream of it . . . but I think maybe . . . just possibly . . . having an affair might bring us closer together."

"Forget it," said his wife, without even looking up from her magazine. "I've tried it, and it's never worked."

Little Johnny's mother had been away for five days at a convention, and when she arrived home she was eager to hear about his week.

"One night," said Johnny, "we had a terrible thunderstorm, and I was scared. So Daddy and me slept together."

"Johnny," interrupted the family's Swedish blonde au pair, "don't you mean Daddy and I?"

"No," said Johnny. "That was Thursday. I'm talking about Tuesday night."

A man was cleaning his car one morning when a neighbour came over and said tearfully: "My wife's just told me she's been having an affair with Alex the mailman."

"What? That fat ugly fucker I see every morning outside your house?"

"Yes," laughed the neighbour, cheering up.

"Why would Alex the mailman want to shag that?"

A wife arrived home late from work one evening in a badly dishevelled state. "Where have you been?" asked her husband.

"I didn't have enough money for the bus fare home," she answered. "So I had to give the bus driver a blow job."

"But you're two hours late," he went on. "It couldn't have taken you that long!"

"I know, but then the ticket inspector got on . . ."

Two married women neighbours were talking about their new mailman. One said: "He's very handsome, punctual and always dresses so smartly."

"And so quickly, too," added the other.

A woman went to the pub sporting a black eye.

"How'd ya get that?" asked the bartender.

"From my husband," she replied.

"But I thought he was out of town," he said.

"So did I!" she said.

A little girl was upset when she came down one morning to find her pet cat lying on the floor with its legs in the air.

"I'm afraid Smokey is dead," said her father.

The girl wiped away her tears and asked: "But Daddy, why is Smokey lying with his legs in the air?"

Thinking on his feet, the father replied: "Because that way it's easier for Jesus to come down, take hold of Smokey's legs and carry him off to heaven."

The little girl was satisfied with the explanation and the father went off to work. But when he came home in the evening, she ran sobbing to the door.

"Daddy! Daddy!" she cried. "Mummy nearly died this morning."

"Why? What happened?" asked the father anxiously.

"Well," said the little girl, "soon after you left for work, I found her lying on the floor with her legs in the air. She was shouting 'Jesus, I'm coming, I'm coming', and if it hadn't been for the mailman holding her down, Daddy, she would definitely have gone."

Starting the car for the long trip back into the city, Jim and Kev said goodbye to their best mate, Bazza.

"Thanks for putting us up for the weekend, mate," said Jim. "The food was great, the booze and dope were superb, and I really enjoyed fuckin' your wife."

At the first petrol stop, Kev turned to Jim and said: "I hope you weren't serious about enjoying fuckin' his wife!"

"No," Jim confessed, "I can't say that I enjoyed it, but I didn't want to hurt Bazza's feelings!"

Looking for a bit of rough, a posh married woman picked up a builder in a bar and took him back to her place for a bout of energetic sex over the coffee table. No sooner had they finished than she heard a car pull up outside. "Oh no!" she said, peeking through the curtains. "It's my husband. He's home early!"

"Shit!" exclaimed the builder, grabbing his jeans. "Where's the back door?"

"There isn't a back door," she gasped.

"Okay," said the builder. "Where would you like one?"

A man arrived home carrying a bunch of flowers. "Okay, what have you done now?" asked his wife suspiciously.

"I slept with your sister," he replied.

"What?!" she screamed. "And you think a lousy bunch of flowers will make me forgive you?"

"What are you on about?" he said. "They're *for* your sister."

A jealous husband hired a private detective to check on his wife's movements. The husband demanded more than just a written report – he wanted a video of his wife's activities. A week later, the detective returned with a tape and sat down to watch it with the husband. As the tape played, he saw his wife meeting another man. He saw the two of them laughing in the park. He saw them enjoying themselves at an outdoor café. He saw them having a playful fight in the street. He saw them dancing in a dimly lit nightclub.

When the tape ended, the distraught husband said: "I can't believe this!"

"What's not to believe?" asked the detective. "It's right up there on the screen. The camera never lies."

The husband replied: "What I mean is, I can't believe my wife is so much fun!"

"Mummy," asked the little girl, "is our au pair bionic?"

"Heavens, no!" said the mother. "What made you think that?"

"Well," said the girl, "it's just that I overheard Daddy telling Uncle Bob that he screwed the arse off the au pair last night."

A guy told his buddy: "Last night I confessed to my wife that I had cheated on her four times over the past year."

"Hey, that was a brave thing to do."

"Well, I believe that honesty is the most important thing in a relationship. Besides, now we won't have any secrets between us when she comes out of the coma."

Airplanes

Two airplane mechanics from Houston were regular drinking buddies. However, thick fog one Friday night meant they were unable to get into town for their weekly drinking session and were left stranded in the hangar instead. The only liquid on tap there was jet fuel, but although it sounded revolting they decided to give it a try.

They each drank four pints of jet fuel and slept it off. In the morning, one guy woke expecting a massive hangover, but he felt surprisingly good. However, there was no sign of his buddy. Just then the phone rang. It was his buddy.

"How are you feeling?" asked the voice on the other end of the phone,

"Fine."

"Well, whatever you do, don't fart."

"Why not?"

"Because I'm in St Louis!"

After a small airplane crashed in the middle of the desert, the pilot and co-pilot wandered around for days in search of something to eat. Finally the co-pilot produced an axe and announced: "I'm so hungry, I'm going to chop off my dick and eat it."

"Don't do that," the pilot urged. "Just think of your girlfriend."

"What's the point?" said the co-pilot. "At this rate I'll never see her again anyway."

"I don't mean it like that," said the pilot. "It's just that if you think of her first, hopefully there will be enough for both of us."

An airplane crashed into the Pacific and the only two survivors, a man and a woman, made it to an uninhabited island. They were almost instantly attracted to each other, and their love made their situation bearable as they built a large hut, cultivated food, and tamed some wild goats and pigs as livestock.

But about a year later, shortly after the birth of their child, the man began to get homesick. He went on and on about how he'd like to be back in the city, sitting at a ball game, drinking beer and eating a hot dog. Finally, his obsession got so strong that the woman couldn't stand it anymore. One day, he came back from collecting water to find that she had made a chair for him out of bamboo. "Just like a ball-park seat," she said. "Sit."

Surprised, he sat down. She disappeared for a moment before returning wearing a hat and shouting: "Get your beer, ice cold beer!"

She handed him a cup. He took a sip and said excitedly: "This tastes great. What is it?"

She replied: "I've been experimenting for months until I got the perfect recipe using wild rice and fruit. I cooled it in the lagoon."

"That's amazing," he said. "But . . ."

"I know," she said. She left the hut, and then returned, shouting: "Hot dogs, get your hot dogs!" She handed him a bun.

He took a bite and asked: "How did you get this?"

She hesitated for a second, and then answered: "Well, I hope you're not turned off, but that hot dog is really a pig's penis."

To her delight, he said: "So, who cares what part of a pig I eat? It tastes like the real thing. Honey, I can't believe you've gone to all this trouble for me. You really are the most amazing woman. And how did you get this delicious yellow mustard?"

"Oh, that," she said. "That's baby shit."

Alcohol

My wife says she doesn't like me when I drink. Unfortunately that's the only time I like her.

A man went to a doctor and said he had a problem making love. "My dick is too small," he told the medic.

The doctor examined him and said: "Yes, I see what you mean. Tell me, what beer do you drink?"

"Budweiser," replied the man, bemused by the question.

"That explains it," said the doctor. "You don't want to drink those weak beers like Budweiser – they shrink things. You want to drink Guinness – that makes things grow."

Two months later, the man returned to the doctor with a big smile on his face. He said: "Doc, I want to thank you for all you've done."

"I take it you now drink Guinness?" asked the doctor.

"No," said the man, "but I've got my wife drinking Budweiser."

Alcohol does not make ugly people attractive. It makes it so you could care less that they're ugly. (Doug Stanhope)

One bitterly cold winter, a man told his drinking buddy: "I've started cooling my beer outside on the front doorstep."

"What made you think of doing that?" asked the friend.

"As a matter of fact, I got the idea from the old lady next door – she's been doing the same with her milk bottles."

A married couple were shopping in the supermarket when the husband picked up a crate of Budweiser and put it in the trolley.

"What do you think you're doing?" asked the wife.

"They're on offer – only $25 for twelve cans," he explained.

"Put them back," she demanded. "We can't afford it."

A few aisles later, she picked up a $50 jar of face cream and put it in the trolley.

"What do you think you're doing?" asked the husband indignantly.

"It's my face cream," she said. "It makes me look beautiful."

He said: "So do twelve cans of Bud and they're half the price!"

I once saw an English guy in Glasgow trying to order a pint of lager and lime, and the barman went: "We don't do cocktails." (Frankie Boyle)

Sitting alone in an upmarket restaurant, a gentleman asked a waiter to take a bottle of expensive Chablis to an attractive woman who was dining at another table. The waiter took the Chablis to the woman and said: "This is from the gentleman at the table by the window."

Without looking at the sender, she studied the bottle for a moment and then decided to send a note of reply. The waiter, who was lingering for a response, took the note from her and conveyed it to the gentleman. The note read: "For me to accept this bottle, you need to have a Mercedes in your garage, a million dollars in the bank, and seven inches in your pants."

After reading the note, the man decided to compose one of his own in return. He folded the note, handed it to the waiter and instructed him to return it to the woman. It read: "For your information, I have a Ferrari Maranello, a BMW Z8, a Mercedes CL600, and a Porsche Turbo in my garages, plus beautiful homes in California, Aspen, Colorado and Miami. There are over $20 million in my bank account. But not even for a woman as beautiful as you would I cut three inches off. Send the bottle back!"

Beer vs Vagina

1 Beer is always wet. Vagina needs a little work. One point to BEER
2 Warm beer tastes awful. One point to VAGINA
3 A really cold beer is satisfying. One point to BEER
4 If after taking a swig of your favourite beer you find a hair between your teeth, you may vomit. One point to VAGINA
5 Ten beers in one night and you can't drive home. Ten vaginas in one night and you don't want to drive anywhere. One point to VAGINA
6 If you have a lot of beer in a public place, your reputation may suffer. If you eat any vagina in public, you become a legend. One point to VAGINA

7 If a cop stops you and you smell of beer you may get arrested. If you smell of vagina he may buy you a beer. One point to VAGINA

8 Too much beer and you'll think you can see flying saucers. Too much vagina and you'll think you've seen God. One point to VAGINA

9 Pulling off a beer bottle label is boring. Pulling off panties is fun. One point to VAGINA

10 If you have another beer, the first one never gets pissed off. One point to BEER

11 You can always be sure if you're the first one to open a bottle or a can. One point to BEER

12 You always know how much beer is going to cost. One point to BEER

13 Beer doesn't have a mother. One point to BEER

14 Beer never expects to be hugged for half an hour after you drink it. One point to BEER

15 Beer with yeast in it still tastes rather nice. One point to BEER

FINAL SCORE: BEER: 8 VAGINA: 7

Alzheimer's

My friends have recently been teasing me about my Alzheimer's. The joke's on them, though. I don't have a toaster.

A woman received a phone call from her husband's doctor, who told her in a state of panic: "I'm afraid we've made a terrible mistake. We mixed up your husband's test results. He's either got Alzheimer's or AIDS."

"What shall I do?" wailed the woman.

The doctor thought for a moment and suggested: "Send him out for a walk. If he comes back, don't sleep with him."

I cried as my nan called my brother an ambulance today. Her Alzheimer's is getting worse.

"Who's been eating my porridge?" said Father Bear.

Mother Bear sighed and poured him another bowl. Life was tough for her now that her husband was suffering from Alzheimer's.

A young man went to visit his old grandma. As soon as he walked in, she said: "Oh, Bert, is that you?"

Knowing that she tended to get a bit confused in her old age, he explained patiently: "No, Nan, Granddad died twenty years ago. It's me, Simon."

She carried on: "Oh Bert, how I've missed you so!"

"Nan! Granddad is dead! I'm your grandson!"

"Come over here, so I can give you a big passionate kiss."

"I'm not him, you daft bitch!"

"Now, bend me over the kitchen table and take me from behind, the way you used to when we were courting."

"Oh, Mabel, I've missed you so much!"

They say you never get a second chance to make a first impression – unless you work in an Alzheimer's hospice. (Patrick Monahan)

My uncle came out of the closet yesterday. He's not gay, but he's got Alzheimer's, and he thought it was the car.

Three elderly Alzheimer's patients attended a memory test at their local hospital. The doctor asked the first old man: "What is two times two?"

"A hundred and seventy-eight," replied the old man.

The doctor turned to the second old man and asked: "What is two times two?"

"Thursday," replied the second old man.

Finally the doctor asked the third old man: "What is two times two?"

"Four," answered the third old man.

"That's right," said the doctor, impressed. "How did you get that?"

"Easy," said the third old man. "I subtracted 178 from Thursday."

Polly put the kettle on, Polly put the kettle on, Polly put the kettle on. Polly has Alzheimer's.

A boy confided to his school friend: "My poor grandmother has had Alzheimer's for nine years now. But I guess I should be grateful for the £10 I get for my birthday every week."

A comedian landed a gig playing at a home for Alzheimer's patients. They liked his first joke so much that he told it over and over again, forty-one times in all.

After the show one old lady went up to him, with tears of laughter running down her face, and said: "I just don't know how you remember them all."

What's the best thing about Alzheimer's? – You meet new people every day.

They say laughter is the best medicine, but my granddad has Alzheimer's and we've been laughing at him for years, and he hasn't got any better.

A ninety-year-old man was sobbing his heart out in the street. Seeing his distress, a young man asked him what the problem was.

"I'm in love with a twenty-one-year-old girl," wailed the old man. "She's beautiful with a fabulous figure, she's kind, caring, she's a fantastic cook and we have amazing sex three times a day, every day."

"So why are you crying?"

"I've forgotten where we live!"

Knock, knock.

Who's there?

Richard.

Richard who?

Richard fights back the tears as he realizes his mother's Alzheimer's is getting worse.

Americans

Back in the 1980s, an American, a Mexican and an Italian robbed a bank, and escaped with a haul in dollars, pesos and lira.

Back at their hideout, the American distributed the money in three even shares: "1,000 dollars for me, 1,000 pesos for you, 1,000 lira for you . . . 1,000 dollars for me, 1,000 pesos for you, 1,000 lira for you . . . 1,000 dollars for me, 1,000 pesos for you, 1,000 lira for you . . ."

As the counting continued, the Mexican whispered to the Italian: "I can't stand Americans, but you have to admit they are fair."

What's worse than being captured by the Taliban? – Being rescued by the Americans.

A study predicts nearly half of all Americans will be obese by 2030. But with a little American ingenuity I bet we can get there by 2025. (Stephen Colbert)

In New York City, a Scotsman and an American were discussing how far each could make a dime go. They agreed to meet up again a few days later to see who had got the most out of a dime.

The Scotsman revealed how he had bought a cigar with his dime. He had smoked one-third of the cigar the first day and saved the ashes. He smoked another third the second day and saved the ashes. On the third day, he smoked the final third and again saved the ashes, and on the fourth day he gave the ashes to his wife to use as fertilizer on her roses. He told the American proudly: "How's that for stretching a dime!"

The American said: "Very good, but I got you beat. I bought a Polish sausage for a dime, and the first day I ate half of it. On the second day, I ate the other half. The third day, I used the skin for a condom, and the fourth day I took a shit in the skin and sewed it back up. The fifth day, I took it back to the butcher and told him it smelled like shit. He agreed with me and gave me my dime back!"

A Canadian bought a new car but returned to the showroom the next day complaining that the radio didn't work. The salesman explained that the radio was voice-activated. "Watch this!" he said. "Nelson!" The radio replied: "Ricky or Willie?" "Willie!" he continued – and "On the Road Again" came from the speakers.

The Canadian drove away happy and, for the next few days, every time he said, "Beethoven", he'd get beautiful classical music, if he said, "Beatles!" he'd get one of their biggest hits, and so on. He was so pleased and impressed with his car.

Then one day, he was driving through Montreal when a carload of teenagers ran a red light and nearly smashed into his new car, but luckily he managed to swerve in time to avoid them. As they drove off, he yelled, "Assholes!" . . . and immediately on the radio the American National Anthem began to play.

An English visitor to the United States was taken by a work colleague to his first football game, one that was also being screened live on TV. Afterwards his host family asked him whether he had enjoyed it.

"Not really," he admitted. "I found it boring. It was all very stop-start. Every thirty seconds or so, the referee would blow his whistle, and the game would then take a few minutes to resume."

"Well, you know why that is?"

"No."

"Snack breaks for the audience."

What do you call an elevator with a group of slim, quietly spoken, intelligent people inside? – A lift.

The United Nations carried out a worldwide survey. The only question was: "Would you please give your honest opinion about solutions to the food shortage in the rest of the world?"

The survey was a total failure. In Africa they didn't know what "food" meant. In Eastern Europe they didn't know what "honest" meant. In Western Europe they didn't know what "shortage" meant. In China they didn't know what "opinion" meant. In the Middle East they didn't know what "solution" meant. In South America they didn't know what "please" meant. And in the USA they didn't know what "rest of the world" meant.

An American walked into a London pub and asked for a Budweiser. The barman said: "You're American, aren't you?"

"Sure am," said the American. "How could you tell? Was it the drink I ordered or my accent?"

"Neither," said the barman. "It's just that you're the fattest bloke I've ever seen."

Did you know most Americans pray before they eat? Can you imagine praying eighteen times a day? (Stewart Francis)

A police officer in London pulled over a driver who had been weaving in and out of the traffic. He approached the car window and said: "Sir, I need you to blow into this breathalyser."

The man reached into his pocket and produced a doctor's note. On it was written: "This man suffers from chronic asthma. Do not make him perform any action that may leave him short of breath."

The officer said: "Okay, then, I need you to come and give a blood sample."

The man produced another letter, which read: "This man is a haemophiliac. Please do not cause him to bleed in any way."

So the officer said: "Right, I need a urine sample then."

The man produced a third letter from his pocket. It read: "This man is an American. Please don't take the piss out of him."

Animals

What do you do if you come across a lion in the jungle? – Wipe it off and say you're sorry.

Two American sociologists were attending a conference in Egypt. Having accidently left their watches at their hotel, they had completely lost track of the time. So when they spotted an old camel herder sitting on a stool by the side of the street next to his camel, they decided to ask him the time.

The old man calmly reached beneath the camel, raised its testicles, held them in his hands for a few moments and announced: "Eleven forty-five."

The sociologists thanked him and went on their way, and over lunch they told their colleagues about the amazing camel herder who could tell the time simply by feeling the camel's testicles. Was it some little-known Arab tradition, they wondered.

Later that day they saw the old man again, still perched on a stool beside his camel.

"Excuse me," they said. "Can you tell us the time?"

As before, the old man reached beneath the camel, raised its testicles, held them in his hands for a few moments and declared: "Five twenty."

"That's incredible," said one of the sociologists. "Can you show us how you are able to tell the time just from the touch of the camel's testicles?"

"Very well," said the old man. "Squat down next to me. Now grasp his balls gently and lift them up to his belly."

"Okay," said the sociologist, following his directions to the letter. "What now?"

"Well," said the old man, "if you look through the gap where his balls were, you can see the clock tower."

Why do elephants have four feet? – Because they'd look silly with only six inches.

An elephant in the zoo called across the fence of his enclosure to the camel and said: "Hey, camel, why are your tits on your back?"

"I don't know," said the camel. "Why is your dick on your face?"

A guy just back from a safari trip to Kenya recounted his experiences to a friend. "It was one hell of a trip, I can tell you. On the second day, I was out in the jungle when I suddenly heard a noise about fifteen feet away. I turned round to see this huge lion sizing me up for dinner. I froze for a second, then ran for my life. The lion bounded after me. He was almost at my shoulder when he slipped and I managed to edge ahead. But seconds later he had caught me up again and I could feel his hot breath on the back of my neck. He was just about to pounce but luckily for me, he slipped again.

"In the distance I could see this house and so I ran for it as fast as I could. But as I got close, the lion caught up again and was almost on top of me when he slipped for a third time. That enabled me to escape into the house and to slam the door in the lion's face. It was a really close shave!"

"Hey! That's some story," said the friend. "If I'd been in that situation, I would have shit my pants."

The guy said: "What do you think the lion kept slipping on?"

I recently adopted a whale and a monkey from an animal charity, which is all very well. But one day I'm going to have to be the one who explains to them why they don't look like each other. (Mark Restuccia)

What did Santa call the reindeer with an injured leg? – Dinner.

Three old men – Ted, George and Tom – were sitting on a park bench debating what the meanest animal in the world was.

Ted said: "The meanest animal in the world is the hippopotamus, because it's got such huge jaws. One bite and you're gone!"

George shook his head and said: "No, the hippopotamus may be mean but he's a pussycat compared to an alligator. An alligator's got attitude, and one bite from those teeth, followed by the death roll, and you're gone!"

Tom thought for a moment before saying: "As a matter of fact, you're both wrong. The meanest animal in the world is a hippogator."

Ted and George laughed. "What the hell's a hippogator?" they asked. "There's no such creature."

"A hippogator," explained Tom, "has got a hippo head on one end and an alligator head on the other."

"Wait a minute!" interrupted Ted and George. "If he has a head on both ends, how does he shit?"

"He doesn't," said Tom. "That's what makes him so mean."

I took my young daughter on a trip to see her favourite farm animals and she did nothing but cry all day. Before we left I had to apologize to the abattoir staff.

They can see every man's bald spot and down every woman's blouse. That's why giraffes are always smirking. (Conan O'Brien)

What do you get if you insert human DNA into a goat? – Banned from the petting zoo.

A guy walked into a bar with his pet monkey. The monkey immediately snatched handfuls of olives, limes and peanuts and started eating them. Then it grabbed the cue ball from the pool table, stuck it in its mouth and swallowed it whole.

The bartender complained about the monkey's behaviour, but the owner said: "I can't stop him. He'll eat anything that's lying around."

Two weeks later, the man and the monkey were back in the same bar. The monkey immediately snatched a maraschino cherry from the bar, stuck it up its arse, pulled it out and ate it.

"Did you see what your monkey just did?" asked the bartender. "It put a cherry up its butt, pulled it out and then ate it. That's gross!"

"I know," said the owner. "You see, he still eats anything that's lying around but ever since he ate that cue ball, he measures everything first."

What do you get when you cross an elephant with a kitten? – A dead kitten with an eighteen-inch asshole.

How many mice does it take to screw in a light bulb? – Two. But how did they get in there?

A bear needed to go for a poop in the woods. As he squatted down behind a large bush, he found a rabbit doing the same.

"Hey," said the bear. "Do you have trouble with shit sticking to your fur?"

"No," said the rabbit.

So the bear picked up the rabbit and wiped his arse with it.

Squirrels: nature's speed bumps.

A man was sitting in a bar with his dog. After a few minutes an attractive woman came in and began to make a fuss of the dog. The man told her that his dog possessed a unique talent – it could perform oral sex on women. The woman was initially horrified but after a few drinks she started to become intrigued by the idea and suggested that perhaps the dog could demonstrate its special trick on her.

So they all went to her apartment, where she took off her clothes and lay on the bed in anticipation. The man stood next to the dog and gave the command: "Okay, boy, go get it."

The dog didn't move an inch.

The man issued the command again, but the dog remained motionless. He tried a third time, but still the dog did nothing.

Finally in exasperation, the man said: "Okay, boy, I guess I'll have to show you one last time . . ."

"I'm not a racist. Some of my best friend is black," said the zebra.

Twelve guys decided to take a trip through the Sahara Desert, so they went to the Arab camel-hire post to buy some transport. The Arab told them it was 1,000 dinars per camel, which they said was too expensive as it would work out at a total of 12,000 dinars. So they decided to hire just the one camel, which they would all ride, sitting on the beast from head to tail.

Riding like this, they set off into the desert, but after a mile or so, the camel started staggering under its heavy load. It could hardly take another step. The first guy, the one on the camel's snout, turned to the second man and said: "I guess the camel is fucked." The second turned to the third and relayed: "I guess the camel is fucked." The third passed it on to the fourth and so on, until the eleventh man turned to the twelfth, who was sitting on the camel's very end, and said: "I guess the camel is fucked."

"So what do you want me to do?" said the twelfth. "If I pull it out, I'll fall off!"

Why do hippos mate in the water? – Have you ever tried to keep a fanny that big moist?

I love animals, but I like eating 'em more. Fun to pet, better to chew. (Jim Gaffigan)

A polar bear was out driving in the wilds of Canada when his car broke down. He pushed it for twenty-five miles to the nearest town, where he took it to a garage.

While the mechanic tried to fix the car, the polar bear went to a supermarket to cool down after all the exertion. With no members of staff around, he wandered over to the freezer and proceeded to eat several boxes of ice cream. In doing so, he completely lost track of the time and had to hurry back to the garage, his face covered in ice cream.

The mechanic walked towards him, shaking his head, and said: "Looks like you blew a seal."

"No," said the polar bear, "it's just ice cream."

A contest was being held at the circus with a £1,000 prize being offered to the first person who could make the elephant nod his head up and down. Dozens of people tried and failed. Finally, a little old man walked over to the elephant, grabbed his balls, and squeezed as hard as he could. The elephant roared in pain and tossed its head up and down. The old man collected his prize money and departed.

The next year a similar contest was held using the same elephant, the only difference being that this time the winner had to make the elephant shake its head from side to side. Again dozens tried and failed. Finally, the same little old man who walked off with the prize money the previous year, appeared. He walked up to the elephant.

"Remember me?" he asked.

The elephant shook its head up and down.

"Want me to do what I did to you last year?"

The elephant shook its head back and forth violently. The old man walked off again with the prize money.

A young circus assistant was on his first day of training to be a tiger tamer. The trainer was telling him what to do. "Firstly, if the tiger growls, move back slightly. Secondly, if the tiger keeps growling, and moves towards you, move back a little more. Thirdly, if the tiger is still growling and advancing on you, throw a load of shit in its face."

The assistant asked: "But what if there is no shit to throw?"

"Don't worry," said the trainer, "if a tiger is advancing on you, there will be!"

Anorexia

Why did the anorexic cross the road? – There was a strong breeze.

What do you call an annoying anorexic that gets under your skin? – A splinter.

My girlfriend is a blonde anorexic. I've stuck with her through thick and thin.

What do you get when you hang a bunch of anorexics next to each other? – Wind chimes.

Why do art teachers in elementary schools hire anorexics to model for their students? – Because kids can only draw stick figures anyway.

My anorexic friend died doing what she loved. Starving.

Why do anorexics scream during sex? – Because you're breaking their bones.

How do you find a lost anorexic? – Tell your dog, "Fetch!"

Why do rock bands prefer anorexic groupies? – Because there will always be a spare set of drumsticks around just in case.

In these difficult times, my friend has had to tighten her belt, but that's anorexia for you.

Art

The curator of a famous American art gallery commissioned an artist to create a painting depicting General Custer's last thoughts. For six months, the artist kept his work a closely guarded secret, so its unveiling was eagerly anticipated. But when the big day came, the curator was horrified to see the result. Instead of a spectacular battle scene, the painting showed a large lake with fish leaping from the water. Bizarrely, the fish had halos around their heads. Meanwhile, on the shore of the lake hundreds of Indians were fornicating.

The curator was furious. "What on earth is this supposed to be?"

The artist said: "You asked for a painting representing Custer's last thoughts. Well, this is it. Custer was thinking: "Holy mackerel! Where did all those fucking Indians come from?'"

I'm taking an art class and the nude model quit. Because I like to finger-paint. (Wendy Liebman)

An art class teacher had asked his students to sketch a naked man from memory. As he walked round the class looking at the drawings, he noticed that an attractive girl student had sketched the man with an erection.

"No," said the teacher. "I wanted it the other way."

The girl said: "What other way?"

A couple went to an art gallery. One painting was of a beautiful, naked woman with only a little foliage covering her private areas. The wife thought the picture was in bad taste and moved on quickly, but the husband lingered, completely transfixed.

"What are you waiting for?" she called out.

"Autumn," he replied.

The thing about glitter is if you get it on you, be prepared to have it on you forever. Glitter is the herpes of craft supplies. (Demetri Martin)

A world-famous artist was visiting Rome painting landscapes and portraits. A nobleman requested an audience with the artist, which was granted.

The nobleman said: "Sir, I will give you 1,000 pieces of gold to paint my mistress nude."

The elderly artist stated that he did not do that type of work as his moral standards would not allow it.

The nobleman returned a week later and said: "Sir, I know that you are an honourable man but my mistress is very impressed with your work. I will give you 5,000 pieces of gold if you will paint her nude."

Once again the artist refused, stating his moral code as an excuse.

A month later, the nobleman returned and said: "Sir, I will give you 10,000 gold pieces to paint my mistress nude."

The artist thought for a while and said: "Come back tomorrow and I will give you my answer."

The nobleman arrived bright and early the following day. He repeated his offer – 10,000 gold pieces to paint his mistress nude.

The artist said: "My wife gave me permission to paint your mistress nude, on one condition."

"Certainly, sir," said the nobleman. "Name it."

The artist said: "I must keep my socks on as I suffer from arthritis."

Australians

Backpacking in Australia, a young Englishman found himself with time to kill in a remote outback town before the next leg of his journey. With over two hours until his bus was due, he decided to call in to the town's only hotel for a beer and something to eat.

As he walked in, every head at the bar turned to stare out the stranger. The silence was deafening until one of the regulars stood up and announced: "I hope you're not a pervert, because perverts aren't welcome in this town."

"No," said the young man, "I assure you I'm not. I'm just waiting for my bus."

He ordered a beer and a burger, and after his meal needed to use the toilet, particularly with the prospect of a seven-hour bus ride ahead. So he asked the bartender where the toilet was.

"The dunny's out the back," growled the bartender, "and don't make a mess!"

Venturing outside, the young man was horrified to see that the toilets were nothing more than two pits piled high with festering poop. One pile was six feet high, the other four feet high. Bracing himself, he climbed to the top of the smaller pile and did his business. As he climbed down, the guy from the bar appeared and grabbed him around the throat.

"I knew you were a pervert!" he snarled. "You were in the ladies!"

Two Australian men were sitting on a rocky ledge above a quiet beach, with a rope going down into the sea and a little Chinese guy frantically trying to climb up it. While they were sitting there a passing priest called over and said: "God bless you, my children. I am so proud to witness Christianity at work, helping a fellow man in his hour of need." With that, the priest continued on his way.

One Australian looked at the other and said: "Who the fuck was that?"

"Oh," said the other, "that's Father O'Brien. He knows all there is to know about the Bible."

The first guy said: "Well, he knows fuck all about shark fishing!"

A wealthy American woman finally decided that at the age of sixty-two it was time she got married. She was very specific about her future husband, and wanted a man who had never before had sex with a woman. During months of searching, she took out personal ads in newspapers and magazines all over the world, and eventually found a man who met her criteria – a guy who had lived his entire life in the Australian outback.

After a brief correspondence, they got married in Miami. On their wedding night she went to the bathroom to freshen up but when she returned to the hotel bedroom she found her new husband standing naked in the middle of the room with all the furniture piled in a corner.

"Why have you moved all the furniture?" she asked.

"Well," he replied, "I may never have been with a woman, but if it's anything like screwing a kangaroo, I'm gonna need all the room I can get!"

You Know You're Australian If . . .

- You think Woolloomooloo is a perfectly reasonable name for a place.
- You get old-age concessions at forty-five for having survived the killer wildlife.
- When you hear that an American "roots for his team", you wonder how often and with whom.
- You've ever had a crush on your neighbour's sheep.
- You believe that cooked-down axle grease makes a good breakfast spread.
- You know at least a dozen women called Kylie.
- Your idea of foreplay is, "You awake?"
- You feel the need to apologize if you go to a bar and order a non-alcoholic drink.

The United States government funded a study to determine why the head of a man's penis is larger than the shaft. After ten months and at a cost of $500,000 they decided that the head is larger than the shaft in order to give the man greater pleasure during sex.

The Italian government also funded a study to find out why the head of a man's penis is larger than the shaft. After nine months and at a cost of $400,000, they, too, decided that the head is larger than the shaft so that the man can experience greater pleasure during sex.

Dissatisfied with these findings, the Australian government conducted their own study. After two weeks and at a cost of $40.55 plus six cases of beer, they concluded that the head of a penis is larger than the shaft to prevent the man's hand flying off and hitting himself in the forehead.

On his second day in Los Angeles, an Australian tourist got lost and ended up in gang territory. He was soon ambushed by a group of young thugs who threatened him with a knife.

"Have you come here to die?" sneered one.

"No, mate," said the Aussie. "I came here yesterday."

I love the irony that you get in Australia. They sell Steve Irwin DVDs on Blu-ray. (Daniel Sloss)

An Australian wedding reception was in full swing, but one of the guests, Joe, had been delayed and arrived late. When he finally reached the hotel, his mate Stewie was just leaving the party.

"I wouldn't go in there if I were you, mate," warned Stewie. "There's bound to be trouble. They've run out of beer and the best man has just rooted the bride."

So Joe decided to turn back towards his car but just as he was about to leave, another guest came out of the hotel and shouted: "Don't go, fellas. Everything's sorted. There's another keg on the way and the best man has apologized."

An Aussie guy approached a pretty woman on the beach and said: "Will you have sex with me?"

"No," she replied firmly.

"That's a shame. Well, would you consider lying down while I have some?"

Differences between Australians, Brits, Americans and Canadians

Aussies: Dislike being mistaken for Brits when abroad.

Canadians: Are rather indignant about being mistaken for Americans when abroad.

Americans: Encourage being mistaken for Canadians when abroad.

Brits: Can't possibly be mistaken for anyone else when abroad.

Americans: Drink weak, pissy-tasting beer.

Canadians: Drink strong, pissy-tasting beer.

Brits: Drink warm, beery-tasting piss.

Aussies: Drink anything with alcohol in it.

Americans: Seem to think that poverty and failure are morally suspect.
Canadians: Seem to believe that wealth and success are morally suspect.
Brits: Seem to believe that wealth, poverty, success and failure are inherited.
Aussies: Seem to think that none of this matters after several beers.

Americans: Are flag-waving, anthem-singing, and obsessively patriotic to the point of blindness.
Canadians: Can't agree on the words to their anthem, in either language, when they can be bothered to sing them.
Brits: Do not sing at all but prefer a large brass band to perform the anthem.
Aussies: Are extremely patriotic about their beer.

Brits: Are justifiably proud of the accomplishments of their past citizens.
Americans: Are justifiably proud of the accomplishments of their present citizens.
Canadians: Prattle on about how some of those great Americans were once Canadian.
Aussies: Waffle on about how some of their past citizens were once Outlaw Pommies, but that was okay so long as they could hold their beer.

Two Sydney construction workers, Bazza and Bruce, were on the roof of a twenty-one-storey skyscraper. Bazza turned to Bruce and said: "Mate, I need a piss, and the lav's down on the ground."

Thinking quickly, Bruce suggested: "Why don't you stand on the end of a plank and piss off the edge? The winds will disperse the liquid and no one will be any the wiser. I'll stand on this side of the plank to stop you falling off."

Bazza agreed that it was a good idea, and so he stepped out on to the plank to do his business, while Bruce stood on the other end.

Then suddenly the lunch horn sounded, and Bruce instinctively walked away, leaving Bazza to plummet downwards.

Two months later, an Englishman, a Frenchman and an Australian were sitting in a London pub arguing about which country's men pulled out all the stops to pursue beautiful ladies. The Englishman boasted: "Lads, we treat our ladies like queens, we take them out to dinner, a movie, maybe even to a club, before we pop home for a kiss and cuddle."

The Frenchman scoffed: "Mon ami, you 'ave no idea. We French, we woo our ladies, we treat them to fine wines and chocolate, to roses and dancing. We romance them like no other countrymen in the world."

Having quietly listened to the other two, the Australian finished his pint, leaned forward and said: "Mates, you two know nothing. We Aussies do the most to chase woman. Case in point: I was walking through Sydney a couple of months ago when I spied these two beautiful lasses. Well, not being one to hang about I made my way in their direction. At that point I was surprised by the sheer dedication of another of my countrymen, as he came flying out of the air, dick in hand, screaming 'Cuuuunt!' "

Automobiles

What do you call a man with a car on his head? – An ambulance.

A car broke down on the highway. The driver pulled over to the side of the road and jumped out of the vehicle. Then he opened the trunk and pulled out two men wearing trenchcoats. The men stood behind the car, opened up their coats and began exposing themselves to oncoming traffic. The result was a horrific pile-up.

A police officer soon arrived on the scene and surveyed the wreckage. He yelled at the car driver. "Why the hell did you put those two perverts at the side of the road?"

"My car broke down," he explained, "and I was simply using my emergency flashers."

My driving instructor told me: "Never brake if there's an animal in the road." I'm not sure that mounted policeman agrees.

I got flashed by a speed camera on my way home. So that's three more points on my wife's licence. (Jack Dee)

Why should the roof on a convertible car be called a foreskin? – Because when you pull it back, it reveals the bell-end underneath.

Two paramedics arrived at the scene of a car crash. The driver of the car was sitting in his seat, screaming hysterically.

One of the paramedics tried to calm him. "Take deep breaths and pull yourself together." Pointing at a girl lying unconscious by the side of the road, the paramedic added: "Be grateful that at least you haven't gone through the windshield like your passenger. She looks in a really bad state."

Still crying uncontrollably, the driver yelled: "You haven't seen what's in her mouth!"

What's the difference between a porcupine and a stretch limo? – The porcupine has pricks on the outside.

A little old lady was driving her VW beetle along the road when, without warning, it suddenly ground to a halt. She got out, went to the front of the car, and raised the hood. While she stood there looking, another elderly lady pulled up, also in a VW Beetle, and offered some assistance.

"What's wrong?" the second old lady asked the first.

"I seem to have lost my engine!"

"Oh! How lucky! I just happen to have a spare in my trunk!"

What's the difference between eating pussy and driving in fog? – When you're eating pussy you can see the asshole in front of you.

I was driving along the highway last week when I saw a sign that said: "Turnoff, 500 metres." Sure enough, 500 metres further on, standing by the side of the road was my granny, wearing no knickers, lifting up her dress.

I actually got pulled over once for driving in the diamond lane. Cop said to me, "You know you have to have more than one person in the car to drive in the car pool lane." I said, "Check the trunk." (Doug Benson)

Babies

Nervously pacing up and down a hospital corridor, a man waited as his wife gave birth to their first child. After a long and difficult labour, the doctor came out and told the man that he was now the father of a baby boy.

The man was overjoyed and rushed in to see his wife, who drowsily handed him the new arrival. Seeing how tired his wife was, he asked the midwife whether there was anything he could do to help and, aware that he wanted to be part of things, she suggested that he take the baby into the next room and bathe him.

A few minutes later, the midwife popped her head round the door to see how he was getting on. She was horrified by what she saw: he had two fingers firmly lodged up the baby's nose and was dragging the infant through the water in figures-of-eight.

"Good God, man!" she shouted. "That's not how to bathe a newborn baby!"

"It bloody well is," he replied, "when the water's this hot!"

My mother tried to kill me when I was a baby. She denied it, of course. She said she thought the plastic bag would keep me fresh.

There were three unborn baby boys in a woman's stomach, and they were discussing what they would like to be when they were older.

The first one said: "I want to be a plumber."

The others laughed at this and asked: "Why a plumber?"

He replied: "So I can fix the pipes in here; it's kinda leaky."

The second baby said: "I want to be an electrician."

The others laughed at this and asked: "Why an electrician?"

He replied: "So I can get some lights in here; it's dark!"

The third baby said: "I want to be a boxer."

The others roared with laughter and asked: "Why in God's name do you want to be a boxer?"

He replied: "So I can beat the hell out of that bald guy who keeps coming in here and spitting on us!"

All babies look like Renée Zellweger pushed against a glass window. My friend insisted on showing me a picture of her new baby. I said at least he's not a twin. (Joan Rivers)

A man was sitting on a bus when a beautiful young mother sat down next to him and started breastfeeding her baby. The baby was reluctant to take it, so the mother said: "Come on, eat it all up or I'll give it to this nice man here."

Five minutes later, the baby was still not feeding properly, so the mother repeated: "Eat it all up or I'll give it to this nice man here."

At this, the man said: "Listen, love, will you make your bloody mind up? I should have got off four stops ago!"

A girl gave birth and told one of her ex-boyfriends that he was the father.

He was not convinced. "You were seeing plenty of men behind my back. How do I know this baby's mine?"

"He's got your characteristics," she said.

"Huh!" he scoffed. "Like what?"

"He was premature."

Which sexual position produces the ugliest children? – Ask your mother.

A young couple had been living together for two volatile years. He was happy going down to the pub every evening with his mates, but she began to feel broody, so one day she asked him: "When are we going to have a baby?"

He put down his bottle of beer, looked her in the eye and said: "What about all the shit and piss, the vomit, the smell, and the screaming in the middle of the night? Is that the sort of environment you want to bring a baby into?"

Little Timmy had just got a little sister. His father came home from the hospital to fetch Timmy so he could visit his new sister for the first time. While driving to the hospital, the father decided to break some news to the boy.

"Timmy," he said, searching for the right words. "Your sister . . . she isn't . . ."

"Yes, Dad?"

"Well, she isn't . . . like other girls . . ."

"Is something wrong with her, Dad?"

"Well . . . er . . . you'll see, okay, you'll see."

Finally they arrived at the hospital, and as they rode in the elevator up to the ward, the father again tried to raise the difficult subject.

"Timmy, your sister . . . well . . . she . . ."

"Yes, Dad?"

"Well . . . she . . . oh, you'll see, okay, you'll see."

They stepped out of the elevator and into a room full of little cute and cuddly babies.

"Dad," said Timmy eagerly, "which one is my sister, which one, which one?"

The father replied hesitantly: "Your sister is not in this room . . . you see . . . when she was born . . . well . . . she . . . you'll see, okay, you'll see."

They entered the next room. There were only two babies there, and both were missing one leg.

"Dad," said Timmy. "Is one of these my sister?"

Swallowing hard, the father replied: "Well . . . actually . . . it's none of these . . . you see . . . it's even wor— Well . . . you'll see, okay, you'll see."

They stepped into the next room, where there was one just baby, with both legs missing.

Timmy asked nervously: "Dad, is that my sister?"

"Well, Timmy . . . no . . . because . . . well . . ." The father paused, wiped his forehead with a handkerchief, and then continued: "You'll see, okay, you'll see . . ."

They stepped into the next room, where there was a baby with no legs and no arms and one ear missing.

Pointing at the poor baby, Timmy asked softly: "Dad, is that my sister?"

The father replied: "Well . . . unfortunately . . . oh, you'll see, okay, you'll see . . ."

The father dragged Timmy into the next room, and there was just one head – no arms, no legs and no body. Timmy raised his little finger, pointed trembling to the little head, and asked: "Dad, is that my sister?"

With tears running down his cheek, the father said: "No, it's even wor— Your sis— Oh . . . you'll see, okay, you'll see."

They went into the next room, and there, on a red silk pillow lay one solitary eye – no arms, no legs, no body, no head, no nothing, just one, single, eye.

Timmy didn't know what to think. He lifted his trembling arm, pointed to the eye and sobbed: "Dad, is that my sister?"

"Yes," said the father, by now in floods of tears. "That is your sister."

Timmy thought for a second and then asked tenderly: "Can I wave to her?"

"There's not much point," said the father. "Unfortunately, she's blind."

You have to change a baby's diapers every day. When those directions on the side of the Pampers box say, "holds 6–12 pounds" they're not kidding! (Jeff Foxworthy)

Gazing adoringly at his new son lying in the cot, a husband said with a cheeky grin: "He's quite big down there, isn't he?"

"Yes," said the wife. "But at least he's got your eyes."

Bankers

A consultant surgeon asked a doctor: "Have you told the banker in bed number eleven that he only has a week to live?"

"Yes, I have," replied the doctor.

"Damn!" said the consultant. "I wanted to tell him!"

What's the difference between a guy who lost everything in Las Vegas and an investment banker? – A tie.

A local charity office realized that it had never received a donation from the town's leading banker. So they called him, hoping to get a contribution. "Our research shows that out of a yearly income of at least £750,000, you haven't given a single penny to charity. Wouldn't you like to give back to the community in some way?"

The banker replied frostily: "First, did your research also show that my mother is dying after a long illness, and has medical bills that are several times her annual income?"

Embarrassed, the charity caller mumbled: "Um . . . no."

"Or," continued the banker, "that my brother, a disabled veteran, is blind and confined to a wheelchair?"

The charity caller began to stammer out an apology but was interrupted as the banker's voice rose with indignation. "Or that my sister's husband died in a car accident, leaving her penniless with three children?!"

The humiliated caller said simply: "Sorry, I had no idea."

"So," barked the banker, "if I don't give any money to them, why the hell would I give any to you?"

How do you save a banker from drowning? – Take your foot off his head.

A city banker was involved in a terrible car crash. The entire side of his Porsche was ripped away, along with his arm. When a police patrolman arrived on the scene, the banker was in a state of shock. "My car! My car!" he wailed.

Seeing the banker's injuries, the patrolman said: "Sir, I think you ought to be more concerned about your arm than your car."

The banker looked down in horror at where his arm used to be and screamed: "My Rolex! My Rolex!"

What's the difference between a banker and an onion? – You cry when you cut up an onion.

A man had been found guilty of pushing a city banker off the roof of a twelve-storey building. The judge said: "Quite frankly, I am appalled. In all my years on the bench this is the most flagrant disregard for human life I have ever had the misfortune to witness. In passing the most severe of sentences I can only hope to protect society from any further endangerment, but before I announce my judgement I would just like to ask you one question: Did it not occur to you that you could have hit somebody?"

A wife opened the fridge at breakfast one morning and said to her husband: "Michael, where have the eggs gone?"

The husband replied: "You know the city banker who's moved in next door? I gave them to him last night. I wanted to let him know how welcome he was."

"All twenty-four of them?" she asked.

"Yes, take a look at his windows!"

Did you hear about the banker's wife who had "severe penalty for early withdrawal" tattooed on her thigh?

A man went into a bar with a tiger and said: "Do you serve bankers?"

"Of course we do," said the bartender.

"Excellent. That's a beer for me and a banker for the tiger."

A senior banking executive arrived for work in a brand-new BMW. One of the young bankers couldn't help admiring it. "Nice car," he said.

"Well," said the executive, "work hard, put the hours in, and next year I'll have an even better one."

A banker was knocked down and killed by a truck outside my house yesterday. I thought, "Wow, that could have been me." Except I can't drive a truck.

Bars

A horse walked into a bar. The bartender said: "Why the long face?"

The horse said: "One theory is that in our early ancestors the skull lengthened so that when grazing, our eyes were positioned above the grass, thereby enabling us to spot oncoming predators."

"So it's not because you're unhappy, then?"

"Goodness me, no!" exclaimed the horse. "It's an evolutionary feature."

Then the horse did a massive dump on the floor.

A guy was chatting up a girl in a bar. He said: "You remind me of my little toe."

"Ah," she said. "Is that because I'm small and cute?"

"No, it's because I'll probably end up banging you on the coffee table."

While sitting at a bar, a guy glanced across the room and saw a pretty young woman waving at him and mouthing "hello". But he was puzzled because he couldn't place her. So when he had finished his drink, he went over and asked her: "Do you know me?"

"I think you're the father of one of my kids," she replied.

He started to panic. His mind raced back to the only time he had ever been unfaithful to his wife and he blurted out: "My God, are you the stripper from my bachelor party that got me so aroused I had to lay you right there and then on the pool table while all my buddies sprayed whipped cream on us?"

"No," she replied calmly. "Actually, I'm your son's math teacher."

Chat-up line in a bar: "Does this rag smell like chloroform to you?"

A woman and her husband were out having a few drinks in a bar. As they were discussing different drinks, she remembered a new cocktail she had heard about and begged her husband to try one.

After a little persuasion, he relented and allowed her to order the drink for him. The bartender subsequently placed the following items on the bar: a salt shaker, a shot of Baileys and a shot of lime juice.

The husband looked at the ingredients quizzically and the woman explained: "First you put a bit of salt on your tongue. Next you drink the shot of Baileys and hold it in your mouth. Then finally you drink the lime juice."

So the husband, trying to please her, went along with it. He put the salt on his tongue – it was salty, obviously, but okay. He drank the shot of Baileys – smooth, rich, cool, very pleasant. He thought it was quite a good drink – until he drank the lime juice.

At one second, the sharp lime taste hit. At two seconds, the Baileys curdled. At three seconds, the salty, curdled taste and mucous-like constituency hit. At four seconds, it felt as if he had a mouth full of catarrh. This triggered his gag reflex, but being manly and not wanting to disappoint his wife, he swallowed the now foul-tasting drink.

After finally choking it down, he turned to his wife and said: "My God, what do you call that drink?"

She smiled at him and answered: "Blow Job Revenge."

A guy walked into an empty Montana bar and ordered a beer. As he approached the bar, he noticed a table about six foot by four foot with some lines marked six to ten inches from one edge. Next to each line there were initials. So he asked the bartender: "What are all those marks on that table?"

"It's a game the locals play," said the bartender. "They pull out their dicks, stretch them as far as they can and mark a line."

Well, this guy was hung like a horse and reckoned he could beat all the lines on the table, so he asked: "Can I have a go?"

"Sure," said the bartender.

So the guy pulled out his dick and it was a clear winner by about three inches. He started to mark his line down when the bartender said: "No mate, the locals start from the other side."

A man walked into a bar with an octopus. He perched the octopus on a stool and announced that it was the smartest octopus in the world. "This octopus," he boasted, "is a musical genius. In fact, I'm so confident of his ability that I will pay £100 to anyone here who can find a musical instrument that my octopus can't play."

A man stepped forward with a guitar. The octopus picked it up and played better than Jimi Hendrix.

Another customer produced a trumpet. The octopus picked it up and played better than Louis Armstrong.

Then a third man handed the octopus a set of bagpipes. The octopus looked bewildered.

"Ha!" exclaimed the challenger. "You can't play it!"

"Play it?" said the octopus. "I'm going to fuck it as soon as I get its pyjamas off!"

A thirteen-year-old girl walked into a bar and demanded of the bartender: "Give me a double Scotch on the rocks."

"Do you want to get me into trouble?" asked the bartender, incredulous.

"Maybe later," said the girl. "Right now, I just want the Scotch."

A man walked into a bar and said to the barman: "Anything but a pint of Stella."

"What's wrong with Stella?" asked the barman.

"I had fifteen pints last night and woke up fucking skint."

"Well," said the barman, "I suppose fifteen pints would leave you a bit short."

"No, you don't understand. Skint is the name of my Jack Russell."

A sexy young woman walked up to a bartender and purred: "May I speak with your manager?"

The smitten bartender was eager to be of service. "Can I help you?" he asked.

"Well, it's kinda personal."

"I'm sure I can help," he insisted.

She smiled and slipped two of her fingers suggestively into his mouth. He was instantly turned on and began sucking them.

Then she leaned forward and whispered in his ear: "Tell your manager there's no toilet paper in the ladies' restroom."

A man wanks into a bar. The bartender says: "Sorry, we don't serve your typo in here."

An attractive woman was standing at the bar when she turned to the man next to her and purred: "I love the strong silent type."

Thinking he was being chatted up, he replied: "You mean a man like me?"

"No," she said moving away. "Farts – like the one I've just done."

Three guys were sitting in a bar talking about the scariest sound they'd ever heard.

The first said: "My car broke down on a level-crossing one night, and I heard this train coming down the track. I was so scared I thought I was going to have a heart attack on the spot!"

The second said: "I was skiing in the mountains last winter, and suddenly I heard this sinister rumble getting nearer and nearer by the second. It was an avalanche. I was so scared all the snow around me was brown!"

The third said: "I remember when I was down in Houston. I picked up this chick in a bar and she took me back to her penthouse flat. Just when I started giving it to her, the door was kicked in. 'Shit!' she screamed. 'That's my husband!' So I climbed out the window on to this six-inch ledge. Just then the husband reached out of the window and grabbed my balls in his right hand."

"Hang on," interrupted the first guy. "What's that got to do with the most frightening sound you ever heard?"

"Well," said the third guy. "Have you ever heard a bloke trying to open a straight razor with his teeth?"

Bestiality

Five men were stranded on a tropical island. The only female around was a gorilla that lived on the other side of the island. After a month, the sexual frustration was so great that one of the men, Wayne, announced: "I'm so horny, I can't bear it anymore!"

So he grabbed a bag and stormed off to the other side of the island, closely followed by his four friends. They managed to catch the gorilla and each guy grabbed an arm or a leg while Wayne put the bag over the gorilla's head. He then climbed on top of the gorilla and started to have sex with her.

The gorilla fought and struggled until she finally got an arm free and wrapped it around Wayne's back. Then she got both feet free and wrapped them around Wayne's waist. Finally she got her other arm free, grabbed on to his hips and started pulling him in harder and harder.

Wayne yelled to his buddies: "Get it off! Get it off!"

"What do you mean?" they said. "You're on top – we can't get her off you."

"No," said Wayne. "I mean get the bag off. I want to kiss the bitch!"

A woman walked in to find her husband giving their dog a blow job.

"That's disgusting!" she screamed. "What have you got to say for yourself?"

The husband just sat there and said nothing.

She yelled: "The cat got your tongue?"

He said: "Sometimes."

A lonely newspaper reporter, sent out to cover the Gold Rush, walked into a smalltown bar. He asked one of the prospectors what they did for female companionship and was told: "We shag sheep."

The reporter was disgusted by the thought but after seeing the handful of local women, he had to agree that the sheep were prettier. Even so, he resisted temptation for several months until his frustration finally became too much to bear. So he caught a nice sheep, took it to the town hotel and bedded it. The next day he took his four-legged lover into the bar. As he and the ewe walked in, everyone put down their drinks and stared at him as if he were crazy.

"You goddam bunch of hypocrites!" he raged. "You've all been shagging sheep for years and now that I've finally stooped to your level, you all stare at me like I'm some kind of weird pervert."

A lone cowboy spoke up from the back. "But tenderfoot, don't you know? That's the sheriff's gal!"

Old Macdonald abused his sheep, RSPCA.

Once upon a time in a far-off land, three princes declared that they wanted to marry the king's beautiful daughter, but as a test to prove their worth, they first had to perform three difficult tasks: vanquish a giant, turn lead to gold, and have sex with a sheep.

The first suitor was slain by the giant, the second failed to turn lead into gold, but the third successfully completed all three tasks.

"Congratulations," the king said to him. "You may now have my daughter's hand in marriage."

"Sod that!" said the prince. "I want the sheep!"

Why is the camel called the ship of the desert? – Because it's full of Arab semen.

A woman came downstairs to find the heating engineer shagging her dog. She phoned the police but they said there was nothing they could do because he was Corgi Registered.

I don't know how long I could be a vet before I got bored and started shagging stuff. (Frankie Boyle)

A farmer had been having sex with one of his pigs for five years until all of a sudden he started to feel guilty about it. It preyed on his conscience so much that he decided to confess everything to his priest.

The priest was shocked to hear the farmer's tale and could only ask: "Was the pig male or female?"

"Female, of course," said the farmer indignantly. "What do you think I am, some kind of pervert?"

If God had not meant man to have sex with goats, why put the horns in such a handy position?

A man appeared in court accused of having sex with dogs. The judge remarked: "This is absolutely disgusting. How low can you go?"

The man said: "A Chihuahua."

A captain in the Foreign Legion was transferred to a desert outpost. On his tour of inspection, he noticed a camel tethered at the rear of the enlisted men's barracks, so he asked the sergeant for an explanation.

"Well," replied the sergeant, "we're miles from civilization here and understandably the men have certain sexual urges. So when they do, we have the camel."

"I see," said the captain. "Well, if it's good for morale, it's fine by me."

After six months at the camp, the captain was starting to feel sexual urges of his own. So one night he ordered the sergeant to fetch the camel. The sergeant then watched in surprise as the captain climbed on to a foot stool and proceeded to have passionate sex with the camel. As he stepped down from the stool with a smile of satisfaction, he said: "Well, Sergeant, is that how the enlisted men do it with the camel?"

"Actually, sir," replied the sergeant, "mostly they just use the camel to ride into town."

Bikers

A surgeon, an accountant and a biker were standing at a bar talking. The surgeon finished his gin and said: "Tomorrow is my wedding anniversary. I bought my wife a diamond ring and a Mercedes. I figure that if she doesn't like the diamond ring, at least she'll like the Mercedes and will know that I love her."

The accountant finished his Scotch and said: "On my last anniversary, I bought my wife a pearl necklace and a vacation in the Bahamas. I figured that if she didn't like the necklace, she'd like the Bahamas and would know that I love her."

The biker finished his beer and snarled: "For my last anniversary, I got my bitch a T-shirt and a vibrator. I figured if she didn't like the T-shirt, she could go fuck herself."

A middle-aged guy was sitting quietly in a truck stop when three burly bikers strode in. The first biker walked over to the man and stubbed a cigarette into his lunch. Then the second biker spat into the man's cup of tea. Finally, the third biker picked up the man's full plate of food and hurled it across the room, splattering it all over the wall. Without saying a word, the man got up and left.

"He wasn't much of a man, was he?" sneered one of the bikers to the waitress.

"Not much of a truck driver either," she said. "He just backed his truck over three motorbikes."

A little man walked into a bar and slipped on a pile of dog poop by the door. Moments later, a burly biker came in and slipped on it as well.

The little man said: "I just did that."

So the biker hit him.

A rough biker decided to take his classy new girlfriend out to a trendy restaurant for a rare treat. While they were enjoying their meal, they overheard the man at the next table ask his wife: "Pass the honey, honey."

Then on the other side, a man was saying to his date: "Pass the sugar, sugar."

Determined not to be outdone and to show that he, too, could be romantic, the biker leaned over to his girlfriend and growled: "Pass the bacon, pig."

Two bikers were sitting in a bar. One suddenly turned to the other and said: "Jesus! What's that smell? Have you just farted or shit yourself?"

"I've shit myself," said the first biker nonchalantly.

"Bloody hell, mate! Why don't you go and clean yourself up?"

Sipping his pint, the first biker replied: "Because I haven't finished yet."

Birds

A man had been shipwrecked on a desert island for nine years. Then one day he spotted a ship on the horizon. He frantically waved his arms and jumped up and down shouting, until he spied a rowboat being let down into the water from the ship. About ten minutes later, the rowboat reached the shore carrying a man in a captain's uniform.

"Thank God!" said the shipwrecked man. "I thought I was never going to be rescued."

"How long have you been here?" asked the captain.

"Nine long years," replied the man.

"Nine years?" said the captain. "How have you coped all that time on your own?"

"Well, I'm quite resourceful. I've built my own house . . ."

"But nine years!" said the captain. "Nine years without sex!"

"Ah well, that's not quite true," said the man shyly.

"What do you mean?" inquired the captain.

"Well, about six months ago I was down here on the shore washing my feet when I noticed an ostrich further up the beach with its head buried in the sand and its arse facing me. I thought it's been eight-and-a-half years since I last had sex, so I crept up behind it and WALLOP!"

"Ugh, that must have been disgusting!" cried the captain.

"Actually, it was okay for the first three miles, but then we got out of step."

Little Johnny said to his dad: "Do you and Mum keep birds in your bedroom?"

"No," said the father. "Why do you ask?"

"Well," said Johnny, "last night I was passing by your room and I heard you say to Mum: 'Do you want to swallow or should I let it fly?'"

My pet budgie broke his leg, so I made him a little splint out of two matchsticks. His face lit up when he tried to walk — mainly because I'd forgotten to remove the sandpaper from the bottom of his cage.

Old natural history books document the existence of a now extinct bird called the ono. From the same family as the albatross, it was a sea bird that roamed the Pacific until the late nineteenth century and was renowned for its huge wingspan and short legs. The male was particularly distinctive, possessing large, bright-red testicles.

The ono bird was given its unusual name by American sailors who observed it coming in to land on desert island beaches. While the females of the species landed in silence, the males were heard to cry "Oh no, oh no, oh no" just before touching down on their short 15 cm legs — and large 22 cm testicles.

Two eagles were flying along when a jet screamed past them.

One eagle said: "Wow! Did you see how fast that thing was going?"

The other eagle said: "You'd go that fast, too, if your asshole was on fire!"

A bird was flying south for the winter, but had set off too late and found itself frozen solid in a blizzard. It dropped to earth in a field of cows, landing in a massive cow pat, just as it was being deposited by the fattest cow in the field. At first, the bird was disgusted until it realized that the pile of poop was actually thawing him out. As the ice melted and his feathers returned to normal, he tweeted joyously, but the sounds were heard by a nearby cat, which promptly crept over and ate the bird.

There are three morals to this story:

1 Not everyone who gets you into shit is your enemy.
2 Not everyone who gets you out of shit is your friend.
3 If you are in shit, keep your mouth shut.

Birth

A man and a woman were discussing the worst pain that anyone could possibly experience. The woman said: "Without doubt, there is nothing more painful in life than childbirth."

"Nonsense," said the man, "a kick in the bollocks is much more painful. Ask any guy."

"You're so wrong," insisted the woman. "Childbirth is far more painful."

The man was not about to yield to her argument and announced: "I have proof that I am right."

"What proof?" she asked scornfully.

"Well," he continued, "a few years after giving birth, a woman will say to her partner: 'Do you want to try for another baby?' But I have never, ever, ever heard a man say — even years later — 'You know what I'd really like? Another kick in the bollocks!'"

A woman in labour was screaming in agony: "Get this thing out of me! Give me the drugs now!"

Between outbursts she turned to her boyfriend and snarled: "You did this to me, you bastard! It's all your fault."

The boyfriend replied calmly: "If you remember, I wanted to fuck you up the arse, but you said: 'No way, it'll be too painful.'"

A little town had a high birth rate that had attracted the attention of the sociologists at the state university. They wrote a grant proposal for their study and received a sizeable amount of money to enable them to carry out detailed research. They used the grant to hire a few additional sociologists, an anthropologist, a family-planning and birth-control specialist, and rented an office in the town.

While the researchers set up their computers and began designing their questionnaires, the project director decided to go to the local drugstore for a cup of coffee. He sat down at the counter, ordered his coffee, and while he was drinking it, he told the druggist what his purpose was in town, then asked him if he had any idea why the birth rate was so high.

"Sure," said the druggist. "Every morning the six o'clock train comes through here and blows for the crossing. It wakes everybody up, and, well, it's too late to go back to sleep, and it's too early to get up . . ."

A middle-aged couple had two beautiful daughters but always talked about having a son. They decided to try one last time for the son they always wanted, and at last the wife got pregnant and delivered a healthy baby boy. The joyful father rushed to the hospital to see his new son, but was horrified at the ugliest child he had ever set eyes upon.

He told his wife: "There's no way I can be the father of this baby. Look at the two beautiful daughters I fathered! Have you been fooling around behind my back?"

The wife smiled sweetly and replied: "Not this time!"

An old country doctor drove out in to the wilds to deliver a baby at a remote farmhouse that had no electricity. When the doctor arrived, no one was home except for the mother in labour and her five-year-old daughter.

The doctor instructed the child to hold up a lantern so he could see while he helped the woman deliver the baby. The girl did so, the mother pushed and, after a little while, the doctor lifted the newborn baby by the feet and spanked him gently on the bottom to get him to take his first breath. The doctor then asked the girl what she thought of her new baby brother.

"Hit him again," she said. "He shouldn't have crawled up there in the first place!"

A white guy was pacing around the hospital room waiting for his wife to give birth. Eventually a doctor entered and said: "Congratulations, sir! You are the father of four bouncing baby boys."

"Four?!" exclaimed the man. "Wow! How about that? Mind you, I'm not surprised, because between you and me, Doc, I've got a dick like a chimney stack!"

"Well," said the doctor, "you might want to get it swept, because they're all black."

Birth Control

Visiting his local health centre, a man saw a sign that read: "Family Planning – Use Rear Entrance." He said to a passing nurse: "That's bloody good advice!"

A devout Catholic told his priest: "I've had it up to here with my wife. I'm filing for divorce."

"That's a big step to take," said the priest. "May I ask why?"

"I discovered her secret supply of birth-control pills, Father."

"I realize that contraception goes against our religious beliefs," said the priest, "but is it sufficient justification for ending your marriage, which after all is also considered sacred in God's eyes?"

"It's not just that, Father. You see, I had a vasectomy four years ago . . ."

My girlfriend's father asked me what form of contraception we used. Apparently "facial cumshot" wasn't the answer he was hoping for.

Have you heard about the new mint-flavoured birth-control pills for women that they take immediately before sex? – They're called Predickamints.

A teenage boy came home out of breath. He said to his father: "Hey, Dad, I've just had sex with Marie from down the street. It was my first time."

"Well done, son," said the father proudly, before adding: "But I hope you remembered to wear something."

"Yeah, I did," said the boy. "A balaclava."

A man called his priest and told him that he and his wife didn't want any more children. "Should we try the pill?" the man asked.

The priest suggested: "Have you tried the rhythm method?"

The man said: "Where am I going to get a band at three o'clock in the morning?"

Blindness

Despite being blind from birth, Charlie Bishop was extremely popular with the ladies, and being a responsible person every month he would pay a visit to the pharmacy to stock up on condoms. The taxi would always drop him off at the same spot on Main Street and he would then pace out the distance to the chemist shop to collect his rubbers.

However, one day he had a different taxi driver who was unable to park in the usual spot. So when Charlie measured out his steps he actually ended up in the shoe shop next door to the pharmacy.

Unaware of his error, Charlie approached the counter. The young lady assistant asked: "How can I help you, sir?"

"I've come for a box of the usual," said Charlie.

"Oh, what size do you take?" asked the girl.

"I've never been asked that before," said Charlie. "To be honest, I don't know."

"No problem. I'll take a quick measure."

"Fair enough," said Charlie, whipping out his dick.

The girl cried in horror: "That's not a foot!"

Charlie said: "It bloody nearly is!"

A pilot and co-pilot boarded an airplane. The pilot had a white stick and kept bumping into passengers while the co-pilot had a guide dog. Both men wore dark glasses. At first, the passengers thought it was a joke but when the engines started up they began to grow concerned. As the plane built up speed along the runway, they became really worried. They looked to the flight attendants for words of comfort but when none were forthcoming, panic set in. The end of the runway moved closer and closer. The passengers became hysterical. Finally, with the plane less than twenty feet from the end of the runway, everybody screamed. Immediately the plane soared into the air.

Up in the cockpit, the co-pilot breathed a huge sigh of relief. He turned to the pilot and said: "One of these days the passengers aren't going to scream, and we're going to get killed!"

How did the blind boy's parents punish him for being naughty? – They rearranged the furniture.

How did the blind girl's parents punish her for being naughty? – They left the plunger in the toilet.

A woman walked into a fishing shop and found a blind man serving behind the cash desk. She asked for a fishing line for her husband but, taking advantage of the man's blindness, she sneaked a £90 reel into her bag. The blind man was just about to ring up the purchase when the phone rang. It was the store manager, who had positioned himself behind a two-way mirror at the back counter.

The manager spoke quietly into the phone. "The lady whose purchase you are ringing up just put a £90 reel into her bag. Don't make a big deal about it, but make sure you charge her for it."

The blind man put down the phone and told the woman: "That'll be £6.50 for the line and £90 for the reel."

The woman was so embarrassed at being caught that she farted loudly.

The blind man went on: "And that'll be £3.50 more for the duck call and £1.50 for the musk scent!"

What's the fastest thing on land? – Stevie Wonder's speedboat.

A blind man with a guide dog went into a store. Suddenly, the man picked the dog up by the tail and started swinging the animal above his head.

The store owner was alarmed by this behaviour and demanded: "Can I help you, sir?"

"No, it's all right," said the blind man. "Just looking around."

Dating a blind girl is challenging but rewarding. It took me ages to get her husband's voice right.

A blind man walked into a restaurant. He told the owner: "I can't read the menu, but if you bring me a dirty fork from the previous customer, I'll sniff it and order from that."

The owner was taken aback by the request, but decided to go along with it. So he went into the kitchen, fetched a dirty fork and handed it to the blind man, who smelled it and promptly ordered the Irish stew.

The following week, the blind man went to the restaurant again and repeated his request for a dirty fork. The owner produced a dirty fork from the kitchen; the blind man smelled it and ordered spaghetti bolognese.

The third time the blind man visited the restaurant, the owner decided to play a trick on him. He went into the kitchen and said to his wife Erica: "Will you rub this fork around your vagina before I take it to the blind customer?"

The wife did as he asked, and then the owner took the fork out to the blind man who sniffed it and exclaimed: "Hey, I didn't know Erica worked here!"

I was in bed with a blind girl last night and she said I had the biggest penis she had ever laid her hands on. I said: "You're pulling my leg."

A blind man went to a brothel and because he couldn't see what he was getting, he was given the roughest old whore in town. They went upstairs and she undressed, but when he started to run his hands over her spotty butt, he recoiled in horror.

"Don't worry," she said. "It's just a touch of acne."

"Thank God!" said the blind man. "I thought it was the price list!"

What goes tap, tap, tap, boom? – A blind man in a minefield.

Poor little Michael had been blind from birth. One night, before he went to bed, his mother told him that the next day was very special. She told him that if he prayed very hard to God, he'd be able to see when he woke up.

Michael was so excited at the thought of finally being able to see that he prayed really hard for two hours.

The next morning, his mother came into his room. She smiled at her son and said: "Wake up, Michael. Open your eyes and all of your prayers will be answered."

Michael opened his eyes and wailed: "Mummy, mummy, I still can't see!"

"I know darling," said his mother. "April Fool!"

Blondes

Chatting up a blonde in a London bar, an American guy asked her: "Where are you from?"

"Birmingham," she replied.

"Hey!" he said. "Do you know there's a place in America that shares the same name?"

"Really?" said the blonde. "What's it called?"

Why can't a blonde waterski? – Because her legs spread the moment her crotch gets wet.

How can you tell when a blonde is dating? – By the buckle print on her forehead.

An interior designer was talking with a female client about decorating her apartment. The woman said she would like the lounge painted cream. The designer wrote this down, went over to the open window and shouted: "Green side up!"

Moving to the kitchen, the woman said she would like tangerine. The designer wrote this down, went over to the open window and yelled: "Green side up!"

When they reached the bedroom, the woman said she wanted it pink. The designer wrote this down, went over to the open window and shouted: "Green side up!"

The woman was puzzled and asked him: "Why do you keep going to the window and shouting, 'Green side up!'?"

The designer explained: "Because across the street I've got a crew of blondes laying turf."

A blonde was in bed with her boyfriend when they started to argue. She yelled: "How dare you call me a slapper! Get out of my bed right now – and take your fucking mates with you!"

How is a blonde like a shotgun? – Four cocks and she's loaded.

What is a bellybutton for? – It gives a blonde a place to park her gum on the way down.

A blonde went to the doctor's to complain of a sore throat. The doctor sat her down, got out his flashlight and said: "Open wide."

"I can't," replied the blonde. "The arms on this chair get in my way."

Why do blondes get married? – So they can appear in *Readers" Wives*.

A blonde went to a dry cleaner's and said to the deaf old guy behind the counter: "Can you get the stains out of this dress?"

"Come again?" he said, cupping his hand to his ear.

"No," said the blonde, "this time it's just mayonnaise."

How does a blonde get rid of unwanted pubic hair? – She spits it out.

Why did God create blondes? – Because sheep can't fetch a beer from the fridge.

Unable to log on to the internet, a blonde phoned the help desk. The adviser asked her: "Are you sure you used the correct password?"

"Yes, I'm sure," said the blonde. "I saw the guy doing it when he set everything up."

"Can you tell me what the password was?"

"Yes. Six stars."

Did you hear about the blonde who had two chances to get pregnant but she blew them both?

What happened to the blonde who tried sniffing coke? – The ice cubes got stuck in her nose.

What is sixty-eight to a blonde? – Where she goes down on you and you owe her one.

A blonde asked her brunette flatmate: "Do you have Oxfam's number?"

"Why do you want their number?" said the brunette.

"Well," explained the blonde, "we've just had our water bill for £248, but I heard on TV that Oxfam can supply a family with water for just £2 a month."

A brunette said to a blonde: "My boyfriend is so sweet."

"Oh," said the blonde. "I always thought he tasted a bit salty."

Did you hear about the best blonde secretary? – She never missed a period.

A blonde showed her boyfriend the pregnancy test she had taken. The result was positive.

"Should we keep it?" he asked.

"No point," she said. "You can only use them once."

How can you break a blonde's nose? – Take your underwear off and lie down under a glass table.

A man went on a date with a blonde. "Do you have any kids?" she asked.

"Yes," he replied, "I have one child that's under two."

"I might be blonde," she said indignantly, "but I know how many one is!"

A gang of bank robbers ordered the staff to take off their clothes and lie face down on the floor. But a nervous blonde pulled off her clothes and lay on her back.

"Turn over, Cindy," said the brunette lying next to her. "This is a stick-up, not the office party!"

What do you get when a naked blonde does a handstand? – A brunette with bad breath.

A blonde at a party was telling her friend that she'd gone off men for life. "They lie, they cheat, and they're just no good," she moaned. "From now on when I want sex, I'm going to use my tried and tested plastic companion."

"What happens when the batteries run out?" asked her friend.

"That's simple," replied the blonde. "I'll just fake an orgasm as usual!"

What important question does a blonde ask before sex? – "Do you want me to charge by the hour or for all night?"

A guy wanted to get an all-over tan before going on a hot date with a gorgeous blonde. So he went sunbathing on the flat roof of his house, but unfortunately he fell asleep and ended up with terrible sunburn on his dick.

Even so, he went to the blonde's apartment and they sat watching a video, but as the film went on, his sunburn started to cause him considerable pain. Eventually he could bear it no longer and made an excuse to go to the kitchen, where he went to the fridge, poured a glass of ice cold milk and dipped his burning penis into it. The relief was instant.

Just then the blonde, wondering where he had gone, peered around the kitchen door. "Oh," she said. "So that's how you guys load those things!"

How is a blonde like a screen door? – The more you bang it, the looser it gets.

What do you call a blonde with a bag of sugar on her head? – Sweet Fuck All.

A blonde thought she might be pregnant, so her boyfriend went out and bought her a pregnancy-testing kit. He said: "Now take this into the bathroom, do your business on it and see if it changes colour."

Five minutes later, he called out: "Has it turned blue yet?"

"No," said the blonde. "It's still brown."

Why was the blonde nicknamed "Éclair"? – Because she loved to be filled with cream.

How do you know when a blonde has just lost her virginity? – Her crayons are still sticky.

A man arrived home to find his blonde wife propping up their washing machine on one side with two bricks.

"What are you doing?" he asked.

She said: "I'm doing the washing at thirty degrees."

A blonde went to a hospital to visit a friend. She hadn't been inside a hospital for several years and felt very ignorant about all the new technology. A technician followed her into the elevator, wheeling a large, intimidating-looking machine with numerous tubes, wires and dials.

The blonde looked at it and smiled: "I certainly wouldn't want to be hooked up to that!"

"Neither would I," replied the technician. "It's a floor-cleaning machine."

What did the blonde's right leg say to the left leg? – Between us we can make a lot of money.

What's the difference between a blonde and a rooster? – A blonde crows, "Any-cock'll-do."

A movie at the cinema had just started when a blonde from the middle of the row suddenly stood up and said she needed to go. Everyone muttered their disapproval about having to stand up to let the blonde out and she apologized profusely as she clambered over people's legs and bags. When she finally reached the end of the row, the guy in the last seat complained: "Couldn't you have done this earlier?"

"Sorry but no," said the blonde. "The 'Turn Off Your Cell Phone, Please' message only just flashed up on screen."

The man was mystified. "So why did you need to get up?"

The blonde said: "Because mine is in the car."

Why did the blonde have sex in the microwave oven? – She wanted to have a baby in nine minutes.

How are saunas like blondes? – They're both hot and wet when you enter, and they don't mind if you bring friends.

A traffic cop stopped a blonde who was driving erratically. "Can I see your driver's licence?" he asked.

The blonde looked blank. "What's a driver's licence?"

"A little card with your picture on it," explained the cop.

"Oh, that," she said. "Here it is." And she handed him the licence.

"And may I have your car insurance?" he asked.

"What's that?" asked the blonde.

"It's the document that says you're allowed to drive the car."

"Oh, that," she said. "Here it is." And she handed him the car insurance.

The cop then reached into his trousers and whipped out his cock.

"Oh, no," groaned the blonde. "Not another breathalyser test!"

Why did the blonde have a hysterectomy? – She wanted to stop having grand-children.

A blonde went to the doctor and said: "It's been six weeks since my last visit, Doctor, but I'm not feeling any better."

"I see," said the doctor, "and did you follow the instructions on the medicine I gave you?"

"I sure did," replied the blonde. "The bottle said: 'Keep tightly closed.'"

Did you hear about the blonde who almost killed her toy poodle? – She tried to insert batteries.

A blonde walked into a bar holding a lump of fresh dog poop. "How lucky was that!" she said to the bartender. "I very nearly stepped in this!"

A disabled man was sick of life and decided to commit suicide. So he positioned his wheelchair near the ledge of the fifth floor of a multi-storey car park, but couldn't quite manage to get over the barrier so that he could plunge to his death. In desperation, he pleaded with passers-by to help him end his life but they either ignored him or refused.

Eventually, a beautiful blonde went over to him, but just he was about to ask her to help him die, she looked him in the eye and gave him the most magical, compassionate smile. Dazzled by her beauty, he instinctively smiled back and realized that all of a sudden the world no longer seemed such a terrible place.

"I'm so glad we met," she said tenderly. "You are just the sort of guy I've been looking for. You look so honest and kind, unlike all the other men I've known! What are you doing up here, anyway?"

She took his hand as he replied: "You know, it's hard to believe, but when I first came up here I was just desperate for someone to toss me off, but none of these men would do it. But now I've seen you, I don't feel the need anymore!"

Her face dropped instantly. "You dirty queer," she yelled, and pushed him over the barrier.

Two blondes were doing a crossword puzzle. The first blonde said: "Flightless bird from Iceland, six and seven letters."

"That's easy," said the second blonde. "Frozen chicken."

How is a blonde like a refrigerator? – Everyone likes to put their meat in her.

The popular blonde cheerleader bounced into the local card shop, looked around, and then approached the clerk. "Do you have any, like, really, really special birthday cards?" she asked.

"Yes, we do," he replied. "As a matter of fact, here's a new one inscribed 'To the Boy Who Got My Cherry.'"

"Wow, neat!" she squealed. "I'll take the whole box."

What's the difference between a counterfeit dollar and a skinny blonde? – One's a phony buck.

A blonde and a brunette were talking in the office. The blonde complained that she had a sore throat.

"When I have a sore throat," said the brunette, "I give my husband a blow job, and then the next day my throat feels much better. You should try it."

"Okay," said the blonde. "I will."

The next day at work, the brunette asked the blonde how her throat was.

"Fine," said the blonde. "Your suggestion was great. Your husband couldn't believe it was your idea!"

Blow Jobs

A man bumped into a girl and her boyfriend in town. The man said: "Hey, you still owe me a blow job."

"You disgusting man!" she cried. "I wouldn't suck your dick if you were the last guy on earth. Tell him, Steve."

"Uh, this is awkward," said the man. "It was actually Steve I was talking to."

A wife was halfway through giving her husband a blow job when she broke off to plead: "Don't come in my mouth."

"Of course I won't, honey," he replied. "I know you don't like it, and anyway this is a nice restaurant."

My father always said to me: "Son, you can't call yourself a real man until you've made a girl gag on your dick whilst she's giving you head." Which is why I haven't washed mine for nine months.

A man visited a whorehouse which advertised a hooker who could sing and give blow jobs at the same time. He was intrigued by this, so he asked the Madam for the singing whore. The Madam took him upstairs to a room and then left. A minute later, a plain young woman entered and told him: "If you want a singing blow job, it has to be in the dark."

The man agreed, so she turned out the light and set to work, giving him the best blow job he had ever experienced – and she was singing "The Star Spangled Banner" at the same time. He soon blew his load, but by the time he had zipped up his fly and turned the light back on, the girl had already gone.

He paid the Madam and left, but he was still curious as to how someone could give such a fantastic blow job and sing at the same time. Determined to find out, he returned the following night and again asked for the singing whore. The same routine occurred, but before he had finished he whipped out a flashlight and turned it on. Again the girl was too quick for him and had fled the room. Still in the dark, he turned the room light on and found a glass eye on the floor.

After giving her boyfriend a blow job, a girl said to him: "I bet you wish you could suck your own cock, don't you?"

"No way!" he said. "I haven't washed the thing in weeks!"

> Penis breath, a lover's dread
> Is what you get when you give head.
> Unpleasant as it tends to be,
> Be grateful that he doesn't pee.
> It's times like this, you wonder why
> You bothered reaching for his fly;
> But it's too late, can't be a tease –
> Accept the facts, get on your knees.
> You know you've got a job to do,
> So open wide and shove it through,
> Lick the tip then take it all,
> Don't drag your teeth or he might bawl.
> Slide up and down, use your tongue
> And feel the precum start to run;

Your jaw it aches, your neck is numb,
So when the fuck's he gonna cum?
Just, when you can't take any more
You hear your lover's mighty roar,
And when he hits that real high note
You feel it oozing down your throat.
Salty, fishy, sticky stuff —
Okay already, that's enough;
Let's switch, you say, before you gag,
And what revenge, you're on the rag.

Bungee jumping is like getting a blow job from your grandmother — a lot of fun until you look down.

A nun climbed into a taxi cab one evening. As they set off, the driver glanced in his mirror and confessed: "I've always wanted to have a nun give me a blow job."

"Well," said the nun, "I suppose that might be possible provided you are single and a Catholic."

"As a matter of fact I am single and Catholic," replied the driver.

"Very well," said the nun. "Pull into this side street."

So the driver pulled into a quiet, dark side street but as he stopped the car he suddenly burst into tears.

"What's wrong?" asked the nun.

"I have a confession to make," sobbed the driver. "I'm married and Jewish."

"That's okay," said the nun. "My real name's David and I'm on my way to a Halloween party!"

My girlfriend's just had her teeth whitened, although to be honest most of it landed on her chin.

A couple of nights ago I was licking jelly off my boyfriend's penis. And I thought, "Oh my God! I'm turning into my mother!" — Sarah Silverman

Trapped in an unhappy marriage, a guy decided he needed some companionship. So he went to a pet store with a view to buying a dog or a cat. He explained his situation to the pet store owner who said: "I've got the ideal pet for you — a South American toothless rat."

"No, I don't think it's for me," said the man.

"But," continued the store owner, "it gives great head."

So the guy bought the rat and took it home. His wife took one look at it and screamed: "What the hell is that thing?"

"Never mind what it is!" said the husband. "Just teach it to cook, and pack your bags!"

I've been dating this girl, and she said she doesn't give blow jobs in the first six months. So I told her to ring me nearer the time.

A businessman had stayed the night at a Wyoming hotel. When he checked out the next morning, the desk clerk noticed that he looked a bit edgy.

"Was everything okay with your room?" the clerk asked.

"The hell it was!" snapped the businessman. "At two o'clock this morning I was woken up by this masked cowboy holding two guns to my head. He told me to unzip his jeans and then he sat on my chest and said that if I didn't suck his dick he was going to blow my fucking head off!"

"What did you do?" asked the clerk.

The businessman replied: "Did you hear any shooting?"

A young man walked into a bar and ordered six tequila shots.

"Six shots?" said the bartender. "Are you celebrating something?"

"Yeah," replied the young man. "My first blow job."

"In that case," said the bartender, "let me give you a seventh – on the house."

"No offence," said the young man, "but if six shots won't get rid of the taste, nothing will."

A family were watching TV together when the wife suddenly stood up and led her husband out of the room by the hand, leaving their two young sons behind. "Excuse us for a few minutes, boys," she said. "We just need a bit of time to ourselves in our room."

Ten minutes later, one of the boys became curious, so he decided to creep upstairs to investigate. Spotting that the door to his parents' bedroom was ajar, he peeked in to see what was going on. Then he crept back downstairs, fetched his little brother and took him up to peek into the bedroom. "Before you look in there," he whispered, "remember this is the same woman who used to tell us off for sucking our thumbs!"

How do you know who gives good blow jobs? – Word of mouth.

During a date with a girl, a young man asked her to give him oral sex.

"No," she said firmly. "You won't respect me."

So the young man was content to wait. After they had been going out together for six months, he again asked her for oral sex.

"No," she said. "You won't respect me."

Eventually the couple got married and on their wedding night he turned to her and said: "Honey, we're married now. You know I love you and respect you, so please will you give me oral sex?"

"No," she said. "I just know that if I do, you won't respect me."

So the man waited . . . and waited . . . and waited. On their silver wedding anniversary, he looked at her tenderly and said: "Darling, we've been married for twenty-five wonderful years now. We've raised two fantastic kids. You know that I love you and respect you totally. So how about you finally give me oral sex? Just the once? Please?"

Moved by his words, the wife at last agreed to his request and performed oral sex on him.

After she had finished, they were lying in bed relaxing when the phone rang. He turned to her and said: "Answer that, you dirty cocksucker."

My wife swallowed after a blow job for the first time in eight years last night. I wonder if it's a sign that she's coming out of her coma.

A man was hiking up a mountain when he spotted a woman standing at the edge of a cliff, sobbing her heart out.

"What's the matter?" he called out.

"I'm going to kill myself," she replied.

"Well," he said, "if you're going to jump, how about giving me a blow job before you do it?"

"I guess I might as well," wailed the woman. "My life's been nothing but misery."

After she had finished, the man said: "Wow! That was great! Why are you so depressed anyway?"

She replied: "My family disowned me for dressing like a woman."

Blow Job Etiquette – A Woman's Perspective

1 We are not obligated to do it, so if you get one, be grateful. Really grateful . . . like diamond necklace grateful.
2 I don't care what they did in the porn video you saw – it is not standard practice to cum on someone's face.
3 It is not essential for me to swallow.
4 My ears are not handles.
5 Do not push on the top of my head – unless you want to risk ending up with puke on your dick.
6 I don't care how relaxed you get; it is never okay to fart.
7 Having my period does not automatically mean that I'm going to blow you instead. I could just feel like shit and have no interest in sex for a week.
8 If I have to pause to remove a pubic hair from my teeth, don't tell me I've just "wrecked it" for you.
9 If you like how we do it, it's probably best not to speculate how we acquired our expertise. Just enjoy the moment.
10 No, it doesn't taste particularly good – and I don't care about the protein content.
11 No, I will not do it while you watch TV.
12 Just because "it's awake" when you get up does not mean I have to "kiss it good morning".
13 When you hear your friends complain about how they don't get blow jobs often enough, keep your mouth shut. It is neither appropriate to sympathize nor brag.

How do you stop your girlfriend from giving you a blow job? – Marry her.

A young girl asked her mother: "Where do babies come from?"

"Well," explained the mother, "Mummy and Daddy fall in love and get married and then they have sex. That means Daddy puts his penis into Mummy's vagina. That's how you get a baby."

"But," the girl continued, "the other night when I came into your room, you had Daddy's penis in your mouth. What do you get when you do that?"

"Jewellery, darling."

Body Jewellery

Belly piercings aren't sexy. Men just think they are because it reminds them of the staple in the middle of a porno mag. (Frankie Boyle)

A guy walked into a sleazy bar and ordered a drink. After a while he said to the rough-looking barmaid: "You should get your bellybutton pierced."
  "Why would I want to do that?" she asked.
  "Because it would be a great place to hang an air freshener."

I don't get the point of vajazzling. I mean, no guy has ever gone down there and thought, "Oh, this could do with redecorating." (Jack Whitehall)

My wife bought a DIY vajazzle kit, so I said I'd do it for her. But I got a bit carried away and she ended up with a glitteris as well.

A girl told her boyfriend: "I'm going off now to have a vajazzle."
  "What's a vajazzle?" he asked.
  She said: "It's where they put sequins all over a cunt."
  "Oh," he said. "So you're going to be on *Strictly Come Dancing*?"

Books

A man went into a bookshop and asked quietly: "I'd like to buy that book about coping with a small penis."
  The bookseller said: "I'm not sure if it's in yet."
  "Yes," said the man. "That's the one."

There's a new book out today – *The Korean Canine Training Manual: Fifty Ways to Wok Your Dog*.

I was disappointed with *Fifty Shades of Grey*. Despite being labelled "mummy porn", it didn't satisfy my fetish for Ancient Egypt.

Rejected children's book titles:

What Is That Dog Doing to That Other Dog?

Nancy Drew and the Mysterious Case of Recurring Crabs
Jodie Was So Bad Her Mum Stopped Loving Her
Good Kids Don't Move the Crackpipe
Babar, the Ivory Coat Rack
Why Can't Mr Fork and Mrs Electrical Outlet Be Friends?
Strangers Have the Best Candy
Peter Rabbit Gets Myxomatosis
The Little Sissy Who Snitched
Fun Games to Play with Fire
Alice's Adventures in the Red-Light District
The Pop-Up Book of Human Anatomy
Some Kittens Can Fly!
Johnny's Two Daddies
Curious George and the Busy Intersection
Controlling the Playground: Respect through Fear
Getting More Chocolate on Your Face
Making Grown-Up Friends on the Internet
Billy's Adventure in the Medicine Cabinet
The Final Straw: I'm Putting You Up for Adoption
Harry Potter and the Magic Spliff
Your Nightmares Are Real
POP! Goes the Hamster . . . and Other Great Microwave Games

A man went into a library and asked to borrow a book on suicide.

"No way," said the librarian. "You won't bring it back."

A young woman walked into a bookstore and while browsing the shelves she phoned a friend and started whispering about the amazing sex she had last night.

After a couple of minutes, the young man working at the cash desk shouted over: "Hey, this isn't a library!"

"I'm going to buy it," she replied, looking at the book in her hand.

"I'm not bothered about that," he replied. "I just mean you don't have to talk so quietly."

Anne Frank had time to write a novel. Mind you, it ends a bit abruptly. No sequel. Lazy. (Ricky Gervais)

Bill said to his friend Jim: "I've been reading a book called *The Secret Life of Adolf Hitler*. It told me things about him that I never knew."

"Like what?" asked Jim.

"Well, for instance, when he was having sex he liked to piss on people."

"Really?"

"Yes. It put me right off him."

Students at a school were assigned to read two books – *Titanic*, the story of the movie, and *My Life* by Bill Clinton. One student turned in the following book report, with the proposition that they were nearly identical stories! His professor gave him an A+ for this report.

Titanic: Cost – $29.99.

Clinton: Cost – $29.99.

Titanic: Over three hours to read.

Clinton: Over three hours to read.

Titanic: The story of Jack and Rose, their forbidden love, and subsequent catastrophe.

Clinton: The story of Bill and Monica, their forbidden love, and subsequent catastrophe.

Titanic: Jack is a starving artist.

Clinton: Bill is a bullshit artist.

Titanic: In one scene, Jack enjoys a good cigar.

Clinton: Ditto for Bill.

Titanic: During the ordeal, Rose's dress gets ruined.

Clinton: Ditto for Monica.

Titanic: Jack teaches Rose to spit.

Clinton: Let's not go there.

Titanic: Rose gets to keep her jewellery.

Clinton: Monica is forced to return her gifts.

Titanic: Rose remembers Jack for the rest of her life.

Clinton: Clinton doesn't remember Jack.

Titanic: Rose goes down on a vessel full of seamen.

Clinton: Monica . . . Oh, let's not go there, either.

Titanic: Jack surrenders to an icy death.

Clinton: Bill goes home to Hillary – basically the same thing.

Breasts

A flat-chested young woman went to the doctor about having her tiny breasts enlarged. Dr Woodgate told her: "Every morning after your shower, rub your chest and say, 'Scooby doobie doobies, I want bigger boobies.'"

So she did this for several months, and amazingly it worked. She grew magnificent D-cup boobs. Then one morning she was running late and in her haste to catch the train, she realized that she had forgotten her morning ritual. Fearing that she might lose her lovely breasts if she didn't recite the rhyme, she stood in the middle of the crowded train and said: "Scooby doobie doobies, I want bigger boobies."

Hearing this, the guy standing next to her said: "Excuse me, are you by any chance a patient of Dr Woodgate?"

"Why yes," she replied. "How did you know?"

He leaned closer, winked and whispered: "Hickory dickory dock . . ."

A new study shows that women with big breasts are smarter than women with smaller breasts. Though to be fair, the guy who conducted the study admits he wasn't really listening. (Conan O'Brien)

A man was walking through a hotel lobby when he accidentally bumped into a woman, his elbow hitting her in the right breast.

"Ma'am," he said by way of apology, "if your heart is as soft as your breast, I know you'll forgive me."

"Sir," she replied, "if your penis is as hard as your elbow, I'm in room 341."

A guy said to a girl in a bar: "I can tell what day a woman was born just by feeling her breasts."

"I don't believe you," she said.

"It's true," he insisted.

"Okay, then show me."

So he fondled her breasts for thirty seconds, by which time she was starting to get impatient.

"Come on," she demanded. "What day was I born?"

"Yesterday," he replied.

My buddy and I planned to go to a fancy-dress party as a pair of breasts. He didn't turn up. I looked a right tit.

Girl: What colour are my eyes?
Boy: 34C.

A man walked into the living room to find his wife breastfeeding their son. "How long do you have to do that for?" asked the husband. "When is he too old for it?"

"Well, it's a physical bond between a mother and her child, isn't it? It's only society that deems the practice to be unacceptable above a certain age."

"Shut up, Dennis," said the father. "I was talking to your mother."

I took a shower with my boyfriend. Ladies, I guarantee you if you take a shower with your boyfriend by the time you step out of that shower your breasts will be sparkling clean. (Sarah Silverman)

A man was walking down the street when he spotted a woman with magnificent breasts. He immediately offered her £100 if she would let him bite them.

"No way!" she exclaimed indignantly.

"What about for £1,000?" he persisted.

"No, certainly not. What kind of woman do you think I am?"

"You wouldn't even do it for £10,000?" he asked.

The woman looked astounded. "You'll pay me £10,000 if I let you bite my breasts?"

"That's right."

"Okay," she said. "Let's go over to that dark alley."

Once there she took off her blouse, and the man began caressing her breasts, kissing them, sucking them and fondling them.

She was beginning to get impatient. "Are you going to bite them or what?" she snapped.

"No," he said. "Too expensive."

My girlfriend's got a training bra. So her breasts have learned to sit up and beg to be played with.

Bulimia

How do you know when a survey of bulimics has been successful? – There's plenty of feedback.

Why do bulimics love KFC? – Because it comes with a bucket.

Did you hear about the guy who had bulimia and OCD? – He would bring up Alphabetti Spaghetti and then put it in alphabetical order.

What does a bulimic call two fingers? – Dessert.

California

An innocent young girl from a small town was visiting friends in San Francisco. She phoned her mother to let her know how she was getting along. "Things are rather strange here," said the daughter. "I see men who hold hands, kiss and hug each other. They're called 'gays' or 'homosexuals'. Even more surprising, there are women here who do the same things and they are referred to as 'lesbians'. You probably won't believe this, but some men here put their heads down on a woman's private parts and do things with their tongues."

"My God!" her mother exclaimed. "What do they call them?"

The daughter said: "Well, after I caught my breath I called one of them 'Gorgeous'."

Math Test for Los Angeles Junior Gang Members

1 Duane has an AK-47 with a 30-round clip. If he misses 6 out of 10 shots and shoots 13 times at each drive-by shooting, how many drive-by shootings can he attempt before he has to reload?

2 If José has 2 ounces of cocaine and he sells an 8-ball to Jackson for $320 and 2 grams to Billy for $85 per gram, what is the street value of the balance of the cocaine if he doesn't cut it?

3 Rufus is pimping for 3 girls. If the price is $65 for each trick, how many tricks will each girl have to turn so Rufus can pay for his $800-per-day crack habit?

4 Jarome wants to cut his half-pound of heroin to make 20 per cent more profit. How many ounces of cut will he need?

5 Willie gets $200 for stealing a BMW, $50 for a Chevy and $100 for a 4x4. If he has stolen 2 BMWs and 3 4x4s, how many Chevys will he have to steal to make $800?

6 Raoul is in prison for 6 years for murder. He got $10,000 for the hit. If his common-law wife is spending $100 per month, how much money will he have left when he gets out of prison and how many years will he get for killing her since she spent his money?

7 If the average spray-paint can cover 22 square feet and the average letter is 3 square feet, how many letters can a tagger spray with 3 cans of paint?
8 Hector knocked up 6 girls in his gang. There are 27 girls in the gang. What percentage of the girls in the gang has Hector knocked up?

What's the only thing that grows in Oakland? – The crime rate.

Why are people surprised by predictions that San Francisco's birth rate will decline sharply over the next ten years? – Most people didn't know San Francisco had a birth rate!

A Californian, a Texan and a guy from Colorado were attending a bus convention in Las Vegas. On their first night, they went out on the town together for a drink.

The Californian drank a wine spritzer, which he downed in one before hurling his empty glass against the wall, smashing the glass in pieces. Explaining his actions to the bartender, he said: "The standard of living is so high where I live in Orange County, California, that we never drink out of the same glass twice."

Next the Texan drank a margarita and threw the empty glass against the wall. He explained: "In Texas, we're all so rich from the oil industry that we never drink out of the same glass twice."

Then it was the turn of the guy from Colorado. He drank his beer but then suddenly pulled a gun and shot his two companions dead. He explained to the bartender: "In Colorado, we have so many Californians and Texans that we never have to drink with the same ones twice."

Canadians

An Englishman, a Canadian and an American were captured by terrorists. The terrorist leader said: "Before we shoot you, you will be allowed last words. Tell me what you would like to talk about."

The Englishman said: "I want to talk about loyalty and service to the crown."

The Canadian said: 'Since you are involved in a question of national purpose, national identity and secession, I wish to talk about the history of constitutional process in Canada, special status, distinct society and uniqueness within diversity."

The American said: "Just shoot me before the Canadian starts talking."

During a bitterly cold winter when temperatures dropped to minus thirty, two Canadian neighbours, Barney and Jake, had a bet as to who could sit out on the porch of their house the longer with a bare ass.

After two hours, Barney's wife came home and asked him: "What on earth are you doing? Come inside, or you'll freeze your ass off!"

Barney explained the bet to her and insisted on staying outside so he could win.

"You're crazy," she said, "but there is a way you could win your bet without freezing to death. When Jake's looking the other way, why don't I swap places with you?"

Barney thought it was a great idea, and so his wife put on a baggy sweater and cap and traded places with her husband when Jake wasn't looking.

Half an hour later, Jake's wife came home and asked him what he was doing.

Jake told her about the bet, but she told him to forget about it and come inside where it was warm.

"No way," said Jake, "I'm already winning. Barney lost his balls half an hour ago."

Cannibals

Two cannibals stumbled across a missionary in the jungle. After killing him, they decided to divide the body up evenly. The first cannibal said: "I'll start at the head, you start at the feet, and we'll meet in the middle."

So the two began to devour the missionary. After a while, the first cannibal called out: "How's it going down there?"

"I'm having a ball," replied the second cannibal.

"In that case slow down!" shouted the first cannibal. "You're eating too fast!"

Did you hear about the cannibal who got married? – At the wedding reception he toasted his mother-in-law.

After getting lost in the jungle, three explorers were captured by cannibals. The cannibal king told the men they could live if they completed a trial successfully.

The first step of the trial was for each to go into the forest and collect ten pieces of the same type of fruit, so the three went their separate ways into the forest. Soon the first returned with ten lemons. The king then explained the trial: "You have to shove the fruits up your arse without any expression on your face. If you make any expression or sound, you will be boiled alive and eaten."

The first explorer managed to ram the first lemon up his arse, but on the second lemon he cried out in pain and was promptly eaten by the cannibals.

Then the second explorer returned with ten berries. He inserted the first nine up his arse without making a sound, but on the tenth he suddenly burst out laughing and was eaten by the cannibals.

The two dead explorers met up in heaven. The first said: "Why did you laugh on the tenth berry? You had almost completed the trial."

"I know," said the second, "but then I saw the third guy coming with an armful of pineapples."

Entering the clearing that his tribe used as a toilet, a cannibal chief saw a fellow cannibal squatting down and crying his eyes out.

"What's the matter?" asked the chief.

The cannibal sobbed: "I've just dumped my girlfriend."

One cannibal said to the other: "You know what I miss most about my wife? The smell of her cooking."

A cannibal returned from a family vacation with part of his leg missing.

"How was your holiday?" asked one of his friends.

"It was great," said the cannibal.

"Hey, but why is part of your leg missing?"

"Oh," said the cannibal, "we went self-catering."

Cats

A tomcat was running all over the neighbourhood, down alleys, up fire escapes, into deserted buildings and down into cellars. Eventually a neighbour became so concerned that he called on the cat's owner.

"Your cat has been going crazy," said the neighbour. "He's been rushing around like mad."

"I know," said the owner. "He's just been neutered, and he's running around cancelling engagements."

How do you make a cat flap? – Throw it off a cliff.

A veterinarian had endured a long day, but when he got home from tending to all the sick animals, his wife was waiting with a long cool drink and a romantic candlelit dinner, after which they had a few more drinks and went happily to bed.

At about 11.30 p.m. the phone rang.

"Is this the vet?" asked an elderly lady's voice.

"Yes, it is," replied the vet. "Is this an emergency?"

"Well, sort of," said the elderly lady. "There's a whole bunch of cats on the roof outside making a terrible noise mating and I can't get to sleep. What can I do about it?"

There was a sharp intake of breath from the vet, who then patiently replied: "Open the window and tell them they're wanted on the phone."

"Really?" said the elderly lady. "Will that will that stop them?"

"Should do," said the vet. "It stopped me!"

Studies have shown that cats are smarter than dogs. After all, how many cats do you see sitting beside a homeless person?

One day a couple found an old stray cat at their door. She was a sorry sight – starving, dirty, smelled terrible, skinny and hair all matted down. Feeling sorry for her, they put her in a carrier and took her to the vet. She had no name, so they simply called her Pussy until they could think of something more imaginative. Since she was in such a poor state, the vet decided to keep her for observation for a couple of days and said he would let them know when they could come and collect her. "Make sure you give her a good wash," the husband told the vet. "She really stinks!"

It so happened that two days later the husband had an appointment with his doctor, whose office adjoined the vet's. The doctor's waiting room was full of people when the side door opened and the vet, who had seen the husband arrive, called over to him: "Your wife's pussy is finally clean and shaved. She now smells like a rose. And by the way, I think she's pregnant. God knows who the father is!"

The schoolteacher asked Little Johnny what he did over the weekend. He said: "My cat died. I knew he was dead because I pissed in his ear."

"You did what?!" exclaimed the teacher.

"I leant over and went 'Psssst' and the cat didn't move."

Chavs

How do you know if a chav is a bad father? – He lets his thirteen-year-old daughter smoke in front of her kids.

What's the difference between a phone battery and a chav just out of prison? – The battery will go a couple of days before being charged again.

How do you make a chav run faster? – Tuck a DVD player under his arm.

A chavette was washing the dishes when her three-year-old daughter asked her: "Mummy, why are your hands so soft?"
    The mother replied: "It's 'cos I'm only fifteen, innit?"

Where does a chavette go to lose weight? – The abortion clinic.

What's the difference between a chavette and a broom cupboard? – Only two men can fit inside a broom cupboard at once.

Why doesn't Viagra work on chavs? – Because they only get hard when they've got their mates with them.

A chavette came home late one evening. Her mother was still up, and when the girl walked in the door, the mother noticed she had rice in her hair.
    "Chantelle," she said, "you didn't tell me you were going to a wedding!"
    "I didn't," replied the girl. "I was giving a blow job to a Chinese guy and he threw up on me."

A chavette gave birth prematurely to a baby boy. Everyone was so proud of him – he was the first one in the family to have been inside for less than nine months.

What's a chav's favourite type of car? – One without an alarm.

What's the difference between a chavette and a toilet? – The toilet's hole is smaller and smells better.

A chav was walking down the road when he spotted a truck on fire. He stopped and saw that the truck driver was trapped in the cab with flames all around him. Gasping for breath through the thick black smoke, the truck driver yelled: "There's an extinguisher in the back."

"Cheers, mate," said the chav. "That's very generous of you." And he walked off with it.

Children

Little Annie came home from school and told her mother that the boys kept asking her to do cartwheels because she's so good at them.

Her mother said: "You should say no, because the boys only want to look at your knickers when your skirt falls."

"I know they do," said Little Annie. "That's why I hide my knickers in my bag."

One day, a young brother and sister – Timmy and Jenny – were playing naked in their garden paddling pool. As they studied each other's body, they became increasingly curious as to why they had different bits.

So when Timmy went indoors, he asked their mother: "Why does Jenny have a hole and I have a stick?"

Choosing a metaphor, his mother replied: "Jenny has a garage, and you have a Ferrari. Men park their cars in the garage when they are ready."

"Oh," said Timmy.

Meanwhile, Jenny was upstairs asking their father the same question: "Why does Timmy have a stick between his legs and I have a hole?"

Using the same familiar metaphor, the father replied: "He has a Ferrari and you have a garage. You must never let him park his Ferrari in your garage."

"Okay," she said.

The next day, Timmy and Jenny were playing naked again in the paddling pool. Timmy suddenly said: "Please, Jenny, let me park my Ferrari."

"No way!" said Jenny.

"But I want to!" protested Timmy.

A couple of minutes later, Jenny ran indoors. Her mother asked: "Jenny, why is there blood on your hands?"

Jenny said: "Timmy tried to park his Ferrari, so I pulled the back wheels off."

Three kids were smoking behind the shed. The first boy boasted: "My dad can blow smoke through his nose!"

"Ha!" said the second boy. "Mine can blow smoke through his ears!"

"That's nothing," said the third boy. "My dad can blow smoke through his arse!"

"How do you know?" asked the others.

"Because I've seen the nicotine stains on his underpants."

I just donated £1,000 to a blind-children's charity. Not that the kids will ever see any of it.

Little Johnny and his dad were walking through the park one day when Johnny noticed two dogs humping furiously.

"What are those two dogs doing, Dad?" asked Johnny.

"They're making puppies," replied his father.

That evening at home, Johnny was awoken by noises coming from his parents' bedroom. He went to investigate and caught his father on top of his mother. They were having sex.

"What are you doing?" asked Johnny.

His father replied: "We're making you a little brother or sister."

"Well, can you flip her over," said Johnny, "because I'd rather have a puppy?"

Why do paedophiles love Halloween? – Free delivery.

The thing I don't like about my children is that when things go wrong they have a tendency to blame other people. They get that from their mum. (Stewart Francis)

A young boy came home early to find his mum and dad on the sofa having sex. Coming up with a quick explanation, the dad said: "It's okay, son. I'm just filling Mummy up with petrol."

The boy said: "Well she doesn't do many miles to the gallon because the mailman filled her up this morning!"

Did you hear about the boy who got kicked out of the Scouts for eating a Brownie?

A mother was sitting in the garden with her three daughters. "Mummy," said the first daughter. "Why am I called Rose?"

"Because when you were born a rose petal fell from that bush and landed on your forehead."

"Mummy," asked the second daughter, "why am I called Lily?"

"Because when you were born a lily petal fell from that plant and landed on your forehead."

The third daughter moaned slowly: "Maaamaaranaammaagh."

"Be quiet, Fridge," said the mother.

Johnny was five years old and wanted to know everything there was to know about courting. His mother was too embarrassed to tell him, so instead she suggested that he hide behind the living-room curtains one night and watch his teenage sister and her boyfriend. The following morning he told his mother what he had seen.

"Sis and Darren talked for a bit, then he turned off the lights. Then he started kissing her. I could tell she was feeling sick because her face looked funny. Darren must have thought so too because he put his hand inside her blouse to feel her heart. But he seemed to have problems finding it. I guess he was getting sick, too, because he started panting and getting out of breath. His other hand must have been cold because he put it under her skirt. That was when she started to moan. I guess she was feeling feverish because she told Darren she felt really hot and a bit wet.

"Then I saw what was making them both sick — a big eel had somehow got into his trousers. It just jumped out and stood there, about eight inches long. He had to grab it with one hand to stop it getting away. When Sis saw it, you could tell she was really scared. Her eyes got big, her mouth was open and she screamed to God. She said it was the biggest one she'd seen. She got brave and tried to kill the eel by biting its head off. Then she grabbed it with both hands while Darren took a muzzle out of his pocket and slipped it over the eel's head to stop it biting her.

"Next she lay back and spread her legs so she could get a scissor lock on it. The eel kept on fighting but after a minute or two I thought it must be dead because it just hung there and some of its insides were hanging out. Sis and Darren were so happy about this that they kissed and hugged each other but then, what do you know, the eel suddenly came back to life again. It wasn't dead after all and began to straighten up and fight again. This time Sis jumped up and tried to kill the pesky eel by sitting on it. After about five minutes, they finally killed it. I knew it was dead for sure this time because Darren peeled off its skin and flushed it down the toilet."

"One man's rubbish is another man's treasure" is an awesome phrase, but a cruel way to tell your kid he's adopted.

A father asked his ten-year-old son if he knew about the birds and the bees.

"I don't want to know," said the boy in some distress.

"Why not?" asked his father, puzzled.

"Because," explained the boy, "at seven years old I was told there was no Tooth Fairy, at eight I was told there was no Easter Bunny, at nine I was told there was no Father Christmas. So if you're now going to tell me that grown-ups don't get laid, there's nothing to live for."

A young boy came home early from school and found his father in bed with the maid. When his mother arrived home half an hour later, the boy hurried to tell her. "Mum, when I got home from school today, I saw Dad in bed with the maid. They were—"

His mother interrupted him. "Wait till dinner tonight, and when the maid serves the meal, I'll wink at you, and then you can tell the story."

That evening the maid served dinner as usual. She had just started serving the vegetables when the boy's mother winked at him. The boy took the hint and said: "Mum, when I got home from school today I saw Dad in bed with the maid. They were doing the same thing I saw you and Uncle Ken doing at the cottage last summer."

A five-year-old boy returned home from Sunday School and wanted to discuss what he had learned.

"Dad," he said, "have any of the men in our family had their penises criticized?"

The father laughed and told him that the word was "circumcised" but that the answer was still "yes".

A little boy was playing with something in the road. The local priest went over to him and said: "Hello, Johnny. What are you playing with?"

Little Johnny replied: "It's sulphuric acid."

"You mustn't play with that," said the priest. "It's dangerous."

"I don't tell you not to play with holy water," said Little Johnny defiantly.

"But holy water isn't dangerous," said the priest. "On the contrary, it is good. Why, the other day I put holy water on a pregnant woman's tummy and she passed a baby boy."

"That's nothing," said Little Johnny. "The other day I put sulphuric acid on my dog's bollocks and he passed a Ferrari!"

I just had a water fight in the park with a group of kids. I won. No one's a match for me and my kettle.

Little Johnny and Susie were only nine, but they were convinced that they were in love. One day they decided they wanted to get married, so Johnny went to Susie's father to ask him for her hand.

Johnny bravely walked up to him and said: "Mr Robinson, Susie and me are in love and I'm asking for her hand in marriage."

Thinking that this was the cutest thing, Mr Robinson replied: "Well, Johnny, you are only nine. Where will the two of you live?"

Without even taking a moment to think about it, Johnny replied: "In Susie's room. It's bigger than mine and we can both fit there nicely."

Still thinking this was just adorable, Mr Robinson smiled: "Okay, then, how will you live? You're not old enough to get a job. You'll need to support Susie."

Again, Johnny instantly replied: "We'll use our pocket money. Susie gets £5 a week and I get £10, and I can make an extra £10 from doing odd jobs. That's a potential £100 a month – that should do us just fine."

By this time Mr Robinson was becoming a little concerned that Johnny had put so much thought into this. So he thought for a moment, trying to come up with something that Johnny wouldn't have an answer to. Eventually he said: "Well, Johnny, it seems like you have got everything all figured out. I just have one more question for you. What will you do if the two of you should have little ones of your own?"

"There's no need to worry, Mr Robinson," said Johnny. "That won't happen. She only lets me shag her up the arse."

A little girl ran up to her mother and asked: "Mummy, Mummy, can I lick the bowl?"

"No, sweetheart," said the mother. "You can flush like everyone else."

Amy came home from nursery school one day and told her mother: "William did a pee in the school yard today."

As Amy was one of the older children at the nursery, her mother wanted to impress upon her the need to help the younger children learn right from wrong. So she asked her daughter: "Well, Amy, how big is William?"

Amy held her two index fingers an inch or so apart and replied: "Oh, about this big."

Little Johnny had a habit of sucking his thumb. His mother tried everything to cure him until one day in the street she pointed to a fat man and told Johnny: "That man has a huge stomach because he didn't stop sucking his thumb."

The next day in the supermarket, Johnny and his mother were waiting in line opposite a heavily pregnant woman. Johnny kept staring at the woman, who eventually lost her temper and told him: "Stop staring at me like that. You don't know who I am."

"No," he said, "but I know what you've been doing."

A father watched his young daughter playing in the garden, and smiled as he reflected on how sweet and pure the little girl was. Tears formed as he thought about her seeing the wonders of nature through such innocent eyes. Suddenly, she just stopped and stared intently at the ground, so he went over to see what work of God had captured her attention. He found that she was watching two crane flies mating.

"Daddy, what are those two insects doing?" she asked.

"They're mating," replied her father.

"What do you call the insect on top?"

"That's a Daddy Longlegs."

"So the other one is a Mummy Longlegs?" suggested the little girl.

Enchanted by such a cute and innocent question, he replied: "No, darling. Both of them are Daddy Longlegs."

Looking puzzled, the little girl thought for a moment, then lifted her foot and stamped the two insects flat, saying firmly: "We're not having any of that poofter shit in our garden!"

You can say lots of bad things about paedophiles but at least they drive slowly past schools.

A little boy walked in to the living room one Sunday morning while his dad was reading the paper and asked: "Where does poo come from?"

The father, feeling a little perturbed that his five-year-old son was already asking difficult questions, thought for a moment before choosing his words carefully. "Well," he began, "you know we just ate breakfast? Well, the food goes into our tummies and our bodies take out all the good stuff, and then whatever is left over comes out of our bottoms when we go to the toilet, and that is poo."

The little boy looked perplexed, and stared at him in stunned silence for a few seconds before asking: "And Tigger?"

A man came out of the bedroom to find his eleven-year-old son waiting for him.

"Dad," he said, "I'm doing my science homework and I want to know how you spell clitoris."

"Gee, I don't know, son, but it was on the tip of my tongue just a moment ago."

Two paedophiles saw a fifteen-year-old girl walking through the park. One turned to the other and said: "I bet she was a looker in her day."

Little Johnny was excited because the circus had come to town and his mum had got front row tickets for him. Finally, the evening came and Little Johnny and his mum went off to the big top. Little Johnny sat there and enjoyed the lions and the tigers and the jugglers and the trapeze artists, and finally out came his favourites, the clowns.

Johnny was loving the clowns and their humorous japes until one of the clowns went up to him and said: "Little boy, are you the front end of an ass?"

"No," replied Little Johnny.

"Are you the rear end of an ass?" asked the clown.

"No," replied Little Johnny again.

"In that case," said the clown, "you must be no end of an ass!"

And the clown sounded his horn and the rest of the audience roared with laughter.

But Little Johnny was distraught and he ran out of the circus and all the way home in tears.

When his mum caught up with him she said: "Johnny, don't worry, your Uncle Dennis, the master of lightning wit, backchat and repartee, is coming to stay tomorrow. We'll take him to the circus and he will sort that nasty clown out."

At this news Little Johnny cheered up and looked forward to the next night.

The next night came and, sure enough, Uncle Dennis, the master of lightning wit, backchat and repartee, arrived and the three of them set off for the circus.

When they got there, Little Johnny, his mum and Uncle Dennis, the master of lightning wit, backchat and repartee, sat down and enjoyed the lions, the tigers, the jugglers and the trapeze artists, and then out came the clowns. Again Little Johnny was enjoying their antics until one of the clowns went up to him and asked: "Little boy, are you the front end of an ass?"

Quick as a flash, Uncle Dennis, the master of lightning wit, backchat and repartee, jumped up and shouted at the very top of his voice: "Fuck off, you red-nosed cunt!"

British scientists have demonstrated that cigarettes can harm your children. Fair enough. Use an ashtray. (Jimmy Carr)

A little boy asked his mother: "Where do babies come from?"

She answered: "The stork brings them, dear."

The boy looked puzzled for a moment and then asked: "So who fucks the stork?"

I took my kids to the National Space Centre today. There was fuck all there.

A mother and her young son were walking through the park one day when the boy spotted two ducks mating.

"What are they doing, Mummy?" he asked.

Embarrassed, his mother replied: "Oh, they're making sandwiches, darling."

Shortly afterwards, the boy saw two dogs mating.

"What are they doing, Mummy?"

"Uh, they're making sandwiches, too, darling."

That night the boy was in bed when he heard noises coming from his parents' room. He called out for his mother, and thinking something was wrong, she rushed straight to his room.

"What's the matter, darling?" she said.

The boy replied: "You were making sandwiches."

She blushed and said: "How can you tell?"

"Because you've got mayonnaise all over your face."

Two paedophiles were walking down the street. One said to the other: "I'll swap you two fives for a ten."

A little boy ran into the kitchen and said to his mother: "Mum, is it wrong to have a willy?"

Shocked, she replied: "Of course not, sweetie. Why do you ask?"

"Well, Dad's upstairs in the bedroom trying to pull his one off."

Two twins, Timmy and Tommy, were asked by their parents what they each would like for their tenth birthday.

"I'd like a new bike." said Timmy. "Then I could ride around and see everything that happens in the neighbourhood."

"And I'd like a digital radio for my room," said Tommy. "Then I would hear all the news that goes on in town."

So their parents bought them the gifts. Later that day, Timmy was out on his new bike when he came upon a serious car crash. There were bodies and emergency vehicles everywhere.

"I've got to tell Mum," thought Timmy, so he raced back to the house and shouted: "Mum! There's been a terrible accident!"

"Yeah, yeah," said his brother. "We heard all about it on my new radio."

Timmy was disappointed that he could not be first with the news, so he left on his bike. A little while later, he came upon a burning orphanage.

"Wow! I've got to go tell Mum," he thought. So he raced home again and yelled for his mother, but again Tommy interrupted and said: "We heard it all on my new radio."

Once again Timmy left disappointed. He rode and rode until he was out in the country. Then he saw a big, fat pig all alone in a field and decided, since there was no one around, to fuck the pig. He had his first orgasm and was so excited he thought: "I got to go tell Mum!"

He raced home and yelled: "Mum, Mum! I lost my virginity!"

"In a pig's arse you did!" sneered his brother.

Timmy shook his head and groaned: "That fucking radio!"

A girl was given a tea set for her second birthday. It became one of her favourite toys, and when her mother went away for a few weeks to care for her sick aunt, the toddler loved to take her father a little cup of tea, which was just water really, while he was engrossed watching the news on TV.

He sipped each "cup of tea" he was brought and lavished generous praise on the taste, leaving the little girl immensely proud.

Eventually the mother returned home and the father couldn't wait to show her how his little princess had been looking after him. On cue, the girl took him his "cup of tea" and he sipped it before praising it to the heavens.

The mother watched him drink it and then said to him: "Did it ever occur to you that the only place that a toddler can reach to get water is the toilet?"

A guy pulled a girl and persuaded her to go to a hotel room with him. They were just about to have sex when it occurred to him that she looked rather young.

"How old are you?" he asked.

"Thirteen," she replied.

"Oh, my God!" he exclaimed. He immediately grabbed his trousers, got dressed and ran out of the room.

Shaking her head in bewilderment, the girl sighed: "Men are so super-stitious."

We bought our young son a jigsaw to keep him occupied while we were out. We came back to find he'd cut his fingers off.

Little Johnny's mother decided to give him an anatomy lesson one day, so she took off all her clothes, pointed to her vagina and said: "See, Johnny, this is where you came from."

Johnny went to school the next day with a big smile on his face and insisted that in future all his friends should call him Lucky Johnny.

"Why?" asked one.

Holding his fingers an inch apart, Johnny said: "Because I came this close to being a turd."

What bounces and makes children cry? – My cheque to Children in Need.

A father was playing with his four-year-old daughter. At one point, she exclaimed excitedly: "Daddy, look at this!" and stuck out two of her fingers.

To keep her entertained, he playfully grabbed the fingers, put them in his mouth and said: "Daddy's going to eat your fingers!" She shrieked with laughter, and he ran from the room.

When he returned moments later, the laughter had stopped. Instead, she was looking glum.

"What's the matter, sweetheart?" he asked.

She said: "Daddy, where's my bogie?"

The Chinese

A man was walking through Chinatown when he saw a sign saying "Hans Schmidt's Chinese Laundry". Being curious, he went into the shop and was greeted by an elderly Chinese man who introduced himself as Hans Schmidt.

"How come you have a name like that?" inquired the stranger. "You don't look very German!"

"Is simple," said the Chinese shop owner. "Many, many year ago when come to this country I stand in immigration line behind big German guy. Immigration lady look at him and go, 'What your name?' He say, 'Hans Schmidt.' Then she look at me and go, 'What your name?' I say, 'Sam Ting.'"

How do you know if a Chinese guy has burgled your house? – Your kids' homework is done, your computer is upgraded, but two hours later the robber is still trying to back his getaway car out of your driveway.

Three Chinese brothers, Bu, Chu and Fu, wanted to live illegally in America and decided to change their names so that they sounded authentically American. Bu changed his name to Buck. Chu changed his name to Chuck. And Fu got sent back to China.

An American soldier serving in Asia met this lovely Chinese girl in the park. They ended up having dinner and, that night in the hotel, while having sex, the girl let out a very loud fart.

The soldier jumped out of bed to get away from the smell. The embarrassed girl looked at him and said: "Oh, so sorry but front hole so happy, back hole must cheer."

An American on a business trip to Shanghai stayed in a smart city-centre hotel. When he got to his room, he noticed a leaflet next to the bed saying: "Try our oriental massage."

So after a couple of drinks from the mini bar, he rang down to reception and told the clerk that he would like to try one of the hotel's special massages. About ten minutes later, a pretty Chinese girl came up to the room and started giving him a massage.

He lay on his stomach while she worked her hands tenderly around his body, and it wasn't long before he had a huge boner. When she then asked him to turn over, she saw that his dick was standing to attention. She giggled: "Ah, you want wanky!"

"Oh, yes please," he groaned.

With that, she disappeared into the bathroom, leaving him on the bed waiting. A few minutes later, she stuck her head out from behind the door and said: "You finished yet?"

Suspecting his wife of having an affair, a husband hired a famous Chinese detective to follow her. A week later, the husband received the following report from the detective:

You leave house.
He come house.
I watch.
He and she leave house.
I follow.
He and she get on train.
I follow.
He and she go in hotel.
I climb tree, look in window.
He kiss she.
She kiss he.
He strip she.
She strip he.
He play with she.
She play with he.
I play with me.
Fall out of tree, not see.
No fee.

A Chinese guy went to a Jewish lingerie shop to buy black bras, size 38FF. The Jewish owner, renowned for his skills as a businessman, said that black bras were rare and that he was finding it very difficult to buy them from his suppliers. Therefore, he had to charge £50 each for them. The Chinese guy bought twenty-five.

A few days later, the Chinese guy returned to the shop and ordered fifty more black bras, size 38FF. The Jew told him that they had become even harder to get and charged him £60 each.

A month later, the Chinese guy returned and bought the Jew's remaining stock of fifty bras, this time for £75 each.

The Jew was puzzled by the sudden large demand for black size 38FF bras and so he asked the Chinese guy: "What do you do with all these black bras?"

The Chinese guy answered: "I cut them in half and sell them as skull caps to you Jews for £200 each."

The Church

The Revd Michael Flapps was walking along the street one day when he spotted a female member of his congregation staggering around in a drunken manner. He tried to assist her, but they stumbled and he fell on top of her.

Just then a passing police officer called out: "Hey, you can't do that in the street!"

"You don't understand," protested the man of the cloth. "I'm Pastor Flapps."

"Oh, well," said the cop, "I guess if you're that far in, you may as well finish."

A window cleaner went to a monastery looking for work. The Head Abbot told him to clean all the windows except the top three. For the next six years, the window cleaner dutifully cleaned the windows as requested until curiosity finally got the better of him and he decided to investigate what took place behind the top three windows.

He put his ladder up against the first window, looked in and saw a dozen monks with their robes up and their dicks lying on a table with a mouse running around on the top of the table. The window cleaner then moved to the second window, through which he saw a monk in bed with a beautiful woman. Finally, the window cleaner put his ladder up against the third window, looked in and saw a monk tied up, stripped to the waist and being flogged.

Climbing down the ladder, the window cleaner found the Head Abbot waiting for him at the bottom. The window cleaner said: "Look, I know you're going to sack me, but please, at least tell me what is going on."

"Well," explained the Abbot, "in the first window you saw a 'lucky monk' competition: wherever the mouse stops is the lucky monk. And in the second window you saw a lucky monk with his prize."

"But what about the third window?" the window cleaner asked.

"That monk," said the Abbot grimly, "was caught with a piece of cheese in his foreskin."

The pastor of the church was speaking to his Sunday School class about heaven and hell. By way of introduction, he asked a small boy in the front row: "Johnny, do you know where little boys and girls go when they do bad things?"

"Sure," said Johnny. "The back of the church yard."

Once there was a fundamentalist preacher who was known all over the state for his strong views against alcohol. He was even working on a petition to the lawmakers to bring back prohibition.

One day the preacher walked into the local drugstore and asked for some Vaseline.

The young man behind the counter said: "I'm sorry, Reverend, but we have completely sold out."

So the preacher left empty-handed.

Overhearing the conversation, the owner of the store asked the clerk why he had said that, pointing out that there was an entire shelf of Vaseline in the back-room.

The clerk said: "That was the preacher who is advocating the return of prohibition. He wants it dry – he gets it dry!"

A Catholic went to a dry ski slope in Northern Ireland and asked to go on the ski jump. So the woman behind the desk said: "Certainly, sir. It's £5 for Protestants or £15 for Catholics."

So the man said: "That's terrible, it's discrimination. I'm taking my custom elsewhere."

Off he went to another dry ski slope and he asked the woman behind the desk if he could go on the ski jump. She replied: "Certainly, sir. It's £4 for Protestants or £10 for Catholics."

Again, the man was disgusted and walked out.

Arriving at a third dry ski slope, he asked to go on the ski slope and the woman behind the desk replied: "Certainly, sir, it's Catholics only and it's free."

So he climbed to the top, put on his skis and the last thing he heard was a voice shouting "pull" followed by a loud bang.

John raised his glass and said: "Here's to spending the rest of my life between the legs of my wife!" That won him the top prize at the pub for the best toast of the night.

He went home and told his wife, Mary: "I won the prize for the best toast of the night."

"Well done," she said. "And what was your toast?"

John said: "Here's to spending the rest of my life sitting in church beside my wife."

"Oh, that's lovely, John!" said Mary.

The next day, Mary ran into one of John's drinking buddies. The friend chuckled leeringly and said: "John won the prize the other night at the pub with a toast about you, Mary."

She said: "Yes, he told me, and I was a bit surprised myself. You know, he's only been there twice in the last four years. Once he fell asleep, and the other time I had to pull him by the ears to make him come."

Clothes

A boss gave his personal assistant an expensive leather dress as a birthday present. As she admired herself in the mirror, he said: "Your panties are coming down."

Embarrassed, she quickly looked down to check. "No, they're not," she said.

"They are," he said, "or the dress goes back to the shop!"

Standing in front of a full-length mirror, a middle-aged woman said to her husband: "Tell me honestly, do these jeans make my butt look like the side of the house?"

"No," he answered. "The side of the house isn't blue."

A Muslim woman wearing a burka was going around door to door handing out leaflets for her local mosque. When she rang the doorbell at one house, the occupant, instead of opening the door, peered at her through the letterbox and asked what she wanted.

"Why are you speaking to me through the letterbox?" she asked.

"To see how you like it!" he replied.

One evening, a teenage girl was just leaving the house to meet up with her friends when her father called out: "Stop right there! Where do you think you're going dressed like that?"

"Like what?" she asked.

"What about the see-through top and lacy bra," he said, "and the miniskirt with the stockings?"

"For the last time, I'm not wearing them, Dad! I've told you, I just want to go out in my jeans and T-shirt."

All the women in my family wear the hijab. Which is good because it means they can share the one bus pass. (Shazia Mirza)

A middle-aged wife was frustrated over her lousy sex life, so she talked to her next-door neighbour. The neighbour asked her what she wore to bed.

The wife replied: "I have this white nightgown with a high lacy front and low-cut back. Derek used to think it was sexy, but now he doesn't even look at me."

"Turn it around so it's cut low in front," the neighbour advised. "It's sure to turn Derek on."

That night, Derek climbed into bed and turned on the television news, as usual. His wife went into the bathroom, put her nightgown on backwards, moved seductively out the door and across the room, turned off the TV, got into bed and nibbled on Derek's ear. Derek just grunted and rolled over.

She slapped him angrily on the arm. "Derek, I want to make love," she said. "Don't you notice anything different about my nightgown?"

"Yeah," he said. "The shit stains are on the front."

Getting ready for a night out with the girls, a young woman appeared wearing a low-cut top, short, tight skirt and thigh-length boots.

"You look like you're going to a brothel!" scoffed her boyfriend.

"Well, what if I am?" she said defiantly.

He replied: "You could give me a lift."

College

Passing through his son's college town late one night on a business trip, a father thought he would pay him a surprise visit.

Arriving at the fraternity house, he knocked on the door and waited for an answer. Eventually a sleepy voice opened a second-floor window and called down: "What do you want?"

"Does Bobby Richards live here?" asked the father.

"Yeah," replied the voice. "Just dump him on the front porch and we'll take care of him in the morning."

During a college lecture on sex education, the professor asked the students how many sex positions they knew. A girl in the front row put up her hand and said: "Twelve."

The professor nodded approval but as he got ready to call on another hand, a female voice shouted from the far back row: "A hundred and five!"

The professor looked over his thick glasses but couldn't make out who had spoken. So he called on a young man down in the front row who replied: "Eight."

And once again from the very back a female voice called out: "A hundred and five!"

Finally, the professor asked a shy girl in the second row how many sexual positions she knew. She replied timidly: "Only one."

The professor said: "Well, young lady, that is unusual. And what position would that be?"

"With the man on top and the woman on the bottom," she replied.

And from the back of the room came that same voice: "A hundred and six!"

Two male math students were chilling out one evening over a few beers. Before long their topic of conversation turned to the human body, and one said: "If you had a dick growing out of your forehead, how long would it have to be before you could see it?"

The other thought carefully for a moment and replied: "I don't know. I guess about seven inches."

His friend laughed: "It wouldn't matter, because your balls would be in your eyes!"

At a California college dance, an American guy made a move on a pretty Swedish girl. While they were dancing, he gave her a little squeeze, and said: "In America we call this a hug."

She replied: "For sure, in Sweden we call it a hug too."

A little later, he gave her a peck on the cheek, and said: "In America we call this a kiss."

She replied: "For sure, in Sweden we call it a kiss too."

Towards the end of the night, and several drinks later, he took her out on the campus lawn, and proceeded to have sex with her. He said: "In America we call this a grass sandwich."

She said: "For sure, in Sweden we call it a grass sandwich too, but we usually put more meat in it."

Condoms

A man bought some flavoured condoms and suggested to his wife in bed: "Let's play a game. I put one on and you have to guess what flavour it is."

So she closed her eyes, dived under the duvet, grabbed his dick, sniffed and said: "Cheese-and-onion flavour."

He said: "Give me a chance to put one on!"

A guy at a fancy-dress party had a condom fixed to his face.

"What are you supposed to be?" asked the host.

"Fuck nose!"

A man was walking past a house when a used condom fell from a second-storey window and landed squarely on his head. Disgusted, he marched angrily up to the front door and started pounding on it. An elderly man opened the door and asked him why he was knocking so loudly.

The passer-by demanded: "Who's in your upstairs room?"

The elderly man replied: "I can't see how it's any of your business but if you must know, my daughter and intended son-in-law are upstairs."

The passer-by handed him the used condom and said: "Well, I just wanted you to know that your intended grandchild fell out the window!"

What do gay men have against condoms? – Their cheeks.

A young man walked into a pharmacy to buy condoms. The sales assistant persuaded him to buy some multicoloured condoms, which were on special offer.

Nine months later, the young man returned to the pharmacy to buy a maternity bra.

"What bust?" asked the clerk.

"I think it was the blue one," said the young man.

A deaf mute nervously approached the chemist shop counter to buy some condoms. He opened his fly, placed his six-inch dick on the counter, pointed to it and placed a £5 note next to it.

With an understanding nod, the pharmacist whipped out his seven-inch dick, laid it beside the deaf mute's, grinned in triumph, took the cash and walked away.

Little Johnny went into a pharmacy and asked the chemist for some rubbers. The chemist put a pack of rubbers on the counter, but Little Johnny looked at them and asked the chemist if he had any other kind. So the chemist went into the back and brought out a different pack.

Little Johnny shook his head and said: "What else do you have?"

"Well," the chemist replied, "the only other kind that I have are the ones with all the bumps and ridges on them. Do you know what these will do to a woman?"

"No," said Little Johnny, "but I do know they'll make a goat jump about two feet off of the ground!"

A man phoned the emergency services and said agitatedly: "Come as quick as you can. My young son has swallowed a condom!"

A couple of minutes later, he phoned again and said: "It's okay. I've found another one."

A teenage boy went to buy his first-ever packet of condoms at the pharmacy. Standing behind the counter was a beautiful assistant who could sense that this was not something the boy had done before. She handed him the pack of condoms and asked if he knew how to wear one.

Embarrassed, he answered: "No, this is my first time."

She unwrapped the pack, took one condom out and slipped it over her thumb. She told him to make sure it was on tight and secure, but he appeared confused. So she looked all around the store to check it was empty, and when she was sure there was no one else about, she walked to the door and locked it. Then taking the boy by the hand, she led him into the back room, unbuttoned her blouse and removed it. She unhooked her bra and laid it aside. "Do these excite you?" she asked.

The boy was so dumbstruck that all he could do was nod his head. She then said it was time to slip the condom on.

As he was slipping it on, she dropped her skirt, removed her knickers and sat down at a desk.

"Hurry up," she said. "We don't have much time."

So he climbed on top of her, and it was all so wonderful that he came within thirty seconds.

She then looked at him with a bit of a frown. "Did you put that condom on?" she asked.

He said, "I sure did," and he held up his thumb to show her.

She fainted.

A sales representative for a condom company was on her way to an international condom convention. Hurrying through the busy airport, she dropped her briefcase carrying her samples, scattering dozens and dozens of condoms all over the terminal floor.

She noticed fellow travellers staring at her as she tried to put the condoms back into her briefcase. "It's okay," she explained. "I'm going to a convention."

A guy spotted a sign in a pharmacy window which read "Condoms Hand-Fitted". He went inside and walked up to the pretty, blonde, blue-eyed assistant and asked: "Do *you* hand fit the condoms?"

"Yes, sir," she replied.

"You personally?" he emphasized.

"Yes, sir."

"Where? Here?"

"No, sir. In the privacy of the back room."

"Well, go and wash your hands then. I want a ham sandwich."

Two old ladies were smoking cigarettes while waiting for a bus. When it started to rain, one of the women reached into her purse, took out a condom, cut off the tip, slipped it over the cigarette and continued smoking. Her friend was so impressed by the idea that the next day she went into a pharmacy and asked for a condom.

"What size?" asked the pharmacist.

The old lady replied: "One that will fit a Camel."

After having sex with her boyfriend, a young woman looked in the box of condoms but was surprised to see there were only five left from the box of twelve.

"What happened to the other six?" she asked.

"Uh, I masturbated with them," he replied nervously.

The next day, she related the story to one of her male friends in the office and asked him: "Have you ever done that?"

"Yeah, once or twice," he answered.

"Really?" she said incredulously. "You have masturbated while wearing a condom?"

"Oh," he said, "I thought you were asking if I'd ever lied to my girlfriend."

A guy walked into a pharmacy and went up to the counter where a lady pharmacist was filling out prescriptions. When she finally served him, he said: "I'd like ninety-nine condoms, please."

With a surprised look on her face, the pharmacist exclaimed: "Ninety-nine condoms?! Fuck me!"

To which the guy replied: "Better make it a hundred, then!"

Many years ago, a Welshman came up with the idea that sheep intestines would make good condoms. A few years later, an Englishman decided that it would be an even better idea to take the intestine out of the sheep first.

Two young brothers were playing in a sandpit in the park when one of them found a condom. Not knowing what it was, they took it home to show their mother.

"Mummy, what's this?" asked one of the boys.

The mother took one look at it, flew into a rage and sent them both straight up to their room without their supper.

There, one boy said: "Mum sure was mad. She's never stopped us having supper before."

"I know," said her brother. "It's a good job we sucked the yoghurt out of that thing first."

After having sex with a girl, there's nothing worse than looking down to see a split, leaking condom hanging off the end of your dick, especially when you weren't wearing one to start with.

A few days before his son was due to leave for his first semester at university, a father sat him down for a quiet chat.

"Son," he said, "in college you're going to be surrounded by beautiful girls, so I got you something from the chemist."

"Dad, you didn't need to. I've already got condoms."

"With a face like yours, you won't be needing condoms, son. I bought you some anti-depressants."

A guy went into a pharmacy to buy condoms. The girl behind the counter asked: "What size?"

He said: "I don't know."

So she held up a finger and said: "That big?"

"Bigger."

So she held up three fingers and said: "That big?"

"Smaller."

Then she held up two fingers and he said: "That's it."

She put the two fingers in her mouth and said: "Medium."

Conjoined Twins

A woman was shocked when she met her blind date for the first time. He admitted: "I may have cropped my Siamese twin out of my Facebook photo."

Did you hear about the conjoined twin boys? – Everything goes in one ear and out the brother.

Did you hear about the guy who set up a matchmaking website exclusively for conjoined twins? – It's called Connect 4.

My neighbour just gave birth to Siamese twins. I knitted them a W-neck sweater as a gift.

A guy was going out with a Siamese twin but she dumped him because she found out he was screwing her sister behind her back.

Next time you're having a bad day, imagine this: You're a Siamese twin. Your brother attached at your shoulder is gay, but you're not. He has a date coming round tonight but you only have one arsehole . . .

Cosmetic Surgery

A cosmetic surgeon was sitting in his consulting room chatting to a friend when a beautiful woman walked in, kissed the surgeon and said: "Thank you so much for everything you have done for me. I felt ugly before, but now you have turned me into a princess."

When the gorgeous lady left the room, the friend asked: "Wow, who was that? You've certainly done a good job on her."

The surgeon replied: "Oh, that was my mother." And they continued their conversation.

A few minutes later, another beautiful lady walked into the room. Even more stunning than the first, she, too, kissed the surgeon and said: "Thank you so much. You have made me look twenty years younger. The facelift and liposuction have done wonders for me."

As she left, the friend exclaimed: "Wow, she looks like a supermodel! Who was she?"

"Oh," replied the surgeon nonchalantly, "that was my wife." And they carried on with their conversation.

A few minutes later, a third beautiful woman walked in, this one even more gorgeous than the other two. She had a perfect body with breasts to die for. She walked over to the surgeon, slapped him hard around the face and yelled: "You bastard! Look what you have done to my body! You've ruined my life!"

As the woman stormed out, the friend looked at the surgeon in bewilderment.

The surgeon shook his head sadly and said: "Let's not talk about it. That was my father."

Over lunch, two women were discussing the merits of cosmetic surgery. After a while, the first woman leaned over and confided: "I'm thinking about having a boob job."

"Oh, that's nothing," said her friend. "I'm thinking of having my asshole bleached."

"Really?" said the first. "I can't quite picture your husband as a blond!"

Two plastic surgeons were talking about operations they had carried out recently, and one mentioned that three months ago he had grafted breasts on to a sailor's back.

"Was it a success?" asked the other.

"Amazingly, it was," said the first. "I did it on a percentage basis, and if his arsehole holds out, I should be a millionaire pretty soon."

A hooker went to a plastic surgeon and asked him to make another hole near her asshole. The surgeon was surprised at such a request and asked: "Why on earth would you want such a procedure?"

The girl explained: "Business is booming, and I want to be rich at a young age. So I'm opening another branch."

A fifty-five-year-old woman went to see a cosmetic surgeon. "What can you do to make me look younger?" she asked.

"Well," he said, "it depends on how much you are willing to pay. You have bags under your eyes – I can remove those for you. And you have crow's feet around your eyes – I can tighten up the skin there."

"I want more than that," she said

"Okay," he continued, "you have a few wrinkles on your forehead – I can remove them. Also, your jowls droop a little – I can sort that out."

"I still want more," the woman insisted. "Money is not an issue."

"In that case," said the surgeon, "I can give you the full treatment from the neck up. I can fix your double chin. Your neck and throat are a bit baggy – I can pull that skin tight. What I'll do is insert a small screw in the back of your neck beneath your hair. No one will be able to see it. When your wrinkles start to reappear, all you need to do is come in and I'll tighten the screw a little. That will tighten your skin right up and take years off you."

The woman had the work done and looked great. But six months later, she turned up at the surgeon's office in a state of high anxiety. "Doctor, see these huge bags under my eyes? They've never been this bad before. You have to do something about them."

"Madam," replied the surgeon, "those aren't bags – they're your breasts. And if you don't stop turning that screw, you're going to end up with a goatee!"

Crime and Punishment

Two men were talking in the pub. The topic of conversation turned to crime, prompting one to recall a personal experience. "I ought to warn you," he began, "that over the last month I've become a victim of a clever scam while out shopping at that DIY megastore on the north of town. Simply going out to buy a few bits and pieces has proved to be quite traumatic. Here's how the scam works: two seriously good-looking twenty-one-year-old girls come over to your car as you are packing away your shopping. They both start wiping your windshield with a rag and cleaner, with their breasts almost falling out of their skimpy T-shirts. It is impossible not to look. When you thank them and offer them a tip, they say, 'No,' but instead ask you for a ride back into town. You agree and they get in the back seat. On the way, they start having sex with each other. Then one of them climbs over into the front seat and performs oral sex on you, while the other one steals your wallet."

"Thanks for the warning," said the other guy. "When did this happen to you?

"Let me see," he said. "I had my wallet stolen March 7th, 8th, 9th, 14th, twice on the 15th, three times yesterday and very likely again this coming weekend!"

A man was in court on a charge of paying a hooker for sex.

"How do you plead?" asked the judge.

"Not guilty," replied the defendant.

Showing him a videotape of the alleged act, the prosecutor said to the defendant: "How can you possibly convince the court of your innocence if we have the sex act plus your subsequent payment to the prostitute right here on tape?"

"Easy," said the defendant. "Whilst I deny that I was involved in an act of prostitution, I will plead guilty to gambling."

"What do you mean, gambling?" asked the prosecutor. "Explain yourself."

"You see," continued the defendant, "I went up to that young lady earlier in the night while she was working in a topless bar and I said to her: 'I bet you £200 that you won't get to have sex with me tonight.' The videotape is just footage of me losing the bet."

I dumped my girlfriend's body in a green wheelie bin, and now I'm in real trouble. The council said it should have gone in a brown bin.

A man arrived home from the pub to find his wife in bed crying.
    "What's the matter, darling?" he asked.
    "We've had a burglar," she sobbed.
    "Did he get anything?" asked the husband.
    "Too right he did!" she wailed. "I thought it was you home early!"

The judge asked a surly defendant if he had anything to say before passing sentence.
    The defendant muttered: "Fuck all!"
    "What did he say?" inquired the judge.
    The clerk of the court turned to the judge and solemnly replied: "The defendant said 'Fuck all', your honour."
    "Really?" said the judge. "I could have sworn I saw his lips move."

A man was sitting downstairs watching late-night TV when he heard his wife screaming from the bedroom. He rushed upstairs just in time to see a figure jumping out of the window.
    The wife cried: "That guy just fucked me twice!"
    "Twice?" queried the husband. "Why didn't you scream after he fucked you the first time?"
    "Because," she replied, "I thought it was you until he started for the second time."

I got caught shoplifting by the security guard in French Connection. What a cnut!

The teenage daughter of a wealthy businessman was kidnapped. Eventually the kidnappers phoned the father and demanded a ransom of £2 million.
    "Two million pounds?!" exclaimed the father. "Listen, it will take me a few days to raise that amount of cash. But first I want to speak to my daughter."

The daughter was handed the phone and spoke to her father quite calmly. "Daddy, I'm okay," she reassured him.

"Are those dogs treating you well, my princess?" asked the father.

"Yes, Daddy, I'm fine," she repeated as one of the kidnappers snatched the phone from her and warned: "Two million . . . in cash . . . in small unmarked bills . . . no cops . . . no publicity . . . you have three days." Then he hung up.

The father started immediately by getting the cash he had in his safe and going to the bank to withdraw the money he kept in an emergency account. However, most of his money was invested in managed trust funds, which required a week's notice for withdrawals. He could only raise just over half a million pounds. He tried asking a couple of business associates for help, but they were out of the country. He was too scared to go to the police in case the kidnappers killed his daughter.

After three days, the telephone rang as arranged. The father picked it up nervously and asked the kidnapper if he could speak to his daughter.

"Hello, Daddy," she said brightly.

"Are you okay, my princess?"

"Daddy, I'm fine," she said.

"Princess, I have some bad news. I wasn't able to get all of the ransom money. I will try and convince them to take the half a million I have now while I cash in my managed funds. I hope they don't harm you because of this."

"Daddy, don't worry," she said. "I struck a deal with them. Each time I fulfil one of their warped sexual desires, they will rebate you £1,000."

"Oh, my God, no, my princess!" wailed the father.

"Daddy, don't worry, they currently owe us £13,000."

Before a burglary trial, the judge explained to the defendant: "You can either let me try your case, or you can choose to have a jury of your peers."

The defendant thought for a moment and then asked: "What are peers?"

"They're people just like you," replied the judge. "They're your equals."

"Forget it," said the defendant. "I don't want to be tried by a bunch of thieves."

Two men were sitting in the pub discussing miscarriages of justice. One said: "My mate Terry is serving a life sentence for something he didn't do."

"Really?"

"Yes, he didn't wipe his fingerprints off the gun."

A seventeen-year-old girl was in court, testifying against her uncle, who had sexually abused her. The prosecution lawyer said: "In your own words, tell the court what happened."

Speaking quietly and tearfully, the girl began: "He came into my room and got into bed with me. Then he touched me here and here and started kissing me, first on my neck, then all the way down my chest. Then he started licking my breasts and caressing the insides of my thighs before slipping his hand down my panties. I don't remember what happened after that."

The judge, masturbating furiously, yelled: "Well, make something up, then!"

I called that Rape Advice Line earlier today. Unfortunately it's only for victims. (Gary Delaney)

A kidnapper phoned a husband and said: "We're holding your wife hostage. A hundred thousand pounds or you never get her back."

The husband said: "I'll take the 100k then."

What did the heartless thief do after robbing a deaf, dumb and blind woman? – He broke her fingers so she couldn't tell anyone.

When his wife went missing without any explanation, a husband became concerned and informed the police. Then, two days later, he returned home to find her waiting in the kitchen.

"Where have you been?" he asked. "I've been so worried about you."

She said: "I was kidnapped by three masked men and they took me to this remote farm where they had rough sex with me for a week."

"What do you mean, a week? You've only been gone two days."

She said: "I'm only here to get something to eat."

Statistically, nine out of ten people enjoy gang rape.

A bartender was getting ready to close for the night when a robber with a ski-mask burst in and pulled a gun. He yelled to the bartender: "This is a stick-up! Put all your dough in this bag!"

The scared bartender pleaded: "Don't shoot, please! I'll do as you say!"

The robber barked: "Shut up and empty the cash register!"

"Okay, okay!" said the bartender. "Just don't shoot! I have a wife and kids! I'll do whatever you say!"

The robber snatched the money but instead of making his escape he put the gun to the bartender's head and said: "Right, now give me a blow job!"

"Anything!" cried the bartender. "Just don't shoot!"

So the bartender started to blow the robber, who soon became so excited that he dropped his gun. Spotting the gun lying on the floor, the bartender quickly picked it up, handed it back to the robber and hissed: "Hold the gun, damn it! Someone I know might walk in!"

Cross-Dressing

A cross-dresser was hitchhiking through Arkansas and managed to get a ride from a mean-looking trucker. After riding about thirty miles in silence, the cross-dresser finally said: "Well, aren't you going to ask me?"

"Ask ya what?" replied the trucker.

"If I'm a man or a woman," answered the cross-dresser.

"Don't matter," replied the trucker. "Gonna fuck ya anyway."

Did you hear about the TV repairman? – He wore a dress and high heels.

What's the biggest crime committed by transvestites? – Male fraud.

The one thing women don't want to find in their stockings on Christmas morning is their husband. (Joan Rivers)

How do you know your husband is a transvestite? – When he wants to eat, drink and be Mary.

What's the best thing about shagging a transvestite? – When you reach round, it feels like it's gone all the way through.

Dating

Two young lovers went off into the mountains for a romantic weekend away. On arrival, the guy went out to chop some wood, but when he got back he complained that his hands were icy cold.

"Okay," said his girlfriend, "put them here between my thighs and that will warm them up."

After lunch, he went out to chop some more wood and again he came back complaining that his hands were freezing.

"Just put them between my thighs," said his girlfriend, "and that will warm them up." So he did.

After dinner, he went out to chop some more wood to get them through the night. When he came back, he said: "Honey, my hands are really, really freezing!"

She looked at him and said: "For crying out loud, don't your ears ever get cold?"

Two strangers met in a bar and over the course of several drinks they established that they both had new girlfriends.

One said: "We've only been dating three weeks but I already know all of my girlfriend's likes and dislikes – food, movies, music, everything."

"Well, after just two weeks I know every part of my girlfriend's body," smiled the other.

"You don't say?"

"Yeah, they're all neatly labelled in the freezer."

Things Not to Say to Your New Girlfriend's Parents

- Can I put my car in your garage . . . just in case the cops come around?
- Kelly is so pretty I've decided to give up being bisexual just for her.
- Nice place you got here. That painting looks expensive. I bet a nice home like this came with a safe already built in?
- Once I pop her cherry, I'll probably lose interest. You know how it is.
- I didn't want to say it in front of her but I'm only going out with Kelly for a bet.
- We're going to keep our relationship quiet for now. My wife can be rather vindictive at times.
- They always say a girl grows up to look like her mother. Let's hope Kelly's the exception to that rule, huh?
- There's nothing that beats that great feeling of knowing your HIV tests are negative.
- Which one of you taught Kelly to give such great head?
- Your daughter is safe with me. If I can handle prison, I can handle anything.
- I bet you were a terrific lay in your day, Mrs Finkelstein.
- Six different dates in one week! I'm really on a roll right now.

- So roughly how much does Kelly have in her savings account?
- Kelly's sister's pretty hot, too. Is she legal yet?
- Do either of you know anything about genital rashes?
- Have you seen the price of condoms lately?
- You have a lovely house. It reminds me of this article I read about these devil-worshippers who went on a murder spree in Detroit.
- Do you happen to know if she does anal? Even if she doesn't, it's no big deal. It's not a deal-breaker . . . yet.
- In my experience those home pregnancy tests aren't very reliable.
- My parole officer says Kelly has a calming influence on me.
- I can't believe I'm going to bang your daughter tonight!

I've got a hot date tonight. She's a burns victim.

A guy had been on a couple of dates with a nurse, and then one night they ended up in bed. As he stripped off, he said to her: "You must have seen a few cocks where you work. How does mine rate?"

She said: "It's slightly bigger than average."

"Thanks," he said. "By the way, what sort of nursing do you do?"

She said: "I'm a midwife."

I think my girlfriend must have had sixty-one boyfriends before me, because she calls me her sixty-second lover.

Don was setting his friend Al up on a blind date with a friend of a woman at work. Al was unsure whether to go through with it and asked: "What should I do if when I get to her house I discover she's really ugly?"

"No problem," said Don. "You just do a loud 'Atchoo', pretend you have a really bad cold and say that you're sorry but you're going to have to cancel. I know it's a bit sneaky but a guy has to look after his own interests. You don't want to waste an evening on an ugly bitch."

"Okay," said Al, "now that you've given me a get-out clause, I'll give the date thing a go."

So, two nights later Al drove over to the woman's house and when she answered the door, he could hardly believe his eyes. She was absolutely gorgeous. She took one look at Al and went "Atchoo!"

I know someone who is trying to set up a "speed-groping" night. It's touch and go whether it happens. (Andrew Lawrence)

A guy joined a dating agency but went on a series of unsuccessful dates. So he went back to the agency and said to its female proprietor: "Have you got someone on your books who doesn't care what I look like, isn't concerned about my personal hygiene and has a lovely big pair of boobs?"

The woman checked the computer database and said: "Actually, we do have one. But it's you."

What a Woman's Rejection Lines Really Mean

- I think of you as a brother = You remind me of that inbred banjo geek in *Deliverance*.
- There's a slight difference in our ages = I don't want to do my dad.
- I'm just not attracted to you in that way = You ugly dork.
- My life is too complicated right now = I don't want you staying the whole night or else you may hear phone calls from all the other guys I'm seeing.
- I've got a boyfriend = I prefer to spend an evening with my male cat and half a gallon of Ben & Jerry's ice cream.
- I don't date men where I work = It's bad enough that you're in the same solar system as me, much less the same building.
- It's not you, it's me = It's you.
- I'm concentrating on my career = Even something as boring and unfulfilling as my job is better than dating you.
- I'm celibate = I've sworn off the likes of you.
- Let's be friends = I want you to stay around so I can tell you in excruciating detail about all the other men I meet and have sex with.

What a Man's Rejection Lines Really Mean

- I think of you as a sister = You're ugly.
- There's a slight difference in our ages = You're ugly.
- I'm not attracted to you in that way = You're ugly.
- My life is too complicated right now = You're ugly.
- I've got a girlfriend = You're ugly.
- I don't date women where I work = You're ugly.
- It's not you, it's me = You're ugly.
- I'm concentrating on my career = You're ugly.

- I'm celibate = You're ugly.
- Let's be friends = You're pigging ugly.

How can you tell if your girlfriend's too young for you? — You have to make airplane noises to get your dick in her mouth.

A man met a beautiful girl and agreed to spend the night with her for £500. So they did. Before he left, he told her that he did not have any cash with him, but that he would have his secretary write a cheque and mail it to her, calling the payment "Rent for Apartment".

On the way to the office, however, he regretted what he had done and realized that their night together was not worth the price. So he had his secretary send a cheque for £250 and enclosed the following note:

"Dear Madam, Enclosed find a cheque in the amount of £250 for rent of your apartment. I am not sending the amount agreed upon, because when I rented the apartment, I was under the impression that: it had never been occupied; that there was plenty of heat; and it was small enough to make me feel cosy and at home. Last night, however, I found out that it had been previously occupied, that there wasn't any heat, and it was far too large."

Upon receipt of the note, the girl immediately returned the cheque for £250 with the following note:

"Dear Sir, First of all, I cannot understand how you expect a beautiful apartment to remain unoccupied indefinitely. As for the heat, there is plenty of it, if you know how to turn it on. Regarding the space, the apartment is indeed of regular size, but if you don't have enough furniture to fill it, please do not blame the landlady."

After not being in a relationship with a girl for nearly five years, Ben began dating again. Three weeks later, he met his pal Jack in the street.

"How's it going with your new girlfriend?" asked Jack.

"Yeah, it's okay," said Ben. "But there are so many things you have to get used to in a new relationship, things you forget about after nearly five years of being single."

"Like what?"

"Well, like after sex, as we're lying there, I have to keep repeating to myself: 'Don't hand her cash . . . don't hand her cash.'"

My girlfriend has eyes like spanners. When I look into them, my nuts tighten.

A guy joined an internet dating site, and his first date was with a girl at a hospital. She said: "I don't know if the website told you, but I only have a few weeks to live."

He replied: "That's okay. I don't know if the website told you, but I'm only looking for a short-term relationship."

I once dated a girl who wore an eye patch. She said she wanted to stop seeing me, so I poked her in her good eye.

What's the best thing about dating a homeless girl? – Afterwards you can drop her off wherever you like.

A girl told her boyfriend: "You have to make sacrifices in a relationship." So he went out and slaughtered a goat.

A wealthy playboy was dating three different girls at the same time. He wanted to settle down and get married, but couldn't decide which of the three to choose. So he decided to conduct a test. He gave each girl £10,000 to spend and closely monitored what each did with the money.

The first girl spent the money on an entirely new wardrobe. She told him: "I always want to look my best for you because I love you so much." He was impressed.

The second girl used the money to buy an expensive watch which she then presented to him as a gift. She told him: "I want you to have this because I love you so much." He was impressed.

The third girl invested the money in the stock market, tripled her initial investment and gave him his £10,000 back plus interest. She then re-invested the remainder "for our future because I love you so much". He was impressed.

At the end of the task, the man was left with a difficult choice as to which girl to make his bride. He thought about it for several days before coming to the only rational conclusion – he chose the one with the biggest tits.

A quick way to start a conversation is to say something like "What's your favourite colour?" A quick way to end a conversation is to say something like "What's your favourite colour . . . person?" (Demetri Martin)

How a Girl Should Interpret Her New Date's Actions

- He insists on going to a brand-new restaurant but gets lost on the way – a virgin.
- Can't hail a cab – impotent.
- Gets in the car without opening door for you – no foreplay.
- Doesn't give the cabbie a tip – small penis.
- Insists on going to a candlelit restaurant – love rat.
- Refuses to sit at a window table – love rat.
- Takes ages to decide what to order – has trouble reaching orgasm.
- Fills up on bread and crackers – premature ejaculator.
- Asks what the specials are – will want you to use handcuffs.
- Asks to change tables – love rat.
- Gives explicit orders to waiter – will expect incredible gymnastics in bed.
- Asks for the "usual" – missionary position only.
- Sends food back – will sleep with you, brag to all his friends, then try to borrow money.
- Insists on having some of whatever you ordered – will expect you to sleep on the wet spot.
- Asks for detailed descriptions of the desserts – needs you to talk dirty during sex.
- Uses a toothpick – is trying to tell you size isn't everything.
- His credit card is refused – low sperm count.

I'll never join one of those online dating services. I prefer to meet women the old-fashioned way – through alcohol and poor judgement.

Two guys were chatting in the pub. After a while, one said: "Can I tell you a true story with a moral to it?"

"Okay," said his friend, taken aback by the sudden serious tone of the conversation. "Go ahead."

The first guy began: "My lovely girlfriend and I had been dating for over a year, and so we decided to get married. There was only one little thing bothering me. It was her beautiful younger sister. My prospective sister-in-law was twenty-two, wore very tight miniskirts and generally was braless. She would regularly bend down when she was near me, and I always got more than a pleasant view. She never did it when she was near anyone else. One day, 'little' sister called and asked me to come over to check the wedding invitations. She was alone when I arrived, and she whispered to me that she had feelings and desires for me that she couldn't overcome. She told me that she wanted to make love to me just once before I got married and committed my life to her sister. Well, I was in total shock and couldn't say a word. She said: 'I'm going upstairs to my bedroom, and if you want one last wild fling, just come up and get me.' I was stunned, frozen in shock as I watched her go up the stairs. She pulled off her panties and threw them down the stairs at me. I stood there for a moment, then turned and made a beeline for the front door. I opened the door, and headed straight towards my car. Lo and behold, my entire future family was standing outside, all clapping! With tears in his eyes, my future father-in-law hugged me and said: 'We are very happy that you have passed our little test . . . we couldn't ask for a better man for our daughter. Welcome to the family.' "

"And what's the moral of the story?" asked his friend.

"The moral of the story is: always keep your condoms in the car!"

Deafness

Accompanied by his wife, a deaf old man went to the doctor. Since her hearing was better than his, she acted as an interpreter.

"Okay," began the doctor, addressing the old man, "would you please take off your shirt?"

"What did he say?" asked the old man.

"They want your shirt," replied the wife.

The old man took off his shirt, which was encrusted with food.

Next the doctor said: "Would you please take off your socks so that I can examine your feet?"

"What did he say?" yelled the old man.

"They want your socks," explained the wife.

As the old man was removing his smelly docks, the nurse said: "We also need a stool sample and a urine sample."

"What did she say?" boomed the old man.

His wife said: "They want your underpants."

Can deaf people tell the difference between a yawn and a scream?

A man was sitting in a bar telling the bartender about the break-up of his relationship. He said: "My ex-girlfriend is profoundly deaf and she left me for a deaf friend of hers, and I blame myself."

"Why?" asked the bartender.

"Well, I should have seen the signs."

At a retirement-home dance, two deaf old men were eyeing up an attractive lady who was sitting by herself. Eventually one of the men plucked up the courage to ask the lady for a dance.

She replied: "I'm sorry, but right now I'm contemplating on matrimony, and I'd rather sit than dance."

So the man returned chastened to his friend.

"What did she say?" asked the friend.

"I didn't quite catch it all, but she said she's constipated on macaroni and would rather shit in her pants."

A young man was sitting on the bus chewing gum and staring into space. After a minute or so, the old woman sitting opposite him said: "It's no good you talking to me, young man. I'm stone deaf!"

A man realized he needed to purchase a hearing aid, but didn't want to spend a lot of money. "How much do they cost?" he asked the salesman.

"Anything from £2 to £2,000."

"Can I see the £2 model?" said the customer.

The salesman put the device around the man's neck, and said: "You just stick this button in your ear and run this little string down to your pocket."

"How does it work?" asked the customer.

"For £2, it doesn't work," said the salesman. "But when people see it on you, they'll talk louder!"

Twin sisters at a retirement home were celebrating their one hundredth birthdays. To mark the occasion, the local newspaper sent along a photographer to take some pictures. One of the twins, Mabel, was a bit deaf but the other, Agnes, could hear quite well.

Firstly the photographer asked the sisters to sit on the sofa.

The deaf sister, Mabel, shouted to her twin: "What did he say?"

"He wants us to sit over there on the sofa," said Agnes.

So they sat on the sofa.

"Now move a little closer together," said the photographer.

"What did he say?" yelled Mabel.

"He wants us to squeeze together a little," replied Agnes.

So they huddled up next to each other.

"Now just hold that pose for a few seconds," said the photographer. "I've got to focus."

"What did he say?" barked Mabel.

"He says he's gonna focus," answered Agnes.

"Oh my God!" shrieked Mabel. "Both of us?"

Little Johnny took his girlfriend to his house to meet his parents but warned her that they were both deaf and dumb. When the youngsters walked into the living room, Johnny's mother had a beer bottle up her fanny and his father had both testicles hanging out and a match propping one eye open.

"What's all this about?" asked Johnny's girlfriend, startled.

"Oh, it's just sign language," replied Johnny. "Mom is saying, 'Get the beers in ya cunt,' and Dad is saying, 'Bollocks, I'm watching the match.'"

I asked my deaf-mute neighbour to stop parking his car across the entrance to my drive. He got really angry. You should have seen the language.

A deaf-mute guy had worked his way up in the Triads to the point where he was trusted to collect protection money on a small patch in Chinatown. After a few weeks, however, he became greedy and started to cream off some of the money, which he then hid in a safe place. Unfortunately for him, the Triad bosses soon realized that they were about $50,000 short and sent their most feared enforcer to sort it out. He tracked down the deaf-mute collector and asked him where the money was but they couldn't communicate, so the enforcer dragged the guy to one of the impoverished restaurant owners who could use sign language.

"Ask him where the money is," barked the enforcer. The restaurant owner signed to the man who had been terrorizing the neighbourhood for weeks: "Where's the money?"

The deaf mute replied: "I don't know what you're talking about."

The interpreter relayed this to the enforcer, who immediately pulled out a gun and rammed it in the collector's mouth. "*Now* ask him where the money is!"

The terrified deaf mute signed back: "The $50,000 is in deposit box 298 at Grand Central Station and the key is in the glove compartment of my car."

The restaurant owner told the Triad enforcer: "He says he still doesn't know what you're talking about, doesn't think you have the balls to pull the trigger, and says your mother sucks cock for money."

Death

A man went into a newspaper shop and asked: "Do you sell bereavement cards?"

"Yes, we do," said the sales clerk.

"In that case, could I exchange one for this Get Well Soon card I bought yesterday?"

How did the bearded lady and the three-legged dwarf die? – In a freak accident.

Three insurance salesmen were sitting in a restaurant boasting about their companies' speed of service.

The first said: "When one of our policyholders died suddenly on Monday, we got the news that evening and were able to process the claim for the wife so quickly that she received the cheque by Thursday morning."

The second said: "When one of our insured died on Monday, we were able to hand-deliver a cheque to his widow the same evening."

The third said: "That's nothing. Our office is on the sixth floor. One of our insured, who was washing a window on the thirty-first floor, slipped and fell on Monday. We handed him his cheque as he passed our floor!"

When you die at seventy-two, no matter what you die of, it's natural causes. Even if you get hit by a truck, it's natural causes. Because if you were younger, you'd get out of the way! (Chris Rock)

My uncle died last week. He drank a bottle of varnish. The doctor said he had a terrible end but a lovely finish.

A woman was walking through a cemetery when she spotted a man hiding behind a gravestone.

"Morning," she called out.

"No," he said, "just having a shit."

My wife's star sign was cancer, which is quite ironic considering the way she died. She was attacked by a giant crab. (Bo Burnham)

The mortician was laying out the body of a man with an unbelievably long penis. He called in his elderly receptionist to show her. She took a look, and then said: "That's just like my husband's."

The mortician asked: "You mean he's got one that long?"

"No," she replied. "That dead!"

Three morticians were trading stories in a bar one night. The first one said: "What a day I had today. The guy wasn't wearing his seatbelt and his head flew into the windshield. It took me all day to make the face look natural."

Not to be outdone, the second mortician said: "You think that's bad? I had this guy in who got hit by a train while he was riding his bike. It took me two days to put all the pieces back together!"

The third mortician just shook his head. "You guys have it easy," he said. "I had this female parachutist whose chute didn't open. She landed on a flagpole and it took me all week just to wipe the smile off her face!"

I was sitting opposite an Indian lady on the train. Her eyes were shut and she seemed to have stopped breathing. I thought she was dead but then I saw the red dot on her head and I realized she was just on standby.

The emergency services were called to the home of an elderly couple after the man had suffered a suspected heart attack, but they were too late and the man had already died. While consoling the wife, one of the paramedics noticed that the bed was a mess. He asked the lady what symptoms the man had experienced and whether anything had precipitated the heart attack.

The lady replied: "Well, we were in the bed making love and he started moaning, groaning, thrashing about the bed, panting and sweating. I thought he was coming, but I guess he was going."

Did you hear about the highway protestor who died of a heart attack? – His doctor had warned him weeks ago but the idiot wouldn't have a bypass.

I'm going to spend some time by my wife's grave today. She doesn't know – she thinks I'm digging a pond.

The day after losing his wife in a boating accident, a man answered the door to two police officers. They said: "We have some bad news, some good news and some great news. Which would you like to hear first?"

"Give me the bad news first," said the man.

"I'm afraid we've found your wife's body in the sea near the harbour."

"Oh, no," sobbed the man. "My poor wife. My poor lovely wife. What can be the good news?"

"When we pulled her up, she had two five-pound lobsters and a dozen large edible crabs on her."

"That's terrible!" gasped the man. "So what's the great news?"

"We're going to pull her up again tomorrow."

Dentists

An old lady went to the dentist, sat in the chair, lowered her pants and lifted her legs in the air.

"I'm not a gynaecologist," said the dentist.

"I know," said the old lady. "I want you to take my husband's teeth out."

I had to have a brace because I had big teeth. If I'd gone to Africa, I would have got poached. (Alan Carr)

A young married woman fell madly in love with her handsome new dentist and pretty soon had lured him into a series of passionate encounters in the dental clinic after hours. But one day he said sadly: "Jennifer, we have to stop seeing each other. Your husband's bound to get suspicious."

"No way, sweetie, he's dumb as a post," she assured him. "Besides, we've been fooling around for six months now and he doesn't suspect a thing."

"True," agreed the dentist, "but you're down to one tooth!"

What's red and bad for your teeth? – A brick.

A mother walked into the bathroom one day and found Little Johnny furiously scrubbing his dick with a toothbrush and toothpaste.

"What on earth do you think you're doing?!" she exclaimed.

Johnny replied: "I'm going to do this three times a day, because there's no way I'm going to get a cavity that looks and smells as bad as my sister's."

Diarrhoea

A woman stormed into the room and yelled: "Which one of you has diarrhoea and splashed it all up the seat?"

Her son-in-law said sheepishly: "Sorry, Anne, it was me. There wasn't any toilet paper to wipe it off."

"And why the fuck would I keep toilet paper in my Vauxhall Nova?!"

What's the definition of bravery? – A man with diarrhoea chancing a fart.

Did you know that diarrhoea can kill you, even if you only drink a bit?

A man went into a pharmacy and said: "Do you have anything that will clear up diarrhoea?"

The pharmacist said: "We have these tablets . . ."

"No, you don't understand," said the man. "I was thinking more of a mop. I just shat on your floor."

Dieting

A guy urgently needed to lose weight. He went to the doctor's office and said: "Doc, I just can't seem to find a diet that works. I've tried them all. You got to help me."

The doctor said: "Well, there is a new drastic diet I've read about in the *Medical Journal*. It's called the Anal Diet. The idea is you don't eat anything until you are desperate. Then, nothing by mouth: if you want it bad enough, you insert it anally."

The patient shook his head and said: "I don't think I could do that."

But the doctor reminded him: "If you really are desperate to lose weight, it's guaranteed to work."

"Okay," agreed the patient reluctantly, "I'll give it a try." The doctor told him to come back in a month so that he could evaluate his progress.

A month later, the patient returned with a huge grin on his face. He walked back and forth in front of the doctor's desk proclaiming: "That's the best damn diet I've ever tried. It took a little time to get used to but look at me: I've lost forty-seven pounds."

With this, the patient raised and lowered his right leg several times, shuffled back and forth from foot to foot, and paced back and forth.

The doctor said: "You look great but have you noticed any side-effects?"

The patient, still pacing back and forth, said: "No; no side effects at all. Why would you ask that?"

The doctor said: "Well, it seems to me that you can't sit still. All this moving about and pacing: what's wrong?"

The patient laughed, smacked himself on the arse and said: "I'm okay. I'm just chewing gum."

A balanced American diet is when every McNugget weighs the same.

A woman had been urged by her doctor to go on a strict diet, but she had no willpower and continued snacking throughout the day. As her weight ballooned, one day she got stuck on the toilet seat.

"Bill!" she cried out to her husband. "The toilet seat's stuck to my butt. Fetch the doctor."

The husband asked the doctor to come out as soon as he could but didn't explain the nature of the problem. In the meantime, the husband managed to remove the seat from the toilet bowl although it remained wedged fast to his wife's backside. He suggested she go and kneel on the bed until the doctor arrived.

When the doctor turned up, the husband showed him straight into the bedroom where the wife was kneeling with her back to the door.

"What do you think, Doc?" asked the husband.

"I think it's very nice," replied the doctor, "but why such a cheap frame?"

Disability

A woman met her one-armed neighbour in the elevator. "Where are you going?" she asked.

"To change a light bulb," he replied.

"Oh. Will you able to manage that?"

"Sure," he said. "I've got the receipt."

After losing one of his arms in an accident, a man became very depressed because he had previously been a keen sportsman.

One day, in the depths of despair, he decided to commit suicide. He got in an elevator and went to the top of a five-storey office block with the intention of jumping off. He was standing on the ledge staring down at the street below when he saw a man skipping along, whistling and kicking up his heels. On closer inspection, he saw that this man didn't have any arms at all.

He started thinking, What am I doing up here, feeling sorry for myself when there are people much worse off than me? I still have one good arm to do things with. There goes a guy with no arms skipping down the sidewalk, so happy and just getting on with life.

So he abandoned his plans, hurried down and caught up with the man with no arms. He told him how, having lost one arm, he had felt useless and had been ready to kill himself, but that seeing him had been an inspiration. He thanked him for saving his life and said: "I now realize that I can survive with one arm if you can enjoy life with no arms."

The man with no arms began skipping and whistling and kicking up his heels again. The guy felt compelled to ask him: "Why *are* you so happy anyway?"

The man with no arms said: "I'm not happy – my balls itch!"

A man in his twenties was sitting in a bar when he noticed a woman going round the tables talking to the customers. Eventually she reached his table and asked him: "Would you like to run a marathon?"

"No chance," he said.

"But," she explained, "it's for disabled children."

"Oh, okay then," he said. "I could win that one."

Just got back from the World Strawberry Picking Championships. Lost in the final to a girl with no legs. Jammy cunt.

Little Johnny went over to Billy's house and rang the bell. Billy's mother answered the door.

Little Johnny said: "Can Billy come and play war in the street with his friends?"

Billy's mother replied: "You know Billy doesn't have any arms or legs."

"I know," said Little Johnny, "but we want to use him as a sandbag."

A vicar was travelling on a train when a pregnant woman got on and sat down opposite him. He carried on reading his newspaper while she got out her knitting. As she was knitting, she would stop every ten minutes, reach into her bag, pull out a bottle of pills, take one pill from the bottle and then swallow it. This went on for about an hour until the vicar happened to glance at the bottle and saw the label "Thalidomide".

"Excuse me," said the vicar. "Do you know the effect those pills could have on your unborn child?"

"Don't worry, I know what I'm doing," said the woman. "You see, I could never knit sleeves."

Girl: Mummy, can I have a cookie, please?
Mother: Yeah, sure.
Girl: But Mummy, I don't have any arms.
Mother: No arms, no cookies.

If I need directions I ask a man with one leg 'cause he definitely knows the easiest way to get there. Yup, if there's a shortcut that one-legged fucker knows where it is. You won't be hoppin' fences neither. (Dave Attell)

Henry was delighted when he finally found a young woman who accepted his proposal of marriage as he was sensitive about his wooden leg and was afraid that no one would have him. He was so conscious of his disability that he couldn't bring himself to tell his fiancée about his leg when he popped the question, when they held the engagement party or when they named the wedding day. All he kept saying was, "Darling, I've got a big surprise for you," at which she blushed and smiled bewitchingly.

On their wedding night, the young couple were at last alone in their hotel room.

"Now don't forget, Henry, you promised me a big surprise," said the bride.

Silently Henry turned out the lights, unstrapped his wooden leg, slipped into bed and placed his wife's hand on the stump.

"Mmm," she said softly, "that *is* a surprise. But pass me the Vaseline and I'll see what I can do!"

Ironically people with club feet generally aren't very good dancers.

A man applied to the council for a job. The interviewer asked him: "Have you been in the Armed Services?"

"Yes, I was in Afghanistan for eighteen months."

"Good," said the interviewer, making a note of the answer, "that will give you extra points towards getting the job. And are you disabled in any way?"

"Yes, a landmine blew my testicles off."

"Okay," said the interviewer, writing it down. Then he broke into a smile and announced. "I'm pleased to say we can offer you the job. The hours are 8 a.m. till 4 p.m. You can start tomorrow. Come in at 10 a.m."

The man was puzzled. "If the hours are eight to four, why don't you want me to come in till ten?"

"This is a council job," replied the interviewer. "For the first two hours we sit around scratching our balls — no point in you coming in for that."

Diseases and Conditions

Two men were sitting in a bar. One said: "My wife has gonorrhoea, diarrhoea and ascariasis."

"Why do you stay with her?" said the other.

"Because I love to fish and she has great worms."

A boy arrived home from school and sobbed: "Mum, everyone says I'm too hairy."

The mother called to her husband: "Honey, the dog is talking!"

An American guy contracted a terrible disease of the penis while on vacation in Bangkok. Every American doctor he consulted told him that it would have to be amputated, but as a desperate last resort he decided to fly back out to Thailand and seek medical advice in the hope that doctors there might be more familiar with the condition.

The Thai doctor examined him thoroughly before announcing: "There is absolutely no need to amputate your penis."

"That's great news!" the American enthused.

"Yes," continued the doctor, "any medical man worth his salt can see that it will drop off anyway in three weeks."

A man told the doctor: "I've got AIDS, syphilis, herpes and gonorrhoea."

"Ah," said the doctor, "you're what we call an incurable romantic."

My wife suffers from photosensitive epilepsy. Whenever I view porn, she has a fit.

A mother said to her grown-up daughter: "Honey, I don't want you to think I have diabetes because I'm fat. I have diabetes because it runs in our family."

The daughter shook her head in despair. "No, Mum," she replied, "you have diabetes because no one runs in our family."

A man went to see his doctor. The doctor said: "I have good news and bad news."

"What's the bad news?" asked the man.

"Your wife has syphilis."

"My God! What could possibly be the good news?"

"She didn't catch it from you."

A guy was reading his emails and there was one from his boss. It said: "Dear Mr Wilkins, I regret to inform you that although I thought this company could tolerate your Attention Deficit Disorder, I'm afraid you're just not productive enough. You may turn up Wednesday to collect your things. I sincerely hope you will be OK."

And the guy thought to himself, doesn't OK look like a sideways person?

A worried woman went to see her doctor who told her: "Mrs Phillips, the results of your tests are back, and I'm afraid to say you have gonorrhoea."

Embarrassed, the woman said: "Er, I think I must have caught it from a toilet seat."

"Well, you must have been chewing it then," said the doctor, "because it's in your gums!"

Why did God invent thrush? — So women would know what it was like to live with an irritating cunt.

Wife: I'm leaving you because of your OCD.

Husband: Close the door seven times on your way out.

A man had just married a beautiful woman who had epilepsy. As he lay in the hotel bed that first night waiting, his anticipation grew and grew. Finally, his new bride emerged from the bathroom and slid into bed next to him. Things were tentative at first, as this was their first time together, but after a bit of kissing and petting things really picked up and they began to make love.

Things were going just as he'd hoped when suddenly she began to have a seizure. Frightened, he ran into the hotel lobby, yelling: "My wife! My wife!"

The concerned hotel staff followed him back to the room to find his new bride still in the midst of a horrible seizure.

"Tie her hands, tie her hands!" the husband yelled to the hotel staff. They immediately tied her hands to the bed.

"Tie he feet, tie her feet!" cried the husband. They tied her feet to the bed.

Then the husband jumped on top of her, and with the hotel staff wondering what was going on, he raised one arm up behind his head and shouted: "All right, boys. Cut her loose!"

A young man went to the doctor and said nervously: "My best mate and I went to a brothel and he's afraid he may have caught some kind of disease. What should he do?"

"Okay," said the doctor. "Get your pants down and let's have a look at your best mate."

They say a problem shared is a problem halved. Not if it's AIDS.

If I had a penny for every time someone said I have OCD, I'd have 893,451 pence.

What does an American with Parkinson's eat? – Beef jerky.

An eighty-year-old woman thought she had crabs, so she went to the doctor.

"Doctor," she said. "I think I have the crabs."

"When was the last time you had sex?" the doctor asked.

"I have never had sex. I'm still a virgin," she replied.

The doctor thought this was a very strange thing to hear in the twenty-first century so he told her to get on the table and he would examine her. After the examination he said: "I have some good news and bad news for you. The good news is you don't have crabs. The bad news is you've got fruit flies. Your cherry rotted."

I shagged a girl with brittle-bone disease last night. Right little cracker she was!

A worried father telephoned his family doctor and said that he was afraid that his teenage son had come down with VD. "He says he hasn't had sex with anyone but the maid, so it has to be her."

"Don't worry too much," advised the doctor. "These things happen."

"I know, doctor," said the father, "but I have to admit that I've been sleeping with the maid, too. I seem to have the same symptoms."

"That's unfortunate."

"Not only that, I think I've passed it to my wife."

"Bugger!" said the doctor. "That means we've all got it."

Two old men with Parkinson's disease went up to an ice-cream van and asked the driver: "Can we have two vanilla cones, please?"

"Sure," said the driver. "Would you like chocolate or strawberry sauce on them?"

"It doesn't really matter, pal," they said. "We're going to drop them anyway."

What do you do if your wife has a fit in the bath? – Put the dishes in.

I used to think my friend had OCD because he kept sending me the same email forty times. It turns out he just had Parkinson's.

What's the cruellest thing you can do to someone with OCD? – Buy them a picture of the Leaning Tower of Pisa and watch while they drive themselves crazy trying to get it to hang straight.

Two medical students were walking along the street when they noticed an old man walking with his legs spread wide apart. One of the students said to his friend: "I bet he has Karpinsky Syndrome. That's how people with that condition walk."

The other student disagreed. "No, I reckon he has Wavell Syndrome. Remember, we learned about it in class? That's how those people walk – a classic case if ever I saw one!"

Since they were unable to agree, they decided to ask the old man. "We're medical students," they said, "and we couldn't help noticing the distinctive way you walk. But we can't agree on what syndrome you have. Could you tell us what it is, please?"

The old man said: "I'll tell you, but first you must let me know what you think it is."

The first student said: "I think it's Karpinsky Syndrome."

The old man said: "You thought, but you are wrong."

The second student said: "I think it's Wavell Syndrome."

The old man said: "You thought, but you are wrong."

"So what do you have?" they asked.

The old man said: "I thought it was wind, but I was wrong."

My girlfriend is epileptic and flashing lights can give her a seizure. That's why I always carry a torch when she's giving me a hand job.

The doctor gave me the all-clear on my OCD tests today. I couldn't thank him enough.

A ten-year-old boy walked into a brothel carrying a dead frog on a stick. He went up to the Madam and said: "I want a hooker."

"Go away, kid," she replied. "You're way too young."

Then the boy pulled a $100 bill from his pocket and repeated: "I want a hooker."

Swayed by the money, she relented. "Okay, kid. I'll sort you a girl."

"And I want her to have the clap," added the boy.

The Madam looked at the boy in disbelief. "Listen, kid, I'll fix you up with a hooker, but a hooker with the clap, no."

The boy then pulled out another $100 bill and said firmly: "I want a hooker with the clap."

"Okay, kid . . ."

"And herpes."

"Whoa!" the Madam exclaimed. "For $200, I'll sort out a girl with the clap, but herpes is going too far."

So he pulled out another $100. "I said I want a hooker with the clap and herpes."

"Okay, kid. Fine. Whatever."

"And AIDS."

The Madam stared at the kid with wide-eyed horror. "No way. I'm not going to be responsible for giving you AIDS!"

He pulled out another $100. "I said I want a hooker with the clap, herpes and AIDS."

"No," said the Madam. "This is just wrong. How would I live with myself?"

He threw out another hundred. The Madam looked at the boy and decided that he wasn't going to back down. She figured that if she didn't give him what he wanted, someone else probably would. "Fine," she sighed. "Up the stairs, third door on the left."

The boy walked up the stairs, the stick with the dead frog bouncing as he went. He entered the room and shut the door. Fifteen minutes later he emerged, came downstairs and was about to walk out the front door when the Madam stopped him.

"Hey, kid," she called out. "Why did you want to throw your life away like that? I mean, you're ten years old and you have the clap. And worse, you have herpes. And even worse, you have AIDS. Why would you do that?"

The boy turned to her and said: "When I get home, I'm going to jerk off on my babysitter's tampon. Sometime later, after I'm in bed, my dad is going to gently caress her. Sometime in the next month, my dad is going to gently caress my mom. And the next morning, my mom is going to gently caress the mailman. And the mailman – he's the one that ran over my frog!"

Divorce

What's the difference between getting a divorce and getting circumcised? – When you get a divorce, you get rid of the whole prick.

The judge in a divorce case asked for the representatives to make their final statements.

The lawyer for the husband rose to his feet and said: "M'lud, may I just remind you once again that one of the key incidents in this case was, in actual fact, an act of chivalry? Since when has it been wrong for a husband to open a door for his wife?"

The lawyer for the wife stood up immediately and said: "I think my learned friend is overlooking the fact that the car was travelling at eighty miles an hour at the time."

A man told his neighbour that he was getting a divorce.

"I'm sorry to hear that," said the neighbour. "What finally pushed you over the edge?"

"We hosted a wife-swapping party this weekend."

"Oh, and she behaved worse than you had expected?"

"No. It was just that to get any action, I had to throw in our maid!"

I've finally come to terms with my hideous deformity. She's agreed to a divorce.

A bitter divorced guy bumped into his ex-wife's new husband at a party. After a few drinks, he sauntered arrogantly over to him and sneered: "So, how do you like using second-hand goods?"

"It doesn't bother me," said the new husband. "From what I hear, once you get past the first three inches it's all brand new."

A wife was driving her wealthy husband home from a party one night when their car smashed into a tree. The wife was knocked unconscious by the impact and the car burst into flames. Seeing blood pouring from her head wound, the husband somehow managed to drag her to safety from the flames. He then wrapped her in a blanket, flagged down a passing car and rushed her to the nearest hospital. Over the next six months, he regularly donated blood to keep her alive. It was touch and go whether she would pull through, but eventually she did recover.

Their marriage had always been volatile, but for the next eighteen months the accident seemed to bring them closer together. However, eventually old tensions started to rise to the surface and once back in full health she decided to leave him. As she came downstairs one morning, carrying two large suitcases and a set of car keys, he challenged her: "Where are you going?"

"I'm leaving you," she said coldly. "I want a divorce."

"What are you doing with the car keys?" he demanded.

"I'm leaving in the Mercedes."

"No, you're not. It's my car. I paid for that. You're not having it."

"Fine," she said, and threw the keys at him.

"And what's in those bulging suitcases?" he asked.

"My clothes," she said.

"You mean the clothes I've paid for over the years? They're not going anywhere!"

"Fine," she said, tipping out the cases before stripping off completely and hurling her clothes at him.

"And," he continued, warming to the theme, "what about the blood in your body? I sat with you for six months in the hospital. You know half of the blood is mine. You're not going anywhere."

With that, she whipped out her tampon and said: "Here! I'll pay you back in monthly instalments!"

Why is it that when a couple get divorced the guy has to pay his ex-wife a share of his future earnings but the woman doesn't have to do his future housework?

Mickey Mouse wanted a divorce from Minnie, but the lawyer said that buck teeth were not grounds for a divorce.

"I didn't say she had buck teeth," said Mickey. "I said she was fucking Goofy!"

I'm going through a divorce at the moment, and my daughters aged three and five are devastated. I told them it was their fault.

A husband and wife were driving along the motorway at 50 mph when she suddenly announced: "I know we've been married for twenty-two years but I want a divorce."

The husband said nothing but slowly increased the car's speed to 60 mph.

His wife continued: "I don't want you trying to talk me out of it, I've made my decision. If you must know, I've been having an affair with your best friend, and he's a much better lover than you."

Again the husband said nothing, but increased the speed to 70 mph.

His wife demanded: "I want the house; it's the least I deserve after giving up my career for you."

The husband remained silent but accelerated to 80 mph.

"I want the kids, too," she added.

He put his foot down so that they were now doing 90 mph.

"And," she went on, "I want the car, the yacht, the villa in the Bahamas and another £200,000 in spending money."

He accelerated further and gradually started to steer the car towards a concrete bridge as she inquired: "Is there anything you want?"

Finally, he spoke. "No thanks," he said. "I've got everything I need."

"What's that, then?" she sneered.

Just before they hit the wall at 90 mph, he replied: "I've got the airbag."

The Divorce Letter

Dear Connie,

I know the counsellor said we shouldn't contact each other during our "cooling off" period, but I couldn't wait anymore. The day you left, I swore I'd never talk to you again. But that was just the wounded little boy in me talking. Still, I never wanted to be the first one to make contact. In my fantasies, it was always you who would come crawling back to me. I guess my pride needed that. But now I see that my pride's cost me a lot of things. I'm tired of pretending I don't miss you. I don't care about looking bad anymore. I don't care who makes the first move as long as one of us does. Maybe it's time we let our hearts speak as loudly as our hurt. And this is what my heart says: "There's no one like you, Connie."

I look for you in the eyes and breasts of every woman I see, but they're not you. They're not even close. Two weeks ago, I met this girl at Flamingos and brought her home with me. I don't say this to hurt you, but just to illustrate the depth of my desperation. She was young, maybe nineteen, with one of those perfect bodies that only youth and maybe a childhood spent ice skating can give you. I mean, just a perfect body: tits like you wouldn't believe and an ass that just wouldn't quit. Every man's dream, right? But as I sat on the couch being blown by this stunner, I thought, look at the stuff we've made important in our lives. It's all so superficial. What does a perfect body mean? Does it make her better in bed? Well, in this case, yes, but you see what I'm getting at. Does it make her a better person? Does she have a better heart than my moderately attractive Connie? I doubt it.

And I'd never really thought of that before.

I don't know, maybe I'm just growing up a little. Later, after I'd tossed her about a half a pint of throat yoghurt, I found myself thinking, "Why do I feel so drained and empty?" It wasn't just her flawless technique or her slutty, shameless hunger, but something else: some nagging feeling of loss. Why did it feel so incomplete? And then it hit me. It didn't feel the same because you weren't there to watch. Do you know what I mean? Nothing feels the same without you. Jesus, Connie, I'm just going crazy without you. And everything I do just reminds me of you.

Do you remember Carol, that single mum we met at the Holiday Inn lounge last year? Well, she dropped by last week with a lasagne. She said she figured I wasn't eating right without a woman around. I didn't know what she meant till later, but that's not the real story. Anyway, we had a few glasses of wine and the next thing you know, we're banging away in our old bedroom. And this tart's a total monster in the sack. She's giving me everything, you know, like a real woman does when she's not hung up about her weight or her career and whether the kids can hear us. And all of a sudden, she spots that tilting mirror on your grandmother's old vanity. So she puts it on the floor and we straddle it, right, so we can watch ourselves. And it's totally hot, but it makes me sad, too. 'Cause I can't help thinking, "Why didn't Connie ever put the mirror on the floor? We've had this old vanity for what, fourteen years, and we never used it as a sex toy."

Saturday, your sister drops by with my copy of the restraining order. I mean, Vicky's just a kid and all, but she's got a pretty good head on her shoulders and she's been a real friend to me during this painful time. She's given me lots of good advice about you and about women in general.

She's pulling for us to get back together, Connie, she really is. So we're doing Jell-O shots in a hot bubble bath and talking about happier times. Here's this teenage girl with the same DNA as you and all I can do is think of how much she looked like you when you were eighteen. And that just about makes me cry. And when it turns out Vicky's really into the whole anal thing, that gets me to thinking about how many times I pressured you about trying it and how that probably fuelled some of the bitterness between us. But do you see how even then, when I'm thrusting inside your baby sister's cinnamon ring, all I can do is think of you?

It's true, Connie. In your heart you must know it. Don't you think we could start over? Just wipe out all the grievances away and start fresh? I think we can. If you feel the same please, please, please let me know. Otherwise, can you let me know where the fucking remote is?

Love, Dan

Doctors

Doctor: Have you ever given yourself a prostate examination?
Patient: Not deliberately, but my wife sometimes buys cheap toilet paper.

A girl went to the doctor and admitted that she had such low self-esteem that she had tried to pay men to have sex with her, but all of them fled, complaining that her pussy stank. She couldn't see how that could be true, because when she bent over, she couldn't smell a thing.

The doctor examined her, then said: "You need an operation."

"On my pussy?" she asked.

"On your nose," the doctor replied.

A woman went to the doctor complaining of stomach cramps. The doctor sent her for some tests and when the results came through he told her: "You're going to have to prepare yourself for long sleepless nights full of crying and changing diapers."

"Why?" she asked. "Am I pregnant?"

"No," he said, "you've got bowel cancer."

One day a young man and his wife were in their bedroom making love. All of a sudden a bumble bee entered the bedroom window. As the woman parted her legs, the bee entered her vagina. She started screaming: "Oh my God, help me, there's a bee in my vagina!"

The husband immediately took her to the local doctor and explained what had happened. The doctor thought for a moment and said: "This is a delicate problem, but I may have a solution if you are agreeable to it."

"Do whatever it takes," said the husband. "Just get the damn bee out of my wife's vagina!"

"Okay," said the doctor, "what I'm going to do is rub some honey over the top of my penis and insert it into your wife's vagina. When I feel the bee getting closer to the tip of my dick I shall withdraw it and the bee should hopefully follow my penis out of your wife's vagina."

The husband nodded and gave his approval. The wife said: "Yes, yes, whatever, just get on with it."

So the doctor, after covering the tip of his penis with honey, inserted it into the young woman's vagina. After a few gentle strokes, the doctor said: "I don't think the bee has noticed the honey yet. Perhaps I should go a bit deeper."

So the doctor went deeper and deeper. After a while the doctor began shafting the wife very hard indeed. She began to quiver with excitement, and moan and groan aloud: "Oh Doctor, Doctor!" The doctor, concentrating very hard, looked like he was enjoying himself. He then put his hands on the young woman's breasts and started making loud noises.

At this point, the husband suddenly became very annoyed and shouted: "Now wait a minute, what do you think you're doing?"

The doctor, still deep in concentration, replied: "Change of plan, I'm going to drown the bugger."

A man took his young son to the doctor. "Doctor, my son has just swallowed a camera."

The doctor smiled: "Well, let's leave it a few days and see what develops."

At which the boy interrupted: "It's a fucking digital camera, you stupid old fool!"

A doctor told his patient: "I have some good news and some bad news."

"Give me the bad news first," said the patient.

"You've only got two weeks to live."

"Only two weeks to live?" cried the patient. "That's terrible. What's the good news?"

"My lottery numbers came up!"

A young man went to the doctor and was stunned to be greeted by a new, gorgeous young female doctor. He could hardly take his eyes off her luscious lips and ample breasts, and his trousers soon started to bulge visibly.

Sensing that he was embarrassed, she said: "Don't worry. I'm a professional. I've seen it all before. Just tell me what's wrong and I'll do my best to help you."

He said: "I think my cock tastes funny . . ."

A man went to the doctor and told him: "Doctor, I have a golf ball stuck up my arse." The doctor examined him and said: "Hmm. That's up a fair way."

A woman went to the doctor and complained of feeling listless and lethargic. After examining her thoroughly, he prescribed a six-week course of the male hormone, testosterone.

A month later she returned to the doctor in a state of high agitation.

"The hormones you prescribed have definitely helped," she said, "but I'm worried that the dosage is too high because I've started growing hair in places where I've never grown hair before."

"That's nothing to worry about," said the doctor reassuringly. "A little hair growth is a perfectly normal side effect of testosterone. Now, where exactly has the hair appeared?"

She said: "On my balls."

Man: I've badly bruised my penis in a surfing accident.

Doctor: Did you fall off your board?

Man: No, when my girlfriend walked in I had to shut my laptop quickly.

A young woman went to the doctor for an examination. After thoroughly examining her, the doctor said: "You are in excellent health except for those bruises on your knees. They seem to be developing into calluses. Can you tell me where they're coming from?"

The young woman started to blush and said: "I guess they have to do with my sexual activity. Whenever we make love we do it doggie style."

"Well, that should be easy to take care of," said the doctor. "Surely you must know other ways to have sexual intercourse."

"Yes, I do," said the woman, "but my dog doesn't."

Old Mr Johnson was rushed into the hospital in the middle of the night, apparently with a massive heart attack. The doctors worked on him all night and morning and finally moved him to the Intensive Care Unit, where his recovery continued. A couple of days later, his doctor came into his room and said: "George, I'm happy to tell you that you are completely well. You have the heart function that you did when you were a fifteen-year-old boy. We're going to send you home tomorrow. You don't have to worry about your heart; do any physical exercise that you like."

Mr Johnson went home and that evening was talking with his wife: "Doris, you'll never believe it. I'm completely well. I have no worries with my heart. Tonight, darling, you and I are going to have sex like you've never had before – wild, passionate and you're going to love it!"

Doris thought for a minute and said: "I don't know, George. I've heard about active sex and heart conditions. I don't want it to be on my head if you croak while we are making love. Maybe, just maybe, if your doctor wrote a note to me saying that everything was okay then maybe I would have such sex with you."

So the next day he visited the doctor to get the note. His doctor told him: "Sure, George, no problem. I'll write the note."

The note read: "This is to certify that Mr George Johnson, a patient of mine, has the heart function of a fifteen-year-old boy and can have mad, passionate, adventurous sex any time that he so desires. Signed, Dr Peter Barrett."

The doctor then asked: "Now all I need is your wife's first name?"

"Uh, doctor, could you just make that out 'To Whom It May Concern'?"

A man went to the doctor and said: "Doc, I bought some steroids, and they've had nasty side effects. I've grown an extra penis."

"Anabolic?"

"No, just a penis."

Two men were sitting in the doctor's office. The first man looked at the second and said: "What are you here for?"

The second replied: "I have a red ring around my pecker. What are you here for?"

The first said: "I have a green ring around my pecker."

The doctor called the man with the red ring first in his office and examined him. As he was walking out he told the other guy it was no problem.

Then the doctor called in the man with the green ring around his pecker and examined him. The doctor said: "Your pecker is going to fall off and you are going to die."

The man said: "What?! You told the guy with the red ring he was okay, but I'm going to die? How do you work that out?"

The doctor said: "There's a lot of difference lipstick and gangrene."

A middle-aged woman went to the doctor and said: "Doctor, I've got a terrible discharge. I think it must be some kind of infection because it smells really bad."

The doctor immediately asked her to lie down on the bed and told her to remove her panties. Before she could say anything, he then started swabbing her vagina.

After a couple of minutes, he asked her: "Now, how does that feel?"

"It feels wonderful, Doctor," she replied, "but the discharge was in my ear."

A woman was lying on the doctor's bed, waiting for her annual smear test. The doctor came in, and as he was preparing himself, she mentioned that she had six children. "Yes," I can tell," he said. "You have the biggest box I have ever seen!"

She was understandably offended by the remark, and when she got home, she went into the bathroom, took the mirror off the wall, and laid it on the floor so she could have a look for herself. As she squatted over the mirror, her husband walked in and saw her.

When he asked her what she was doing, she said: "I am doing my exercises."

"Well, be careful," he warned. "You're about to fall into that huge hole in the floor!"

Dogging

I went dogging with my wife last night. Never again! By the time she'd parked the car, everyone had gone home.

Petrol is so expensive these days that I can no longer afford to run a car. The last time I went dogging I had to ask my mum to give me a lift there.

A man was sitting at the bar looking glum. A friend went over to him and asked: "What's up with you?"

"Well," he explained, "I was driving around the other day and feeling really horny. So I decided to drop by at a well-known dogging spot nearby. There were a few other cars there so I pulled up and joined in."

"Sounds great. So why are you looking so miserable?"

"I'm pretty sure that's why I failed my driving test."

A blind couple were caught having sex in a car. They were arrested for guide-dogging.

Dogs

A poodle and a Great Dane were waiting in separate cages at the vet's. To ease the tension and pass the time, the poodle struck up conversation with his large neighbour.

"I did a really stupid thing yesterday," confessed the poodle. "My owner is devoutly religious and he invited some church friends round for tea. I don't know what came over me but I saw this woman's leg and I started humping it furiously. Three of them had to drag me off and throw a bucket of cold water over me. Now I'm here to be castrated."

"I know how you feel," said the Great Dane. "My owner is an elderly spinster who never lets me out. Yesterday, she bent over the bathtub after taking a shower and the sight of her bare butt in the air was simply too much for me. I lost control, mounted her and rode her for all she was worth. I stayed on for half an hour."

The poodle said: "So I guess you're here to be castrated, too?"

"No," replied the Great Dane. "I'm here to get my nails clipped."

Apparently animals make different sounds according to which part of the world they are in. For example, in Korea a dog makes a sizzling noise.

A man said to his stupid friend: "I'm thinking of getting a dog."

"What sort?" asked the friend.

"A Labrador retriever."

"No, you don't want to get one of those," said the friend shaking his head. "Have you seen how many of their owners go blind?"

What's the best way to give your dog a bone? – Tickle his balls.

Why are all the dogs at dog shows really nice dogs? You never see a pit bull with a ribbon round his head going, "If you say one fucking word . . ." (Lee Evans)

A man said to his wife: "You know how they say owners come to resemble their dogs? Well, I think it's happening to your mother and her poodle."

"What?" said the wife. "You mean her new perm and the way she prances about?"

"No," replied the husband. "I mean the way she shits in the garden!"

A young girl loved walking her dog after school but when the dog came on heat the girl's father suggested the pet be kept indoors for a few days. However, the girl was so upset that the father felt obliged to find a solution. So he sprayed some gasoline on the dog's butt to deter any male dogs.

The girl took her pet out as usual but came home half an hour later without the dog.

"Where's Missy?" asked the father.

"Oh," said the girl, "she ran out of gas a few blocks back and is being pushed home by another dog."

How do you make a dog drink? – Put it in a blender.

Why Dogs Are Like Men

- Both take up too much space on the bed.
- Both have irrational fears about vacuum cleaning.
- Both mark their territory.
- Neither tells you what's bothering them.
- The smaller ones tend to be more nervous.
- Both have an inordinate fascination with women's crotches.
- Both fart shamelessly.
- Neither of them notices when you get your hair cut.
- Both are suspicious of the postman.
- Neither understands what you see in cats.

An old lady took her dog to the vet as it seemed to be having problems with its hearing. The vet cleaned the dog's ears and advised her to use hair removal cream on them once a month as a means to reduce build-up and avoid a recurrence of the problem.

The old lady left the vet and headed straight to the pharmacist to buy hair removal cream. The pharmacist advised: "If you're using it on your legs, wear a dress for a couple of days to avoid any irritation. If you're using it on your armpits, wear a singlet for a couple of days to avoid any irritation. By the way, where are you using the cream?"

"On my schnauzer," said the old lady.

The pharmacist replied: "In that case, I'd avoid riding a bike for the next week."

Ninety per cent of dogs in Korea are inbred – in a sandwich or something.

Whereas other people name their dogs Rover or Spot, this guy decided to call his dog Sex. It caused him no end of embarrassment: "When I went to the City Hall to renew the dog's licence, I told the clerk I would like a licence for Sex.

"The clerk said: 'I would like to have one too!'

"Then I said: 'But she is a dog.'

"He said he didn't care what she looked like.

"I said: 'You don't understand, I have had Sex since I was nine years old.'

"He replied: 'You must have been quite a strong boy.'

"Then when I decided to get married, I told the minister that I would like to have Sex at the wedding. He told me to wait until the ceremony was over.

"I said: 'But Sex has played a big part in my life, and my whole world revolves around Sex.'

"He said he didn't want to hear about my personal life and would not marry us in his church.

"When my wife and I went on our honeymoon, I took the dog with me. When we checked into the motel, I told the clerk that I wanted a room for me and my wife and a special room for Sex. He said that every room in the motel is a place for Sex. I said: 'You don't understand. Sex keeps me awake at night.'

"The clerk said: 'Me too!'

"One day I entered Sex in a contest, but before the competition began the dog ran away. I told one of the other dog owners that I was desperate to have Sex in the contest. She said I was perverted. 'You don't understand,' I said. 'I want to have Sex on TV.' She called me an exhibitionist.

"When my wife and I separated, we went to court to fight for custody of the dog. I said: 'Your Honour, I had Sex before I was married but Sex left me after I was married.'

"The judge said: 'Me too!'

"Last night Sex ran off again. I spent hours searching for her. A police officer came over and asked me what I was doing in the alley at four o'clock in the morning. I said: 'I'm looking for Sex.' My case comes up next Thursday.

"Well, now I've been thrown in jail, divorced and had more troubles with that dog than I ever foresaw. Just the other day when I went for my first session with a psychiatrist, she asked me: 'What seems to be the trouble?'

"I replied: 'Sex has been my best friend all my life and I don't know what I'd do without it. I just wouldn't be able to carry on. Life wouldn't be worth living.'

"The doctor said: 'Listen, you need to understand that sex isn't a man's best friend. What you need is companionship. Why don't you get yourself a dog?'"

Drugs

What's the difference between a drug pusher and a hooker? – A hooker can wash her crack and sell it again.

I'm not addicted to cocaine – I just like the way it smells.

A guy was talking to his friend in a bar. "You might not believe this, but I once went twelve years without sex, drugs or alcohol."

"Really?"

"Yeah. But my God, my dad knew how to throw a good thirteenth birthday party!"

My friend died doing what he loved – heroin.

You know you're too high when you're eating cereal naked and your girlfriend says, "Put your clothes on," and then you realize it's not your girlfriend, it's some woman on a bus. (Dov Davidoff)

A junkie was out walking one evening when he found a poor person on the street and helped him up. The poor person said: "I am a genie, and since you helped me I'll give you three wishes."

The junkie said: "I want a big bag of meth."

The genie said: "Okay," and POOF, the bag appeared! They prepared some thick, long white lines and shared it with each other.

The next morning the genie asked: "What's your second wish?"

The junkie said: "I want two big bags of meth."

"Okay," said the genie, and POOF, two bags appeared. And they prepared it and snorted it between the two of them.

The next morning, the genie asked: "And your third wish?"

The junkie said: "I want four big bags of meth."

The genie granted the wish and POOF, the four bags appeared. They then prepared lots of big lines and shared it between the two of them.

Much later, the genie got up and said: "It's time for me to go." The genie took a couple of steps, paused, turned around and said: "Okay, just one more wish."

There were nine flies on a woman's fanny. Four of them were smoking dope. What were the other five doing? – Sniffing crack.

A house was raided by cops in a dawn bust. During the search the male occupant was approached by an officer with a sniffer dog. The officer said to him: "This dog tells me you're on drugs."

The man replied: "You reckon I'm on drugs? You're the one who thinks his dog talks to him!"

You Know You're a Junkie When . . .

- Mosquitoes get a buzz after attacking you.
- You're a Bob Marley fan and you don't even like reggae.
- Your cigarette gets way too heavy.
- You think everybody is staring at you, but there's nobody in the room.
- Everything goes better with coke.
- Your best friend just happens to be your dealer.
- The lab technician testing your urine sample gets high off the fumes.
- You forget your friends' names.
- You forget your own name.

My doctor told me to stay away from drugs. So I bought a fifteen-foot straw.

Cocaine is never a solution – unless, of course, you dissolve it in water.

A giraffe, a crocodile and an elephant stopped a man in the street. The giraffe pulled out a police badge and said: "Sir, we have reason to believe you are carrying substances of a hallucinogenic nature."

Drugs. I can take them or leave them. But they're much more effective when I take them. (Ronnie Shakes)

What do you get when you take ecstasy and birth-control pills? – A trip without the kids.

Drunks

A rough, middle-aged woman was sitting at a bar. She had incredibly hairy armpits so that whenever she raised her arm to order a drink, a mass of hair was visible to all her fellow drinkers. Eventually at closing time a drunken guy at the far end of the bar pointed to the woman and said to the bartender: "I'd like to buy the ballerina a drink."

"She's not a ballerina," said the bartender. "What makes you think she's a ballerina?"

The drunk replied: "Any girl who can lift her leg that high must be a ballerina!"

An old drunk was wandering the streets with tears streaming down his face.

"What's wrong?" asked a sympathetic passer-by.

"I've lost all my worldly belongings," sobbed the drunk.

"How did that happen?"

"The cork fell out."

A drunk was walking through a park when he saw a woman in the lake, flapping her arms about and screaming: "Help me, I can't swim!"

He shouted back: "Neither can I, but I don't go around making a great fuss about it!"

Two drunks were lying in an alley with their heads resting against a wall. The first drunk said: "Have you ever been so drunk that when you tried to kiss a woman on the lips, you went down too low and kissed her on the bellybutton instead?"

The second drunk took a swig out of his whisky bottle and said: "Even drunker than that."

A drunk guy went up to a girl in the street and leered: "If you show me your tits, I'll let you feel my cock."

"I don't want to feel your cock!" she raged.

The drunk said: "Well, it's a nice change to meet a girl who doesn't want something in return."

Two drunks in London were discussing their lives. One of them was happy, but the other was sad.

The happy one asked the other: "What's your problem?"

The sad one explained: "Whenever I come home drunk, my wife locks the door. I have to walk the streets for hours, and get into trouble with the police."

"You know, I had that problem in the past," said the happy drunk, "but I found a solution. When I'm drunk, I get undressed naked in the stairway, then press the bell button. When my wife opens the door, I throw my clothes inside. She is afraid of the scandal, so she lets me in."

"That sounds a good idea," said the sad drunk. "I think I'll try it."

A few weeks later, they met again and the sad guy was even worse than usual.

"What happened?" asked the happy guy. "Did you try my method?"

"I'll tell you what happened!" said the sad drunk. "I undressed, pressed the button. The door opened. I threw all of my clothes inside, the doors closed. And then I heard: 'Next station – Leicester Square.'"

A young guy went clubbing and got seriously drunk. He was swaying all over the place. Eventually he went up to a beautiful girl and said: "Duck my sick."

Realizing he was drunk, she said: "Don't you mean 'suck my dick'?"

He immediately threw up over her and said: "No."

Half a dozen men were sitting around a table in a bar. One took a long swig of beer, then said: "Hey, listen to this. Last night while I was in here with you guys, a burglar broke into my house."

"Did he get anything?" his buddies asked.

"Yeah, a broken jaw, six teeth knocked out and a pair of broken nuts. The wife thought it was me coming home drunk!"

A drunk staggered out of the pub one night, unzipped his flies and started peeing in the town fountain. At that point, a police officer walked past and shouted: "Hey, stop that and put it away!"

The drunk shoved his dick back into his jeans and zipped up. The officer was just about to continue on his way when the drunk started giggling.

"What's so funny?" asked the officer.

"I fooled you," said the drunk. "I may have put it away but I didn't stop."

A drunk bought a camel from a guy on a street corner and proudly rode it into the pub car park, causing a bit of a stir with the local drinkers.

"Nice camel, mate," one of his drinking buddies commented. "Is it male or female?"

"Female," the drunk beamed.

"How do you know?" his friend asked.

"Well," the drunk explained, "on the way here today, at least twenty people yelled out: 'Hey, look at the cunt on the camel!' "

A drunk stumbled into the back of a taxi. He leaned towards the driver and said: "Excuse me, have you got room for a lobster and three bottles of wine on your front seat?"

"I think so," said the driver.

"Good," replied the drunk, and he threw up.

Jerry arrived home from the pub late one Saturday night drunk as usual, and crept into bed beside his wife, who was already asleep. He kissed her clumsily on the cheek and fell asleep. When he awoke, he found a strange man standing at the end of his bed. "Who the hell are you?" asked Jerry. "And what are you doing in my bedroom?"

The mysterious man answered: "I am St Peter and this is not your bedroom."

Jerry was stunned. "You mean I'm dead? I can't be, I have so much to live for, and I haven't said goodbye to my family. You have to send me back straightaway."

St Peter replied: "Yes, you can be reincarnated, but there is a condition. We can only send you back as a fish or a hen."

Jerry was devastated, but knowing there was a farm not far from his house, he asked to be sent back as a hen. A flash of light later, he was covered in feathers and clucking around, pecking the ground.

"This isn't so bad," he thought until he experienced a strange feeling welling up inside him.

The farmyard rooster strolled over and said: "So you're the new hen. How are you enjoying your first day here?"

"It's okay," said Jerry, "but I have this strange feeling inside like I'm about to explode."

"You're ovulating," explained the rooster. "Don't tell me you've never laid an egg before?!"

"Never," replied Jerry.

"Well, just relax," advised the rooster, "and let it happen."

So he did and after a few uncomfortable seconds, an egg popped out from under Jerry's tail. An immense sense of relief swept over him and his emotions got the better of him as he experienced motherhood for the first time. When he then laid his second egg, the feeling of happiness was overwhelming and he knew that being reincarnated as a hen was the best thing that had ever happened to him.

The joy kept coming but just as he was about to lay his third egg, he felt an enormous smack on the back of his head and heard his wife shouting: "Jerry, wake up, you drunken bastard! You've shit the bed!"

Dwarfs

One day a man was having a pee in a public toilet when a dwarf walked in and set up a stepladder. When the man looked down, he noticed the dwarf staring at his balls.

"Excuse me, sir," said the dwarf. "I was just admiring your balls. Do you mind if I hold them?"

The man was taken aback by the bizarre request, but figured that it couldn't do any harm. So he said: "Okay, then, go ahead."

The dwarf then grabbed on to one of the man's balls and said: "Now give me your wallet or I'll jump!"

A woman was driving along the road when the car in front braked suddenly and she ploughed into the back of it.

When the driver got out, the woman saw that he was a dwarf. He said: "I'm not happy."

The woman said: "Well, which one *are* you?"

I met a dwarf with one bollock. He was a little testy.

A man arrived home from work early and found his wife in bed with a dwarf. "This is the third time this week I've caught you cheating on me," he bellowed. "First, it was with a lumberjack, then it was with a salesman, now it's with a dwarf!"

She replied: "At least I'm cutting back."

What's the best thing about fucking a dwarf? – Your dick looks huge in the photos.

A guy walked into a bar with his dwarf wife and sat down on a stool, with his wife standing next to him. The bartender was busy at the other end and didn't see them when they walked in. When he had finished serving the customers there, he walked down the bar and asked the new customer what he would like.

He asked for two glasses of beer, which the barman then brought. After leaving him, the bartender went about serving other patrons, but then he noticed that the man had finished his beers.

The bartender asked if he would like a refill, and the man said: "Yes. I'll have a couple more."

The bartender fetched two more beers and set them in front of the man. Never having seen anyone with the guy, he became curious and asked him: "Why do you order two drinks at a time?"

The man replied: "Oh, one is for me, and the other is for my wife."

Having not seen the dwarf wife, the bartender was mystified and said: "Your wife? Where is she?"

"She's standing here next to me."

The bartender stood on tiptoe, leaned forward over the edge of the bar and exclaimed: "Well, I'll be damned, she ain't any bigger than your fist!"

The man replied: "No, but she's a lot better!"

Did you hear about the dwarf who was charged with sexual harassment after going up to a woman and telling her that her hair smelled nice?

A dwarf went into a whorehouse. None of the girls really wanted to serve him, so they decided to draw lots. Candy was the unlucky one, so she went up to the room with him. A minute later there was a loud scream.

The Madam and all of the girls charged up the stairs and into the room, where they found Candy had fainted. Standing next to the bed was the naked dwarf, with a three-foot dick hanging down and almost touching the floor. The girls were stunned by the sight. Finally, one of them regained sufficient composure to ask him: "Would you mind if we felt it? We've never seen anything like that before."

The dwarf sighed: "Okay, honey. But only touching, no sucking; I used to be six feet tall."

My ex-girlfriend tried to make me jealous by sucking off a dwarf. To be honest I thought it was a low blow.

A dwarf woman went to the doctor and said: "Doctor, every time it rains my vagina gets sore."

The doctor was at a loss to know how to treat the condition, so he suggested that she came back and saw him when it was raining and then he would see what he could do.

A couple of days later, it was pouring with rain and the dwarf woman returned to the doctor.

"Okay," he said, "stand on the chair and I'll take a look at you."

So she stood on the chair and he examined the sore area. Producing his scalpel from his desk drawer, he said: "Right, I just need to make a couple of cuts here and there."

"Just do what it takes, Doctor – anything to relieve the soreness around my vagina."

A couple of minutes later, he told her to climb down from the chair. "There. How does that feel now?"

"It feels great. There's no soreness at all. That's amazing, Doctor. What did you do?"

"I just took a couple of inches off the top of your gumboots."

Did you hear about the dwarf juggler? – He wasn't very good: he dropped all the dwarfs.

Dyslexia

A farmer arrived home to find his wife gone and a John Deere parked outside. He sighed: "I never should have married a dyslexic."

Did you hear about the dyslexic who cried "fowl"? – Nobody listened and the wolf ate him.

Dyslexic IT technicians wait ages for a USB, then three come along at once.

What do you call dyslexic owls? – Slow.

Breaking news: Riot at seafood restaurant. Dyslexic customer appeals for clam.

What do we want? A cure for dyslexia. When do we want it? Own.

Did you hear about the dyslexic who was found dead in bed? – He had choked on his own Vimto.

England and the English

On a train from London to Birmingham, an American was berating the English-man sitting across from him in the compartment. "You English are too stiff. You set yourself apart too much. You think your stiff upper lip make you above the rest of us. Look at me. I have Italian blood, French blood, a little Indian blood and some Swedish blood. What do you say to that?"

The Englishman replied: "Very sporting of your mother."

A whingeing English tourist was sitting in a pub in the Australian outback. "I really don't like all these flies you have here," he moaned.

A fed-up Australian standing next to him at the bar replied sarcastically: "Well, why don't you just pick out the one you like and I'll kill all the rest?!"

Why did audiences scream so loudly at Beatles concerts? – It was the shock of seeing four Liverpudlians working.

Why aren't Scousers as strong as they used to be? – TVs are getting lighter.

As a guy stumbled out of a Liverpool pub, a local prostitute said to him: "Fancy a shag?"

"Sorry, love," he replied. "I've only got a fiver on me."

"No worries," she said. "I've got change."

The following letter was sent to the problem page of a UK national newspaper:

"Dear Agony Aunt, I am a sailor in the merchant navy. My parents live in South London and one of my sisters, who lives in Brixton, is married to a guy from Liverpool. My mother and father have recently been arrested for growing and selling marijuana and are currently dependent on my two sisters who are prostitutes. I have two brothers, one who is currently serving a non-parole life sentence in Wormwood Scrubs prison for the rape and murder of a teenage boy in 2002, while the other is currently being held in Wandsworth jail on charges of incest on his three children. I have recently become engaged to marry a former Thai prostitute who is still a part-time 'working girl' in a brothel although her time there is limited as she has recently been infected with an STD. We intend to marry as soon as possible and are currently looking into the possibility of opening our own brothel, with my fiancée utilizing her knowledge of the industry working as a manager. I am hoping my two sisters would be interested in joining our team. Although I would prefer them not to prostitute themselves, it would at least get them off the streets, and hopefully the heroin. My problem is this: I love my fiancée and look forward to bringing her into the family, and of course I want to be totally honest with her. So should I tell her about my brother-in-law being a Scouser?"

In New York, flipping the bird means an offensive gesture using your middle finger. In London, flipping the bird means it's time for anal.

An Englishman told his wife that he was going fishing with his mates, but instead he sneaked off to see his mistress. He came home later and his wife asked him what happened to the fish.

"Er," he said, "we didn't catch any."

"Liar!" screeched his wife. "You've been cavorting with a French girl, haven't you?" And she hit him with a rolling pin until he confessed.

Nursing his bruises, he said: "How did you know?"

She said: "Because you smell of eau de cologne."

Next day, he again told his wife that he was going fishing with his mates, but instead he sneaked off to see his other mistress. He came home later and again his wife wanted to know why he didn't have any fish. He tried the same lame excuse, but she screamed: "You liar! You've been at it with a Spanish girl, haven't you?" And she hit him with a rolling pin until he admitted the truth. When he asked her how she knew, she said it was because he smelled of sangria.

After two beatings, he decided never to cheat on his wife again. The next day, he really did go fishing with his mates. He caught a load of mackerel and thought to himself: "She'll be pleased with this lot."

But as he was carrying the fish home, he tripped and dropped them all down a manhole. So he had to go home to his wife without the mackerel. He was just about to explain what had happened when his wife hit him over the head with the rolling pin and screamed: "You've been out with an Essex girl, haven't you?"

What do Las Vegas and Sunderland have in common? – They're the only two places in the world where you can pay for sex with chips.

Signs That You've Been in London Too Long

- Somebody speaks to you on the Tube and you freak out because you think she must be a stalker.
- The UK west of Heathrow is theoretical to you.
- American tourists no longer annoy you.
- You have twenty-two different takeaway menus next to your phone.
- The countryside makes you nervous.
- Your idea of personal space is no one physically standing on you.
- Homeless people are invisible.
- You call a six-foot-square patch of scrubland your garden.
- You can't remember the last time you got up to 30 mph in your car.
- You can get into an hour-long argument about the best way to get from Hackney to Richmond, but you can't find Lancashire on a map.
- You're oblivious to sirens.
- You pay more each month to park your car than most people in the UK pay in rent.
- You step over people who collapse on the Tube.
- You have a minimum of five "worst cab-ride ever" stories.

Erections

A young man was travelling home from work on a crowded subway train when an attractive businesswoman in her thirties got on and stood next to him. He was instantly attracted to her and could feel his pants start to bulge. As the train swayed back and forth, he relished the opportunity to press his body against hers.

Eventually she turned to him and said: "Listen, if you don't stop poking me with your thing, I'm going to call the police."

"I don't know what you're talking about," he protested innocently. "It's just my wage packet in my pocket."

"Oh really?!" she said scornfully. "Well, that's some job you must have because that's the fifth raise you've had in the last fifteen minutes!"

I was sitting on the train this morning opposite a really sexy Thai woman. I thought to myself, "Please don't get an erection. Please don't get an erection." But she did.

Three women neighbours in their seventies were hanging out their washing. Over a period of several months, the other two had noticed that on a day when it rained Sheryl never put her washing on the line. It was as if she always knew what the weather was going to be. So finally they decided to ask her what her secret was.

"It's easy," said Sheryl. "When I wake up in the morning, I look over at my husband. If his penis is hanging over his right leg, I know it will be sunny and I can hang out the washing. If his penis is hanging over his left leg, I know it's going to rain, so I don't hang out the washing."

"What if he has an erection?" asked one of the neighbours.

"Honey," smiled Sheryl, "on a day like that, you don't do the washing!"

A doctor was examining a young man who had a testicular condition. As he cupped the young man's balls in his hand, the doctor said: "Don't worry, it's perfectly normal to get an erection in a situation like this."

"But I haven't got an erection," said the young man.

"No," said the doctor, "but I have."

A husband took his wife and young daughter to the zoo. While he went off to fetch the ice creams, his wife and daughter went to see the elephant, which happened to be sporting a massive erection.

"What's that, Mummy?" asked the little girl.

"Oh, it's nothing," said the wife, embarrassed. Then she quickly changed the subject.

A few minutes later, the husband returned. The little girl ran up to him and pointed to the elephant's huge member.

"What's that, Daddy?" she asked.

The husband was flustered. "Uh, well, darling, what, uh, did your mother say?"

"She said it was nothing," replied the little girl.

"Well, darling, your mother's been spoilt."

Following a mix-up at the hospital, a man scheduled for a vasectomy was given a sex-change operation instead. When informed of the blunder, the man was understandably distraught.

"I'll never be able to experience an erection again," he cried.

"Of course you'll be able to experience an erection," said the surgeon, trying to console him. "It's just that it will have to be someone else's."

An old man was kneeling by the side of the bed while his wife was lying naked on the sheets. She turned to him and asked: "What are you praying for?"

"Guidance," he replied.

"Pray for stiffness," she said. "I'll guide it in myself!"

Did you hear about the guy who entered an erection contest, but only got through to the semis?

An undertaker arrived home sporting a black eye. "What happened to you?" asked his wife.

"I've had a terrible day," he said. "I had to go to a hotel and collect a man who had died in his sleep. When I got there, the manager said they couldn't fit him into a body bag because he had this huge erection. Anyway, I found the room and, sure enough, there was this big, naked guy lying on the bed with a huge erection. So I did what I always do in such situations – I grabbed it with both hands and tried to snap it in half."

"Okay," said his wife. "But how did you get the black eye?"

The undertaker replied: "Wrong room."

Whoever said "laughter is the best medicine" never suffered from erectile dysfunction.

While away at a conference, a business executive met a young woman who was pretty, witty and intelligent. When he persuaded her to disrobe in his hotel room, he found out she had a superb body as well. Unfortunately, despite being enormously attracted to her, the executive found himself unable to perform and so the evening ended in disappointment

On his first night home, the executive walked from the shower into the bedroom to find his wife wearing a crumpled old bathrobe, her hair in curlers, her face covered in cream, and chewing gum loudly while she pored over a tacky celebrity magazine. Then, without warning, he felt the onset of a magnificent erection.

Looking down at his pants, he snarled: "Why, you ungrateful, mixed-up son of a bitch. Now I know why they call you a prick!"

One morning a farmer's simple teenage son woke with a huge erection. Not knowing what to do, he consulted his father, who told him: "Go out to the stables and shovel manure for a while and that should take care of it."

So the boy began shovelling. After a while, the pretty young milkmaid walked by and asked the boy what he was doing.

"Well, Miss Daisy," he said in a slow drawl, "I woke up with a huge hard-on and I didn't know what to do with it. Pa told me to come out here and shovel manure for a while."

Raising her dress enough to expose herself, the girl purred: "Why don't you just stick it in here, Jethro?"

The boy said: "The whole shovel full, Miss Daisy?"

Ben walked into a bar and saw his friend Steve slumped morosely in the corner. So he walked over and asked Steve what was wrong.

"Well," replied Steve, "you know that sexy blonde I wanted to ask out, but I got an erection every time I saw her?"

"Yes," Ben said, laughing.

"Well," said Steve, "I finally plucked up the courage to ask her out, and she agreed."

"That's great!" said Ben. "When are you going out?"

"I went to meet her this evening," continued Steve, "but I was worried I'd get an erection again. So I got some duct tape and taped my penis to my leg, so if I did, it wouldn't show."

"Good idea," said Ben.

"So I got to her door," Steve went on, "and I rang her doorbell, and she answered it in the sheerest, tiniest dress you ever saw."

"And what happened then?"

"I kicked her in the face."

When a clown gets an erection, does he call it his funny bone?

A young man went into a pharmacy and asked the little old lady behind the counter if he could speak to the pharmacist.

"That's me," she replied. "My sister and I have been pharmacists for fifty-three years, and there's nothing we haven't heard. So what's your problem?"

The man explained sheepishly: "I have a problem with my erections. Once I get hard, it won't go soft for hours and hours, no matter how many times I have intercourse. It's really embarrassing. Please can you give me something for it?"

The old lady said: "I'll have to go out the back and talk to my sister. Wait there."

Five minutes later she returned. "Young man, I have consulted with my sister and the best we can give you is £2,500 a month and a one-third interest in the pharmacy."

Excrement

My dad once said to me: "Son, if you throw enough shit, eventually some will stick."

I said: "Dad, can't we just *paint* the wall?"

What's the best way of keeping flies out of your kitchen? – Keep a bucket of shit in the hall.

A man was having a shit in the train toilet when there was a knock on the door.

"Can I see your ticket please?" asked the inspector.

"Not right now," said the man. "I'm having a shit."

"I don't believe you," said the inspector. "Can you pass it under the door?"

"Okay," said the man, sliding it under. "The yellow bits are sweetcorn."

After thirty-five years working in a town's sewers, Bill's achievement was recognized by a visit from the mayor, who wanted to see for himself the valuable service that Bill performed. So the mayor climbed down into the sewer and asked Bill why he liked his job so much.

"Well," said Bill, "my job is fascinating. You see that big poop floating past us now? That's from the carpenter. I can tell because you can see sawdust in it. Now, this next poop, that's from the gardener. I can tell because it's got grass clippings in it. And this big poop coming into view now is from my wife."

The mayor was amazed. "Bill, I can understand the logic behind the carpenter and the gardener, but how on earth do you know that that poop out of all the millions of poops in the sewer is from your wife?"

"Easy," said Bill. "It's got my lunch tied to it."

The upside to having your own place: shitting with the bathroom door open. The downside: forgetting your builders have keys. (Daniel Sloss)

Walking down the street, a man saw a sign in a restaurant window advertising that the chef would prepare anything no matter how unusual it might be. The man went inside and told the waiter: "I want a big steaming plate of shit."

"I'm sorry, sir," said the waiter. "We can't do that." So the man reminded him about the sign in the window and threatened to sue the restaurant for misleading advertising.

"Very well," the waiter sighed. "I'll have a word with the chef."

The waiter disappeared into the kitchen and explained the man's gross request. The chef reluctantly agreed that the customer did have a point about the sign in the window and so he and the waiter dropped their trousers and crapped on a plate. The waiter then took the plate of fresh, steaming poop out to the customer.

Five minutes later, the waiter returned to the kitchen covered from head to toe in shit. The chef asked: "What the hell just happened?"

The waiter replied: "He said there was a hair in it!"

I caught my wife taking a dump last night. Our trapeze act in the Cirque du Macabre is really starting to take off.

A man walked into a hospital carrying a Tupperware container. He handed it to a nurse, who was alarmed to see that it contained an enormous hard poop.

"Why have you brought this in?" she asked.

"Because I need to see an optician," he replied.

"Don't you mean a dietician?"

"No, I need an optician, because every time I do one of these, my eyes start to water."

Constipation: same shit, different day.

A flash young city banker called into a rough downtown bar one night, put ten $100 notes on the bar and claimed that he could eat the sloppiest turd ever produced. He said that if he couldn't eat the pile of poop, then whoever produced it would be a grand richer.

The first guy to take up the challenge was a trucker who proceeded to produce a turd that was so runny it started to run down the cracks in the floor. The city banker licked it up in no time.

The next guy to have a go was a builder who unleashed a loose crap that went from his chair over the table and on to the next chair. The city banker panicked for a second but still ate it in five seconds flat.

Now everybody in the bar was amazed and it looked like the city guy was going to keep his money. Then this biker walked into the bar and decided to have a go. He stood on the bar and laid the meanest, smelliest shit ever seen. It went up the length of the bar, down across the barstools and right to the banker's feet. Undeterred, he got down and started chomping but all of a sudden heaved his guts out all over the place. The biker sauntered up to the bar, picked up his winnings and headed for the door.

Just then the city guy, wiping the vomit from his mouth, looked up and said to the biker: "Hey, buddy, it wasn't your turd that made me sick; it was that little bastard picking his nose in the corner."

Some Euphemisms for Taking a Dump

Releasing the chocolate hostage

Firing a torpedo out to sea

Saying goodbye to Mr Brown

Dropping a wad in the porcelain god

Letting a brown snake out of the cave

Dropping one from the poopdeck

William Shatnering

Doing business with John

Giving birth to the brown eel

Giving birth to a lawyer

Stocking the pond with brown trout

Logging into the toilet and making a huge download

Poking out the turtle's head

Freeing the slaves

Taking a trip to the oval office

Backing the big brown motor-home out of the garage

Making a deposit in the porcelain bank

Blowing the butt trumpet

Dropping the Browns off at the Super Bowl

Dropping some friends off at the pool

Feeding the sewer gators

Download a brownload

Elvis has left the building

A new manager at a country hotel found two of his elderly regulars waiting on the doorstep at opening time.

"Good morning," they said, ordering a pint of beer. But as they stood at the bar, their faces fell. "Where's the snuff?" they asked.

"Snuff?" queried the manager.

They said: "Your predecessor always used to leave snuff on the bar in a big blue saucer for his most important customers. And that's us because we're here every lunchtime, 365 days a year."

"Well, it's the first I've heard of it," explained the manager by way of apology, "but rest assured, there will be snuff on the bar for you tomorrow lunchtime. We always look after our customers."

The manager was so busy settling into his new post and getting to know the staff and regulars that he completely forgot about the snuff until he saw the two old men slowly walking up the lane the following lunchtime. He hurriedly put the big blue saucer on the bar and searched in the back room for the snuff. He rummaged through every cupboard in the place, but to no avail. Then he remembered that surplus stock was sometimes kept in an old building in the yard. So he looked there, too, but still had no luck.

On his way back across the yard, he spotted a dried-up piece of dog poop in his path. In frustration, he kicked out at it and it crumbled into dozens of tiny pieces as it splattered against the wall. This gave him an idea. He dashed back into the hotel, grabbed the blue saucer and, using a piece of paper towel, he picked up the remains of the poop and crumbled it into the saucer. He then went back into the hotel and put the saucer on the bar just as his two old regulars entered.

"Morning," said one of the men, eyeing the saucer on the bar. "Glad to see you found some snuff."

"I promised I would," said the manager, quietly keeping his fingers crossed as the old man helped himself to a large portion.

The man sniffed intently and said to the manager: "Can you smell dog shit?"

"No," mumbled the manager unconvincingly.

Then the second man, who had been hanging up his coat, wandered over and took a pinch from the saucer. "There's a smell of dog shit around here!" he exclaimed.

Again the manager mumbled that he couldn't smell anything.

Just then, a third elderly man entered. "George," the first man called, "come over here!"

George strolled over.

"Can you smell dog shit?" asked the first man. "Because I can and Alec can, but the hotel manager can't."

George sniffed the air deeply, twice. "Can't smell a thing," he said. "But wait a minute." He then took two big pinches of the "snuff" – one in each nostril – from the saucer on the bar, and sniffed again. "Ah, I can smell dog shit now, right enough," he said. "This must be good snuff – it really clears your nose."

My girlfriend said I'm too immature for her. I said: "If I'm immature, how come I've got an arsfor?"

She said: "What's an arsfor?"

"Shitting," I replied, and giggled for fifteen minutes.

Two flies were sitting on a turd. One turned to the other and said: "I haven't seen you around for a while. Where have you been?"

"Yeah, I know," said the other fly. "I've been on the sick."

A girl asked her boyfriend: "Have you ever pissed in the shower?"

"A couple of times," he replied. "Accidentally, of course."

"Ugh!" she exclaimed. "What do you mean, accidentally?"

"Well, these things can happen when you're having a crap!"

A fly was buzzing around a barn one day when he noticed a pile of fresh cow manure. As it had been hours since his last meal, he flew down and began to eat. He ate and ate and ate. Finally, he decided he had eaten enough and tried to fly away. He had eaten too much, however, and couldn't get off the ground. Looking around, wondering what to do, he spotted a pitchfork leaning against the wall. So he climbed to the top of the handle and jumped off, thinking that once he got airborne he would be able to take flight. Unfortunately, he was wrong. He dropped like a rock, splattering hard against the floor.

The moral of the story: never fly off the handle when you know you're full of shit.

Fairy Tales

I've started dating Little Red Riding Hood's gran. She's an animal in bed.

In the heart of the woods, the Three Bears woke up one morning. Baby Bear went downstairs, sat in the small chair at the table, looked in his bowl and saw it was empty. "Who's been eating my porridge?" he squealed.

Then Daddy Bear arrived at the table, sat in the big chair, looked in his bowl and saw it was empty. "Who's been eating my porridge?" he roared.

Mummy Bear put her head around the door and yelled: "For God's sake, how many times do we have to go through this? I haven't made the fucking porridge yet!"

The Big Bad Wolf growled: "I'm going to eat you up."

"Oh," wailed Little Red Riding Hood. "Are you going to eat me whole?"

"Nah," said the Big Bad Wolf, "I'll spit that part out."

The Fairy Godmother was out for a stroll in the forest one day, when she saw Cinderella sobbing quietly under a tree.

"What's wrong, dear child?" asked the kindly godmother.

"It's not fair!" sobbed Cinderella. "All the other girls have got boyfriends, but I've got nothing or no one!"

Now the Fairy Godmother didn't think this was fair either, so she reached into her fairy godmothering bag and pulled out a giant dildo for Cinderella, and said: "Here you go Cinderella, this is as good as anything."

"Oh, thank you!" squealed Cinderella, and she skipped off happily with her new toy. The Fairy Godmother wandered off in happy spirits, too, as she had done her good deed for the day.

The next day, the Fairy Godmother was walking back through the forest again when she saw Cinderella sitting under a tree, but this time she was screaming and her dress was covered in blood.

"What's wrong? What's wrong?" cried the Fairy Godmother.

Cinderella glared up at her, and said: "You never told me it turned back into the fucking great pumpkin at midnight!"

How the Seven Dwarfs Got Their Names

Miss Snow White was a randy cow
And desperate for a fuck,
So off she went into the woods
To try to get some luck.
She'd almost given up looking
When she saw some chimney smoke,
Then she stumbled on the cottage
And went in for a poke.
Her clothes came off in seconds
And she'd just removed her pants,
When seven dwarfs came marching in
With a merry song and dance.
Snow White just stood there speechless,
And thought she was in heaven.
Originally after one good shag,
But now she could have seven.
Straightaway she took command,
"My fanny needs a lick!"
And when one dwarf moved forward,
She said, "You'd better drop your pick."
So down he went on to all fours,
And said, "I ain't licking that."
"Not there, that is my arsehole,
You DOPEY little brat!"
The next dwarf started blushing,
"Do we have to do it here?"
Snow White said, "Don't be BASHFUL,
Unless you're some kind of queer."
So reluctantly he whipped it out,
To prove he was no fool.
And Snow White gave a big "Hi-Ho"
As she rode upon his tool.
Now one dwarf wasn't smiling,
'Cos he hadn't had a sniff,
And due to his impatience,
He couldn't raise a stiff.
"Relax, you GRUMPY bastard,"
So he did as he was told,

And as soon as he was hard enough,
He shot his creamy load.
The next dwarf got a blow job,
And she took him deep quite easy,
But the relief went directly to his head,
And when he sneezed, she called him SNEEZY.
With three dwarfs left, she turned and said,
"You're next, I want your knob!"
But no sooner had he entered her,
He was sleeping on the job.
"Wake up you SLEEPY bastard!"
She wanted more from him,
And he woke with such excitement
That he filled her hairy quim.
The next dwarf rammed his dick up her,
And shagged her fanny raw.
A dazed Snow White then whimpered,
"That should be against the law."
He made poor Snow White tremble,
He was so big and thick.
"No wonder you're so HAPPY,
With that fucking great big dick!"
With one dwarf still remaining,
But feeling rather sore,
She said, "You'll have to use your tongue,
My twat can't take no more!"
So he put his tongue to work
Where others had placed their cocks,
And 'cos he made Snow White feel better,
She named the last one DOC.
So there's the truth about the dwarfs,
And how they got their names,
By satisfying Miss Snow White,
And joining in her games.

Little Red Riding Hood was walking through the woods on her way to visit her grandmother, when suddenly the Big Bad Wolf jumped out from behind a tree.

"Ah ha!" grinned the Big Bad Wolf menacingly. "Now I've got you and I'm going to eat you! Eat! Eat! Eat!"

Little Red Riding Hood said angrily: "Damn it, doesn't anybody fuck anymore?"

What did the Seven Dwarfs say when the Prince woke Snow White from her deep sleep? – "Oh well, I guess it's back to jerking off!"

Families

Grandma, who was living with her daughter's family, let her eleven-year-old grandson in from school. "What did you learn today?" she asked.

"Sex education," the boy replied matter-of-factly. "Penises, vaginas, intercourse and stuff."

The old lady was shocked and reported the conversation to her daughter.

"Mother, this is the twenty-first century," said the daughter. "These days it's all part of the curriculum."

An hour later, the grandmother was reading when her daughter announced that dinner was ready. The old lady went upstairs to summon her grandson but found him masturbating furiously on the bed.

"Son," she said, "when you've finished doing your homework, come downstairs to eat."

My mother hates it when I call my stepfather Bernie. Apparently he's still sensitive about the scars.

A man was walking along the street when he was stopped by a woman carrying a clipboard.

"Excuse me, sir," she said, "but have you had an accident in the last three years that wasn't your fault?"

"Yes," he replied. "She's nearly two now."

I have two brothers – well three, actually, but one has learning difficulties so he doesn't count.

Walking past his thirteen-year-old son's bedroom, a father couldn't help hearing part of a conversation. "It gets longer when it's pulled," said the boy, "it fits between boobs and it inserts neatly into a hole. Plus it works best when it's jerked."

At that point the shocked father burst in and said: "Son, I think we need to talk about your penis."

"Okay, Dad," said the boy, "but first let me finish my technology project on car seatbelts."

Two young brothers aged five and six were listening through the door while their older sister was frolicking on the bed with her boyfriend. After a while they heard her say: "Oh, Neil, you're going where no man has gone before!"

The six-year-old turned to his brother and whispered: "He must be fucking her up the arse."

I hate crushing up pills and putting them in my gran's dinner. It feels underhand and sneaky, but if I ever got her pregnant I'd never be able to forgive myself.

What My Mother Taught Me

My mother taught me TO APPRECIATE A JOB WELL DONE –
"If you're going to kill each other, do it outside. I just finished cleaning!"

My mother taught me RELIGION –
"You better pray that will come out of the carpet."

My mother taught me about TIME TRAVEL –
"If you don't straighten up, I'm going to knock you into the middle of next week!"

My mother taught me LOGIC –
"Because I said so, that's why."

My mother taught me more LOGIC –
"If you fall out of that swing and break your leg, don't come running to me!"

My mother taught me IRONY –
"Keep crying and I'll give you something to cry about!"

My mother taught me about the science of OSMOSIS –
"Shut your mouth and eat your supper!"

My mother taught me about CONTORTION –
"Will you look at the dirt on the back of your neck!"

My mother taught me about WEATHER –
"It looks as if a tornado swept through your room!"

My mother taught me about HYPOCRISY —
"If I've told you once, I've told you a million times: don't exaggerate!"

My mother taught me THE CIRCLE OF LIFE —
"I brought you into this world, and I can take you out!"

My mother taught me about BEHAVIOUR MODIFICATION —
"Stop acting like your father!"

My mother taught me about ENVY —
"There are millions of less fortunate children in this world who don't have
    wonderful parents like you do!"

My mother taught me about ANTICIPATION —
"Just wait until we get home!"

My mother taught me about RECEIVING —
"You are going to get it when we get home!"

My mother taught me MEDICAL SCIENCE —
"If you don't stop crossing your eyes, they are going to stay that way!"

My mother taught me how to BECOME AN ADULT —
"If you don't eat your vegetables, you'll never grow up!"

My mother taught me about GENETICS —
"You're just like your father!"

My mother taught me about my ROOTS —
"Do you think you were born in a barn?"

And my mother taught me about JUSTICE —
"One day you'll have kids . . . and I hope they turn out just like you!"

My sister said she'd go down in history, which is probably why the history
teacher always gave her such good marks.

A little boy was helping his grandpa in the garden. The boy watched as an earth-
worm tried to get back into its hole.

"Grandpa," said the boy, "I bet I can put that worm back into that hole."

"I'll bet you £5 you can't. It's too wriggly and limp to put back in that little
hole. You'll never get it in."

The boy went into the house, came back with a can of hairspray and sprayed the
worm until it went straight and stiff. Then he stuffed the worm back into the hole.

His grandpa gave him the £5 and went indoors with a broad grin on his face. Half an hour later, he reappeared and gave his grandson another £5.

"But grandpa," said the boy, "you already gave me £5."

"I know. That's from your grandma."

My friend's dad always referred to teenagers as "strapping young lads". I often wondered why. Then one day I looked in his basement . . .

A man was waiting for his teenage daughter when she arrived home late from a party. He told her: "I hope you've been good."

"Good?!" she said. "If that guy I met was telling the truth, I was fucking fantastic!"

My sister was with two men in one night. She could hardly walk after that. Can you imagine? Two dinners. (Sarah Silverman)

I went round to my mum and dad's house last night and we ended up watching a movie. But I was really embarrassed when the sex bit started. So I made them stop and go upstairs.

Little Johnny woke up in the middle of the night after hearing a noise coming from his parents' bedroom. He peered through the half-open door and saw his mother and father enjoying wild sex. He immediately fled in alarm, but his father saw this and a few minutes later went to check that the boy was okay.

Hearing a commotion coming from Little Johnny's room, the father walked in to find Johnny shagging his grandma.

"What the hell is going on here?" screamed the father.

Little Johnny looked up and said: "It's not so funny when it's *your* mum, is it?"

My wife left me speechless today. I hate looking after our mute son.

Young Jenny's grandfather usually drove her to school, but one day he wasn't feeling well, so his wife drove her instead. That evening, Jenny's parents asked her what it was like being taken to school by Grandma instead of Grandpa.

"It was so different," said Jenny.

"In what way?" asked her parents.

"Well, Gran and I didn't see a single tosser, blind bastard, dickhead or total and utter wanker on our way to school today."

Why did the guy sleep with his sister-in-law? – He had it in for his brother.

Even though her sister died five years ago, my wife still gets upset whenever I say her name – especially during sex.

A young man arrived home in a state of exhaustion.

"Are you okay?" asked his mother. "How did your day out with Grandma go?"

"Never again!" he said. "I've never been so embarrassed in my life. I couldn't believe some of the things she said, things like: 'What are you doing here? We don't want your sort in this country! Go on, get back to Africa, get back to India!' Everybody was staring at us. Eventually I had to tell her: 'Gran, it's a zoo.'"

Famous People

Appearing on a US TV chat show, Sean Connery boasted that despite his advanced years, he could still manage sex three times a night. Paris Hilton was a guest on the same show, and afterwards she made a beeline for Sean in the green room.

"I hope I'm not being too forward," she gushed, "but I've always had a thing about older men. I'd love to test your sexual prowess tonight. Would you like to come back to my place?"

So they went back to her house and had great sex. Afterwards Sean said: "If you think that was good, let me sleep for half an hour, and then we'll have even better sex. But while I'm sleeping, hold my balls in your left hand and my dick in your right hand."

Paris was a bit puzzled by the request, but agreed to go along with it. Half an hour later, he woke up and, as promised, they had even better sex.

Sean said: "Paris, my dear, that was wonderful. But if you let me sleep for an hour, we can have the best sex yet. But again while I'm sleeping, hold my balls in your left hand and my dick in your right hand."

Paris did as he asked, and when he woke up an hour later, they had truly fantastic sex.

As she basked in the afterglow, Paris turned to Sean and said: "Tell me, does holding your balls in my left hand and your dick in my right hand stimulate you while you're sleeping?"

"No," said Sean. "But the last time I had a one-night stand, the bitch stole my wallet."

Paris Hilton had a nightmare. She was being chaste.

Paris Hilton, a brunette and a redhead found a magical mirror that would zap you away in an instant if it believed you were wrong.

The brunette stepped up and said: "I think that I have the best-looking breasts in the world!" POOF! She disappeared.

The redhead went in front of the mirror and said: "I think that I have the sexiest legs in the world!" POOF! She disappeared.

Paris Hilton said: "I think . . ." POOF!

What did Paris Hilton say to King Kong? – "Is it in yet?"

Anne Frank's last diary entry was: "It's my birthday and Dad bought me a drum kit." (David Mitchell)

Why have incidents of global terrorism fallen with the rise of Susan Boyle? – Because jihadists have finally seen what a virgin looks like.

Despite Tiger Woods's fall from grace, he still boasts a number of female admirers, including a young bride who, much to her husband's dismay, couldn't stop talking about her golfing hero all through their honeymoon.

After the newlyweds had made love at the hotel for the first time, the husband picked up the phone to order room service, but the wife quickly grabbed it and said: "Tiger wouldn't do that – he'd make love to me again."

The husband obliged and then picked up the phone to order some food. Again, she snatched it from him, saying: "Tiger wouldn't do that – he'd make love to me again."

Somehow the husband summoned up the energy to make love for a third time. By now he was really hungry but the wife still wouldn't let him order food. Instead, she seized the phone and said: "Tiger wouldn't do that – he'd make love to me again."

So they had sex for a fourth time, and afterwards the exhausted husband reached wearily for the phone.

"Are you calling room service?" she asked accusingly.

"No," he said, "I'm calling Tiger Woods to find out what par is for this hole!"

What do you call the space between Pamela Anderson's breasts? – Silicon Valley.

Donald Trump went to the doctor and said: "Can you give me something to boost my esteem?" The doctor handed him a huge pair of stick-on ears.
"Will these make me more attractive and powerful?" asked Trump.
"No," said the doctor, "but they'll stop people laughing about your hair."

A fan asked Bruce Forsyth: "Have you ever met Frank Sinatra?"
"No, I haven't," replied Bruce.
"Never mind," said the fan, "it won't be long now."

Bill Gates bumped into Hugh Grant at a Hollywood party. Gates said: "I've seen some fabulous pictures of Divine Brown lately. I'd really like to get together with her some time. Any chance you could fix me up?"
Grant said: "You have to remember that ever since that unfortunate incident with me, her prices have rocketed."
"Money's no object," said Gates. "Now what's her number?"
So Gates phoned Divine Brown and set up a date. Afterwards, as they lay on the bed together, he turned to her and mumbled breathlessly: "Now I know why you chose the name Divine."
She replied: "And sadly now I know why you chose the name Microsoft."

What did Mike Tyson and Dr Harold Shipman have in common? – They both had a killer jab.

Why was there confusion when Stephen Hawking suffered a heart attack? – His carer didn't know whether to take him to A & E or PC World.

What did doctors do when Stephen Hawking was taken ill? – They tried turning him off and then back on again.

How does Stephen Hawking recover from a hangover? – He presses F5.

Stephen Hawking was admitted to hospital with a sprained wrist, fractured collar bone and broken leg. Apparently his date stood him up.

I don't understand these new degrees. Sport science? There's a reason they're kept apart. Take Stephen Hawking. Brilliant scientist, always last to be picked for football. Although he is an excellent dribbler. (Frankie Boyle)

Madonna went into an African florist's shop and said: "I'd like some flowers, please."
   "Orchids?"
   "No, just the flowers, thanks."

What's the difference between a Madonna video and a porn video? – The music is better in a porn video.

What's the difference between Jesus and Madonna? – Jesus has only been resurrected once.

Madonna and her driver were cruising along a country road one evening when a cow ran in front of the car. The driver tried to avoid it but couldn't – the cow was killed. Madonna told her driver to go up to the farmhouse and explain to the owners what had happened.
   About an hour later, the driver staggered back to the car with his clothes in disarray. He was holding a bottle of wine in one hand, a cigar in the other and smiling happily.
   "What happened?" asked Madonna.
   "Well," replied the driver, "the farmer gave me the wine, his wife gave me the cigar, and their beautiful daughter made mad passionate love to me."
   "My God, what did you tell them?" asked Madonna.
   "I said, 'I'm Madonna's driver, and I just killed the cow.' "

A hidden episode of *Scooby Doo* has emerged featuring Jimmy Savile as the villain. He'd have got away with it, too, if it wasn't for meddling with those kids.

Steve Irwin should have known better than to go swimming without sunscreen on. It would have protected him from harmful rays.

When astronaut Neil Armstrong walked on the moon, he not only gave his famous speech about "one small step for man, one giant leap for mankind", he also made a number of barely heard remarks, either to his fellow astronauts or to Mission Control. Just before he re-entered the landing craft, for example, he was heard to say: "Good luck, Mr Gorsky."

Many people at NASA thought it was a casual greeting to one of the Soviet cosmonauts, but a check through records showed nobody by the name of Gorsky linked to the Soviet space programme. Over the ensuing years, a number of people quizzed Armstrong as to what "Good luck, Mr Gorsky" meant, but he simply smiled enigmatically and refused to elaborate.

Then in 2006, while Armstrong was taking part in a question-and-answer session following a speech, a reporter brought up the old riddle of Mr Gorsky. This time Armstrong finally revealed the origins of the story as, in the intervening period, Mr Gorsky had died.

Apparently when he was a kid, Armstrong was playing baseball with a friend in the backyard. His friend hit a fly ball that landed by the front of his neighbours' bedroom windows. The neighbours were Mr and Mrs Gorsky. As young Neil bent down to retrieve the ball, he heard Mrs Gorsky shouting at Mr Gorsky: "Oral sex? You want oral sex? You'll get oral sex when the kid next door walks on the moon!"

Two Hollywood doctors were discussing their celebrity patients. One said: "I've been treating Jay-Z."

"What's he been in for?" asked the other.

"I've just cured him of a nervous affliction. He's got ninety-nine problems but the twitch ain't one."

How is Cheryl Cole like the Icelandic volcano? – They've both stopped blowing Ash.

Why did Helen Keller masturbate with one hand? – So she could moan with the other.

Roseanne Barr went to see her doctor. He asked her to take off her clothes, and after examining her thoroughly he told her that she needed to lose weight again. "There's just one more thing," he said. "Before you put your clothes back on, get on your hands and knees and put your head in the corner."

She was puzzled by the request, but did as the doctor asked.

"Okay," he continued, "now stay on your hands and knees and crawl to a point mid-wall. Great. Now crawl and put your head in the other corner. Perfect. Thanks. You can get up now and get dressed."

As she got dressed, Roseanne finally asked him: "What was all that about?"

"Oh," he said sheepishly, "I was thinking about buying a white leather couch, and I wanted to see what it might look like."

Victoria and David Beckham were getting ready to attend a glittering awards ceremony when she turned to him and said: "This tampon: does it make me look fat?"

You know who really gives kids a bad name? Posh and Becks. (Stewart Francis)

What did Kermit the Frog say when Jim Henson died? – Fuck all!

Princess Diana, Cary Grant and King Herod were discussing their respective places in history.

Princess Diana said: "I am the most popular person ever." And she phoned *The Guinness Book of Records* who confirmed that she was indeed the most popular person ever.

Cary Grant said: "I am the most handsome person ever." And he phoned *The Guinness Book of Records* who confirmed that he was indeed the most handsome person ever.

King Herod boasted: "That's all very well, but I am the most hated person ever. Nobody has ever been as reviled and loathed as me." So he phoned *The Guinness Book of Records.*

A few minutes later, Herod stormed back into the room in a vile temper, yelling: "Who the fuck is Piers Morgan?!"

Two guys were chatting in the pub. One said: "I just don't understand why Paul McCartney married Heather Mills. He could have had any woman in the world."

His friend replied: "Some people will do anything to get a disabled parking space."

Paul McCartney's finding it hard to adapt to his new wife. When she asks for a foot rub he still keeps reaching for the sandpaper.

When David Copperfield was engaged to Claudia Schiffer back in the 1990s, a regular feature of his shows involved asking if anyone in the audience would like to show him a trick.

One night in Las Vegas, a guy in the audience called out: "I would, David, but I'm going to need your girlfriend and a table."

"Okay," said Copperfield, and, to loud applause, the guy and Claudia Schiffer climbed on stage. He then bent her over the table, pulled down her panties and started screwing her from behind.

Copperfield was furious and yelled: "That isn't a trick!"

"I know," said the guy, grinning from ear to ear. "But it's fucking magic."

In ancient Greece, the great philosopher and teacher Socrates was revered for his wisdom and common sense. One day, he bumped into an acquaintance who said excitedly: "Socrates, do you know what I just heard about one of your students?"

"Wait a moment," replied Socrates. "Before you tell me anything, I would like you to pass a little test. It is called the Triple Filter Test."

"Triple Filter?"

"Yes," continued Socrates. "Before you tell me about my student, it might be advisable to take a minute and filter what you are going to say. The first filter is truth. Have you made absolutely sure that what you are about to tell me is true?"

"Well, er, not really," said the man. "I just heard about it and . . ."

"I see," said Socrates. "So you are not really sure whether the story is true or not. Now let us try the second filter, the filter of goodness. Is what you are about to tell me concerning my student something good?"

"No, just the opposite . . ."

"So," continued Socrates, "you want to tell me something bad about him, but you are not certain that it is true. You may still pass the test, however, because there is one filter remaining: the filter of usefulness. Is what you want to tell me about my student going to be useful to me?"

"No, not really."

"Well," concluded Socrates, "if what you want to tell me is not true, good or even useful, why tell it to me at all?"

And with that he walked off.

This is the reason why Socrates was a great philosopher and was held in such high esteem. It also explains why he never found out that Plato was shagging his wife.

Fantasies

My wife asked me to make love to her like they do in the movies. So I stuck my dick up her arse and then came on her face while shouting, "Take that, bitch!" From the look on her face I'd hazard a guess that we don't watch the same kind of films.

Did you hear about the student whose girlfriend said she wanted something that was nine inches long, hard and full of sperm? So he gave her a sock from under his bed.

A man confided to his friend: "I told my wife last night that my ultimate fantasy was to have a threesome."

"How did she react?" asked the friend.

"She was actually okay about it until I told her it didn't involve her."

To spice up their flagging sex life, a wife decided to surprise her husband by dressing up as a policewoman. Brandishing a pair of handcuffs, she smiled: "You're charged with being good in bed."

Five minutes later, she tossed the handcuffs aside and stormed off to the bathroom.

"What's the matter?" asked the husband.

She replied frostily: "The charges have been dropped due to lack of evidence."

Belinda Carlisle sings, "We dream the same dream." But I can't believe that every night Belinda Carlisle has a wet dream about Wilma Flintstone. (David Baddiel)

A guy went up to a street hooker and told her: "Listen, love, I don't mind paying a bit extra, but I'm a bit kinky and would like to hit you around a bit after I've come."

She asked: "Well, how long would you beat me for?"

He said: "Until you've given me my money back."

A wife asked her husband if he had any fantasies.

"There is one," he said. "I fantasize that we're complete strangers and have never met . . ."

"What," she said, "and then you pick me up in some bar?"

He said: "No, just the first part."

A guy said to his drinking partner: "I tried erotic suffocation on my wife the other night while we were having sex."

"Yeah?" said his friend. "I've always fantasized about that, too. Did she enjoy it?"

"I don't think so. She's just been lying there for five days now giving me the silent treatment."

Farmers

A poor farmer and his wife were lying in bed when he leaned over and started to rub her breasts. "If only these would give milk," he sighed, "we could get rid of the cows."

Then he started massaging her butt. "If only this would lay eggs," he sighed, "we could get rid of the chickens."

Hearing this, she leaned across and started to rub his penis. "If only this would get hard more often," she sighed, "we could get rid of the farmhand!"

A man was showing his grandson around his farm and when they came to the corral, he explained: "That's a bull and a cow, and he's serving her."

Shortly afterwards, they saw two horses. The man told his grandson: "That's a stud and a mare, and he's serving her, too."

That night at supper, after everyone was settled and grace was said, Grandma turned to Grandpa and said: "Will you please serve the turkey?"

The boy jumped to his feet and yelled: "If he does, I'm eating a burger!"

The old farmer was having a pretty bad year. All of his crops had been lost, but fortunately, the peach orchard had done really well. The only way he was going to make it financially was to cut out the middle man and sell the peaches directly to the consumer, so he loaded his pickup truck with peaches and headed into town.

Just on the outskirts of town he came to a house. So he took a basket of peaches and went up and knocked on the door.

A gorgeous blonde in a sheer robe answered the door. In a sexy voice she said: "Hi, handsome, what can I do for you?"

Quite shaken, the old farmer muttered: "I have these here really nice peaches for sale."

The blonde shamelessly opened the top of her robe to reveal her breasts and said: "Are those peaches full and firm like these?"

"Oh yes," he spluttered, "they're really good peaches."

Then she opened the rest of her robe, showing she had on no panties. She teased: "Would they be succulent and delicious like this?"

The old farmer mumbled, but then broke down crying and said: "Oh yes, they're wonderful peaches."

She asked: "Why on earth are you crying?"

The old farmer whimpered: "Lady, the cutworms ruined my tomato crop and the weevils ate all my cotton and now I think you're going to screw me out of my peaches."

A farmer had put his farm up for sale but when a prospective buyer came to look at the property he was alarmed to see a row of beehives just the other side of a hedge.

"Don't worry about them," said the farmer. "Those bees have never stung anyone. They just make honey."

However, the buyer was not convinced. "I'll tell you what I'll do," he said. "I'm going to stand naked all night tied to that tree just a few feet from those hives. If I get stung, I get the farm for free. If I don't get stung, I'll pay you double the asking price."

The farmer decided it was a fair deal and duly tied the buyer naked to the tree.

The following morning, the farmer saw the buyer bent double and looking very pale. "Oh, no," thought the farmer, "he's been stung. I'm going to have to give away my farm for nothing."

As he moved closer, he asked the buyer where he had been stung and if he needed a doctor.

"I haven't been stung," gasped the naked buyer, "so I guess I'll have to pay you double for your farm. But tell me: doesn't that calf have a mother?"

A city guy purchased a farm and decided to purchase his stock from an old farmer.

"I'd like to buy a rooster," he told the farmer.

"Fair enough," said the farmer, "but round here we call 'em cocks."

"Okay, I understand. Also I would like to buy a chicken."

"No problem," said the farmer, "but round here we call 'em pullets."

The city guy paid for the two birds and put each one in a cage. Worried about how he was going to get the cages home, he said: "Maybe I ought to buy a donkey, too."

"Good idea," said the farmer, "but round here we call 'em asses. I'll let you have old Ned. He's a good animal but, like most donkeys, a bit stubborn. Sometimes you have to scratch him between the ears to get him to move."

"Okay, I'll remember that," said the city guy.

So he set off with the donkey and the cages, but a mile down the road the donkey suddenly stopped and refused to move. Just then an elderly lady passed by on her way home from church.

"Excuse me, ma'am," said the city guy, "would you hold my cock and pullet while I scratch my ass?"

A farmer was looking really fed up in his local bar, so his friend asked him what was wrong. "I can't get the bull to mate with the cows," said the farmer.

His friend said: "I have a tip for you. When you get home, rub your hand over the cows' fannies and then smear it over the bull's nose. You watch: he will fuck them senseless."

So the farmer went home and did as his friend advised and sure enough, the bull started servicing every cow in sight. So the farmer thought, "If it works for the bull, then I'll try it on my wife tonight. Perhaps it will get me in the mood."

So that night, while his wife was asleep, he slid into bed, rubbed his hand over his wife's fanny and then smeared it over his nose. He immediately got a raging erection, so he nudged his wife in the ribs and said: "Take a look at this."

His wife switched on the lamp, turned round, looked at him and said: "You woke me up just to show me you have a nose bleed!"

The greatest truck driver in the world was driving along a country lane late one night when his truck broke down. All he could see was a faint light in the distance, so he headed towards it. He came to an old farmhouse and knocked on the door.

"Hi," he said, by way of introduction, "I'm the greatest truck driver in the world and my truck is broken down. I wonder if I could have a bed for the night?"

"Well," said the farmer, "there are only two rooms, myself and the wife in one, and my eighteen-year-old daughter in the other."

"Look, I'm the greatest truck driver in the world and all I want is a bed for the night. I promise your daughter will be safe with me in her room."

"All right," said the farmer reluctantly, and they all went to bed.

At four in the morning, the farmer heard the headboard in his daughter's room banging against the wall. He got up, poked his head around the door and saw the greatest truck driver in the world frantically screwing his daughter with his bare ass going up and down.

The farmer went downstairs and loaded his shotgun. Then he crept back up, sneaked into the daughter's room and shoved the shotgun up the greatest truck driver in the world's asshole. "All right," yelled the farmer, "if you're the greatest truck driver in the world, try and reverse out of there with a full load."

A farmer's young son ran into the house and said: "Mummy, Mummy, the bull is shagging the cow!"

"Johnny, please!" cried his mother, aghast. "Don't use language like that. You must be polite. You have to say the bull is 'surprising the cow'."

Twenty minutes later, the boy ran in again. "Mummy, Mummy, the bull is surprising all the cows!"

"He can't be surprising *all* the cows, Johnny."

"He can. He's shagging the horse!"

Farting

Once upon a time there was a young man who was addicted to baked beans. He ate them for every meal but they gave him such terrible gas that when he got married he promised his wife that he would give them up. He stuck to his word until, walking home from work on his birthday, he caught a whiff of baked beans coming from a nearby café. So he decided to treat himself and popped inside for a secret plate of his favourite food. Despite consuming a huge portion, he was confident he could get rid of the inevitable gas on the ten-minute walk home.

He arrived home, buttocks clenched, to find his wife waiting for him.

"Darling, I've got a surprise for you tonight," she said. And with that she put a blindfold over his eyes, led him to his chair at the head of the dinner table and made him promise not to look. Just then the phone rang and she went into the hallway to answer it.

Seated on the chair, he was unable to contain his gas any longer. He could hear his wife's voice in the hallway, so he figured it was safe to let a few rip. He leaned first one way and then the other, releasing a volley of farts like machine-gun fire. They were loud and they stank. The smell was so bad that even he felt faint. He tried to wave the stench away with his hands and prayed that it would be gone by the time his wife returned.

Finally, she came back into the room, removed his blindfold and said: "Surprise!"

He opened his eyes to see a dozen dinner guests seated around the table.

What's the difference between a clever spoonerism and a fart? – One's a shaft of wit . . .

One day a Navy ship arrived in town. A small but energetic sailor was the first to leave the ship and rush ashore. As soon as he got to the beach he rapidly searched for a prostitute to satisfy his pent-up desires, and within a minute or so he found one.

It was very sunny and hot. Sand was everywhere. So the sailor, without wasting a second, dragged the prostitute under a pier where they had a fast and furious sex session. The sailor then got up, put his trousers on, paid £20 and hurried off.

Next day, same sailor, same beach, same prostitute, same burning sun and heat, same abundance of sand, same place under the pier, same rapid action . . . but this time during the intimate process, the prostitute could not help letting loose a strong, loud fart.

The sailor continued and, ignoring this little distraction, finished having sex with her. He then got up, put on his trousers, paid £25 and started to leave.

The prostitute stopped him and asked: "Why the £5 tip?"

The sailor said: "That's for blowing the hot sand off my balls!"

A young man was travelling on a train when he let out a loud, involuntary fart. In an attempt to cover his embarrassment, he tried to make conversation with the elderly lady sitting opposite him and asked her: "Do you happen to have today's paper?"

"No," she replied, "but at the next station I'll try and grab you a handful of leaves."

Little Johnny kept annoying his big sister by farting loudly whenever she was around. Eventually she said to him: "Johnny, why do you keep farting? I know you're doing it deliberately."

"Because I can fart better than anyone else," he replied.

"Oh, yeah?" she said. "Well, if I can prove that I can fart better than you, do you promise to stop?"

"Okay," he said. "It's a deal."

So she put two sheets of white paper on the floor with identical amounts of fine, dust-like soil on each. Johnny squatted down, dropped his trousers, farted and blew all but a few particles of soil off his piece of paper. Then his sister squatted down, lifted her skirt, dropped her panties, farted and blew all the soil off her paper.

"I win!" she cried triumphantly.

"No wonder you won," groaned Johnny, peering up her skirt as she stood up. "You've got a double-barrel!"

A young man was so nervous about going to his new girlfriend's parents' for dinner that he couldn't stop himself passing gas throughout the meal. The first time he did it, the girl's father turned pointedly to the family dog, which was sitting next to the table, and said: "Rover, get away from the table." The young man gave an inward sigh of relief and was grateful to the father for getting him out of an embarrassing situation.

Moments later, the young man farted again. Once more, the considerate father turned to the dog and said: "Rover, move away from the table."

Shortly afterwards, the hapless young man let another one go. Again the father spared his blushes by telling the dog: "Rover, move away from the table."

No sooner had the dog been admonished than the young man let out a real snorter – louder and smellier than his previous efforts. The father turned to the dog and said: "Rover, for Christ's sake, hurry up and move before he craps all over you!"

I hate dates. I sit home all day, and I don't fart once. I go on a date and I've got twenty in the bank straightaway. (Carl Barron)

At the end of a hard day digging the garden, a man felt very stiff and sore. His wife said sympathetically: "Have a nice soak in the bath and I'll bring you a drink."

"Good idea," said the husband, relishing the prospect of being waited on. Sure enough, as he was lying in the bath she entered with a glass of Scotch, which she handed to him. "If there's anything else you'd like, just shout," she said as she left the bathroom.

When she got halfway along the landing, the husband relaxed completely and let off an enormous long fart in the bath. A few minutes later, despite it being a very warm summer's evening, the wife came in carrying a fluffy bed warmer.

"What's that for?" he asked.

"Oh," she said, flustered, "I thought I heard you say, 'Whataboutahottawater-bottle?'"

In school, Little Billy put his hand up and said to the teacher: "Please, Miss, I want a piss."

The teacher replied: "Billy, you must say, 'I need a number one.'"

A few minutes later, Billy put his hand up again and said: "Please, Miss, I want a shit."

The teacher said: "Billy, you must say, 'I need a number two.'"

A few minutes later, Little Johnny put his hand up and said to the teacher: "It's not for me, Miss, it's for Billy. He says he wants to fart but doesn't know the code number."

A week or so before her wedding, a girl was watching her mother baking biscuits in the kitchen. "Mum," she asked, "how do you keep Dad so happy after all these years of marriage?"

The mother promptly threw a wad of biscuit dough on the floor, hitched up her dress, squatted down and picked up the dough with her snatch. "Practise this," she said, "and when you can do it, I guarantee your man will be satisfied for the rest of his life."

So the girl practised and practised until her wedding night. While her husband waited for her in bed, she donned a sexy negligee and emerged from the bathroom carrying a can of biscuit dough. She opened the can, threw the dough on the floor, lifted her negligee and squatted over the dough. As rehearsed, she then picked up the dough with her snatch, but in doing so accidentally emitted a thunderous fart.

Her husband immediately leaped out of bed and backed away, ashen-faced.

"What's wrong, honey?" she asked.

"Listen, woman," he said. "If that thing barks like that for a biscuit, I sure as hell ain't throwin' no meat at it!"

An old couple had been married for thirty years and every morning, much to his wife's annoyance, the old man would wake up and give off an enormous fart. And every time he did it, she told him: "One of these days you'll fart your guts out."

After a particularly bad week, she decided to exact revenge. So she got up early and placed some turkey giblets in the bed next to her husband's butt. While making breakfast downstairs, she heard his usual morning fart reverberate through the floorboards followed by a scream. Fifteen minutes later, he staggered downstairs, ashen-faced.

"You were right all along," he stammered. "I finally did fart my guts out, but by the grace of God and these two fingers, I managed to push 'em back in!"

A working-class man had been going out with an upper-class girl for over a month until one weekend he was invited over for dinner at her parents' country mansion. Trying his best not to be intimidated by the sheer size of the house, not to mention the maids and butlers, he engaged in polite pre-dinner small talk and was relieved when everyone laughed at his jokes. They then sat down for a seven-course meal, which he was determined to get through without embarrassing himself by picking up the wrong item of cutlery.

Everything was going smoothly until about halfway through the meal when the combination of the various rich foods made him want to fart. He desperately tried to hold it in, but with four more courses to go, he realized it would be impossible. So he asked to be excused to go to the bathroom and asked for directions as to how to get there. The instructions he received were really complicated, but by then he was busting for a fart, so he decided to set off in search of the bathroom and hope for the best.

After roaming the corridors, hopelessly lost, for a couple of minutes, he could hold it in no longer. Spotting a window in a hallway, he rushed over, opened the window, stuck his butt through it and let out a long, loud, stinky fart that measured 7.2 on the Richter scale. Hugely relieved, he then managed to find his way back to the dinner table where everyone was eating in silence.

Turning to his girlfriend, he whispered: "It's all going rather well, isn't it?"

"It was," she replied frostily, "until you farted through the serving hatch!"

Fish and Fishing

At a senior citizens' luncheon, an elderly gentleman and an elderly lady struck up a conversation and discovered that they both loved to fish. Since both of them were widowed, they decided to go fishing together the next day. The gentleman picked up the lady in his car and they drove to where his boat was moored on the river.

A couple of miles after setting off on their adventure, they came to a fork in the river and the gentleman asked the lady: "Do you want to go up or down?"

Suddenly the lady stripped off her blouse, skirt and panties and made passionate love to the gentleman right there in the boat. When they finished, he couldn't believe what had just happened, but he had experienced the best sex he'd had in years.

They fished for a while and continued on up the river until soon they came to another fork. Again he asked the lady: "Up or down?"

Once more she ripped off her clothes and made wild passionate love to him on the spot.

The elderly gentleman was so impressed by her behaviour that he asked her to go fishing again the next day. She accepted the invitation and they set off along the river in his boat until they came to the first fork. In eager anticipation, he asked: "Up or down?"

"Down," she replied calmly.

Puzzled and disappointed, the gentleman steered the boat down the river until they came to a second fork and he asked the lady: "Up or down?"

"Up," she replied.

By now the gentleman was really confused, so he said: "I don't understand. Yesterday, every time I asked you if you wanted to go up or down, you made wild passionate love to me. But today, nothing! What's going on?"

The lady replied: "Well, yesterday I wasn't wearing my hearing aid and I thought the choices were fuck or drown."

I saw a man at the beach yelling: "Help, shark! Help!" I just laughed – I knew that shark wasn't going to help him.

A man went fishing and hadn't caught a thing in four hours, when all of a sudden the local vicar turned up, cast his rod into the stream and within half an hour his keep net was full. The man was hacked off by this so he decided to ask the vicar for the secret of his success.

The vicar kindly told him: "Well, my son, go home tonight, rub your hand between your wife's legs, and then rub it in with all your worms and the smell will attract the fish."

The man thought it sounded like a good idea so he went home and, seeing his wife standing by the stove cooking dinner, he crept up on her, stuck his hand up her skirt and started rubbing away.

The wife giggled: "Oh hello, Vicar. Off fishing again?"

Why Fishing Is Better Than Sex

- You don't have to hide your fishing magazines.
- When you go fishing and catch something, that's good; when you have sex and catch something, that's bad.
- The Ten Commandments don't say anything about fishing.
- If your partner takes pictures or videotapes of you fishing, you don't have to worry about them showing up on the internet if you become famous.
- It's perfectly respectable to fish with a total stranger.
- Fish don't mind if you fall asleep in the middle of fishing.

- If your regular fishing partner isn't available, he or she won't object if you fish with someone else.
- Nobody will ever tell you that you will go blind if you fish by yourself.
- You can catch and release a fish without having to lie and promise to remain friends after you let it go.
- When dealing with a fishing pro, you never have to wonder if they are really an undercover cop.
- You don't have to go to a sleazy shop in a seedy neighbourhood to buy fishing stuff.
- You can have a fishing calendar on your wall at the office, tell fishing jokes and invite co-workers to fish with you without getting sued for harassment.
- If you want to watch fishing on television, you don't have to subscribe to the Playboy channel.
- You can catch fish in a £1 net; if you want to catch a woman, you're talking dinner and a movie, minimum.
- Nobody expects you to fish with the same partner for the rest of your life.
- Your fishing partner will never say: "Not again? We just fished last week! Is fishing all you ever think about?"

A man took his goldfish to the vet and announced: "I think it's got epilepsy."

The vet said: "It looks calm enough to me."

"Ah," said the man, "I haven't taken it out of the bowl yet."

Flight Attendants

An airline's passengers were being served by a flamboyantly gay flight attendant who entertained them by cracking jokes while handing out the food and drinks.

As the plane prepared to descend, he flounced down the aisle and announced to passengers: "Captain Mikey has asked me to tell you that he'll be landing the big scary plane shortly, lovely people, so if you could just put up your trays that would be super."

On his trip back up the aisle he noticed that a well-dressed, sophisticated woman hadn't moved. He said to her cheerfully: "Perhaps you didn't hear me over those big brute engines. I asked you to raise your trazy-poo so the main man can pitty-pat us on the ground."

She slowly turned to face him and replied haughtily: "In my country I am called a princess. I take orders from no one."

To which the flight attendant answered: "Well, in my country I'm called a queen, so put your tray up, bitch."

What do you call a pregnant flight attendant? – Pilot error.

A man boarded an airplane in New Orleans, with a box of crabs. A female flight attendant took the box and promised to put it in the crew's refrigerator, which she did. The man told her in no uncertain terms that he was holding her personally responsible for the crabs staying frozen, and proceeded to warn her of the consequences should she happen to let the crabs thaw out.

Mindful of this, shortly before landing in New York she announced over the intercom to the entire cabin: "Would the gentleman who gave me the crabs in New Orleans please raise your hand?"

Not one hand went up, so she took them home and ate them herself.

A new female flight attendant was summoned to her boss to be reprimanded. "I heard about the incident on your maiden flight," said the boss sternly. "From now on, whenever a passenger feels faint, I'll thank you to push his head down between his *own* legs!"

During a transatlantic flight, the pilot spoke over the intercom and announced: "Hello, everyone, this is the pilot speaking. We are cruising at an altitude of 35,000 feet but I regret to inform you that we are likely to pass through some turbulence shortly, so if you could return to your seats and fasten your seatbelts. Thank you."

The turbulence turned out to be so bad that the pilot had to wrestle with the controls. Although he was exhausted, eventually they got through it and he decided to address the cabin again.

"Well, ladies and gentlemen, sorry about the bumpiness there. Hope it didn't spoil your journey too much."

There was a pause and the next thing the cabin heard was: "Jeez, I could really do with some coffee and a blow job up here!"

Realizing he had accidentally left the intercom switched on, a stewardess ran to the front of the plane to tell him.

At which point an elderly lady passenger shouted: "Don't forget the coffee, dear!"

Food

A man arrived in Boston, Massachusetts, on a business trip. He stepped out of the airport and flagged a cab. Feeling hungry, he said to the cabbie: "Can you tell me where I can get scrod around here?"

The cabbie laughed: "Buddy, I must have heard that request a thousand times, but that's the first time anyone has ever used the pluperfect subjunctive!"

Restaurants always boast about "home-made cooking". I don't want home-made cooking. That's why I'm here, 'cos I don't like the shit at home! (Lee Evans)

I ate a couple of Scotch eggs yesterday. The nurse in the Glasgow fertility clinic looked horrified.

Two eggs got married. On their wedding night, Mr Egg was lying in bed, when out of the bathroom came Mrs Egg wearing a see-through bra and panties. She said seductively: "I've just slipped into something a bit more comfortable."

On seeing this, Mr Egg said: "Right, I'd better go and slip into something more comfy too." But when he came back out of the bathroom he was wearing a crash helmet.

Mrs Egg said: "Why the hell are you wearing a crash helmet?"

Mr Egg replied: "Because the last time I was this hard, some bastard hit me over the head with a fucking spoon!"

Eggs! They're not a food, they belong in no group! They're just farts clothed in substance. (Dylan Moran)

My mate hates it when I put his chocolate bars in different wrappers. It gets his Snickers in a Twix.

A man went to a French restaurant, where the menu was entirely in French. As the man spoke no French, he struggled to understand the menu and instead simply told the waiter to bring out the restaurant's speciality. He had a truly fantastic main course, after which the waiter asked if he wanted dessert. Again he asked the waiter to bring out the restaurant's speciality. The waiter said that was the peach poosay and he would order it for him. A few minutes later, a waitress came out carrying a covered silver platter. She took the cover off and there was a peach that had been quartered and pitted. The waitress proceeded to raise her skirt and take a piece of the peach and push it in and out of her pussy. Then she picked up the second piece and did the same.

The man called the waiter over and asked: "Am I actually expected to eat the peach after that?"

The waiter responded: "But no, monsieur, you eat the poosay."

Someone told me that carrots are good for your eyes. What they failed to tell me is that you have to take them orally. (Sarah Silverman)

A man walked into his local butcher's and asked for a pound of what's what. The butcher, puzzled by this request, politely informed the man that they didn't sell what's what. So the man left, only to come back the next day and ask for the same. The butcher thought the man was having a joke, so he smiled and told him jovially but firmly that they did not sell what's what. The man left empty-handed.

The next day the man returned, more determined than ever, and asked for a pound of what's what. This time the butcher reacted angrily. "Stop wasting my time," he yelled. "I've told you before; we don't sell what's what, nor have we ever heard of it!"

"What's that then?" asked the man, pointing vaguely at some meat in the window.

"What's what?" said the butcher.

"Well, I'll have a fuckin' pound of that then!"

What's worse than a fly in your soup? – A fly in my soup.

A pretty young woman loved to grow vegetables in her garden, but she could never get her tomatoes to ripen. Admiring her elderly neighbour's garden, which had beautiful, bright-red tomatoes, she asked him his secret.

"It's simple," said the old man. "Twice a day – once in the morning and once in the evening – I expose myself in front of the tomatoes and they turn red with embarrassment. You should try it."

So the young woman took his advice and exposed herself to her plants twice daily. Three weeks later, her neighbour asked her how she was doing.

"Any luck with your tomatoes?" he inquired.

"No," she replied excitedly, "but you should see the size of my cucumbers!"

I only eat non-free-range meat, because those animals are happy to die. Why would you kill a happy free-range chicken? Sick bastards! (Daniel Sloss)

A cucumber was talking to a pickle. The pickle said: "My life sucks. Whenever I get big, fat and juicy, they sprinkle seasoning all over me and stick me in a jar."

"That's nothing!" said the cucumber. "Whenever I get big, fat and juicy, they slice me up and put me in a salad."

A penis was passing and overheard the conversation. "You think that's bad!" said the penis. "Whenever I get big, fat and juicy, they put a plastic bag over my head, stick me in a dark, smelly room and make me do push-ups till I throw up!"

A man walked past an ice-cream stand that advertised: "Every flavour of ice cream in the world." The man was highly sceptical about the boast, so he decided to test it.

"So you say you have every flavour of ice cream in the world?" he said. "Okay, I would like three scoops of fanny-flavoured ice cream, please."

"No problem, sir," said the ice-cream seller who proceeded to give the man three scoops of ice cream in a cone.

The man took a good lick, but immediately grimaced: "Ugh! This doesn't taste like fanny, it tastes like shit!"

The seller said: "Take shorter licks."

I bought some Jamie Oliver sausages from the supermarket. On the side of the packaging it said "Prick with a fork".

Hitler was a vegetarian. Just goes to show: vegetarianism, not always a good thing. Can, in some extreme cases, lead to genocide. (Bill Bailey)

A man sat down in a restaurant and ordered a hot chilli, but the waitress said: "I'm sorry. The customer next to you had the last bowl."

The man looked across the table and saw that the other customer had left most of his chilli. So he asked him: "Would you mind if I have that?"

"Sure," said the other guy.

So he started eating his way through the chilli but then halfway down, he discovered a dead mouse.

"Oh my God!" he exclaimed. "I've just found a dead mouse in the chilli!"

The other guy said: "That's as far as I got, too."

Foreplay

An inexperienced young guy took a girl back to his apartment. As they started fondling each other on the sofa, she sighed: "You haven't removed many bras, have you?"

"What gave it away?" he asked.

She said: "The scissors, mainly."

A couple on a first date were about to go into his apartment, but before he could open his door, the woman said: "Wait a minute, I can tell how a man makes love by how he unlocks his door."

"Give me some examples," said the man.

"Well, the first way is, if a guy shoves his key into the lock, and opens the door hard, then that means he is a rough lover and that isn't for me. The second way is if a man fumbles around and can't seem to find the hole, then that means he is inexperienced and that isn't for me either. So how do you unlock your door?"

"Well," he smiled, "first, before I do anything, I lick the lock."

A guy picked up a girl in a bar, took her home and they started getting it on. As things became more passionate, he began sucking on one of her breasts and milk came out.

Shocked, he asked: "Hey, are you pregnant?"

"No," she said. "That wasn't a nipple; that was a boil!"

A young man and his girlfriend were lying naked on the bed. After five minutes of kissing and cuddling, he said to her: "I'd like you to go downtown, if you know what I mean."

With a weary sigh, she got on her knees in front of him and started peering at his genitals, flicking her head this way and that, studying his equipment in detail without actually touching him.

After a couple of minutes, he began to lose patience. "What exactly are you doing?" he demanded.

She said: "I'm doing what I always do when I'm downtown with no money – just looking."

I had to defrost the fridge before bed last night. Or foreplay as she calls it.

The French

Why does the French flag have Velcro? – So the blue and red sections can be easily removed in times of war.

A teenage boy was playing in his room on his computer when his grandfather came in and sat on the bed.

"I know you love your computer," said the grandfather, "but you really should get out of the house more and experience life. After all, you're eighteen now. When I was eighteen, I went to Paris, went to the Moulin Rouge, drank all night, had my way with the dancers, pissed on the barman and left without paying! Now that is how to have a good time!"

A week later, the grandfather came to visit again. He found the boy still in his room, but this time with a broken arm in plaster, two black eyes and no front teeth.

"What happened to you?" he asked.

The boy said: "I did what you did. I went to Paris, went to the Moulin Rouge, drank all night, had my way with the dancers, pissed on the barman and he beat the hell out of me!"

"Oh dear!" said the grandfather. "Who did you go with?"

"Just some friends. Why? Who did you go with?"

"The Third Panzer Division."

How were the French relay team knocked out of the Olympics? – They saw a German with a baton and surrendered.

Inspired by the Swiss, France has brought out a French Army knife. There are no scissors or tweezers, just six corkscrews and a white flag.

What do you call a Frenchman killed in battle? – The slowest runner.

Cameron Diaz, an Englishman and a Frenchman were all sitting in the same train compartment. All was quiet until the train entered a tunnel. Through the darkness could be heard the sound of a loud slap and a cry of pain. When the train emerged from the tunnel, Cameron Diaz and the Englishman were sitting normally, but the Frenchman was rubbing his cheek and nursing a swollen eye.

Cameron Diaz immediately thought: "The Frenchman must have tried to kiss me when we entered the tunnel, but kissed the Englishman by mistake and got a slap for his trouble."

The Frenchman thought: "The Englishman must have tried to kiss Cameron and she slapped me by mistake."

And the Englishman thought: "This is great. Every time we go into a tunnel, I can smack that French prat!"

What is the difference between a pair of jeans and a Frenchman? – There is only one fly on a pair of jeans.

Why are French Canadians banned from swimming in the St Lawrence River? – Because they leave a ring.

François Hollande, the French President, was sitting in his office when his telephone rang.

"Hello, Mr Hollande," a heavily accented voice said. "This is Paddy down at the Harp Pub in County Clare, Ireland. I am ringing to inform you that we are officially declaring war on you!"

"Well, Paddy," Hollande replied, "this is serious news! How big is your army?"

"Right now," said Paddy, after a moment's calculation, "there is meself, me cousin Declan, me next-door neighbour Seamus, and the entire darts team from the pub. That makes eight!"

Hollande paused and then roared with laughter. "I must tell you, Paddy, that I have 100,000 men in my army waiting to move on my command."

"Bejaysus!" said Paddy. "I'll have to ring you back."

Sure enough, the next day, Paddy called again. "Mr Hollande, the war is still on. We have managed to get us some infantry equipment."

"And what equipment would that be, Paddy?" asked Hollande.

"Well, we have two combines, a bulldozer and Murphy's farm tractor."

Amused, Hollande sighed: "I must tell you, Paddy, that I have 6,000 tanks and 5,000 armoured personnel carriers. Also, I have increased my army to 150,000 since we last spoke."

"Saints preserve us!" said Paddy. "I'll have to get back to you."

Sure enough, Paddy called again the next day. "Mr Hollande, the war is still on! We have managed to get ourselves airborne. We have modified Padraig O'Riordan's ultra-light with a couple of shotguns in the cockpit, and four boys from the Shamrock Bar have joined us as well."

Hollande was silent for a minute and then cleared his throat. "I must tell you, Paddy, that I have 100 bombers and 200 fighter planes. My military bases are surrounded by laser-guided, surface-to-air missile sites. And since we last spoke, I have increased my army to 200,000!"

"Jesus, Mary, and Joseph!" exclaimed Paddy. "I will have to ring you back."

Sure enough, Paddy called again the next day. "Top o' the mornin' to you, Mr Hollande. I am sorry to inform you that we have had to call off the war."

"Really? I am sorry to hear that, Paddy," said President Hollande. "I was looking forward to it. Why the sudden change of heart?"

"Well," said Paddy, "we had a long chat last night over a few pints of Guinness, and decided there is no way in the world we are going to be able to feed 200,000 prisoners!"

Frigidity

How can you tell if your girlfriend's frigid? — When you open her legs, the lights go on.

A guy was in the middle of having sex with his girlfriend when he suddenly stopped and asked her: "Sorry, did I hurt you?"

"No," she said. "What makes you think you might have hurt me?"

"Because you moved."

I don't think I'm good in bed. My husband never said anything, but after we made love he'd take a piece of chalk and outline my body. (Joan Rivers)

During a bitter argument, a husband told his wife: "You're so frigid, I bet you put cold cream between your legs."

She replied: "Well, you must put vanishing cream between yours!"

Two men were sitting at a bar and staring into their drinks. One said: "Have you ever seen an ice cube with a hole in it before?"

"Yeah," his friend replied. "I've been married to one for seventeen years!"

A guy and his wife visited a museum to view an exhibit of King Tutankhamen's treasure. After some time in the museum, the guy was starting to get horny, and since there was no one else around at the time, he suggested to his wife that he and she hop in to King Tut's sarcophagus for some sex.

"Come on, honey," he pleaded. "Why won't you ever do anything daring?"

"Don't be silly," said his wife. "I'd be afraid that we would set off the motion detector."

"You won't have to worry about the motion detector," said the husband. "Just have sex with me like you normally do!"

Funerals

I have a hard time at funerals – I'm a necrophiliac.

A young man was standing by the graveside at his boss's funeral. His boss was a deeply unpleasant man – a lying, cheating bully with misogynist, homophobic and racist views – but everyone in the firm had been ordered to attend his funeral. In view of the deceased's unpopularity, the young man was surprised when the other mourners all burst into a spontaneous round of applause.

Turning to the woman next to him, he asked: "Why is everyone clapping? I thought they all hated the old bastard."

The woman replied: "Oh, that's because the drunk driver who killed him has just arrived."

Did you hear about the two men who were cremated at the same time? – It was a dead heat.

Phoning the florist to order some flowers for her mother-in-law's funeral, a woman was caught off guard when asked what message she wanted on the card.

"Message?" she sputtered. "Well, I guess, 'You will be missed.' "

On the day of the funeral, she was pleased that her floral tribute had arrived but mortified that the card read: "I guess you will be missed."

A man asked his elderly mother: "When you die, do you want to be buried or cremated?"

"Oh, I didn't know," she said. "Surprise me!"

At his wife's funeral, a man was standing next to her casket in the church when her attractive young cousin approached him.

"There's no need for you to be lonely, Tom, now Eileen's gone," she said, fingering his tie.

"I don't think I'm quite ready yet," he replied. "I need a bit more time."

"I'm sorry," she muttered. "Too soon?"

"Yeah," he said. "Your sister's just sucked me off in the vestry, so give me ten minutes."

Did you hear about the guy who died of asbestosis? – It took six months to cremate him.

Gambling

Don had a serious gambling problem, and whenever he came home his wife would ask him how much he had lost at the casino. Then one night, he didn't come home at all. Instead, it was nine o'clock the following morning when he finally walked through the door. His wife was furious.

He smiled at her and said: "Honey, I have a confession to make. I was at the bar last night, got blind drunk, and went home with Shelley the barmaid. I stayed overnight and we had the most fantastic sex ever."

"Don't tell me your lies," snapped his wife. "Come on, tell me, how much did you lose last night?"

Clive was very depressed about the fact that he had three testicles until his friend Adrian suggested they could make a lot of money out of his extra ball. "This could be a gold mine for us," enthused Adrian. "We go from bar to bar, and bet everyone that between you and the bartender you've got five balls. It can't miss!"

Clive agreed that it was a sure-fire earner, and so off they went. At the first bar, Adrian announced: "I'll bet anyone here that the bartender and my friend Clive have five balls between them."

As dozens of people rushed up to place their bets, Adrian turned to the bartender and said: "You don't mind if we use you on this, do you?"

"Not at all," said the bartender. "In fact, I'm very impressed. I've never met a man with four balls before – I've only got one."

Shergar knew his gambling debt was out of control when he woke to find Sarah Jessica Parker's head next to him.

A man came home in the early hours of the morning after playing poker with his friends. His wife had stayed up to give him a piece of her mind.

"Before you start," he said, "don't even bother getting pissed off. Pack your bags. I lost you in the poker game. You're moving in with Kev."

"How could you do such a terrible thing?" she whined.

"It wasn't easy," he said. "You don't normally fold with four aces."

While his father played poker with his friends and relatives one Saturday after-noon, Little Johnny was making a real nuisance of himself, running around the table and yelling out what cards each player held. The father tried everything to get Johnny to occupy himself – video games, TV, ice cream – but nothing seemed to work. The boy's antics became so disruptive that some of the players threat-ened to quit playing and go home.

At that point, Little Johnny's uncle stood up and led him out of the room. Five minutes later, he returned to the poker table without Johnny and the game resumed.

For the rest of the afternoon, Little Johnny was nowhere to be seen, leaving the players to finish their session in peace.

After the game ended, the father asked the uncle what he had said to keep Johnny quiet for so long.

"Not much," replied the uncle. "I just showed him how to masturbate."

Did you hear about the guy who rang Gamblers Anonymous for help with his fruit-machine addiction? – They asked him if he wanted to hold.

A husband arrived home from the pub four hours late one night. "Where the hell have you been?" screamed his wife.

He said: "I've been playing poker with some guys."

"Playing poker with some guys?" she repeated. "Well, you can pack your bags and go!"

"So can you," he said. "This isn't our house anymore."

An old man and his pretty young wife entered a used-car lot. The owner of the lot spotted them and went over to serve them. The old man noticed that the owner couldn't take his eyes off his young wife.

So the old man proposed a wager: "I see you like the look of Maisie here," he said. "Well, if you can do everything to my wife that I can do and still end up the same way as I do, I'll pay you double for the car. If you can't, you'll give it to me for free. Is that a deal?"

Confident that he could outperform an old man, the car-lot owner agreed to the wager.

First, the old man gave his wife a passionate kiss and the owner did the same. Then the old man unbuttoned her blouse and kissed her breasts. The owner did the same. Finally, the old man unzipped his fly, pulled out his dick and bent it in half.

The lot owner said: "What colour car do you want?"

Gays

A guy was jogging through a San Francisco park when he veered off the path to take a pee. However, he accidentally stepped into quicksand and rapidly sank right up to his waist. Unable to get out, he called over to another guy who was jogging: "Hey, can you give me a hand?"

The other jogger said: "I'll help you – for a blow job."

"Fuck no! Goddamned fags!"

So the second jogger shrugged and went on his way.

A few moments later, the sinking jogger was still going down, and another male jogger appeared on the scene. Again, the man in the quicksand asked for some help.

"I'll help you," came the reply. "For a blow job."

"Fuck you – no! Goddamned fags!"

So the jogger shrugged and went on his way.

By this time, the poor man was almost up to his neck in the quicksand and facing imminent death. Just then, another male jogger came by. In desperation, the man in the quicksand shouted: "Hey, if you help me out of here, I'll, I'll . . . I'll give you a blow-job."

The new jogger calmly walked over, put his foot on the guy's head, pushed him down under the quicksand and muttered: "Goddamned fags!"

A guy walked into a bar and quickly realized it was a gay bar but he didn't care because he really wanted a drink. After a minute or so, the gay waiter came over and said to him: "What's the name of your penis?"

The customer said: "Listen, I'm just not into all that. All I want is a drink."

The gay waiter said: "I'm sorry but I can't serve you until you tell me the name of your penis."

So the customer sighed: "All right, what's the name of your penis?"

The waiter said: "NIKE . . . you know, JUST DO IT."

The customer thought for a moment and said: "The name of my penis is SECRET."

The waiter said: "Secret?"

"Yeah," said the customer, "STRONG ENOUGH FOR A MAN BUT MADE FOR A WOMAN!"

Why did they invent glow-in-the-dark condoms? – So gays could have lightsabre fights.

Gay partners Clive and Charles were about to take a shower. The phone rang and Clive said to Charles: "I'll be right back, love, so don't start without me."

After a couple of minutes, Clive returned and saw semen splattered all over the wall of the shower stall. "I thought I told you not to start without me!" he yelled.

"I didn't start without you," said Charles. "I just farted!"

Two gay men were walking through the park one night when it started to rain.

One said: "Shall I put the umbrella up?"

"Yes," answered the other, "but for fuck's sake don't open it!"

Open Mike Night has a whole new meaning in gay bars.

A man walked into a bar and ordered a stiff drink. "You look a bit down," said the bartender. "What's the problem?"

"I've just learned that my eldest son is gay," groaned the man.

A few weeks later, the man returned to the same bar and ordered another stiff drink.

"More problems?" asked the bartender.

"I've just found out that my second son is gay," wailed the man.

Two months later, the man was back in the bar, still looking thoroughly dejected. He told the bartender: "I've just found out that my youngest son is gay."

"Jesus!" exclaimed the bartender. "Doesn't anybody in your house like women?"

"Yeah," sighed the man. "My wife does."

There's a new gay musical based on *The Wizard of Oz*. It's called *Swallow the Yellow Thick Load*.

What's the difference between a microwave oven and a gay man? – A microwave won't turn your meat brown.

A gay guy was told by his doctor that he had AIDS. "Is there anything I can do?" he asked.

"Yes," said the doctor. "I want you to go home and eat five pounds of spicy sausage, a hot curry, twenty jalapeño peppers, a bowl of chilli, and wash it all down with a gallon of prune juice."

"And will that cure me, doc?"

"No, but it will make you realize what your arse is for."

What do you call a fart in the men's toilet of a gay bar? – A love call.

What's the difference between a gay rodeo and a straight rodeo? – At a straight rodeo they yell, "Ride that sucker!"

Just after his wife had given birth, a man asked the male doctor on duty: "How soon do you think we'll be able to have sex?"

The doctor winked and said: "I'm off duty in ten minutes. Meet me in the car park."

A gay man said to his partner: "My asshole's really hurting. Any idea what it is?"

"Ring Sting."

"Why, do you think he'll know?"

Six mates were seated at the bar, trying to impress one another with the size of their dicks. The bragging went on for almost an hour until the bartender got tired of hearing about it. So he said: "Let's put an end to all this crap and find out who's lying and who isn't. Each of you whip out your dong and lay it on the bar." All six of them did.

Just at that moment a gay man walked into the bar, and the bartender asked him if he wanted a drink. The gay guy looked down at the bar, licked his lips and said: "No thanks, I'll just have some of the buffet."

Did you hear about the bisexual pride parade? – It went both ways.

We now have gay bishops in church. Will this filter through to the game of chess? Now bishops can make all the same moves but can only be taken from behind.

Two gay men were caught in an alleyway by a police officer. One man ran off but the cop managed to grab the other and told him menacingly: "If I catch your mate, I'm going to ram this truncheon right up his ass!"

Just then a voice called out: "I'm in the bin!"

Why do gay men like to have lesbian friends? – Someone has to mow the lawn.

Michael and Gary got married in California. They couldn't afford a honeymoon so they went back to Michael's mom and dad's house for their first married night together.

In the morning, Johnny, Michael's little brother, got up and had his breakfast. As he was going out of the door to go to school, he asks his mom if Michael and Gary were up yet.

"No," she replied.

Johnny asked: "Do you know what I think?"

"I don't want to hear what you think," said his mother. "Just go to school."

When Johnny came home for lunch he asked his mom: "Are Michael and Gary up yet?"

"No," she replied.

Johnny said: "Do you know what I think?"

"Never mind what you think!" said his mother. "Eat your lunch and go back to school."

After school, Johnny came home and asked again: "Are Michael and Gary up yet?"

"No," replied his mother.

Johnny said: "Do you know what I think?"

His mom replied wearily: "Okay, now tell me what you think."

Johnny said: "Last night Michael came to my room for the Vaseline and I think I gave him my airplane glue."

Why do so many gay men have moustaches? – To hide the stretch marks.

Jay and Jamie were having gay sex. Suddenly Jay announced: "I've got AIDS."

"Oh, fuck!" exclaimed Jamie.

"Only kidding," said Jay. "I just love the way your arse tightened when I said it."

You Know You're Gay When . . .

- You can be in a crowded bar and still spot a toupee from fifty yards.
- You can tell a woman you love her swimsuit, and mean her swimsuit.
- You understand why God invented spandex.
- Your pets always have great names.

- You know how to make an entrance.
- You know the difference between a latte, a cappuccino, café au lait and a macchiato, and if you don't, you know how to fake it.
- You have a medicine cabinet stocked for any occasion.
- You're Barbra Streisand's biggest fan.
- You know how to "air kiss".
- You never hold a grudge for longer than a decade.
- You understand the importance of lighting.
- You've shaved something other than your face.
- There's a married guy somewhere who is terrified of you.
- You're the only one at the class reunion who looks better than you did in high school.
- You can smile to let someone know you hate them.
- You know that being called a "cheap slut" isn't necessarily an insult.
- You've read the book, seen the movie and done the musical.

A gay man was worried about his lack of chest hair, which he thought made him less attractive to his partner. So he decided to visit a doctor to see if anything could be done.

The doctor suggested that the man smother Vaseline all over his chest once a day in the hope that the skin there would be stimulated sufficiently to produce hair.

So the guy went home and smothered his chest in Vaseline. When his partner came home and jumped into bed with him, he was alarmed by the feel of his boyfriend's chest.

"What the hell have you done?" he asked.

"It's Vaseline."

"But why?"

"Because the doctor said that rubbing it on my chest might encourage hair to grow."

"Deary me! Don't you think if that was true you'd have a ponytail coming out of your arse by now?"

How does a gay guy fake an orgasm? – He spits on his partner's back.

A teenage boy asked his father: "Do you think the minister at the church could be gay?"

"Why do you think that?" asked the father.

"Because he closes his eyes when I kiss him."

Two gay friends – Damien and Jonty – were talking when Damien announced that he had got circumcised the previous week.

"Can I see it?" asked Jonty.

So Damien dropped his trousers and pulled out his dick.

"Ooh!" squealed Jonty. "You look ten years younger."

A guy joined a nudist club. On his first day there, he was wandering through the gardens when he spotted a large sign: "Beware of Gays."

A little further along, he saw another sign: "Beware of Gays." Then turning a corner next to a pretty stream, he noticed a bronze plaque set in the ground. He bent over to read it.

The sign read: "Sorry but you've had two warnings!"

Did you hear about the sewage worker who turned gay after entering so many manholes?

First gay man: What's your ringtone these days?

Second gay man: Same colour as yours, I would imagine.

Three gay men died and were going to be cremated. Their lovers happened to be at the funeral home at the same time and were discussing what they planned to do with the ashes.

The first man said: "My Jonjo loved flying, so I'm going up in a plane to scatter his ashes in the sky."

The second man said: "My Simon loved fishing, so I'm going to scatter his ashes in his favourite lake."

The third man said: "My Larry was such a great lover, I think I'm going to put his ashes in a pot of chilli so that he can tear my ass up one last time."

Germans

A German arrived at London's Heathrow Airport. The customs officer said to him: "Name?"

"Helmut Schnell."

"Occupation?"

"No. Just visiting."

An athlete turned up at London's Olympic Park carrying a long, thin bag. A spectator asked him: "Are you a pole-vaulter?"

The athlete replied: "No, I'm German, and how do you know my name?"

What did the German kid say when he pushed his brother off a cliff? – "Look, Father, no Hans!"

Did you hear about the new German microwave? – It seats twelve.

Gingers

What do you call a ginger guy in a porn movie? – The cameraman.

Why do ginger people get sunburnt easily? – It's nature's way of telling us they should be locked indoors.

What is every ginger's wish? – To go prematurely grey.

Why didn't Indians scalp redheads? – Because the hair from a buffalo's butt was more manageable.

When is the only time you focus on a ginger guy? – When you're aiming through your sniper scope.

What's the difference between a ginger guy and a brick? – A brick will get laid.

What is so unrealistic about the Harry Potter movies? – A ginger kid with two friends . . .

What do you call a ginger kid with two friends? – Schizophrenic.

What's the difference between ginger pussy and a pillow? – You could eat a pillow if you had to.

My wife told me to get our ginger son ready for his first day at school. So I kicked him in the leg and stole his dinner money.

A ginger guy stumbled across a magic lamp and when he rubbed it a genie popped out.

"What is your wish?" asked the genie.

The ginger guy said: "I want a huge mansion with a thousand rooms and a hundred floors, all made of pure gold."

The genie looked at him scornfully and said: "Don't be an idiot. Do you have any idea how much gold that would take? That's impossible. Pick something else."

So the ginger guy said: "Okay. I want everyone to stop taking the piss out of my hair colour."

The genie thought for a moment, then said: "So this mansion, do you want en suite bathrooms?"

Why did God invent colour-blindness? – So someone will fancy the ginger kids.

Boomerangs: frisbees for ginger people.

What should you do if you have a ginger baby? – Shave its head and tell everyone that it's got cancer.

A ginger teenager was leaving the house one evening.

"Where are you going?" asked his father.

"To pull some girls," the boy replied.

"Well, don't forget to wear a . . . you know . . ."

"What?"

"You know."

"Do you mean a condom, Dad?"

"No, I mean a hat!"

What do you call a beautiful woman sitting next to a ginger guy? – A hostage.

The internet: so gingers can have friends, too.

What's the best thing about being ginger? – You know you weren't adopted.

Greeks

A Greek and an Italian were sitting down one day debating who had the superior culture. The Greek said proudly: "We have the Parthenon."

The Italian countered: "We have the Colosseum."

The Greek said: "We had great mathematicians."

The Italian argued: "We had the Roman Empire."

The debate went on like this for a couple of hours, until finally the Greek declared triumphantly: "We invented sex."

"Yes, that is true," conceded the Italian, "but it was us who introduced it to women!"

Why did the Greek boy leave home? – He didn't like the way he was being reared.

And why did he return to Greece? – He couldn't bear to leave his brothers behind.

An Italian, a Greek and a Jew were all killed in a car crash in a city street. The next thing they knew, the three men were standing before God in heaven.

God said to the Italian: "All you ever cared about was stuffing your face with pizza and pasta. I'm willing to give you another chance, but I'm warning you: the next time you walk into a pizzeria, I'm sending you straight to hell!"

Then he turned to the Greek and said: "All you ever cared about was your orgies and your wild sex parties. I'm willing to give you another chance, but the next time you perform anal sex, you're going straight to hell!"

Then he said to the Jew: "All you were ever concerned with was saving money and digging around everywhere for loose change. I'm willing to give you another chance, but the next time you pick up a penny off the ground, I'm sending you straight to hell!"

The three men quickly found themselves back on the same street where they had been killed. They started walking along and came to a pizzeria. The Italian looked in the window and said: "Oh, that pizza smells so good, I've just got to have one slice!" He went through the door and POOF! he disappeared.

The Greek and Jew continued walking down the street until the Jew noticed a penny on the sidewalk. He thought to himself: "Oh, look at that penny! I've just got to have it!" He bent over to pick it up and POOF! the Greek disappeared.

Gynaecologists

An attractive woman went to see a gynaecologist who was so captivated by her beauty that he started behaving in a highly unethical manner. First he told her to undress and then he began stroking her inner thighs. As he did so, he asked her: "Do you know what I'm doing?"

"Yes," she replied. "You're checking for any abrasions or skin abnormalities."

"That's right," said the gynaecologist.

Next he started to fondle her breasts. "Do you know what I'm doing?" he asked her.

"Yes," she answered. "You're checking for lumps."

"That's right," he answered.

Then he started to have sex with her. "Do you know what I'm doing now?" he panted.

"Yes," she replied. "You're getting herpes."

What does a gynaecologist do when he feels sentimental? – He looks up an old girlfriend.

A French gynaecologist was talking to an English gynaecologist. "Ah, Reechard," he said, "we 'ave ze best job in ze world, no? All ze lovely women, they come to us and we solve their problems. Only last week I saw a woman and relieved her problem – she 'ad a cleetoris like a melon."

"Don't exaggerate, Pierre," said the Englishman. "No woman has a clitoris like that."

"Ah, you English, you always think of ze size, never ze taste!"

A ten-year-old boy told his friend: "Yesterday my mum caught me playing gynae-cologists with the girl next door."

"Wow! I bet you were in trouble," said the friend.

"Not at all," said the boy. "It was Wednesday, so we were playing golf."

A woman called her gynaecologist and asked for an emergency appointment. On arrival, she was ushered straight into the examination room.

"What's the problem?" asked the gynaecologist.

"It's rather embarrassing," she said, "but you'll see when you examine my vagina."

So the gynaecologist shone his torch up her vagina. "Right, I see what you mean," he said. "Your vibrator appears to be well and truly stuck up there. I'm afraid removing it is going to involve a delicate and expensive surgical operation."

"I'm not sure I can afford it," she said. "But while I'm here, could you at least replace the batteries?"

A guy went into a job centre in Philadelphia and saw a card advertising for a gynaecologist's assistant. "Can you give me some more details about this?" he asked the clerk behind the desk.

The clerk sifted through his files and replied: "Yes, I've had quite a few enquiries about this job. The job entails you getting female patients ready for the gynaecologist. You have to help them out of their underwear, lie them down and wash their nether regions. Then you need to apply shaving foam, shave off all their pubic hair and finally rub in soothing oils so that they're ready for the gynae-cologist's examination. There's an annual salary of $45,000 but I'm afraid you'll have to travel to Pittsburgh."

"Oh why, is that where the job's based?"

"No, that's where the end of the queue is."

Hair

A middle-aged guy who was bald bought a hairpiece in the hope that it would make him more attractive to women. That night he took it for its first outing to a singles bar, where he picked up a pretty young woman and took her back to his apartment.

To get her into the mood, he switched off the lights but as they started fumbling passionately in the dark, he realized to his horror that his toupee had fallen off. He began groping frantically for it, hoping to put it back on his head before the girl saw that he was really bald. In the zeal of the search, he inadvert-ently ran his hands up the girl's legs.

"Oh! That's it! That's it!" she gasped in ecstasy.

"No, it isn't," he said, momentarily forgetting himself. "Mine's got a side parting."

A little girl went to the barber's with her dad and stood next to the chair eating a cake while her dad got his hair cut.

The barber smiled at her and said: "You're going to get hair on your muffin."

"I know," she said. "I'm going to get tits, too."

What's the best thing about dating a girl with chronic alopecia? – You don't have to hold her hair when she vomits.

I prefer balding men. Why would you want to run your hands through a man's hair when you could shove your fist right into his skull? (Stephanie Hodge)

A man with a bald head and a wooden leg was invited to a fancy-dress party. He didn't know what costume to wear to hide his head and his leg, so he wrote to a fancy-dress company asking for their advice A few days later he received a parcel with a note: "Dear Sir, please find enclosed a pirate's outfit. The spotted handkerchief will cover your bald head and with your wooden leg you will be perfect as a pirate."

The man was annoyed because he felt that the suggestion was emphasizing his wooden leg, so he wrote a rude letter of complaint. A week passed and he received another parcel with a note which said: "Dear Sir, sorry about before, please find enclosed a monk's habit. The long robe will cover your wooden leg and with your bald head you will really look the part."

The man was outraged since the company had gone from emphasizing his wooden leg to emphasizing his bald head, so he wrote an extremely rude letter of complaint. The next day he received a small parcel and a note which read: "Dear Sir, please find enclosed a tin of treacle. Pour the tin of treacle over your bald head, stick your wooden leg up your arse and go as a toffee apple!"

Halitosis

A man went to see a doctor about his bad breath. The doctor said: "Try one tablespoon of horse manure three times a day."

"Will that cure it?" asked the man.

"No," said the doctor, "but it will tone it down a bit."

A woman was about to settle down to a bridge evening with her lady friends when her husband announced that he was going down to the pub. She calmly walked over to him, unzipped his trousers, kissed him on the head of his dick, zipped him back up, said goodbye and sat down to play cards.

Her friends were dumbfounded and, after he had gone, one of them felt obliged to ask: "Why do you kiss your husband goodbye on his thing?"

The wife replied: "Obviously, you've never smelled his breath!"

People are so defensive, especially women. I offered a girl a Tic-Tac one time. She said to me, "Oh, do I need one? Is it my breath? Do you think I need one?" I'm like, I'm just trying to be nice. If I was going to give you something you needed I would give you moustache wax and a T-shirt that says "One Cock at a Time". (Dave Attell)

A guy couldn't get anywhere with girls because of his horrible breath, so he went to his doctor for an examination to discover the root of the problem. The doctor told him: "I'm afraid you need a psychiatrist instead."

"Why a psychiatrist?"

"You have to break one of your two bad habits," the doctor continued. "You either have to stop scratching your arse or biting your fingernails."

Hangovers

A man woke up one morning with the filthiest hangover and no recollection of the night before. Slowly opening his eyes, he saw a bottle of aspirin and a glass of water on the bedside table.

He looked around the room to find his clothes were on the dresser, neatly folded, with a clean shirt on top. The bedroom was immaculate. On the bedside table was a note, which said: "Darling, your breakfast is in the kitchen. I love you."

Downstairs, he found his favourite cereal, croissants, fresh orange juice and coffee laid out waiting for him, along with the morning paper. His teenage son was sitting at the table finishing his own breakfast.

"Tell me, son," asked the man. "What happened last night?"

"Well," said the boy, "you came home so blind drunk you didn't even know your own name. You nearly broke the door down, then you were sick in the hallway, then you knocked the furniture over and when Mum tried to calm you down, you thought she was the police, so you gave her a black eye."

"Christ!" said the man. "Then how come my clothes are all folded, the house is tidy and my breakfast is ready?"

The boy explained: "When Mum dragged you into the bedroom and tried to get your trousers off to put you into bed, you shouted at her: 'Get your filthy hands off me, you whore, I'm married!' "

Degrees of Hangover

1-star hangover:
Although you drink ten bottles of water, you still feel as parched as the Sahara. Even vegetarians have cravings for a cheeseburger and a bag of fries.

2-star hangover:
The coffee you hug to try to remain focused merely serves to exacerbate your rumbling gut and remind you how you could murder a full English breakfast. You spend the workday idly surfing the net, sending scurrilous emails and trying to stay awake.

3-star hangover:
You have a persistently dull headache and your stomach feels like a herd of elephants has just trampled on it. Anytime a girl or lad walks by, you gag because their perfume/aftershave reminds you of the random gin shots you did with your alcoholic friends after the doorman kicked you out at 1.45 in the morning. You long to be in bed with a kebab and a litre of Coke watching daytime TV.

4-star hangover:
Your boss has lambasted you for being late and reeking of booze. Although you somehow managed to grab some decent clothes from your wardrobe this morning, you smell of socks. The cuts on your face are testimony to the problems you had shaving. Girls with four-star hangovers look like they have applied their makeup while riding the dodgems.

5-star hangover:
Vodka vapour is seeping out of every pore. Your body has lost the ability to produce saliva, so your tongue is suffocating you. You feel so bad you could cry, but that would drain the last drop of moisture from your body. Your fellow workers think your dog has just died because you look so pathetic. You should have called in sick because, let's face it, all you can manage to do is breathe – and today you're not even very good at that.

6-star hangover:
You stagger home and collapse straight into bed. You enjoy deep sleep for about two hours before banging noises inside your head wake you up. As you half open your bleary eyes, you notice that your bed has been cleared for take-off and is flying relentlessly around the room. As your throat wells up, you stumble out of bed and – if lucky – you reach the toilet and remember to raise the lid in time before releasing a torrent of diced carrot and tomato pieces. You sit there pitifully on the floor, cuddling your only friend in the world – the toilet. The pattern is repeated three more times in the course of the night. Come daylight, work is out of the question, so you call in sick. Shortly after midday, you lever yourself out of bed and feel momentarily better until a glance in the mirror reveals red eyes and lumps of vomit glued to your hair. You spend the rest of the day trying to avoid anything that might make you sick again, such as moving. You vow never to touch a drop again.

One day a guy got blind drunk – worse than anything he had known. In the morning, he woke up with a terrible hangover in a strange room, and when he turned bleary-eyed to try to make out where he was, he saw to his horror that sleeping peacefully beside him was the ugliest girl he had ever seen.

Very quietly, he slipped his arm out from under her, got up and dressed as fast as he could. He put a £20 note on the bureau and started to tiptoe out. Just then he felt a tug on his trouser leg. Looking down, he saw a girl even uglier than the one in the bed. She looked up at him, smiled a toothless smile, and asked: "Nothing for the bridesmaid?"

Health

A husband said to his wife: "I never want to live in a vegetative state, dependent on some machine and fluids from a bottle. If that ever happens, just pull the plug."

So his wife got up, unplugged the TV and threw out his beer.

While working out at a health club, Dale could not help noticing that another man was looking really depressed. This surprised Dale, who had been thinking that this guy was the luckiest man at the club. "Why are you so down?" Dale asked. "I saw you yesterday leaving with that gorgeous aerobics instructor on your arm."

"Well, we went to her place and had a few drinks," the guy explained. "Then she said, 'Marvin, take off my blouse,' and a moment later, 'Marvin, take off my leotard.' Before long, she said, 'Marvin, take off my bra.' Then, finally, she said, 'Oh, Marvin, take off my panties.'"

"Hey, man, you had it made!" Dale sighed enviously. "Was it great?"

"I suppose it must have been. I really couldn't see past that guy Marvin."

My friend's living the dream. He's in a coma.

It should not be an act of social disobedience to light a cigarette. Unless you're actually a doctor working at an incubator. (Dylan Moran)

What's the difference between an oral and a rectal thermometer? – The taste.

Arriving home early from work, a husband found his wife on the bed having a heart attack. He was just about to call emergency services when his young son said: "Daddy, there's a naked man in the wardrobe."

Startled, the husband opened the wardrobe door and there was his best friend Jim.

"What the hell do you think you're doing?" yelled the husband. "There's Jenny having a heart attack and you're playing games with the kids!"

No one can read my poker face . . . since I had a stroke.

You shouldn't make jokes about strokes. If you ever have one, you'll be laughing on the other side of your face. (Jimmy Carr)

"May contain traces of nuts": for the daredevil among nut allergists.

My daughter's eating for two. She's got a tapeworm.

I went to donate blood the other day, but they wouldn't take it. Apparently they need to know where it comes from.

When a man complained to a friend about a pain in his elbow, the friend recommended a self-diagnosis computer at the local pharmacy. "It's an amazing machine," said the friend. "It can diagnose every known human disease and condition, and it's cheaper and far quicker than a doctor. All you have to do is pay £10, feed in a urine sample and the computer will tell you what you're suffering from. It's as easy as that."

So the man went to the pharmacy, paid his £10 and fed in his urine sample. Sure enough, two minutes later, the computer issued a printout. It read: "You have tennis elbow. Soak your arm in warm water. Avoid heavy labour. It will clear up in two weeks."

The man was fascinated by the computer and that evening he decided to try to outsmart it. He mixed together some tap water, a stool sample from his dog and urine samples from both his wife and his daughter. To complicate the sample still further, he also masturbated into it. Then he went down to the pharmacy, paid his £10, fed in the sample and waited eagerly for the computer's diagnosis.

Two minutes later, the printout appeared. It read: "Your tap water is too hard – get a water softener. Your dog has ringworm – bathe him with anti-fungal

shampoo. Your daughter is using cocaine – put her in rehab. Your wife is pregnant with two girls. They aren't yours – get a lawyer. And if you don't stop jerking
off, you'll never cure your tennis elbow."

It seems unfair that the huge price of my eye test was in the small print. (Milton
Jones)

I went for my routine check-up today, and everything seemed to be going fine
until he stuck his finger up my butt. I think it's time I changed dentists.

My doctor said I need to do something that gets me out of the pub. So I've
started smoking.

Heaven and Hell

God and St Peter were playing golf in heaven. St Peter teed off first and hit a
superb drive 300 yards right down the middle of the fairway.

Next it was God's turn, but he scuffed his tee-shot along the ground. His ball
was heading towards a deep bunker until, out of nowhere, a squirrel caught his
ball in his mouth and dropped it in the middle of the fairway. Then amazingly an
eagle swooped down, picked up God's moving ball, flew towards the green and
dropped it in the hole for a hole-in-one.

St Peter turned to God and said: "Are we going to play golf or are we going
piss about?"

Two women met up in the afterlife.

First woman: "Hi, my name is Kelly."

Second woman: "Hi, I'm Rhona. How did you die?"

"I froze to death."

"How horrible!"

"It wasn't so bad. After I quit shaking from the cold, I began to feel warm and
sleepy, and eventually I died a peaceful death. How about you?"

"I died of a massive heart attack. I suspected that my husband Joel was
cheating, so I came home early one day to catch him in the act. But instead I
found him all by himself watching TV."

"So what happened?"

"I was so sure another woman was in the house that I started running around
looking – up in the loft, down in the basement, I searched the place from top to

bottom. I went through every closet and checked under all the beds. I kept this up until I had looked everywhere, and finally I became so exhausted that I just keeled over with a heart attack and died."

"Too bad you didn't look in the freezer – we'd both still be alive."

Three girls died and were brought to the gates of heaven, where they were met by St Peter and his obedient angel. St Peter told the girls: "Before entering you must answer one simple question."

"Which is . . . ?" they replied in unison.

"Have you been a good girl?" he asked the first girl.

"Oh yes," she said. "I was a virgin before I got married, and was still a virgin even after I got married."

"Very good," said St Peter. "Angel, give this girl . . . the golden key."

Then St Peter asked the second girl: "Have you been a good girl?"

"Quite good," she said. "I was a virgin before I got married, but was not after I got married."

"Very good," said St Peter. "Angel, give this girl . . . the silver key."

Finally, St Peter asked the third girl: "Have you been a good girl?"

"Not at all," she said. "I practically had sex with every guy I met before and after I got married. Anywhere, anytime, that was my motto. I was a real slut."

"Very good," said St Peter. "Angel, give this girl . . . my room key."

Due to an administrative error when Dracula died he went to heaven. There he asked God whether it was possible for him to be reincarnated.

"I don't know," said God sceptically. "What do you want to come back as?"

Trying to combine his sinister passion with a religious symbolism that he hoped would appeal to the Almighty, Dracula replied: "May I be reincarnated as a white angel with wings and still suck blood?"

"Very well," said God. "I'll send you back as a sanitary pad."

A woman died and went to heaven. As St Peter was processing her documentation, she heard another woman screaming in pain. She looked in the room where the cries of anguish were coming from and saw holes being drilled into a woman's shoulders to fasten the wings. Then she heard a man screaming and saw holes being drilled into his head to fasten the halo.

"I've decided I don't want to go to heaven," she told St Peter. "I'll go to that other place."

"You don't want to go there," he replied. "They rape and sodomize you down there."

"I don't care," she answered. "At least I already have holes for that."

Three married couples – one Jewish, one Irish, one American – all died on the same day and arrived in heaven. St Peter was waiting at the gates to take down their names. After telling St Peter about all the good deeds he had done the Jew told him that his wife's name was Penny.

"I'm sorry," said St Peter, "but I can't admit anyone with a name linked to money."

Next in line was the Irishman. He, too, told St Peter of his many charitable works and said that his wife's name was Brandy.

"I'm sorry," said St Peter, "but I can't admit anyone with a name linked to alcohol."

Hearing all this, the American turned to his wife and said: "Fanny, I think we may have a problem . . ."

Hillbillies

Stuck in the wilds of Montana, a lumberjack began to feel sexually frustrated. So he asked the foreman: "Are there any women around here?"

"No," said the foreman, "but if you're looking for excitement there's an old hillbilly named Jed who lives in a cabin about half a mile away. If you don't mind spending a little cash, Jed will show you the time of your life."

The lumberjack was horrified at the idea. "No way," he said. "I don't go in for that kinda stuff!"

Three months later, the lumberjack was feeling more frustrated than ever. He was now desperate for sex, and so he asked the foreman about Jed. "This guy, Jed. How much will it cost?"

"Six hundred dollars," replied the foreman.

"That's a hell of a lot of money. Why so much?"

"Well," explained the foreman, "there's $200 for Jed, and $100 each for the four guys who have to hold Jed down. You see, old Jed doesn't go in for that kinda stuff either."

An old hillbilly woman was busying herself in the kitchen of her wood cabin when she hollered out to her husband: "You need to go fix the outhouse!"

The husband replied: "There ain't nothing wrong with the outhouse!"

"Yes, there is," she yelled back. "Now get out there and fix it!"

So he strolled over to the outhouse, looked around and shouted: "There ain't nothing wrong with the outhouse!"

She yelled: "Stick your head in the hole!"

"I ain't sticking my head in that hole!" he shouted in reply.

She insisted: "You have to stick your head in the hole to see what to fix."

So he stuck his head in the hole, looked around and shouted: "I'm telling you, woman, there ain't nothing wrong with the outhouse!"

She hollered back: "Now take your head out of the hole!"

He proceeded to pull his head out of the hole, but then started screaming: "Help! My beard is stuck in the cracks in the toilet seat!"

To which she replied: "Hurts, don't it?"

How do you get a good ole hillbilly gal pregnant? – Come on her shoes and let the flies do the rest.

After working in the city for twenty-five years, a man decided to take early retirement and escape from the stresses of modern life by buying a remote cabin in the wilds of Montana. His home was so isolated that in the first six months the only visitor he had was the mailman. Then one evening, there was a knock on the door and standing there was a burly hillbilly.

"I'm Caleb," announced the hillbilly, "your neighbour from six miles over the ridge. I'm having a party Saturday night and I thought you might like to come."

"Sure, that sounds great. I'd like to meet some local folks at last."

"Oh, but I gotta warn you," said the hillbilly. "There's gonna be some heavy drinkin'."

"Don't worry about that. I lived in New York for twenty-five years. I can take my drink."

"Oh, and there's almost sure to be some fightin' too."

"That's no problem. I get on with most people."

"Oh, and I've seen some wild sex at these parties."

"Great. After six months' isolation, I'm up for that."

"Right, see you Saturday then," said the hillbilly.

"One thing. What should I wear?"

"Whatever you want – it's just gonna be the two of us."

Ma and Pa were two hillbillies living out on a farm up in the wilds of Montana. When Pa found out that the hole under the outhouse was full he went into the kitchen of the house and told Ma that he didn't know what to do to empty the hole.

Ma suggested: "Why don't you go ask the young'n down the road? He must be smart 'cause he's a college gradjyate."

So Pa drove down to the neighbour's house and asked him: "Mr college grad-jyate, my outhouse hole is full, and I don't know what to do to empty it."

The graduate said: "Get yourself two sticks of dynamite, one with a short fuse and one with a long fuse. Put them both under the outhouse and light them both at the same time. The first one will go off and shoot the outhouse in the air. While it's in the air the second one will then go off and spread the poop all across your farm, fertilizing your ground. The outhouse should then come back down to the same spot atop the now-empty hole."

Pa thanked him, then drove to the hardware store and picked up two sticks of dynamite, one with a short fuse and one with a long fuse. He went home and put them under the outhouse. He then lit them and ran behind a tree.

All of a sudden, Ma came running out of the house and dashed into the outhouse. A split second later, the first stick of dynamite exploded, shooting the outhouse into the air. Then the second stick of dynamite went off, spreading poop all over the farm with a tremendous blast. Finally, the outhouse came crashing back down atop the hole.

Pa raced to the outhouse, threw open the door and asked: "Ma, are you all right?"

As she pulled up her panties, she gasped: "Yeah, but I'm sure glad I didn't let that fart go in the kitchen!"

Driving across the Wild West, a New Yorker stumbled across a small hillbilly town that proudly boasted it had no women. He went for a drink in the local bar and asked the bartender: "How can you live in this town without any women?"

"It's not so bad," said the bartender. "Whenever we get lonely, we go out back where there's a barrel with a knothole in it. It might not sound great, but, believe me, after one try you're hooked."

A few hours later, the New Yorker started to feel lonely, so he took the bartender's advice, found the barrel and inserted his penis into the knothole. Satisfied, he returned to the bar and told the bartender: "You were right. That was great. How much do I owe you?"

"Nothing," said the bartender, "but now it's your turn to get in the barrel."

Hobos

Seeing a homeless guy begging on the street, a woman took pity on him and gave him a handful of change.

"Thank you," said the homeless man. "Your generosity is much appreciated. You know, my life used to be great but just look at the state of me now."

"How do you mean?" asked the woman.

"Well," he explained, "I was a multimillionaire. I had bank accounts all over the world with hundreds of thousands of dollars deposited in each."

"So where did it all go wrong?" she asked.

The homeless man sighed: "I forgot my mother's maiden name."

A hobo said to a businessman in the street: "Mister, I haven't tasted food for a week."

"Don't worry," said the businessman. "It still tastes the same."

Another hobo went up to a smartly dressed woman in the street and said: "I haven't eaten for three days."

"Gosh," said the woman, "I wish I had your willpower," and walked on.

Two hobos were walking along the street early one morning, complaining about their empty stomachs. Soon they found a possum lying dead by the roadside. The first hobo said to the second: "Come on, I'll split it with you."

The second hobo declined, so the first hobo ate the whole possum himself. An hour later, the first hobo started to turn green. He gagged for a few minutes, then spewed up the possum's remains all over the road."

The second hobo smiled and said: "I knew if I waited long enough I'd get a hot meal."

What's red and orange and looks good on hobos? – Fire.

On his way to work, a businessman regularly passed a beggar on a street corner. The beggar would always hold out one hand, and the businessman would usually give him a few coins. Then one morning, the businessman noticed that the beggar was holding out both hands. "Why are you holding out both hands?" he asked.

"Well, sir," replied the beggar, "business has been so good that I decided to open another branch."

A hobo walked into a bar, but the bartender told him to clear off because he was bad for business.

"Okay, okay," said the hobo. "If you give me a cocktail stick, I'll leave."

So the bartender handed him a cocktail stick and he left.

A few minutes later, another hobo walked in, and once again the bartender ordered him out.

"All right, I'll go," said the second hobo, "if you give me a cocktail stick."

So the bartender gave him a cocktail stick and he left.

A few minutes later, a third hobo entered the bar. The bartender said: "If I give you a cocktail stick, will you go?"

"I don't want a cocktail stick," said the hobo. "I want a straw. Give me a straw and I'll leave."

The bartender was puzzled. "How come you want a straw when the other two wanted cocktail sticks?"

"Well," said the hobo, "someone's been sick outside and now all the lumpy bits have gone."

A hobo lived in a battered old shed on the other side of a man's back garden fence. Despite the hobo's impoverished lifestyle, the man couldn't help noticing that he was always smiling. One day, the man asked him: "What's the secret of happiness, buddy?"

The hobo replied: "Throw away all your possessions."

"How can that make you happy?"

"I need your TV and DVD recorder for my shed!"

An old hobo's only possession was a female donkey until one day he won $75,000 on the lottery. He didn't know what to do with his newfound wealth, so he decided to spend a night in a five-star hotel. He asked for the finest room and started going up the stairs with his female donkey, but the manager called out: "Excuse me, sir. Where do you think you're going with that donkey?"

"Anywhere I go, she goes," replied the hobo.

"I'm sorry, sir," said the manager, "but you can't take the donkey upstairs. Leave it down here with us and we'll take good care of her."

So the hobo left the donkey at the front desk and went up to his room. As he opened the door, he saw that everything was made of gold, and there was a table full of food and a huge television. He didn't want to ruin anything, so he took off his shabby coat and slept on the floor.

The next morning the manager came up to the room and asked how his night was. "Great," replied the hobo. "How much do I have to pay?"

The manager said: "A thousand bucks for the food."

"But I haven't touched the food," protested the hobo.

"It was right there," said the manager. "You should have. And it's $2,000 for the TV."

"But I didn't even know how to turn the damn thing on!" said the hobo.

"It was there," said the manager, "so you should have. And it's $5,000 for sleeping on the bed."

"But I slept on the floor!"

"It was there," insisted the manager. "You should have. Anyway your total bill is $8,000."

"Okay," said the hobo defiantly. "In that case you owe me $10,000 for screwing my donkey!"

"But, sir, I didn't screw your donkey."

"It was there," grinned the hobo. "You should have!"

What do you call a dead hobo floating down the river in a sleeping bag? — A drifter.

Two hobos were chatting next to a railroad track. The first hobo said: "I found this gorgeous girl tied to the tracks last week. I managed to drag her clear and then we had fantastic sex for two hours."

"Wow!" said the second hobo. "What was she, blonde or brunette?"

"Don't know. I couldn't find the head."

Finding a $10 bill in the street, a hobo decided to go to the liquor store and buy a bottle of white wine. After knocking back the wine, the hobo fell into a drunken torpor and collapsed in an alleyway. About ten minutes later, a passing gay guy happened upon the sprawled body of the hobo, and, seizing his opportunity, shafted him up the ass. He was just about to leave when he felt a pang of conscience and tucked a $10 bill into the hobo's hand.

Waking up the next day, the hobo discovered the $10, and, hardly able to believe his good fortune, he returned to the liquor store and bought another bottle of white wine. Once again he downed the whole bottle and fell into a drunken sleep in his favourite alleyway. Shortly afterwards, the same gay guy chanced upon the hapless hobo and, with nobody else around, took the opportunity to rear-end him. His lust satisfied, he crammed a $10 bill into the hobo's belt to ease his guilty conscience.

On waking up, the hobo discovered the $10 in his belt and, touched by the charity of humanity, hastened back to the liquor store. There, he picked up a bottle of red wine and took it to the cash desk.

Remembering the hobo's previous purchases, the sales assistant said: "Oh, you're switching to red wine, are you? I thought you usually drank white."

"I do quite like the white wine," said the hobo, "but it doesn't half make my ass sore!"

A hobo walked into a jewellery shop, put his hands down his pants and started fingering his asshole. The sales assistant shouted at him: "Stop what you're doing and get out!"

The hobo said: "You want to make your bloody mind up! You've got a sign in the window that says, 'Come inside and pick your ring in comfort.'"

A wealthy lady had hired a band, a caterer and a clown for her granddaughter's birthday party.

Shortly before the party was due to start, two bums showed up looking for a handout. Feeling sorry for them, the lady promised them a free meal if they would chop some wood out back. Gratefully, they went to the rear of the house.

The guests arrived, the party got under way, and all of the children were enjoying themselves. The only problem was that the clown hadn't arrived, and soon he phoned to say that he was stuck in traffic and wouldn't be able to get there in time.

Disappointed, the lady tried valiantly to entertain the children herself but she was a poor substitute. Just then she happened to look out of the window and saw one of the bums doing cartwheels across the back lawn. She watched in awe as he swung from tree branches, did midair flips and jumped high in the air.

So she went outside and said to the other bum: "What your friend is doing is absolutely marvellous. I have never seen such a thing. Do you think he would consider repeating this performance for the children at the party? I would pay him $75."

"I don't know," said the bum. "Let me ask him. Hey, Denzil! For $75, would you chop off another toe?"

Honeymoon

Two elderly newlyweds arrived at their Florida honeymoon suite. He put his reading glasses on the bedside table and went into the bathroom to freshen up and recover from the demands of the wedding day. While he was in the bathroom, she took off all her clothes and started doing aerobic exercises on the bed in preparation for their night of passion. After touching her toes and flexing her arms, she lay on her back and began cycling with her legs in the air. She then stretched her legs farther back, trying to touch the bed behind her head with her toes, but merely succeeded in getting her feet caught in the headboard.

Just as she was attempting to extricate herself, her husband returned. He squinted at her and said: "For God's sake, comb your hair and put your teeth back in. You look just like your mother!"

Two newlyweds arrived at a hotel and asked for the honeymoon suite. The clerk asked: "Do you have reservations?"

"Only one," said the husband. "She won't take it up the arse."

A hotel porter was peeking through the keyhole of the honeymoon suite. "Look at this," he whispered to a passing maid. "She's really enjoying that."

The maid couldn't resist looking through the keyhole. "Wow!" she gasped. "I wish my boyfriend would do that to me more often!"

A passing waiter overheard and came to join in the fun. He, too, had a quick look through the keyhole. "Unbelievable!" he hissed. "And to think that last night he had the nerve to complain about a hair in his soup . . ."

Three honeymoon couples were staying in rooms on the same floor in a hotel. As he and his wife were getting undressed, the first man said: "Wow! I didn't know your butt was so huge!" His wife was furious and threw him out into the corridor.

Meanwhile, the second couple were also getting undressed. The second man looked at his wife and commented: "What ridiculously large breasts you've got!" His wife livid and threw him out into the corridor.

A few minutes later, the two men were joined in the corridor by third new husband. They asked: "What are you doing out here? Did you put your foot in it?"

"No," he said, "but I could have done."

Two newlyweds were on honeymoon at an English seaside town. Returning one afternoon to the small hotel where they were staying, the bride set off upstairs while the husband looked at some tourist brochures in the reception area. Just then the landlady appeared and said to him: "I have a couple of extra tickets to a play tonight, and I wonder if you and your new bride would like to have them?"

"I'll ask her," said the husband, studying the tickets. Then he called up to her: "Honey, would you like to see *Oliver Twist* tonight?"

"No way!" his bride retorted. "If you show me one more trick with that thing, I'm going home to my mother!"

A man and his new wife checked into a five-star hotel for their honeymoon night. At the front desk, the receptionist gave the groom the key to the bridal suite and said: "Sir, it is now six o'clock, dinner will be served from 7.30 onwards."

"Thank you," said the groom, "but we won't be needing any dinner." And he and his bride headed off to their room.

Throughout the evening the people in the room next door to the bridal suite were phoning down to the main desk to complain about all the moaning, groaning and bouncing of bed springs.

Next morning at 6 a.m., the groom phoned down to room service. "Hi," he said. "Could I get some breakfast brought up here?"

"Sure, what would you like?" asked room service.

The groom said: "Well, I have to replace all the energy I lost last night so you'd better get me four fried eggs, six sausages, five slices of toast and two litres of orange juice!"

"That's quite an appetite you've got there," said room service. "Is that for your wife as well, or just for you?"

"No, that's just for me. But can you also send up six pieces of lettuce for my wife?"

"Why six pieces of lettuce?" asked room service.

The groom replied: "I want to find out if she eats like a rabbit, too!"

A couple on their honeymoon were just preparing to get into bed together when the wife turned to her husband and said: "Darling, I have a confession to make to you. I used to be a hooker."

The husband thought for a moment and said: "Actually, I find that a bit of a turn-on, tell me about it."

She replied: "Well, my name was Kevin and I played for Hull Kingston Rovers."

Two friends had a joint wedding, after which they went to the same place for their honeymoons. As they checked into the hotel, one whispered to the other: "I'll tell you what, we'll see who shags their wife the most. Each time you shag her, make a mark on the headboard, and in the morning the loser buys the winner breakfast."

The other agreed, and they both took their wives to bed early so they could get started. The first guy got into bed, had sex with his wife and then scratched a mark onto the headboard. Halfway through the night, he woke up, roused his wife and made love to her again, after which he made a second mark on the headboard, next to the first. In the morning, he woke up, shagged her again and made a third mark next to the other two on the headboard.

Shortly afterwards there was a knock on the door, and his mate staggered in, on his knees, his overused dick glowing through his trousers. He looked at the headboard and wailed: "You bastard! One hundred and eleven. You beat me by one!"

A woman married a man who did not believe in pre-marital sex, and despite not being a virgin she had managed to convince him that she was. Before going on honeymoon, she asked a friend how she could keep her secret seeing that she would soon be having sex with her husband for the first time. The friend suggested that she shove a piece of raw, bloody meat up her vagina, so that when her husband penetrated her, she would bleed like a true virgin.

So the woman inserted the piece of raw meat in her vagina, and on the first night of their honeymoon she and her husband had great sex. But the following morning she woke up to find him gone. He had left a note on the bedside table. It read: "Sorry, this relationship is too intense for a guy like me. I will always love you. Oh, and your vagina is in the sink."

Hookers

When a man lost his job, he was in such dire straits financially that he sent his wife out on the streets to sell her body. After a few hours she came home with £35.50 in her hand.

He asked: "Who gave you the fifty pence?"

She said: "All of them."

An old sailor went to a brothel and picked a woman for sex. As they got down to it, he asked: "How am I doing?"

"Three knots," she replied.

"Three knots? What do you mean?"

"You're not hard, you're not in, and you're not getting your money back."

A hooker who had been off the game for a while decided to go back into business. Just before the first client arrived at her shabby bedsit, she carefully removed all her scabs and slipped them under the pillow.

After they'd had sex, he asked her: "How much is that?"

"Fifty," she replied.

"Here's fifty-two," he said, handing her the cash.

"Thanks. Is the extra a tip?"

"No, it's for the Pringles."

What's the difference between a cheap hooker and an elephant? – One rolls on its back for peanuts and the other lives in a zoo.

A horny guy only had a small amount of cash in his pocket, but he just had to have sex, so he went to the brothel and asked what he could get for £5. The Madam said she didn't have anything at that price, but the guy insisted he simply had to get laid.

Finally taking pity on him, she took him up to a really old lady who cleaned the place.

"Here," said the Madam, "you can have old Gladys for £5."

So the guy started getting it on with old Gladys, but it was really dry and rough. After a while, however, it became moist and smooth and much more pleasurable. He finally exploded in ecstasy, and afterwards they started talking about it.

He told her how rough it had been initially, but how great it then became once things started moving.

"Yeah, I know what you mean," she said. "Once all those blisters popped, it really felt great for me too!"

What do you call a hooker with two ponytails? – A blow job with handlebars.

A union leader visited a Nevada brothel. As a stickler for the rules of the workplace, the first question he asked the brothel owner was: "Is this a union house?"

"No, it's not," replied the owner.

"So if I pay $100, what do the girls get?"

"The house takes $80 and the girls get $20."

"Well, I don't think that's fair. I shall take my custom elsewhere."

And with that he left.

Further down the street, he found another brothel. "Is this a union house?" he asked the owner.

"Yes, it is," said the owner.

"So if I pay $100, what do the girls get to keep?"

"The girls get $80 and the house takes $20."

"That sounds fair," said the union leader, who then looked around the room, pointed to a buxom young blonde and added: "I'd like to buy two hours with her."

"I'm sure you would sir," said the brothel owner, gesturing at a seventy-five-year-old woman in the corner, "but Ethel here has seniority."

A husky foreigner, looking for sex, accepted the terms of a New Orleans hooker. When she undressed, he noticed that she had no pubic hair. The man shouted: "What, no wool? In my country all women have wool down there!"

"What do you want to do?" replied the hooker. "Knit or fuck?"

On his first visit to Orlando, Florida, Hans, a middle-aged German tourist, found the red-light district and entered a large brothel. The Madam asked him to be seated and sent over a young lady to entertain him.

They sat and talked, frolicked a little, giggled a bit, drank a bit and she sat on his lap. Then he whispered in her ear and she gasped and ran away. Seeing this, the Madam decided to send over a more experienced lady to entertain the gentleman.

They too sat and talked, frolicked a little, giggled a bit, drank a bit and she sat on his lap. Then he whispered in her ear, and she too screamed, "No!" and walked quickly away.

The Madam was surprised that this ordinary-looking man had asked for something so outrageous that her two girls would have nothing to do with him. So she decided that only her most experienced lady, Lola, would do. Lola had never said no to anything and was beyond embarrassment. So the Madam sent her over to Hans. They sat and talked, frolicked a little, giggled a bit, drank a bit and she sat on his lap. Then he whispered in her ear and she screamed: "No way, buddy!" She smacked him hard around the face and stormed off.

By now the Madam was absolutely intrigued, having seen nothing like this in all her years of operating a brothel. She hadn't done the bedroom work herself for a long time, but she was sure she had said yes to everything a man could possibly ask for. She just had to find out what this man wanted that had made her girls so angry, and she also saw it as a way of showing them that she was still queen of the hookers.

So she went over to Hans and told him that she was the best in the house and was available. She sat and talked with him. They frolicked, giggled, drank and then she sat on his lap. Then Hans leaned forward and whispered in her ear: "Can I pay in euros?"

"I'm shocked that you and Janey are getting a divorce," said Rich to his friend Sam. "I've always thought of you as the perfect couple, that you'd be together forever. Surely you can sort things out. What's suddenly gone wrong?"

"Well," explained Sam, "we were driving through a red-light district last week when Janey said: 'Oh look, it's one of those hookers, or prossies, or whores or whatever you call them.' And I said: 'It's Lexi. Her name is Lexi.'"

Rich fell silent for a moment, and then said: "So who do you think will get to keep the house?"

What's the difference between an epileptic corn-husker and a hooker with diarrhoea? – The corn-husker shucks between fits.

Away from home on a business trip, a man arrived at a city hotel around midnight and booked a single room. As the clerk filled out the paperwork, the man noticed a sexy young woman sitting alone in the lobby and smiling at him. He told the clerk to wait while he went over and talked to her. Moments later, he returned with the girl on his arm.

Lying to the clerk, he said: "Fancy meeting my wife here! I'll need a double room instead."

The next morning, he went to settle the bill and was horrified to see that it came to over £5,000.

"What's the meaning of this?" he yelled at the clerk. "I've only been here one night!"

"Yes," said the clerk, "but your 'wife' has been here for three weeks."

What's the difference between a wife and a hooker? – One is contract, the other is pay as you go.

Reaching his fortieth birthday a man was disappointed that he was still a virgin and living with his elderly parents. Having just been paid at work, he decided to venture down to the local brothel and finally lose his virginity to some nice young lady.

Half an hour later, he found himself lying on a bed with a gorgeous brunette hooker slowly stripping in front of him. Unable to contain himself after all the years of sexual frustration, he lunged at her fanny with his tongue and began vigorously eating her out. Almost immediately he found something distasteful within her, but because of his inexperience he thought it might be perfectly normal and so he carried on. A minute or so later, however, he came across a large piece of sweetcorn.

He turned to the hooker and asked: "Excuse me, miss, but are you sick?"

"I'm not," she said, "but the last guy who was in here was."

After striking gold in Montana, a miner headed straight to the nearest bar and announced: "I'm lookin' for the meanest, roughest, toughest whore in town."

The bartender said: "I reckon we can help ya there. She's upstairs, second door on the left."

The miner handed the bartender a gold nugget to pay for the whore and two bottles of beer, then marched upstairs. He flung open the second door on the left and said to the woman in the room: "I'm lookin' for the meanest, roughest, toughest whore in town."

"You sure have found her," said the woman. Then she stripped naked, bent over and grabbed her ankles.

The miner said: "How d'ya know I want to do it in that position?"

"I don't," she said, "but I thought ya might want to open those beers first!"

What's the difference between a call girl and a hooker? – A call girl doesn't have to worry about hitting her head on the steering wheel.

A hooker was on special offer at the town brothel for just £20 a time. Frank was so desperate for sex that he decided to take advantage of the discount, no matter how rough she was. The only rule was that the lights had to remain off the entire time and under no circumstances was the client permitted to go down on her.

At that price, Frank shagged her twice a week for the next month until finally he was unable to resist the urge to eat her pussy that he had repeatedly been warned was off limits. Moments later, the pimp heard Frank vomiting upstairs.

"You went down on her, didn't you?" growled the pimp.

"Yeah," said Frank, horrified, "and I got a mouthful of rice."

"That wasn't rice," said the pimp. "She's been dead for two months."

An inexperienced guy went into a brothel, but wasn't sure exactly what he wanted. To help him make up his mind, the Madam at the front desk told him to go outside to a fence that had three holes. She told him to stick his dick in each of the holes and then make a choice.

He stuck his dick in the first hole and got it sucked for a few seconds. He stuck his dick in the second hole and felt a hand starting to jerk him off. Finally, he stuck his dick in the third hole and felt it slip into a warm pussy. Then he returned to the front desk.

"Well, which woman do you want?" asked the Madam.

"Forget the women," he said. "I want thirty yards of that fence!"

If you have sex with a hooker without her permission, does it count as shoplifting?

A young US sailor was on shore leave in Korea for the first time. While the rest of the guys were enjoying the attractions of the city's red-light district, he was too shy to come right out and ask the hookers what they charged for sex. After enduring two nights of frustration, on the third night he hatched a cunning plan to get laid. So when one of the local girls approached him and asked him his name, he answered: "Rick Peanus."

"Lick Peanus?" she queried.

"Sure," said the sailor. "How much?"

Did you hear about the hooker who had an appendix operation? – Now she's making money on the side.

Three hookers were sitting at a bar. The first one said: "I can get three fingers up my fanny." And she proceeded to give the other two a demonstration.

The second one said: "That's nothing. I can get a whole fist in there." And she duly obliged to show the other two.

The third one slid down the barstool.

A cop approached a teenage hooker on a street corner and sighed: "What would your mother do if she saw you carrying on like this?"

"She'd kill me," said the hooker. "This is her corner!"

One afternoon, a hooker brought a guy home, took him inside and started down the hallway. All along the hallway there were pictures of dicks. Finally, the guy asked to whom they belonged.

"Oh," said the hooker, "they are my favourite clients."

"Shit!" the guy thought to himself. "Mine is only half the size of theirs!"

Just then the hooker said: "Wait here a minute while I go and get ready!"

As soon as she left the room, the guy ran down to the shops and bought the biggest cucumber he could find. When he got back he jumped into bed with the hooker and started to push the cucumber in and out of her.

"Oh yeah, baby!" she moaned ecstatically. "That's great. I love a good fingering before a fuck!"

What's the best thing about having a sister who's a hooker? – The family discount.

A brothel owner answered the door to find a distinguished-looking man in his late forties standing there.

"Can I help you?" she asked.

"I want to see Donna," he replied.

"Sir, I have to tell you that Donna is one of our most expensive ladies," said the brothel owner. "She is in great demand, almost fully booked for months ahead. Perhaps you would prefer someone else?"

But the man was adamant. "No, I must see Donna."

"Very well," said the brothel owner. "I'll see if she can spare you thirty minutes."

A few minutes later, Donna appeared and told the man that she charged $1,000 for half an hour. Without hesitation, he pulled out ten $100 bills, gave them to Donna and they went upstairs. After his allotted time was up, he left.

The next night, the man visited the brothel again and insisted on seeing Donna. The owner was amazed and explained that nobody had ever come back to Donna two nights in a row because she was simply too expensive. When Donna appeared, she reminded the man that she charged $1,000 for half an hour – and no discounts. Again he pulled ten $100 bills from his wallet, handed the money to Donna and they went upstairs. Half an hour later he left.

The following night the man was there again, demanding to see Donna. Nobody at the brothel could believe that he was back for a third successive night but, as before, he paid Donna $1,000 in cash and they went upstairs.

After their session was over, Donna said to him: "Nobody has ever been with me three nights in a row. Where are you from?"

The man replied: "South Dakota."

"Really?" said Donna. "I have family in South Dakota."

"I know," said the man. "Your father died last month, and I am your sister's attorney. She asked me to give you your $3,000 inheritance."

What do bungee jumpers and hookers have in common? – They both cost £100 and if the rubber breaks you're screwed.

A man walked into a brothel late one night. He wanted to get a good-looking girl, but they were all busy with other clients. So he ended up with the most God-awful-looking, saggy old crone, and he was so disgusted, all he could do was shit in her face.

To his surprise, he really enjoyed this. This became a nightly routine for him, as he would ask for the old whore and shit in her face. Unfortunately, after a couple weeks, the novelty wore off, so the next time he went in, he asked for a pretty girl and fucked her.

As he was leaving, the old whore ran up to him, fell at his feet and said: "What's the matter, don't you love me anymore?"

What do you call a hooker with a runny nose? – Full.

An English tourist and his wife were walking around Amsterdam's red-light district. He looked at the hookers sitting in the windows and said to his wife: "There's a job for you."

"What?" she said, quietly flattered. "Do you think I could make good money on the game?"

"Fuck, no!" he exclaimed. "The windows need cleaning."

What do you call a hooker with cum on her face? – A taxi. Her job's done.

Two prostitutes were walking around London's Soho. One said to her friend: "I think I might be pregnant."

"Have you had a check-up?"

"No, I think he was Polish."

A man was walking through the streets of Bangkok when a small girl approached him for sex.

"No," he said. "You're far too young."

The girl said: "How do you know my name?"

Why are hookers like bowling balls? – Both get picked up, fingered and then banged down an alley.

A guy went into a brothel, and said to the Madam: "I have this problem. I take a long time to orgasm, so I need a girl that will outlast me!"

The Madam said: "Okay, we have Lynnette, she lasts a while."

So the guy went into the room, but half an hour later he walked out complaining: "You said she lasts a while, but she only lasted half an hour. I need someone with more staying power."

"Okay," said the Madam, "you can try Shelley. She is in the room at the end of the corridor, and she lasts for ages."

So he tried again. This time he was away for an hour, but he walked out complaining again: "Sorry, but she was still not good enough. I need longer than that before I orgasm."

"Okay," said the Madam, "we have Maxine, but you have to wear this black condom."

"Okay, I will try anything," said the man.

An hour and a half later he came out, with a smile on his face. "That was amazing," he said. "She lasted forever, but why the black condom?"

"Well," said the Madam, "you have to have some respect for the dead!"

Hospital

Two men were in the same hospital ward. "What are you in for?" asked the first.

"Camera down the throat," replied the second.

"Oh, endoscopy?"

"Yes, checking for stomach cancer. What about you?"

"Camera up the arse."

"Oh, colonoscopy. Checking for bowel cancer, are they?"

"No, my neighbour was sunbathing in the nude and my wife caught me taking a photo."

A guy was lying in his hospital bed, wired up with drips and monitors, breathing with the aid of an oxygen mask. A young woman was going round the ward with the tea trolley and when she reached his bed she asked him: "Is there anything you would like?"

"Yes," he answered. "Could you tell me if my testicles are black?"

"I'm sorry, but I'm not medical staff," she replied. "I can't help you with that."

"Oh, please have a look for me," he begged. "I'm really worried. Are my testicles black?"

Taking pity on his obvious distress, the girl glanced around the ward and, seeing no sign of any medical staff, said: "All right, I'll have a look for you." So she pulled back the bedcover, lifted his dick out of the way and, cupping his balls in her hand, told him: "No, they look fine to me."

The patient immediately pulled off his oxygen mask and shouted: "I asked, 'Are my test results back?'"

In hospital, what's grey, sits at the end of the bed and takes the piss out of you? – A kidney dialysis machine.

Four nurses decided to play a trick on a particularly arrogant hospital doctor. Later, each discussed what they had done.

The first nurse said: "I stuffed cotton wool in his stethoscope so that he couldn't hear."

The second nurse said: "I let the mercury out of his thermometers and painted them all to read 105 degrees."

The third nurse said: "I poked holes in all of the condoms he keeps in his desk drawer."

And the fourth nurse fainted.

One of the young children on the Intensive Care Unit is playing with a toy donkey: ICU baby, shaking that ass.

At the end of a twenty-hour hospital shift, an exhausted nurse walked into a bank. Preparing to write a cheque, she unwittingly pulled a rectal thermometer out of her pocket and started to write with it. Realizing her mistake she wailed: "Oh, that's just great! Some asshole's got my pen!"

Did you hear about the nurse who swallowed a razor blade? – She gave herself a tonsillectomy, an appendectomy, a hysterectomy and circumcised three of the doctors on her shift.

A nurse was walking down a hospital corridor when she was spotted by her supervisor. The supervisor couldn't believe what she was seeing. The nurse's hair was unkempt, her skirt was crumpled, and to round things off, her left breast was hanging out of the open front of her uniform.

"Nurse Vickers!" boomed the supervisor. "What is the meaning of this? Why are you walking around the hospital not only looking like a tramp, but with your breast exposed?"

"Oh," said the nurse, stuffing her breast back into her uniform. "It's those damn interns! They never put anything back when they're through using it."

Hygiene

Three personal-hygiene product salesmen were attending a conference. All were envious of a fourth guy, Eric, whose sales figures had gone through the roof. He had won every award available and they were keen to know the secret of his success.

"It's simple," said Eric. "I get a pile of dog shit, garnish it with some lettuce, tomato, onion and a few olives and serve it up on a crispbread in a shopping mall. As soon as people taste it, they go: 'Ugh! This tastes like shit!' And I say: 'That's exactly what it is. Would you like to buy a toothbrush?' "

How can you tell if it's way past time for a woman to douche? – When you spot her odour-eaters crawling up her leg.

How does a woman know if her husband is cheating on her? – He starts taking two showers a week.

A businessman was standing at the bar next to a scruffy guy whose personal hygiene left a lot to be desired. Eventually the stench of stale sweat became so unbearable that the businessman turned to him and asked pointedly: "Do you have a shower after you've had sex?"

"Yes, of course I do," the scruffy man replied.

"Well, don't you think it's about time you went home and had a shag?"

Impotence

What's the difference between anxiety and panic? – Anxiety is when, for the first time, you can't do it the second time; panic is when, for the second time, you can't do it the first time.

A little old couple were sitting on the couch watching the Playboy movie channel. He looked at her and asked: "Do you think we can still do that?"

"We can sure try!" she answered.

So they shuffled off to the bedroom. He went into the bathroom to get ready and she took off all her clothes in the bedroom. When he came out of the bathroom, he saw her standing on her head in the middle of the bedroom floor.

"What are you doing?" he asked.

"Well," she replied, "I thought if you couldn't get it up, maybe you could just drop it in!"

Did you hear about the guy who scheduled an appointment with an impotence clinic? – He had to cancel because something came up.

A man arrived home with a huge tub of ice cream. He asked his wife if she wanted some.

"How hard is it?" she asked.

"As hard as my dick," he smiled.

To which the woman replied: "Okay, then. Pour me some."

A man told his doctor: "Doc, I can't get aroused for my wife anymore."

"Very well," said the doctor. "Bring her with you tomorrow and I'll see what I can do."

The next day the man returned with his wife. The doctor told her to take off all her clothes and to sit on the bed with her legs apart. After a few moments he asked her to get dressed again. While she was getting dressed, the doctor took the husband to one side. "Don't worry," he said. "You're in perfect health – your wife didn't give me an erection either."

An elderly gentleman came home one night to find a girl of about seventeen ransacking the place. He grabbed her by the arm and was just about to call the police when the girl dropped down on her knees and pleaded: "Please don't call the police, mister, oh please! If you don't, I'll let you make love to me and do whatever you want with my body!"

The old man thought for a moment and decided to give in. Soon they were naked and in bed together. The old man tried and tried but he just couldn't get an erection. Finally, he rolled over, exhausted and embarrassed. "I'm sorry, young lady . . . but it's no use," he gasped. "I'm afraid . . . I'm going to have to . . . call the police . . . after all."

A young man was shipwrecked alone on a remote island. Although he had plenty of food and water, there was nothing much for him to do except play with himself. However, after six years of solitary pleasure even that began to become monotonous and he struggled to get an erection. With no sign of happiness on the horizon, he slowly started to lose his sanity. Then one morning while he was lying on the beach, he thought he saw a ship in the distance. He quickly started a fire, and then threw wet seaweed on top until smoke was billowing high into the air. The ship started to come his way.

He became really excited and thought to himself: "At last I'm going to be saved! The first thing I want is to take a long, hot shower. Then they're going to have to give me some clothes and I'll go upstairs and have a nice dinner. I will find a beautiful woman to dance with, then I'll take her to her cabin and we can kiss and I can fondle her body all over. She'll start to take off her clothes and she'll be wearing tiny red silk panties that barely cover her crotch!"

At this, he finally started to get an erection. He quickly slipped his hand into his shorts, grabbed his dick and yelled: "Ha! Ha! Fooled you! I lied about the ship!"

Incest

Swearing is like having sex with your sister – you always feel awkward doing it in front of your mum.

Incest: I can relate to that.

A sixteen-year-old boy went into the bathroom and started pleasuring himself, forgetting that he hadn't locked the door. Suddenly his mother walked in, leaving him hugely embarrassed. "It's okay," she said. "It's nothing to be ashamed about. It's perfectly natural. But here, let me show you, you're not doing it right." With that, she took hold of his dick and soon got so carried away that they ended up having full sex on the bathroom floor.

When they finished, she said: "Wow! You're even better than your father."

The boy replied: "Yep, that's what my sister said, too."

I think pot should be legal. I also think if your cousin is super-hot, you should be able to fuck one time. (Dave Attell)

I think my uncle must have been a ventriloquist. He used to put his hand up my arse and tell me not to talk.

One night, a man said to his wife: "Darling, let's try something new in the bedroom. I'll get some chocolate spread, some whipped cream and a few strawberries. Then I'll paint my cock with the chocolate spread, and invite my sisters round for a 'special treat'. Then, one by one, I'll pop the strawberries up my arse, squirt cream down my crack, and while Kylie deepthroats me for the last of the chocolate, Katie can my lick my arsehole and swallow strawberries as I shit them out. Then I'll finish off by banging them a couple of times before squirting my creamy load over their faces. Shall we give it a go?"

The wife looked stunned. "*Over my dead body!*" she yelled.

"Bloody hell!" he said "You're into some weird stuff!"

My village is staging its annual incest competition. I've entered my sister.

Inflatable Dolls

My new girlfriend really takes my breath away. She's inflatable.

A man went into a sex shop and asked for an inflatable doll.

"Male or female?" asked the shopkeeper.

"Female."

"Black or white?"

"White."

"Christian or Muslim?"

The man was puzzled and asked: "What's religion got to do with it? It's an inflatable doll!"

"Well," said the shopkeeper, "the Muslim one blows itself up."

I had to dump my inflatable doll. I let her down gently.

Internet

The internet: where men are men, women are women, and children are the FBI.

Did you hear about the woman who was such a slag that when she got poked on Facebook it used four fingers?

A husband called out to his wife: "I tried to log on to the internet this morning but it wouldn't let me in. Have you changed the password?"

"Yes," she called back.

"What is it?"

"It's the date of our anniversary."

"Bitch!"

A police officer knocked on the door of a house and told the occupant: "I'm sorry, sir, but we think your wife has been involved in a fatal car crash. We'd like you to come and identify the body."

"I'm a bit busy right now," said the man. "Can't you take a photo of the body and tag me on Facebook? If it's her, I'll click the 'like' button."

The twenty-first century: when deleting history is more important than making it.

I hate those emails where they try to sell you penis enhancers. I got ten just the other day – eight of them from my girlfriend. It's the two from my mum that really hurt. (Jimmy Carr)

Did you hear about the guy who looked up himself on the internet? – Now his webcam smells of poop.

I Googled "Gary Oldman" and got some rather disturbing images. He's really let himself go, I thought. Then I realized I'd accidentally omitted the "r".

The Irish

Paddy phoned his local paper and asked how much it cost to place an advert.

"Five euros an inch," replied the saleswoman.

"That's too expensive," said Paddy.

"Why? What are you selling?"

"A ten-foot ladder," said Paddy.

Paddy's wife was about to give birth, so he rushed her to hospital. On arrival, the nurse asked: "How dilated is she?"

"Oh Jaysus!" beamed Paddy. "We're both over the moon!"

An Irish country doctor was desperate to go away on a midweek fishing trip, so he asked a young family friend to conduct his surgery in his absence even though the friend had no medical training.

"Michael," said the doctor, "I am going fishing tomorrow and I don't want to close the clinic. So I want you to look after the clinic for the day and take care of my patients. It's easy really. Most things you can just look up in the textbook – but anything serious, refer to the hospital."

"Okay," said Michael.

So the doctor went fishing and returned the following day. "So, Michael," he asked. "How was your day?"

Michael told him that he took care of three patients. "The first one had a headache, so I gave him Paracetamol."

"Well done, Michael," said the doctor. "And the second one?"

"The second one had indigestion and I gave him Gaviscon."

"Excellent," said the doctor. "You're good at this. And what about the third one?"

"Well," said Michael, "I was sitting here and suddenly the door flew open and a gorgeous young woman burst in. She tore off all her clothes, including her bra and her panties, and lay down on the table, spreading her legs and shouting: "Do something. I haven't seen a man for five years!"

"My God! What did you do?" asked the doctor.

"I gave her eye drops."

Paddy got a phone call one night to say that his wife had been in an accident. He rushed to the hospital and asked the nurse: "How is she? Can I see her?"

The nurse said: "I'm afraid you're too late."

"Okay," said Paddy. "No problem. I'll come back in the morning."

How many potatoes does it take to kill an Irishman? – None.

Paddy got a job as a carpenter on a building site, but on his first day he forgot to wear his hard hat. As he walked under some scaffolding, a workman above dropped a Stanley knife and it sliced Paddy's ear clean off.

As Paddy screamed in pain, the whole site workforce came running, looking for the lost ear. After a few seconds a guy found an ear in a pile of rubble and shouted: "Is this it!?"

Paddy looked up and shouted back: "No, mine had a pencil behind it!"

When Paddy couldn't get a dance at the local ceilidh, his friend decided to tell him the truth.

"Look, it's the smell from your socks. Go home and change them and you'll have no trouble."

Later in the evening Paddy complained that he still couldn't get a dance.

"Did you change your socks?" asked the friend.

"Of course I did," said Paddy, pulling them from his pocket.

An Irishman walked in to a branch of Home Depot and asked: "Can I order 1,600 bricks please?"

"That's a lot of bricks," said the store assistant. "Are you building a house?"

"No," said the Irishman, "I'm building a barbecue."

"A barbecue? Why do you need 1,600 bricks for a barbecue?"

"Because I live on the eighth floor."

One summer's night, Paddy felt uncomfortably warm in bed. His wife told him: "When I get too hot, I use the other side of the pillow."

Sadly, Paddy died of suffocation a few minutes later.

A student decided to hold a party where his guests came as different emotions – fear, happiness, misery and so on. The first guest turned up covered in green paint with the letters N and V painted on his chest.

"What have you come as?" asked the host.

"I'm green with envy," came the reply.

"Hey, that's brilliant! Come in and have a drink."

A few minutes later, a woman showed up, wearing a pink body-stocking with a feather boa wrapped around her private parts.

"Wow, great outfit!" laughed the host. "And you've come as . . .?"

"I'm tickled pink," she said.

"That's great! Come in and have a drink."

Shortly afterwards, the doorbell rang again, and this time there were two naked Irish guys standing there. One was standing with his penis in a bowl of custard while the other had a pear on the end of his dick.

"What emotions are you two supposed to represent?" asked the host.

"Well," said one of the guys, "I'm fucking dis custard and he's come in dis pear!"

Paddy came home from work to find his wife in a foul mood.

She stormed: "A colleague of mine saw you kissing another woman last night! Come on, who was it?"

"How the hell should I know?" Paddy replied. "You work with over a hundred people."

A man walked into a bar and saw Paddy with an empty pint glass on the table in front of him.

"Would you like another one?" asked the man.

Paddy said: "Now what would I be wanting with two empty glasses?"

Paddy and his two English friends were talking in a bar. The first friend said: "I think my wife is having an affair with a carpenter. The other day I came home and found a hammer under the bed, and it wasn't mine."

The second friend said: "I think my wife is having an affair with an electrician. The other day I came home and found wire cutters under the bed, and they weren't mine."

Paddy said: "I think my wife is having an affair with a horse."

"What on earth makes you think that?" asked his friends.

"Because," said Paddy, "the other day I came home and found a jockey under the bed."

A policeman was called out to a farm in Limerick where the farmer had reported losing 2,033 pigs. The policeman took down the details but when he got back to the station to enter the theft on to the police computer, he decided to double-check the exact number with the farmer.

"Mr O'Donovan," he said, "are you absolutely sure that you lost 2,033 pigs?"

"Oh yeth, dat ith right," said the farmer.

Satisfied, the policeman put down the phone and typed: "Farmer lost two sows and thirty-three pigs."

Two Irish couples decided to swap partners. Afterwards Paddy said to Mick: "That's the best fuck I've ever had. I wonder how the girls got on?"

A guy was flying his hot-air balloon over southern Ireland and was completely lost. He looked down and spotted Paddy fishing on a lake, so he shouted down: "Hello there, could you please tell me where I am?"

Paddy shouted up: "You can't fool me, mister. You're in that feckin' basket!"

An Irishman went for a job interview, but the manager insisted on giving him a maths test before taking him on.

"Right. Here's your first question," said the manager. "Without using numbers, represent the number nine."

"Without numbers?" said the Irishman. "Dat's easy." And he drew three trees.

"What's that supposed to be?" asked the manager.

"It's obvious," said the Irishman. "Tree and tree and tree make nine."

"Okay, I'll let you have that," conceded the manager grudgingly. "Here's your second question. Using the same rules as for the first question, represent the number ninety-nine."

The Irishman thought for a moment, then picked up the picture that he had just drawn and made a smudge on each tree. He then handed the picture to the manager.

The manager looked at it blankly. "How on earth does this represent ninety-nine?"

"Well," explained the Irishman. "Each of da trees is dirty now. So it's dirty tree and dirty tree and dirty tree. Dat's ninety-nine."

Having been outfoxed twice, the manager was growing concerned that he might actually have to hire the Irishman, but he had one more trick up his sleeve. "Okay," he said. "Last question. Using the same rules as before, represent the number one hundred."

The Irishman thought for a few seconds, then picked up the picture again and drew a little mark at the base of each tree. He then handed the drawing triumphantly to the manager with the words: "Dere you go. One hundred!"

The manager was more bewildered than ever. "There is no way that this drawing represents one hundred."

"I think you'll find it does."

"Show me!"

The Irishman leaned across the desk and pointed to the newly drawn marks at the base of each tree. "You see dose?" he said. "A little dog came along and pooped by each tree. So now you've got dirty tree and a turd, dirty tree and a turd, and dirty tree and a turd – and dat makes one hundred. So when do I start?"

Paddy marched into a UK job centre and complained: "I've been ringing 08001730 for two days now trying to get an appointment!"

The clerk behind the counter said: "Did you call the number on our door?"

"Yes," replied Paddy. "That's what I said: 08001730."

"No, sir," said the clerk. "Those are our opening times."

Paddy was walking down the street with one of his shoelaces undone. Mick saw this and called out: "Hey, Paddy, watch you don't trip up over your laces."

"Yeah, it's these bloody instructions," said Paddy.

"What instructions, Paddy?"

"Underneath the shoe, it says 'Taiwan'."

An Irishman applying for a job as a blacksmith was asked whether he had any experience of shoeing horses.

He said: "No, but I once told a donkey to fuck off."

Mick set up Paddy on a blind date. Mick said: "She's a lovely girl, but there's something you should know: she's expecting a baby."

The next day, Mick asked Paddy how the date had gone.

"I remembered what you'd told me," said Paddy, "but I must say she looked surprised when I walked into the bar wearing a romper suit and nappy."

A guy was walking down a street in Cork when he saw two cars in a driveway with a sign saying "Boat for Sale".

He knocked on the door of the house and asked the Irish owner: "Why does your sign say 'Boat for Sale'? I can only see two cars."

"Dat's right," said the Irishman, "and dey're boat for sale."

Limping on crutches, a Yorkshire farmer spotted an Irishman walking down the lane. He hobbled over to the Irishman and said: "I've got 248 sheep. Can you round them up for me?"

"Sure," replied the Irishman. "250."

Paddy walked into a New York City barber's that charged $70 for a haircut.

"How much do you want off?" asked the barber, sitting him in the chair.

"Sixty dollars," said Paddy."

An Irishman had been missing for weeks. His wife told the police. Next day, the police arrived to tell her that her husband's body had been found floating in the river.

"That couldn't be him," she said, "because he couldn't swim."

Paddy phoned a helper at an animal-rescue centre and said: "I've just found a suitcase in the woods containing a cat and four kittens."

"That's terrible," replied the helper. "Are they moving?"

"I'm not sure, to be honest," said Paddy. "But that would explain the suitcase."

Paddy and Mick went into a bar in Scotland. Paddy asked the bartender: "Is there any good fishing around here?"

"Certainly," said the bartender. "The fish are thick in the water. You don't even need to put the rod in – you just reach in and pull them out! Big salmon! On your way home tonight, get your friend to hold you over the bridge by your legs and you can pull the salmon out of the water."

The two agreed: "Yes, we'll try that when we get to the bridge."

So on their way home they came to the bridge and Mick held Paddy upside down by his legs, waiting for the salmon. After three minutes, Paddy suddenly shouted: "Quick! Pull me up!"

Mick shouted back: "Have you caught a salmon?"

"No," said Paddy, "there's a train coming!"

Two Irish terrorists were making letter bombs. After they had finished, one said: "Do you think I put enough explosive in this envelope?"

"I don't know," said the other. "Open it and see."

"But it will explode."

"Don't be stupid! It's not addressed to you!"

As they prepared for a romantic vacation in Florida, Paddy and his wife talked about the kinky things they wanted to do to each other.

The wife said: "I've never told you about this, darling, but I've always wanted to be handcuffed."

So Paddy planted a kilo of cocaine in her suitcase.

An Englishman was chatting to an Irish guy in a Belfast bar and soon the conversation turned to religion and the Troubles.

The Irish guy revealed: "I'm a member of the Lemon Order."

The Englishman said: "Surely you mean the Orange Order?"

"No, we're more bitter than them."

An Englishman, a Scotsman and an Irishman were talking about their families.

The Englishman said: "My son was born on St George's Day, so we called him George."

"What a coincidence!" said the Scotsman. "My son was born on St Andrew's Day, so we called him Andrew."

"That's amazing," said the Irishman. "Wait till I get home and tell our Pancake!"

Italians

An elderly Italian couple arrived in New York. They stopped off at a shopping mall, but somehow became separated. The feisty Italian woman then went from store to store asking: "Hava you seena my Mario, balda head, potta belly and da baggy pants?"

Time after time, no one had seen her Mario until finally a sales clerk said that a man matching his description just ran out the back door "lickety-split".

The woman said: "No, no, that'sa notta my Mario. He may grabba da ass, pincha de tit, but he no lickety-split."

What's the difference between an Italian grandmother and an elephant? – Fifty pounds and a black dress.

Maria was sitting on her stoop eating a slice of pizza. Two of her girlfriends walked by and noticed that she wasn't wearing any underwear.

"Hey, Maria," one of them called out. "Did you take off your panties to keep yourself cool?"

"I don't know about keeping cool," she said, "but it sure keeps the flies away from my pizza!"

A band at an Italian wedding asked for requests from the guests. Antonio walked up to them and said: "Hey, do you guys know 'Strangers in Da Night'?"

"Sure we know that one," replied the bandleader.

"Dat's great!' said Antonio. "But I gotta one favour to ask. Could you play it in 5/4 time?"

"Isn't it played in 4/4 time?" asked the bandleader.

"Yeah, but dis here's a special occasion, you know?"

After briefly consulting his fellow musicians, the bandleader said: "Okay, we can do that."

Hearing this, Antonio turned and called out: "Hey, cousin Roberto! Come up here and sing!"

Cousin Roberto put down his drink, strolled up to the mike, and as the band started to play, he sang: "Strangers in da fuckin' night . . ."

Why don't Italians like Jehovah's Witnesses? – Italians don't like *any* witnesses.

On the night before her wedding, an Italian bride-to-be talked with her mother.

"Mama," she said, "I want you to teach me how to make my new husband happy."

The mother replied tenderly: "When two people adore, honour and respect each other, love can be a beautiful thing . . ."

The daughter interrupted: "I know how to fuck, Mama. I want you to teach me how to make great lasagne!"

How do we know Silvio Berlusconi prefers Ford cars to Fiats? – He likes to get into an Escort.

An Italian guy was recounting the tale of his trip to Toronto. He said: "One daya I go to Toronto and stay in bigga hotel. I go down to eat soma breakfast. I tella the waitress I wanna two pissa toast. She bringa me only one piss. I tella her I wanna two piss. She say, go to toilet. I say, you no understand, I wanna two piss on my plate. She say you betta no piss on plate, you sonna ma bitch. I don't even know da lady, ana she calla me sonna ma bitch!

"Then I go to pharmacia with da cougha. The man he give me candy ana tell me fa cough! Fa cough! I don't even know da guy, ana he tella me fa cough!

"Later I go to eat soma pasta downtown. The waitress she bring me spoon, a knife but no fock. I tella her I wanna fock. She tella me everybody wanna fock. I tella her, you no understand, I wanna fock on table. She say you betta no fock on table, you sonna ma bitch! I don't even know da lady, ana she calla me sonna ma bitch!

"So I go back to ma hotel room, and there's no sheet on da bed. I calla da manager and I tella him I wanna sheet. He tella me to go to toilet. I say, you no understand, I wanna sheet on bed. He say you betta no sheet on bed, you sonna ma bitch! I don't even know da guy, ana he calla me sonna ma bitch!

"I go to check out of hotel, and man at desk he say peace to you. I say, 'Peace on you, too, you sonna ma bitch!' I go back to Italy."

You Know You're Italian When . . .

- You have at least five cousins living on the same block.
- You can bench-press 325 pounds but still cry when your mother yells at you.
- You can only get one good shave from a disposable razor.
- There were more than twenty-five people in your bridal party.
- You netted more than $50,000 on your first communion.
- You have been chased around the kitchen table with a wooden spoon.
- You know at least fifteen different arm-waving gestures to convey the word "no".
- Your plumber, electrician, carpenter, mechanic, builder and lawyer are all your cousins.
- Your sister has back hair.
- If someone in your family grows taller than five foot nine inches, it is presumed his mother had an affair.
- You have to go by your middle name because all of your cousins were also named after your grandfather.

A New York doctor called in his next patient – an elderly Italian immigrant who sometimes struggled to understand the doctor's instructions.

The Italian opened his jacket and proudly put a model of Buzz Lightyear on the doctor's desk.

"I'm sorry. What's this for?" asked the doctor.

The Italian said: "You tell me bring specimen."

At the finish line of the famous Venice Canal Swimming Race, a reporter was waiting to interview Bruno, who had been the hot favourite to win the race but instead finished dead last.

"So, Bruno," asked the reporter. "What went wrong?"

"Well," explained Bruno, "at the start I was in the lead but then as I passed under the first bridge I saw the beautiful Carla standing on top of it looking very sexy. She was calling to me: 'Hey, Bruno, I am yours after the race.' Hearing this, I began to get aroused and this made my swimming trunks uncomfortable. Then when I passed under the second bridge the gorgeous Claudia was standing on it, caressing her breasts. She was calling to me: 'Hey, Bruno, these are for you after the race.' By now I was so aroused I was dragging in the mud and the other swimmers were catching me up. Then when I got to the third bridge the magnificent Maria was standing on top, stroking her fanny. She was calling to me: 'Hey, Bruno, I want you to fuck me every which way after the race.' That was too much for me. I was so aroused, I was stuck in the mud and all the other swimmers passed me. I am so sorry I let my fans down, but there was nothing I could do."

"Why didn't you try the backstroke?" asked the reporter.

Bruno smiled: "But what about the bridges?"

Jargon

404: Someone who's clueless. From the World Wide Web error message "404 Not Found", meaning that the requested document could not be located.

AIRPLANE BLONDE: One who has bleached or dyed her hair but still has a "black box".

AUSSIE KISS: Similar to a French kiss, but given down under.

BEAVER BEATER: A dildo.

BEER COAT: The invisible but warm coat worn when walking home after a booze cruise at 3 a.m.

BEER COMPASS: The invisible device that ensures your safe arrival home after a booze cruise, even though you're too drunk to remember where you live, how you got here and where you've come from.

BITCH: Beautiful Individual That Causes Hard-ons.

BOBFOC: Woman who looks great from behind but hideous from the front – "Body Off *Baywatch*, Face Off *Crimewatch*".

BUDGIE's TONGUE: Female erection.

BUM BEANS: The little bits of crap that get stuck in your rectum hairs.

BUTTERFACE: Everything's nice, but her face.

CANKLES: When you are so fat, your calves and ankles are the same size.

CHUBBY CHASER: Man with a preference for fat women.

DUMPSTER DAY: When you get a week's worth of poo out in one day.

FANNY BATTER: Vaginal excretion.

GNADGER SCRATCHER: A guy who shamelessly sticks his hands down his pants and rearranges the contents in full public view.

GRENADE: An ugly girl with a cute friend. Thus, your buddy has to jump on the grenade to save the team.

GREYHOUND: A very short skirt, only an inch from the hare.

HELIUM HEELS: A girl whose legs go up easily.

HELMET FOR YOUR LITTLE ASTRONAUT: A condom.

HOOVER GIRL: One who sucks hard.

IGNORANUS: Someone who's both ignorant and an asshole.

LAST-TIME BUYER: A person buying a place in a retirement home.

MYSTERY BUS: The bus that arrives at the pub on a Friday night while you're in the toilet after your tenth pint, and whisks away all the unattractive people so the pub is suddenly packed with stunners when you come back in.

MYSTERY TAXI: The taxi that arrives at your place on a Saturday morning before you wake up, whisks away the stunner you slept with, and leaves a Ten-Pinter in your bed instead.

NOONER: Having sex at lunchtime.

NUT-HUGGERS: Extremely tight pants on a man.

OH-NO SECOND: That minuscule fraction of time in which you realize that you've just made a big mistake (e.g. you've hit "reply all").

ORANGA-TRAMP: Long-haired ginger person.

PHANTOM CRAP: When you know you pushed a turd out but there is nothing in the toilet.

PICASSO BUM: A woman whose knickers are too small for her, so she looks like she's got four buttocks.

PIT STOP: Your regular check for armpit smell.

PORN BUDDY: A pact made with a friend so that in the unfortunate event of your death he will clear out of all of your porn stash to lessen the anguish of your poor parents.

RALPH: To vomit.

RANDOM ARM: When you're lying side by side with your partner and one of you has an arm that you don't quite know what to do with.

RAT BUSH: A hairstyle that looks normal at the front but is spiked up and messy at the back.

RESCUE DUMMY: A guy who swims out to sea to impress his girlfriend but ends up having to be rescued by a far more attractive and intelligent lifeguard.

REVERSE KANGA (Australian): Sitting on a toilet backwards to leave a long, filthy skid mark.

ROB: Rolls Over Belt – a fat person.

RPI: Random Pooing Incident.

SALAD DODGER: An overweight person.

SCROTCH: To scratch your crotch.

SCRUD: The dried-out skid marks on a toilet.

SEAGULL MANAGER: A manager who flies in, makes a lot of noise, craps on everything and then leaves.

SHED HEAD: Someone with a really big forehead. Ant McPartlin could be said to be a "shed head".

SINBAD: Single working girls. Single income, no boyfriend and desperate.

SLAG TAG: A big love bite.

SNATCH SPLITTER: A very large penis.

STAIR: Sexually Transmitted Aggressive Itchy Rash.

STELLA VISION: The result that drinking copious amounts of beer has on your opinion of a woman, e.g. "She looked sexy through Stella vision."

STINKPRETTY: Cheap perfume.

SWAMP DONKEY: A deeply unattractive person.

TACTICAL VOM: When you throw up, due to alcohol, so you can drink more.

TESTICULATING: Waving your arms around and talking bollocks.

THUNDER BLUNDER: When you let out a mega fart and the whole room shakes.

THUNDERWARE: Big panties.

WAFFLE CRAPPER: A girl that is so hot she could crap on your waffles every morning and you'd still want more.

WALLET: A girl who spends so much time on a sunbed she becomes brown and leathery.

WANK STAIN: Someone of little or no importance.

WHEELIE BINT: A girl so ugly that she is only taken out once a week.

YESTERGAY: Someone who used to be gay.

ZOO KEEPER: Someone who puts up with your crap.

Jehovah's Witnesses

Why are there no Jehovah's Witnesses in heaven? – Because God and St Peter are behind the pearly gates saying: "Ssssh! Pretend we're not in!"

A Jehovah's Witness gave me an advent calendar one Christmas. I opened the first door and there were two of them standing behind it.

Why don't Jehovah's Witnesses celebrate Halloween? – They don't like total strangers knocking on their door.

What's the world's shortest Jehovah's Witness joke? – Knock, knock.

Jesus Christ

One day, Jesus was sitting in heaven talking to God about how the world had become divided by war and religion. "I was thinking, Father," he said, "the people of the world seem to have lost their way and seem to have forgotten who I am."

"Well, there's an easy solution to that," replied God. "Why don't you go down to earth and visit your people? A personal appearance can work miracles."

So the next day Jesus left heaven and went down to earth. His first port of call was a Baptist church. He walked up to the preacher and asked: "Do you know who I am?"

"No, sir," replied the preacher. "I don't think I do."

Disillusioned, Jesus made his way to a Catholic church and asked the priest: "Do you know who I am?"

"Well, now," said the priest, "let me think. Were you the guy who repaired the church roof last year?"

"No, I wasn't," said Jesus.

"Then I'm afraid I don't know you," said the priest.

Thoroughly dejected because nobody appeared to recognize him, Jesus trudged into a synagogue and asked the rabbi: "Do you know who I am?"

The rabbi said: "Hmm, you look familiar, but let me see you in profile."

So Jesus turned to the side.

"I'm still not sure," said the rabbi. "Let me see the other side of your face."

So Jesus turned again.

"You definitely do look familiar," continued the rabbi, "but I need to be sure. Come here against this wall, spread out your arms and put your feet together."

So Jesus stood against the wall, spread his arms and put his feet together.

Suddenly, the rabbi grabbed a hammer and three nails and banged them into Jesus's hands and feet. "There!" he cackled. "Got you again!"

So what if Jesus turned water into wine? I turned a whole student loan into vodka once. (Sean Lock)

Adolf Hitler escaped from hell and made his way up to heaven. At the pearly gates, he said to St Peter: "I want to come in."

"No way," said St Peter.

"You don't understand," protested Hitler. "I've repented. I'm really sorry for all the terrible things I did and since I left hell I've been going around giving back all the gold and treasures that I stole from the Jews."

At that point, Jesus appeared on the scene and asked what was going on.

"It's Hitler," said St Peter. "The most evil man in history – he wants to come in."

"Get lost!" said Jesus.

"No, please believe me," said Hitler. "I'm a changed man. To prove it, I have here a six-foot solid-gold cross that I can't find the owner of. I could give it to you as a token of my sincerity."

Now Jesus was partial to crosses, so he decided to put the proposition to God. "Hey, Dad," said Jesus, "I've got Hitler outside and he wants to come in now he's repented."

"Tell him to clear off," said God.

"But Dad," continued Jesus, "he's given back all the gold he stole from the

Jews except for a six-foot solid-gold cross he can't find the owner of. He says he wants me to have it."

"And what do you want with a solid-gold cross?" scoffed God. "You couldn't even carry a wooden one!"

A woman was out Christmas shopping with her three young children. After hours of trailing around toy shops and hearing her kids asking for every item on the shelves, she was thoroughly fed up. Weighed down with bags, she squeezed herself and her kids into a crowded shopping mall elevator and sighed aloud, to nobody in particular: "Whoever started this whole Christmas thing should be arrested and strung up!"

A voice from the back of the elevator replied quietly: "Don't worry, ma'am, I believe they crucified him."

When Jesus went to heaven, was that not essentially "moving back in with your parents"? (Iain Stirling)

Jesus was out walking one day, when he came across a stoning. Jesus looked at the crowd and then said: "Those amongst you who have no sin shall throw the first stone."

Hearing this, a man at the back of the crowd yelled: "That's typical of you, Jesus. You always want to go first!"

One evening, a priest was sitting on a pew at the front of his church, quietly praying to the Lord. A hot blonde suddenly came in and the priest asked her: "What can I do for you, my child?"

The blonde immediately jumped on him and said: "I want you now! Take me!"

"I beg your pardon?!" the priest exclaimed.

"Fuck me now!" she said. "Fuck me hard up the ass!"

The priest by now was sweating and trembling at the sight of the blonde lifting up her blouse to reveal a pair of huge breasts. "But, my child," he protested, "you are in the house of the Lord."

"I don't care, take this horny virgin now, you sexy son of a bitch!"

The priest, now shaking, sweating terribly and feeling himself go hard, turned towards the front of the church and, looking up to the Lord, he cried: "Jesus Christ, help me. What should I do?"

A voice came back: "Don't just stand there, you idiot! Get me down off this bloody cross!"

Jewish People

What happens when a Jew with an erection walks into a wall? – He breaks his nose.

Two beggars – one Jewish, the other Catholic – were sitting side by side in a street in Rome. One had the Star of David in front of him; the other had a cross. A number of people passed by and looked at both beggars, but only put money into the hat of the one sitting behind the cross.

Among the crowds was a priest who paused and watched dozens of people giving to the beggar behind the cross while completely ignoring the one behind the Star of David. Eventually he felt so sorry for the beggar behind the Star of David that he went over to offer him a little advice.

"My dear fellow," said the priest, "don't you understand? This is a Catholic country; this city is the home of Catholicism. People aren't going to give money if you sit there with a Star of David in front of you, especially when you're sitting beside a beggar who has a cross. In fact, people who might not ordinarily give to beggars are probably giving him money purely to spite you."

The beggar behind the Star of David listened to the priest, then turned to the beggar behind the cross and said: "Benny, look who's trying to teach the Rosenthal brothers about marketing!"

Why does a British fifty-pence piece have seven sides? – So that you can prise it out of a Jew's hand with a spanner.

At the end of a successful week in his tailoring business, a little Jewish guy decided to treat himself by going to the local brothel. The Madam said: "Well, you can have this nice Chinese girl over there for £20, then I have a redhead for £30 and this terrific blonde for £45." Throwing caution to the wind, the Jewish guy opted for the £30 redhead and had a marvellous time.

More than twenty years later his wife had died and he felt lonely, so once again he went to the brothel. He immediately recognized the redhead, who was now the Madam, and they had a friendly reunion. Then suddenly a strapping young man of about twenty appeared and called out:

"Mum, is this guy bothering you?"

"No, no," said the Madam. "In fact, Ben, I'd like you to meet your father."

"What?" said Ben. "This little Jewish bloke's my father?"

The Jewish guy responded: "Watch your manners! If I hadn't been so generous, you'd have been Chinese!"

I was raped by a doctor, which is so bittersweet for a Jewish girl. (Sarah Silverman)

Three Jews were sentenced to death and put in front of a military firing squad.

The officer asked the first condemned man: "Do you want a blindfold?"

"Yes, sir."

The officer asked the second condemned man: "Do you want a blindfold?"

"Yes, sir."

The officer asked the third condemned man: "Do you want a blindfold?"

"No, I don't want anything from you!"

The second man turned to the third and whispered anxiously in his ear: "Solly, don't make trouble now."

A Jewish mother learned that her daughter's male piano teacher had been charged on twenty-nine counts of indecently assaulting teenage girls. She had to find out whether her daughter had been one of his victims, so she asked her: "When you have your piano lessons with Mr Rose, has he ever made any comments of a sexual nature to you?"

"No, Mum. Never."

"Has he ever looked at you in a way that's made you feel uncomfortable?"

"No, Mum. Never."

"Has he ever rubbed himself up against you?"

"No, Mum. Never."

"Has he ever tried to kiss you?"

"No, Mum. Never."

"Has he ever touched you anywhere strange, like on your chest or inner thighs?"

"No, Mum. Never."

The interrogation over, the mother drove straight to the piano teacher's house and confronted him. "You filthy pervert!" she raged. "So my beautiful daughter's not good enough for you?"

A wealthy Jew owned a company that manufactured nails. His only son had just graduated from college and the father wanted to get him involved in the family business. At first, he sent the young man to learn the ropes in various different departments – research and development, then manufacturing and then sales, but in each the son proved a major disappointment. Determined to find a place for his offspring, the father decided that his son needed his own project.

So the father put him in charge of the firm's new advertising campaign. He told him that he would have no supervision and that all of the resources he needed would be placed at his disposal. In effect, he was his own boss. The son was delighted by the faith his father was showing in him and vowed to repay his confidence.

A month later, the son informed his father that he had devised an advertising campaign and took him to a site in town to look at the billboard. As they drove to the location, the son explained how he had been struggling for ideas until having a sudden flash of inspiration. They turned the corner and, to the father's horror, the giant billboard depicted Christ on a cross with the caption: "Even Then They Used Goldstein Nails."

The father explained to his son that they couldn't portray Christ on a cross because it might offend their Christian clients. Dejected, the son said he would rethink the campaign and report back in due course.

A week later, the son phoned his father to tell him that he had resolved the problem and drove him out to see the billboard. Sure enough, in accordance with his father's instructions, Christ was no longer on the cross; instead he was lying at the base.

The caption read: "This Wouldn't Happen with Goldstein Nails."

How do you get a Jewish woman to go to bed with you? – Have a circumcision: they can't say no to anything that's 10 per cent off.

The Italian guy said: "I'm tired and thirsty, I must have wine."
    The French guy said: "I'm tired and thirsty, I must have cognac."
    The Australian guy said: "I'm tired and thirsty, I must have beer."
    The Russian guy said: "I'm tired and thirsty, I must have vodka."
    The Jewish guy said: "I'm tired and thirsty, I must have diabetes."

At a meeting in a synagogue, Benjamin asked the rabbi: "Rabbi, why are people always so suspicious of us?"

"That's an interesting question," said the rabbi. "How about we all talk about it tomorrow over some vodka? Each one of you should bring a bottle of vodka so we can mix it in a big pot and drink and discuss, and the answer will become clear."

Benjamin went home and thought to himself: "If everyone else is going to bring a bottle of vodka, I can bring a bottle of water and no one will notice the difference."

So the next day, he took along a bottle of water to the meeting. The rabbi poured all the drink together in one pot and started mixing it. "Well, Rabbi," said Benjamin, "what is the answer to my question? Why are people always so suspicious of us?"

The rabbi filled a cup and said: "Drink this, Benjamin."

Benjamin drank it and said: "But this is water!"

"Yes," said the rabbi, "and that is why people are always so suspicious of us."

What's the definition of a Jewish pervert? – Someone who likes girls more than money.

Two Jewish mothers met up for their regular weekly chat. One said: "Before we go any further, I have good news and bad news to impart."

"Tell me the bad news," said the other.

"My Joshua phoned last night to tell me he's gay."

"Oh my! How terrible for you – and after all that you've done for that boy! But you mustn't blame yourself, you've been a wonderful mother. Now tell me the good news."

"He's marrying a doctor."

Look at the insane things the Jews believe. The Jews believe that Barbra Streisand is worth 1,000 bucks a ticket. (Greg Giraldo)

How was copper wire invented? – Years ago, two Jews found the same penny.

A man called on his Jewish friend one evening and found him removing the wallpaper from the walls of his lounge.

"Doing some decorating, are you?" inquired the man.

"No," said the Jewish guy. "We're moving."

I was just offered a job in Palestine. They offered me half a million dollars plus funeral expenses. (Jackie Mason)

How is Christmas celebrated in a Jewish home? – They put parking meters on the roof.

Mrs Goldstein and Mrs Rosenthal got chatting in the park. Mrs Goldstein said: "See that boy over there? Look how big his head is! That's the biggest head on a child I've ever seen!"

Mrs Rosenthal said: "That's my grandson."

"That big head," said Mrs Goldstein, "it suits him."

How do you make a Jewish omelette? – First you borrow three eggs . . .

A daughter phoned her mother to tell her that she was marrying a gentile. The mother seemed surprisingly unconcerned, even when the daughter added that her husband-to-be had been married before, was unemployed and that they would have to live in the family home. The mother even offered her own bed.

"But where will you sleep?" asked the daughter.

"Oh, don't worry about me," replied the mother. "The minute you hang up I'm going to kill myself anyway!"

Mr and Mrs Solomon worked their fingers to the bone just so that their son, Benjamin, could go to college. They were overjoyed and they spared no expense to send him off in style. A few months later he returned home on break, and the Solomons went to the airport to meet him.

When he got off the plane, Mrs Solomon threw her arms around him and cried: "Benjie, it's so good to have you home."

Her son drew back and said: "Please, Mother, you must stop calling me Benjie. I'm eighteen years old now, not a little boy."

His mother apologized meekly and tried a new topic of conversation. "Were you a good boy? Did you eat only kosher like I told you?"

But again Benjamin was firm. "Mother, this is the twenty-first century," he said. "It is foolish to observe all those old dietary laws when everyone knows they were invented only because of dangers to your health. All of those dangers are gone now that we have refrigeration and chemical preservatives. I don't keep kosher, and you shouldn't bother to either."

"Well," said his mother, "did you at least go to synagogue?"

"To tell the truth, Mother, I didn't. All the guys go to the college chapel on Sunday for a non-denominational service."

At this point Mrs Solomon lost control. "Just tell me one thing, Benjamin," she said bitterly. "Are you still circumcised?"

What did the Jewish paedophile say? – "Wanna buy a sweetie, little girl?"

A Jewish woman said to her mother: "I'm divorcing Hymie. All he ever wants is anal sex, and so my asshole is now the size of a fifty-cents piece when it used to be the size of a ten-cents piece."

Her mother said: "You're married to a multimillionaire, you live in an eight-bedroom mansion, you drive a Mercedes, you get a $7,000 weekly allowance, you get seven holidays a year! And you want to throw all that away for forty cents?"

Kissing

What's better than snatching a kiss? – Vice versa.

A guy was sitting on the couch watching a romantic movie with his girlfriend. She was lying with her head in his lap.

At the end of the movie, wiping back the tears, she said: "Give me a kiss."

He said: "If I could reach down that far to kiss you, I wouldn't need you in the first place!"

My girlfriend told me that I kiss like a stroke victim, which is weird that she has that frame of reference.

A young couple were kissing passionately on their first date. After a couple of minutes, the girl pulled away and said: "I think you just passed me your chewing gum."

"Oh, sorry," said the young man. "I've got bronchial asthma."

What's the difference between French kissing and Belgian kissing? – They're much the same, but Belgian kissing is more phlegmish.

A young man took a girl out to dinner. They got on really well, and when he asked her if she wanted to come back to his apartment for a drink, she said yes.

After they had been in his apartment for a while, he asked her: "Do you mind if I give you an old-fashioned kiss?"

She replied: "At a time like this you want me to change positions?"

Lawyers

After graduating from college, a lawyer's son was pondering his future. Unsure about his career path, he asked his father whether he might be permitted to observe his work from a chair in the corner of the office to determine whether the law appealed to him as a profession. The father thought it was an excellent idea, and so the son joined him in the office the following morning.

The first client was an impoverished tenant farmer who proceeded to outline his case. "I work for the Rawlings farm on the north side of town. For many years, I have tended their crops and animals, including some cows. I have raised the cows, fed them and generally looked after them. And I was always led to believe that I was the owner of these cows. Now old Mr Rawlings has died and his son has inherited the farm. He believes that since the cows were raised on his land and ate his hay, the cows are his. In short, we are in dispute over who owns the cows."

"Thank you," said the lawyer. "I have heard enough. I will take your case. Don't worry about the cows."

The next client was a wealthy landowner. "My name is Rawlings," he said by way of introduction, "and I own a farm on the north side of town. We have a tenant farmer who has worked for my family for many years, tending crops and the animals, including some cows. I believe the cows belong to me because they were raised on my land and were fed my hay, but the tenant farmer believes they are his because he raised them and cared for them. In short, we are in dispute over who owns the cows."

"Thank you," said the lawyer. "I have heard enough. I will take your case. Don't worry about the cows."

After the client left, the lawyer's son could not help but express his concern. "Father, I know very little about the law, but isn't there a conflict of interest here? It seems we have a very serious problem concerning these cows."

"Don't worry about the cows," said the lawyer. "The cows will be ours."

How do you get a lawyer out of a tree? – Cut the rope.

Seeing a man drinking from a stream on his land, a farmer shouted: "You don't want to be drinking water from that thar creek, it's full of horse piss and cow shit!"

"I'm terribly sorry, but I'm an educated city lawyer and I didn't understand a word of your babble. Could you please repeat what you said but this time in a language akin to English?"

"Okay," said the farmer. "I said: 'If you use two hands, you'll drink it quicker.'"

A preacher and an attorney were talking one day about the mistakes they made in their respective professions and how they dealt with them. The lawyer boasted that if he made a really big mistake he just shuffled a few papers and used some complex legal jargon to cover it all up. If it was a small mistake he just ignored it and went on.

The attorney turned to the preacher and asked: "How do you do it, Pastor?"

The pastor said: "If it is a really large mistake I just turn to the Lord and ask forgiveness."

The attorney interrupted and asked: "But what about small mistakes, how do you handle them?"

The preacher replied: "Well, just last Sunday in my sermon I was quoting Jesus from the Gospel of John, chapter 8, where he said: 'You are of your father the devil, he was a LIAR from the beginning.' Instead I said: 'You are of your father the devil, he was a LAWYER from the beginning.'"

"So how did you handle that?" demanded the lawyer.

The preacher replied: "It was such a small mistake that I just ignored it and went on."

How can you tell if a lawyer is well hung? – You can't get a finger between the rope and his neck.

An airplane was experiencing engine trouble, and the pilot instructed the cabin crew to have the passengers return to their seats and prepare for an emergency landing.

A few minutes later, the pilot asked the flight attendants if everyone was buckled in and ready.

"All set back here, Captain," came the reply, "except the lawyers are still going around handing out business cards."

The Devil approached a lawyer with a proposal. The Devil promised to arrange for the lawyer to win every case, make twice as much money, work half as hard, be appointed to the Supreme Court Bench at 49 and live to be a hundred. In return, the lawyer had to sell the Devil the souls of his parents, his wife and his four young children.

The lawyer said: "So what's the catch?"

One evening after attending the theatre, two gentlemen were strolling down the avenue when they observed an attractive young lady walking ahead of them. One of them turned to the other and remarked: "I'd give £100 to spend the night with that woman."

Much to their surprise, the young lady overheard the remark, turned around and replied: "I'll take you up on that."

So after bidding his companion goodnight, the man accompanied the young lady to her flat, where they had sex. The following morning the man presented her with £50 as he prepared to leave. She demanded the rest of the money, stating: "If you don't give me the other £50, I'll sue you for it."

He laughed, saying: "I'd like to see you get it on these grounds."

The next day he was surprised when he received a summons ordering his presence in court as a defendant in a lawsuit. He hurried to his lawyer and explained the details of the case.

His lawyer said: "She can't possibly get a judgment against you on such grounds, but it will be interesting to see how her case will be presented."

After the usual preliminaries, the lady's lawyer addressed the court as follows: "Your honour, my client, this lady, is the owner of a piece of property, a garden spot, surrounded by a profuse growth of shrubbery, which property she agreed to rent to the defendant for a specified length of time for the sum of £100. The defendant took possession of the property, used it extensively for the purpose for which it was rented, but upon evacuating the premises, he paid only £50, one-half the amount agreed upon. The rent was not excessive, since it is restricted property, and we ask judgment be granted against the defendant to assure payment of the balance."

The defendant's lawyer was impressed and amused by the way his opponent had presented the case. He therefore changed his own speech to fit the occasion. "Your honour," he began, "my client agrees that the lady has a fine piece of property, that he did rent such property for a time, and a degree of pleasure was derived from the transaction. However, my client found a well on the property around which he placed his own stones, sunk a shaft and erected a pump, all labour performed personally by him. We claim these improvements to the property were sufficient to offset the unpaid amount, and that the plaintiff was adequately compensated for rental of said property. We therefore ask that judgment not be granted."

The young lady's lawyer responded: "Your honour, my client agrees that the defendant did find a well on her property. However, had the defendant not known that the well existed, he would never have rented the property. Also, upon evacuating the premises, the defendant removed the stones, pulled out the shaft, and took the pump with him. In doing so, he not only dragged the equipment through the shrubbery, but left the hole much larger than it was prior to his occupancy, making the property much less desirable to others. We, therefore, ask that judgment be granted."

She won the case.

A lawyer raged at a criminal: "Just when I thought you couldn't possibly get any lower, you go ahead and do something like this. I've seen a lot of lows in my time but this is creepy; even I being a lawyer can't possibly imagine this. This is so low that it gets into negative low. You passed the exam for exceptional lowlife behaviour. Your behaviour would make a dead man sick to the stomach. It is so disgusting and deplorable that I even plan on filing for crimes against humanity. I just don't know how I feel right now. Your act is an embarrassment to anyone that remotely looks like you. One time I was hiking in the Oregon woods and crossing a makeshift bridge, I slipped and grabbed on to the bridge, my life flashed before my eyes, the drop must have been at least 200 feet; that's not even as low as you come. You sank beneath the realm of unrealistic plunges, of immorality, respect or anything else. What do you have to say for your damn self?"

The criminal looked up and said: "So you'll be my lawyer?"

The lawyer replied: "Sure. If the price is right."

Lepers

If a leper gives you the finger, do you have to give it back?

Why was time-out called at the leper hockey game? – There was a face-off in the corner.

What do you call a leper in a bath? – Porridge.

What do you get if you put a leper in a wind tunnel? – Confetti.

A man was sitting in the theatre stalls watching a play. About ten minutes into the play some potato crisps fell down and landed on the seat next to him. As no one else was on the row he picked them up and ate them. A bit later some more crisps fell down, so he ate them as well. After the play ended, he decided to thank whoever it was dropping him all these crisps. So he climbed up the stairs to the balcony. When he got to the top he found that right above his seat there was a leper scratching himself.

Did you hear about the famous Russian leper, Andropov?

How do you make spaghetti? – Hit a leper over the head with a tennis racket.

Why couldn't the leper tie his new running shoes? – They cost him an arm and a leg.

Two boys knocked on the door of a house and said: "Mrs Thomas, can Timmy come out to play?"
    "Now boys," she said, "you know Timmy has leprosy."
    "Then can we come inside and watch him rot?"

What did the leper say to the hooker? – "You can keep the tip."

A leper went into a DVD rental store and said: "Have you got *My Left Foot*?"

Lesbians

A young woman went to the doctor after noticing two small circular rash marks, one on each side of her inner thigh. The doctor asked her to remove her pants, sat her in a chair and, kneeling down to position himself between her legs, examined the marks.
    Eventually he asked her: "Are you by any chance a lesbian?"
    "Yes, I am," blushed the woman.
    Standing up, the doctor said: "Well, don't worry, your rash will go away."
    "Is there anything I need to do?"
    "Yes, go home and tell your girlfriend her earrings aren't real gold."

Two naked lesbians barged into the house today and started wrestling with my girlfriend while she was in the bath. I tried to help, but I could only knock one out.

What do you say to a lesbian with no arms and no legs? – "Nice tits, bitch."

Two elderly lesbians were having sex on a park bench. One said: "Take your glasses off, you're scratching my leg."
　　The other one said: "Put your glasses on, you're licking the bench."

Why did the burka-wearing lesbians split up? – They hadn't been seeing enough of each other.

How many nails are used to make a lesbian's coffin? – None: it's all tongue and groove.

A cowboy was sitting at a bar when a young woman came in and sat next to him. As they started chatting, she asked: "Are you a real cowboy?"
　　"Well, ma'am, I've spent all my life herding cows and breaking horses, so I guess I must be." Pursuing the theme, he asked: "And what are you?"
　　"I'm a lesbian," she said. "I spend all day and night thinking about women. If I'm in the shower, watching TV or on the internet, I'm always thinking about women."
　　Soon she left and was replaced by another woman, who started talking to the cowboy and asked: "Are you a real cowboy?"
　　"Well," he drawled, "I always thought I was but I just found out I'm a lesbian."

Why do lesbians like whales so much? – Because they have twenty-foot-long tongues and breathe out of the top of their heads.

Why were the two blind and deaf lesbians walking down the street with their hands down each other's panties? – They were lip reading.

What did one lesbian vampire say to the other? – "See you next month."

Two lesbians were sharing a bath. One girl asked the other: "How come you have very little pubic hair on your pussy?"

Her friend replied: "Well, have you ever seen tall grass on a busy road?"

What do you call a lesbian with long fingernails? – Single.

How can you tell if a lesbian is butch? – Instead of K-Y, she uses WD-40.

Why do sumo wrestlers shave their legs? – So nobody will mistake them for lesbians.

A lesbian went to see a gynaecologist who complimented her on her personal hygiene. "I have to say, yours is the cleanest pussy I've seen in months."

"Thanks," said the lesbian. "I have a woman in three times a week."

A little Pakistani girl went up to her mother and said: "Mummy, I don't want to be a lesbian when I grow up."

The mother said: "What makes you think you'll be a lesbian, Minjeeta?"

Limericks

There was a young woman named Alice
Who used dynamite as a phallus.
They found her vagina
In North Carolina
And part of her asshole in Dallas.

There once was a girl from Azores
Whose cunt was all covered in sores.
The men who got pussed
Were desperate for lust
And licked up what was left in her drawers.

I'm told of a Bishop of Birmingham
Who buggered young boys while confirming 'em.
To roars of applause,
He tore down their drawers
And pumped the Episcopal sperm in 'em.

There was a young fellow named Cass
Whose bollocks were made out of brass.
When they tinkled together,
They played "Stormy Weather"
And lightning shot out of his ass.

There was a young lady from China
Who had an enormous vagina.
And when she was dead
They painted it red
And used it for docking a liner.

A policeman from near Clapham Junction
Had a penis that just would not function.
For his whole married life,
He deluded his wife
With some snot on the end of his truncheon.

A lighthouse keeper called Crighton
Took to seeing a lady from Brighton.
But ships ran aground
And sailors were drowned
As she wouldn't have sex with the light on.

There once was a hermit called Dave
Who kept a dead whore in a cave.
He said, "I admit,
I'm a bit of a shit,
But think of the money I save."

There once was a lady named Dot
Who lived off of pig shit and snot.
When she ran out of these
She ate the green cheese
That she grew on the sides of her twat.

While once with the Duchess at tea,
She asked, "Do you burp when you pee?"
I said (with some wit),
"Do you fart when you shit?"
And thought, "That's one up to me!"

There was an old man of Duluth,
Whose cock was shot off in his youth.
He fucked with his nose,
And his fingers and toes,
And he came through a hole in his tooth.

There once was a lady from Ealing
Who protested she lacked sexual feeling,
Till a cynic named Boris
Touched her clitoris
And then scraped her off of the ceiling.

A clever young man named Eugene
Invented a wanking machine.
At the twenty-first stroke
The bloody thing broke
And beat both his balls to a cream.

There once was a barmaid named Gail
On whose breasts was the menu for ale.
But since she was kind
For the sake of the blind
On her ass it was printed in Braille.

A mathematician named Hall
Had a hexahedronical ball.
The cube of its weight
Times his foreskin plus eight
Was four-ninths of five-eighths of fuck all.

There once was a mouse called Keith
Who circumcised boys with his teeth.
It wasn't for leisure
Or sexual pleasure
But to get to the cheese underneath.

There was a young lady from Kew
Who filled her vagina with glue.
She said with a grin,
"If they pay to get in,
They'll pay to get out of it, too."

There was a young woman named Kim
Who had an enormous great quim.
It wasn't the size
That attracted the flies.
It was the jelly that hung round the rim.

There once was a plumber called Lee
Who was plumbing a girl by the sea.
Said she, "Stop your plumbing,
There's somebody coming."
Said the plumber, still plumbing, "It's me!"

There once was a young man from Leeds
Who ate a whole packet of seeds.
Within the hour,
His dick was a flower
And his balls were all covered in weeds.

A Scotsman who lived by the Loch
Had holes down the length of his cock.
When he got an erection,
He would play a selection
From Johann Sebastian Bach.

There was a young vampire called Mabel
Whose periods were very stable.
Every full moon
She'd get out a spoon
And drink herself under the table.

There was a young dentist Malone
Who had a charming girl patient alone.
But in his depravity
He filled the wrong cavity,
My, how his practice has grown!

There was a young lady from Moreton,
Who had one long tit and one short one.
On top of all that,
A great hairy twat,
And a fart like an 850 Norton.

There was a young fella named Mort
Whose dick although thick was quite short.
To make up the loss
He had balls like a hoss
And never shot less than a quart.

There once was a lady named Myrtle
Who had an affair with a turtle.
Even more phenomenal
A swelling abdominal
Showed Myrtle the turtle was fertile.

There once was a man from Nantucket
Whose dick was so long he could suck it.
Then he got an erection
In his ass's direction
And said, "Now I think I can fuck it."

"Twas a crazy old man called O'Keefe
Who caused local farmers much grief.
To their cows he would run,
Cut their legs off for fun
And say, "Look, I've invented ground beef!"

There was a young lady from Ongar
Who was shagged in the sea by a conger.
By her squirms and her squeal
You could tell that the eel
Was like her old man's, only longer.

There was a young fellow named Paul
Who confessed, "I have only one ball.
But the size of my dick
Is God's dirtiest trick,
For the girls always ask, 'Is that all?'"

There once was a rabbi from Peru
Who was vainly attempting to screw.
His wife said, "Oy vey,
If you keep up this way,
The Messiah will come before you!"

There was a young girl named Sapphire
Who succumbed to her lover's desire.
She said, "I know it's a sin
But now that it's in
Could you shove it a few inches higher?"

There was a young girl from Seattle
Whose fetish was blowing off cattle,
Till a bull from the south
Shot a load in her mouth
That fair made her tonsils rattle.

Said a disgusting old whore from Silesia,
"Seeing as my cunt doesn't please ya,
You might as well cum
Up me slimy old bum,
But make sure that my tapeworm don't seize ya."

There once was a fellow named Sweeney
Who spilled some gin on his weenie.
Just to be couth
He added vermouth,
Then slipped his girlfriend a martini.

The tantric adept from Vermont
To show his adroitness is wont
To hold it all back
Till his balls turn blue-black
And then spew spouts of sperm like a font.

Said the swell to the belle from Virginia,
"After all that I've done now to win ya!
Dinners, movies and plays,
And it's always me pays –
Tell me, what does it take to get in ya?"

A young man with passions quite gingery
Tore a hole in his sister's best lingerie.
He slapped her behind
And made up his mind
To add incest to insult and injury.

The lass I brought home was a prize
With an alluring pair of brown eyes.
Her breasts, so select,
Were what I'd expect
But her bollocks were quite a surprise!

Though excited, her brother protested,
"If we're caught, we could both be arrested."
But she jerked down his shorts,
Say judicial reports,
And said "I insist", and incested.

Losers

Signs That You're a Loser

- Your date wants to have sex in the back seat, and she wants you to drive.
- Companies have stopped sending you junk mail because you're not worth the postage.
- Your dog would rather rub itself up against a wall than have you pet it.
- Your last girlfriend was inflatable.
- Fantasizing out loud before falling asleep is your idea of pillow talk.
- The last party you went to had jelly, ice cream and musical chairs.
- When you're on the beach, even the tide won't go out with you.
- You're twenty-eight and you still have imaginary friends.
- You have tweeted about a bodily function.
- You advertise for a stalker.
- Your right hand falls asleep while you're masturbating.
- You're not in line to win a prize in the *Reader's Digest* monthly draw.
- You become a Catholic just so you can go to Confession and have someone to talk to.
- You sing karaoke alone in your bedroom on a Friday night.
- The town hooker says she has a headache when you go to her for business.
- Your friends think your parents are cooler than you – and your parents agree.
- The only girl you speak to regularly on the phone costs £4.50 a minute.
- You look forward to dinner-time calls from telemarketers.
- Even your shadow doesn't like being seen with you.
- Your social life consists of your weekly visit to your psychiatrist.

A jealous guy caught his girlfriend talking quietly on the phone and immediately confronted her over his suspicions.

"Who was that you were talking to?" he demanded. "Is there somebody else?"

"Of course not," she groaned. "Do you honestly think I'd be going out with a loser like you if there was somebody else?"

Marriage

A couple were celebrating their golden wedding anniversary, but the husband seemed preoccupied. "There's always something that's bugged me about the children," he said. "I can't help noticing that out of our seven kids, Ricky looks different from all the others. I know it's an awful thing to ask, but does he have a different father?"

The wife couldn't bear to look him in the eye. "Yes, it's true," she admitted, head bowed. "Ricky does have a different father from the other six."

The husband's heart sank. Fighting back the tears, he said: "You have to tell me: who is Ricky's father?"

She looked at him sorrowfully and said: "You."

A woman walked into a gun shop and asked for help in choosing a rifle. "It's for my husband," she said.

"Okay," said the sales clerk. "Did he say what calibre he wanted?"

"No, he didn't," said the woman. "In fact, he doesn't even know I'm going to shoot him yet!"

A husband and wife liked to carry out home-improvement jobs in the nude. While they were decorating the kitchen, he called out to her from the garage: "Do you need more paint?"

"No," she replied. "I've got some on my brush."

He yelled back: "You ought to be more careful."

My wife had been bad-mouthing me all day until I finally flipped. I said: "When are you going to learn how to give a decent blow job?"

A wife said to her husband: "You're just too immature. It's impossible to have a proper grown-up conversation with you. We need to set aside some time where we can sit down as adults and talk things through."

"Yeah?" scoffed the husband. "Like that's going to happen during the conker season!"

Two men were talking in the pub. The first said: "My wife ran off with my best friend yesterday."

The second said: "Sorry to hear that. What was his name?"

"Will."

"I didn't know you had a best friend named Will?"
"I didn't until yesterday."

Two guys were sitting at a bar. One said: "After ten years of marriage, sex is down to three times a year."

"Same here," said the other. "In fact, if my wife didn't sleep with her mouth open, I'd have none at all."

A man was in court for beating his wife. The judge said: "Why do you keep beating her?"

The man replied: "I think it's my weight advantage, hand speed, longer reach and superior footwork."

Husband's Score Ratings

- You visit her parents: +1
- You visit her parents and actually make conversation: +3
- You visit her parents and stare vacantly at the television: -3
- And the television is off: -6

- You spend the day watching college football in your underwear: -6
- And you didn't even go to college: -10
- And it's not really your underwear: -15

- You take her out to dinner: 0
- You take her out to dinner and it's not a sports bar: +1
- Okay, it's a sports bar: -2
- And it's all-you-can-eat night: -3
- It's a sports bar, it's all-you-can-eat night and your face is painted the colours of your favourite team: -10

- You give her a gift: 0
- You give her a gift, and it's a small appliance: -10
- You give her a gift, and it's not a small appliance: +1
- You give her a gift, and it isn't chocolate: +2
- You give her a gift that you'll be paying off for months: +30
- You wait until the last minute and buy her a gift that day: -10

- With her credit card: -30
- And whatever you bought is two sizes too small: -40

- When she wants to talk about a problem, you listen, displaying what looks like a concerned expression: 0
- When she wants to talk, you listen, for over thirty minutes: +5
- You listen for more than thirty minutes, without looking at the television or picking up a newspaper: +10
- She realizes this is because you've fallen asleep: -10

Three guys were in a bar discussing how much their wives bitched at them. To give the women no cause for complaint in future, the men decided that when they got home, they would do the first thing that the women asked.

The next night, the three met up again in the same bar. The first guy said: "Man, I don't think our idea was so great! I was sitting on the couch watching TV and I dropped my cigarette on the couch. My wife said: 'Go on, why don't you burn the whole house down?' That place is still smouldering."

The second guy said: "That ain't nothing. I was working on the car, and dropped my wrench and it nicked the fender. She said: 'Why don't you tear the whole car apart?' I tell you, it took me all night."

The third guy said: "You guys have got nothing on me. When I walked in the door, my wife was doing the dishes, and I felt a little amorous. I reached down, and she said: 'Cut that out!' Ever seen one of these real close?"

How can you stop your husband from going out? – Pour on some more fuel.

A middle-aged man was lying in bed with his wife. While she started to get amorous, he was preoccupied with reading his Kindle. As her frustration grew, she turned to him and whispered in his ear: "Say something dirty to me."

He said: "The dishes."

A wealthy man was so smitten with the beautiful woman he had just met that he proposed to her on only their second date.

"But we don't know anything about each other," she said.

"That doesn't matter. We'll learn about each other as we go along. That will be part of the fun."

So she agreed and they got married. After the ceremony, they went on a luxury honeymoon to the most exclusive hotel in the Maldives. On their first morning, they went to the hotel pool. He climbed to the top of the diving board and, with an elaborate double somersault, plunged into the water.

As he surfaced, he said to his bride: "Impressive, huh? You see, I used to be an Olympic diving champion. I told you we'd learn things about each other as we went along."

Then she jumped into the water and swam twenty lengths of the pool without breaking sweat. As she climbed out, he said: "Wow! That was incredible. Were you an Olympic endurance swimmer?"

"No," she said. "I was a hooker in Venice and I worked both sides of the canal."

I've never slapped my wife although I did once high-five her face.

Two married men were drinking in a bar. One said to the other: "I got my wife a bag and a belt for her birthday. She wasn't happy, but the Hoover works fine now."

A husband and wife were lying in bed. Suddenly she turned to him and said: "If you could compare me to one thing in the universe, what would it be?"

Gazing into the distance, he replied: "The sun."

"Aah, is that because I'm bright, beautiful and you couldn't live without me?"

"No," he said. "It's because nobody can bear to look directly at you."

My wife said she wanted me to put the magic back into our relationship. I don't think sawing her in half was exactly what she had in mind.

A man asked his wife what special gift she wanted for her fortieth birthday. She said: "Something to run around in would be nice."

So he bought her a tracksuit.

---

29 February: the only day in the year when a man doesn't want to see a woman on her knees in front of him.

A young, naïve new bride went to lunch with an older, more experienced girl-friend from work soon after returning from her honeymoon. Her friend asked how she was enjoying married life.

"Well," the new bride responded, "I'm a bit concerned because my husband has this habit of falling asleep with his erect penis inside of me."

"Why is that a problem for you?" her girlfriend asked.

"He walks in his sleep!"

A husband and wife visited a marriage counsellor. First, the wife spoke to the counsellor alone. The counsellor asked her: "You say you've been married for twenty years, so what seems to be the problem?"

The wife replied: "It's my husband – he's driving me crazy! I'm going to leave him if he continues this shit!"

"In what way does he drive you crazy?" asked the counsellor.

"For twenty years," she said, "he's been doing these stupid things. First, whenever we go out, he's always looking at the floor and refuses to go near anyone. It's very embarrassing."

The marriage counsellor was amused. "Anything else?"

"He keeps picking his nose all the time! Even in public!"

"Hmm, anything else?" continued the counsellor.

The wife hesitated before answering: "Whenever we're making love, he never lets me go on top! Once in a while, I'd like to be in control!"

"Okay," said the counsellor, "I think I'll talk to your husband now."

So the wife left the room and the husband came in. The counsellor told him: "Your wife says that you've been driving her crazy. She might even leave you."

The husband looked shocked. "What?! For twenty years I've been loving and considerate and I've always given her what she wants! What could be the problem?"

The counsellor explained: "She says you've got these habits that are driving her crazy. First, you're always acting strange in public – looking at the floor and never going near anyone else."

"Oh, you don't understand!" said the husband. "It's one of the pieces of advice my father gave me on his deathbed and I swore I'd obey everything he said."

"What did he say?"

"He said that I should never step on anyone's toes."

The counsellor smiled: "Actually that means that you shouldn't do anything that would cause anyone else to get angry."

The husband looked sheepish. "Oh. Okay."

The counsellor continued: "And you keep picking your nose in public."

"Well, it's another thing my father specifically commanded me to do! He told me to always keep my nose clean."

The counsellor shook his head in disbelief. "That means that you should not indulge in any criminal activity."

"Oh," said the husband, feeling very stupid.

"And finally, she says that you never allow her to go on top during your lovemaking."

"That," said the husband firmly, "was the last thing my father commanded me to do on his deathbed and it's the most important thing of all."

"What did he say?" asked the counsellor.

The husband replied: "With his dying breath, he said, 'Don't screw up.'"

I once told my wife she looked sexy with black fingernails. Now she thinks I slammed her hand in the car door on purpose.

Good Reasons for Men to Be Single

- You wouldn't have to explain why you're wearing "that" shirt with "those" trousers.
- You could leave the toilet seat in any position you damn well please.
- You could actually tell the bartender: "If anyone calls, I'm here."
- You'd be painting the town instead of the house.
- There's no danger of your ever having to go to the opera.
- You could show your girlfriend where you live.
- The only weeds you'd be concerned with would be the ones you're rolling.
- You would have saved £89,527.61 in groceries by now.
- You wouldn't catch so much grief about those skid-marks in your underwear!
- You'd get to see what your credit cards look like.
- You could have a wank whenever you feel like it, without having to explain breathlessly through a locked door why you're "still in the bathroom".
- You could see a different face when you wake up in the morning, every day of the week!
- Cooking your own meals would be an adventure, not a punishment.
- You could fart as loudly as you want and without ever having to worry about the stench.
- Going to a strip club wouldn't have to be a covert mission.
- Bachelors don't have mothers-in-law.
- You wouldn't have to watch subtitled French films.
- You could go home drunk to sleep, instead of under a bridge.
- You could use your own name at hotels.

- You could watch late-night adult channels on TV without having to keep the sound down to listen for footsteps coming down the stairs.
- You could get home from work five minutes late without being subjected to the Spanish Inquisition.
- You wouldn't have a driving instructor grading you every time you go somewhere.
- When asked his opinion, a single guy can say: "Yes, you're fat!"

Three women were chatting in a bar.

One said: "I call my husband Hawk because he soars to great heights whenever we make love."

The second said: "I call my husband Swan because he is handsome, strong and fiercely loyal."

The third said: "I call my husband Thrush because he's an irritating twat."

A man came home one day and said to his wife: "Honey, what would you do if I said I'd won the lottery?"

She sneered: "I'd take half, and then leave you."

"Okay," he replied. "I had three numbers and won £10. Here's a fiver. Now get the hell out of here!"

Two men were talking in the pub. One said to the other: "I gave my wife some flowers last night."

"Did she like them?"

"No, she found the label."

"What, she found out how much they cost?"

"No, she found out she was not a family who had died in a car crash."

Wife: Does my bum look big in this?

Husband: Do you want the honest truth?

Wife: Yes. Don't hold back.

Husband: Okay. I'm sleeping with your sister.

For their fortieth wedding anniversary celebration, a husband took his wife to a smart restaurant. But halfway through the meal he surprised her by asking her: "Darling, have you ever cheated on me?"

"What a strange question to ask after all these years," she said. "But okay, if you must know, yes, I have cheated on you. Three times."

The husband was dismayed by the revelation but wanted to know the details.

She said: "The first time was when you were twenty-nine. Remember how you wanted to set up in business but no bank would give you a loan? And remember how the bank president came to our house in person and signed the papers? Well . . ."

Instead of being angry, the husband was deeply moved. "You mean, you slept with the president of the bank just so that I could start up my own business? That's the kindest thing anyone's ever done for me. So when was the second occasion?"

"Remember when you were forty-four and had a heart attack and no surgeon would operate on you? And then Dr Kerslake came all the way up here to carry out the surgery himself, and after that you were in good shape again? Well . . ."

The husband was genuinely touched. "So you slept with Dr Kerslake to save my life? What a wonderful woman you are! And when was the third time?"

"Remember how in 2011 you really wanted to be president of the golf club? But you were forty-nine votes short?"

I said to my wife: "Can you hear that? No one whining, moaning or complaining. Just silence. Nothing but silence. Beautiful, isn't it?"

And then I placed her urn back on the mantelpiece.

On the way home from a party, a wife said to her middle-aged husband: "Have I ever told you how sexy and irresistible to women you are?"

"I don't believe you have, dear," he replied, flattered.

"Then what the fuck gave you that idea at the party?"

A guy who had recently got married met up with an old school friend, but instead of being full of the joys of married life the newlywed guy looked really glum.

"What's wrong?" asked the friend. "Marriage not suiting you?"

"It's my wife. She said I was one in a million – but it's only now I've found about her past that I realize what she meant."

A man asked his wife: "How come you never get mad when we argue? How are you always able to control your temper?"

She said: "I clean the toilet."

"How does that help?"

"I use your toothbrush."

I've just bought the new Cluedo Domestic Violence edition. The wife did it in the kitchen, with the cupboard door.

On the night before their first wedding anniversary, a couple agreed that as an erotic treat whoever woke up first in the morning should wake the other with oral sex.

The following morning, the husband woke first and, remembering their pact, he slowly pulled back the covers . . . and stuck his cock in her mouth.

What is a wife? – An attachment you screw on the bed to get the housework done.

"I always worry when you go away for a weekend with the guys," said the attractive young wife.

"Don't worry about me, honey," said the husband reassuringly. "I'll be back before you know it."

"I know," she sighed. "That's what worries me."

I sat on the end of the bed last night pulling off my boxers. My wife looked at me and said: "Please don't do that to the dogs."

A husband and wife were on vacation at the same hotel as an attractive brunette. The husband was flirting with the brunette, much to his wife's annoyance. One day while the three were sitting around the hotel pool watching the children splashing about, the brunette said: "I love kids."

"We'll get on really well, then," said the husband.

"Why?" asked the brunette. "Is it because you have got children?"

"No," said the wife. "It's because he's hung like a four-year-old."

A husband who was a keen gardener told his wife: "That new rose I've grown, I've named it after you."

"What a lovely thought!" said the wife. "Is it because it's pretty, delicate and sweetly scented?"

"No," said the husband. "It's because it's prickly and good against a wall."

My wife always complains that I never notice her. So remembering something for a change, I called her at work today to wish her Happy Birthday. Turns out she died two years ago.

A woman was complaining to a neighbour that no matter what she did to try to stop him, her husband kept coming home late at night.

"Take my advice," said the neighbour, "and do what I did. One time my husband rolled in at three o'clock in the morning, and from my bed I called out: 'Is that you, Ken?' It cured him in an instant."

"How come?"

"His name is Jack."

Masturbation

A man was busy masturbating in the bathroom. As he finished and pulled up his trousers, he was horrified to see the window cleaner staring at him. Two minutes later, the doorbell rang and the man, still red-faced, rushed downstairs to answer it.

"I've done your windows, mate," smirked the window cleaner. "That'll be £100."

The man hurriedly paid up and shut the door. His wife, who had been listening from the kitchen, said: "A hundred pounds, for six small windows! He must have seen you coming!"

A young guy confessed to his friend: "I had a wank over an ex-girlfriend last night. Yeah, I know it's wrong, but I still have a key and she's a heavy sleeper."

One day, Farmer Brown went behind his barn and found to his dismay that his teenage son was jerking off. He promised the boy that he would find him a wife so he wouldn't have to do that anymore. True to his word, Farmer Brown fixed the boy up with a suitable bride and they were married a month later.

Two weeks after the wedding, Farmer Brown happened to look behind his barn and saw to his horror that his son was jerking off again.

Farmer Brown was furious. "Why are you still doing this?" he yelled. "Why aren't you with your wife?"

"Aw, Pa," said the son, "her little arm gets so tired."

I just got home from the World Blindfold Masturbation Championship. No idea where I came.

A doctor said to his patient: "You're going to have to stop masturbating."

"Why?" asked the patient.

"Because I'm trying to examine you."

A man was standing in the kitchen masturbating, when his wife suddenly walked in. Without saying a word, she knelt down in front of him, gave him the best blow job he'd ever had and swallowed the lot.

As she stood up, he said: "We haven't had sex for weeks and then you give me a great blow job. Why?"

She said: "I have just spent half an hour mopping the floor, and it's quicker to go and brush my teeth than it is to mop it again!"

If you are right-handed and masturbate with your left for a change, are you being unfaithful?

A man arrived home from work early to find his wife masturbating in the bedroom.

"What's going on here?" he asked.

"What does it look like?" she replied dismissively.

"A yawning sea lion," he said.

What's the difference between masturbation and basketball? – In basketball, you dribble *before* you shoot.

Alice and Sophie, both in their fifties, were having lunch when Sophie whispered: "It's mine and Harry's twenty-fifth wedding anniversary next month, and I would really like to give him something special. I know he's always wanted a hand job, but I've never given him one and to be honest, I don't really know how to do it. I don't suppose you could give me any tips?"

"Sure," said Alice. "Go and get yourself a ketchup bottle. You have a month to practise with it."

A month later on their anniversary, Sophie and Harry were in bed when she told him that she had a special present for him.

"Oh, what?" he asked excitedly.

"What you've always wanted," she replied with a smile. "A hand job."

He immediately became erect with anticipation. So she grabbed his dick with one hand and said: "Here goes. I hope you like it."

She then took her other hand and smacked the end of his penis with her palm three times."

What happened when the guy with no arms tried to masturbate? – He was stumped.

A woman, her husband and her brother-in-law were drinking together in the pub one night when the guys started talking about masturbation. They remarked that while there were plenty of male terms for jerking off, there weren't many female euphemisms. So they asked the woman what she called it.

Looking scornfully at her husband, she replied: "Finishing the job!"

I found an alien pleasuring himself in my freezer. He said: "I come in peas."

Masturbation Euphemisms

- Visiting Rosy Palm and her five daughters
- Bashing the bishop
- Choking the chicken
- Spanking the monkey
- Whacking the weasel
- Draining the monster
- Milking the snake
- Firing the hand cannon
- Giving Yul Brynner a high-five
- Tugging the tapioca tube
- Jacking the joystick
- Jerkin' the gherkin
- Doing the hand jive
- Playing the pink trombone
- Making the bald man puke
- Shaking hands with the unemployed
- Polishing your helmet
- Pumping the python
- Slapping the salami
- Freeing Willy
- Massaging the one-eyed monk

Did you hear about the guy who climbed to the top of the Empire State Building to masturbate? – Police didn't know whether to arrest him for indecent exposure or hijacking.

A mother walked past her fourteen-year-old son's room and saw him masturbating. Disturbed by what she had witnessed, she decided to have a gentle talk with him and told him that good little boys save it until they are married.

A few weeks later, she asked him: "How are you doing with that little problem we talked about?"

"Great," he answered. "So far I've saved nearly a quart!"

Have you heard about the new salad for wankers? – It tosses itself.

A sex therapist was advising a dysfunctional male patient about the relief that could be obtained through masturbation.

"But I do get some pleasure from my organ," said the man. "I frequently grasp it and hold it tight. It's a habit with me."

"Well," said the therapist, "it's a habit you'll have to shake."

I've just got myself one of those hands-free kits. Or, as most people call them, "a girlfriend".

One day a housewife was going about her usual routine of cleaning the house when she suddenly felt intensely horny. Unfortunately, her husband was still at work, so she resorted to stripping off all her clothes and started to masturbate.

She got very excited, rubbing herself and moaning, and when her husband walked in, she was still writhing around in the middle of the living-room floor.

He glanced through the mail and said to his wife: "Honey, when you're finished vacuuming the floor, could you get started on dinner?"

Looks aren't everything, but you can't wank over personality.

A father told his son: "Don't masturbate too much or you'll go blind."

The boy said: "Dad, I'm over here!"

If a woman is uncomfortable watching you masturbate, do you think?
a) You need more time together.
b) She's a prude.
c) She should have sat somewhere else on the bus.

Paul was sitting at his school desk when his friend Steve turned up late for a lesson with a huge smile on his face. "I bet I know where you've been," whispered Paul. "You've been for a crafty wank, haven't you?"

"Can you tell?" grinned Steve.

"Of course I can," said Paul, jumping to his feet. "Sir, Steve has just been wanking in the toilets!"

A young man walked into his flatmate's room and found him beating his dick with a hammer. "What are you doing?" he asked.

"I'm masturbating."

"Masturbating with a hammer?! Are you enjoying it at all?"

"Yes, each time I miss it."

Media and Entertainment

While his wife was enjoying a night out with her friends, a husband took the opportunity to relax and watch some TV. But he was interrupted when their nine-year-old son, who had been watching his own TV in his room, appeared in the doorway and asked: "What's love juice?"

Choking on his beer, the dad decided that perhaps it was time to explain a few things to the boy. "Well, son," he said, "one day you'll meet a girl you really like and you'll get aroused and your penis will get hard. You will touch the girl all over and when you reach the top of her leg it will feel wet. This is her love juice coming out of her vagina, which means that she is ready for sexual intercourse."

The son looked puzzled and said: "Okay, Dad, thanks."

As the boy was about to leave the room, the dad said: "Hang on, son, what are you watching up there to make you ask such a question?"

The son replied: "Wimbledon."

Unemployment in Britain has risen to 2.6 million, but on the upside Jeremy Kyle's viewing figures have risen to 2.6 million. (Jimmy Carr)

A man came home from the pub to find his wife watching a TV cookery show. "I don't know why you bother watching that stuff," he scoffed. "You can't cook to save your life."

"So what?" she replied. "You watch porn . . ."

I once thought about going on *Britain's Got Talent* because I used to have a pet goldfish that would hump the carpet, although only for about thirty seconds.

A local radio station in California was running a phone-in competition to find words that weren't in the dictionary but could still be used in a sentence that would make logical sense. The first prize was a trip to Bali.

The DJ greeted the first caller: "You're through to KLW-22, your sunshine morning station. What's your name?"

The caller replied: "Mike."

"Okay, Mike. What's your word?"

"'Goan.' Spelled G-O-A-N, pronounced 'goa-an'."

"That's good, Mike. The word 'goan' is not in the dictionary. Now to win that trip of a lifetime to Bali, tell me what sentence can you use that word in where it would make sense?"

"Goan fuck yourself."

The DJ immediately cut him off and took calls from other listeners, all of which were unsuccessful until a guy called Wayne came on the line.

"Okay, Wayne," said the DJ. "You're through to KLW-22, your sunshine morning station. Now what's your word?"

"'Smee.' Spelled S-M-E-E, pronounced 'smee'."

"That's good, Wayne. The word 'smee' is not in the dictionary. Now to win that trip of a lifetime to Bali, tell me what sentence can you use that word in where it would make sense?"

"Smee again. Goan fuck yourself."

I went to see *Walt Disney on Ice*. I was a bit disappointed – it's just an old bloke in a freezer. (Gary Delaney)

A man approached the producers of *Britain's Got Talent* and told them about his act. "I drink two litres of petrol, strap ten sticks of dynamite around my waist, hold a grenade in each hand, climb into a box and set fire to myself."

"Wow! That sounds incredible," they said. "Could you demonstrate it for us?"

"I'd better not. I can only do it once."

A man walked into a talent agent's office, and said: "We're a family act, and we'd like you to represent us."

The agent said: "Sorry, I don't represent family acts. They're a little too old-fashioned."

The man pleaded: "But this is really special."

"Okay," said the agent. "What's the act?"

The man replied: "Well, my wife and I come out on stage and she begins to sing 'The Star-Spangled Banner' while I take her roughly from behind. After a minute of this, my kids come out and begin to do the same, but my daughter's singing '*Pie Jesu*' while my son performs anal sex on her."

The agent shifted uncomfortably in his seat, but the man continued: "Just when my daughter hits the highest note in the song, my son and I switch partners. He turns my wife around and she starts to perform oral sex on him in rhythm to the music. When the song's over and we're both getting close, we all stop and lie down on the stage." The man smiled fondly as he recalled: "This is the best part: our dog then comes out on the stage, and he's trained to lick each one of us to orgasm in turn. He just goes right down the line, looking as happy as can be! Finally, we all get up and take a bow. Well, that's the act. What do you think?"

The agent was lost for words. Shaking his head in amazement, he eventually said: "I have to say, that's not like any other family act I've ever heard of. Tell me, what do you call yourselves?"

"The Aristocrats."

Men

What's the biggest difference between men and women? – What they mean when they say: "I got through a whole box of tissues watching that movie."

Why did God give men penises? – So that there'd be at least one way to shut a woman up.

College Training Courses for Men

Introduction to common household objects I: The mop.

Introduction to common household objects II: The sponge.

Dressing up: Beyond the funeral and the wedding.

Refrigerator forensics: Identifying and removing the dead.

Design pattern or splatter stain on the linoleum?: You CAN tell the difference!

Accepting loss I: If it's empty, you can throw it away.

Accepting loss II: If the milk expired three weeks ago, keeping it in the refrigerator won't bring it back.

Going to the supermarket: It's not just for women anymore!

Recycling skills I: Boxes that the electronics came in.

Recycling skills II: Styrofoam that came in the boxes that the electronics came in.

Bathroom etiquette I: How to remove beard clippings from the sink.

Bathroom etiquette II: Let's wash those towels!

Bathroom etiquette III: Five easy ways to tell when you're about to run out of toilet paper!

Giving back to the community: How to donate fifteen-year-old Levi's to charity.

Retro? Or just hideous?: Re-examining your 1970s polyester shirts.

Knowing the limitations of your kitchenware: No, the dishes won't wash themselves.

Romance: More than a cable channel!

Going out to dinner: Beyond Pizza Hut.

Adventures in housekeeping I: Let's clean the closet.

Adventures in housekeeping II: Let's clean under the bed.

The petrol gauge in your car: Sometimes Empty MEANS Empty,

Directions: It's okay to ask for them.

Listening: It's not just something you do during half-time.

Accepting your limitations: Just because you have power tools doesn't mean you can fix it.

A wife said to her husband: "The trouble with men is that they can't multi-task: they can't do two things at once."

"Actually, I can," replied the husband.

"Oh yes? Give me an example."

"Well, while I was banging you in bed last night, I was thinking about your sister."

If you're a guy you have absolutely no idea what's going on at any time in the relationship, ever. Here's what you know: you know when you're getting laid, and you know when it's all over. Those are the only two things you're aware of. (Adam Carolla)

If Men Wrote Problem Pages . . .

Q: My husband continually asks me to perform oral sex on him.

A: Do it. Semen can help you lose weight and gives a great glow to your skin. Interestingly, men know this. His offer to allow you to perform oral sex on him is totally selfless. This shows he loves you. The best thing to do is to thank him by performing it twice a day; then cook him a nice meal.

Q: My husband doesn't know where my clitoris is.

A: Your clitoris is of no concern to your husband. If you must mess with it, do it in your own time or ask your best friend to help. You may wish to video-tape yourself while doing this, and present it to your husband as a birthday gift. To ease your selfish guilt, perform oral sex on him and cook him a delicious meal.

Q: My husband has too many nights out with the boys.

A: This is perfectly natural behaviour and it should be encouraged. Man is a hunter and he needs to prove his prowess with other men. A night out chasing young single girls is a great stress relief and can foster a more peaceful and relaxing home. Remember, nothing can rekindle your relationship better than the man being away for a day or two (it's a great time to clean the house too)! Just look at how emotional and happy he is when he returns to his stable home. The best thing to do when he gets home is for you and your best friend to perform oral sex on him. Then cook him a nice meal.

Q: My husband wants a threesome with my best friend and me.

A: Obviously your husband cannot get enough of you! Knowing that there is only one of you, he can only settle for the next best thing – your best friend. Far from being an issue, this can bring you closer together. Why not get some of your old college roommates involved too? If you are still apprehensive, maybe you should let him be with your friends without you. If you're still not sure then just perform oral sex on him and cook him a nice meal while you think about it.

Q: My husband is uninterested in foreplay.

A: You are a bad person for bringing it up and should seek sensitivity training. Foreplay to a man is very stressful and time-consuming. Sex should be available to your husband on demand with no pesky requests for foreplay. What this means is that you do not love your man as much as you should. He should never have to work to get you in the mood. Stop being so selfish! Perhaps you can make it up to him by performing oral sex on him and cooking him a nice meal.

Q: My husband always has an orgasm, then rolls over and goes to sleep without giving me one.

A: I'm not sure I understand the problem. Perhaps you've forgotten to cook him a nice meal.

How do you stop a man breaking into your house? – Replace the locks with bra fasteners.

How Do We Know Santa Claus Is a Man?

1 He turns up late.
2 He drinks your booze.
3 He empties his sack.
4 He only comes once.
5 He clears off before you wake up!

A man was fed up with going to work every day while his wife stayed at home, so he prayed for a change in circumstance. "Dear Lord, I go to work every day and put in eight hours while my wife merely stays at home. I want her to know what I go through, so please allow her body to switch with mine for a day. Amen."

God, in his infinite wisdom, granted the man's wish, and the next morning, sure enough, he awoke as a woman. He got up, cooked breakfast for his partner, woke the kids, set out their school clothes, fed them breakfast, packed their lunches, drove them to school, came home and picked up the dry cleaning, took it to the cleaners, stopped off at the bank to withdraw some cash, went grocery shopping, drove home to put away the groceries, paid the bills, balanced the family accounts, cleaned the cat's litter tray and bathed the dog. By that time it was already one o'clock.

Then he rushed around making up the beds, did the laundry, vacuumed, dusted, swept and mopped the kitchen floor, ran to the school to pick up the kids, got into an argument with them on the way home, set out milk and cookies and got the kids organized to do their homework, then set up the ironing board and watched TV while doing the ironing.

At 5 p.m., he began peeling potatoes and washing and chopping vegetables for dinner. He then cooked and served dinner for his partner and kids. After dinner, he tidied up the kitchen, loaded the dishwasher, folded the laundry, bathed the kids and put them to bed.

By 10 p.m. he was exhausted and even though his daily chores weren't finished, he went to bed, where he was expected to make love with a degree of enthusiasm.

The next morning he woke up and immediately knelt by the bed and said: "Lord, I don't know what I was thinking. I was so wrong to envy my wife for being able to stay home all day. Please, please, let us trade back."

The Lord, in his infinite wisdom, replied: "My son, I feel you have learned your lesson and I will be happy to change things back to the way they were. You'll have to wait nine months, though. You got pregnant last night."

What do you call a magic wand that can make a man disappear? – A home pregnancy-test kit.

How do you know if it's time to wash the dishes and clean your house? Look inside your pants. If you find a penis in there, it's not time. (Jo Brand)

What It Means When a Man Says "I Love You"

1 Please sleep with me.
2 I forgot to get you a gift; this will have to do.
3 Stop nagging me.
4 What did I forget? This should buy me a little time.
5 Huh? I'm sorry; I wasn't listening.

Before moving in together, a couple decided to lay down a few ground rules. The girl said: "I know it can be difficult for men to read women's moods, so here are a few pointers: in the evening, if my hair is neat and tidy, that means I don't want sex at all; if my hair is a little dishevelled, that means I may or may not want sex; and if my hair is wild and untamed, that means I want sex."

"Okay, darling," said her boyfriend. "Just remember that when I come home from work, I usually like a drink. If I have only one drink, that means I don't want sex; if I have two drinks, I may or may not want sex; and if I have three drinks, the state of your hair becomes irrelevant."

For a man, what is the downside of a threesome? – He'll probably disappoint two women instead of one.

What do you call a man who expects sex on a second date? – Slow.

Things Men Would Do If They Woke Up and Had a Vagina for a Day

• Go shopping for zucchini and cucumbers.
• Squat over a hand-held mirror for an hour and a half.
• See if they can do the splits.
• Discover if it really is possible to launch a ping-pong ball twenty feet.
• Cross their legs without rearranging their crotch.
• Spend a lot of time sitting on the edge of the bed.
• Have multiple orgasms without the need for a sleep in between.

- Go to a gynaecologist for a pelvic exam and ask for it to be recorded on video.
- Finally locate the G-spot.

What do you call the useless bit of fatty tissue at the end of a penis? – A man.

The five words a woman wants to hear during sex: "I will always love you."
  The five words a man wants to hear during sex: "You can put it anywhere."

Don and George were sitting in a bar reflecting on their lives. After a while, Don said to George: "There's one thing that's always baffled me about you, George: why have you never got married?"

  "Well," replied George, "I guess I just never met the right woman. I guess I've always been looking for the perfect girl."

  "Oh, come on now," said Don. "Surely you must have met at least one girl that you wanted to marry?"

  "Yes, there was one girl . . . once," said George, misty-eyed. "I guess she was the one perfect girl – the only perfect girl I ever met. She was just the right everything, I mean she really was the perfect girl for me."

  "Well, why didn't you marry her?"

  George shrugged his shoulders and replied: "She was looking for the perfect man."

A recent survey was conducted to discover why men get out of bed in the middle of the night. Five per cent said it was to get a glass of water, 12 per cent said it was to go to the toilet, 83 per cent said it was to go home.

WOMAN's DIARY: Saturday, 24 November 2012. Saw him in the evening and he was acting really strangely. I had been shopping in the afternoon with the girls and I did turn up a bit late so thought it might be that. The bar was really crowded and loud so I suggested we go somewhere quieter to talk. He was still very subdued and distracted so I suggested we go somewhere nice to eat. All through dinner he just didn't seem himself; he hardly laughed and didn't seem to be paying any attention to me or to what I was saying. I just knew that something was wrong. He dropped me back home and I wondered if he was going to come in; he hesitated but followed. I asked him again if there was something the matter but he just half shook his head and turned the television on. After about ten minutes of silence, I said I was going upstairs to bed. I put my arms around him and told him that I loved him deeply. He just gave a sigh and a sad sort of smile. He didn't follow me up but later he did, and I was surprised when we made love. He still seemed distant and a bit cold, and I started to think that he was going to leave me and that he had found someone else. I cried myself to sleep.

MAN's DIARY: Saturday, 24 November 2012: United lost at home. Gutted. Got a shag though.

Mental Illness

A nurse at an asylum spotted a male patient walking around his room as if he was driving a car. "What are you doing, Norman?" she asked.

"I'm driving to Seattle."

She said she hoped he had a good trip and continued with her rounds.

The next day she saw him again. He was still pretending to drive a car. "How are you today, Norman?" she asked.

"I just arrived in Seattle."

"That's nice," she said, and continued with her rounds. In the next room she found Alec masturbating furiously.

"Alec, what do you think you're doing?"

"I'm screwing Norman's wife while he's in Seattle."

In desperation, a man called the Paranoia Helpline. A voice on the other end said: "How the hell did you get this number?"

On an official visit to a state asylum, a US senator observed a patient reaching up and then putting something invisible into a basket on the ground.

"What are you doing?" asked the senator.

The patient replied: "I'm taking the stars from the sky."

Puzzled, the senator moved on to the next patient, who appeared to be taking something invisible from the same basket and then reaching up high.

"What are you doing?" inquired the senator.

The patient explained: "I'm putting the stars back in the sky."

More mystified than ever, the senator moved on to the next patient, who was sitting in the middle of the floor making a rowing movement with both arms and shouting out, "Ahoy to starboard!"

"And what are you doing?" asked the senator.

The patient answered: "Trying to get away from those two nutters!"

I've been talking to the press about my battle with mental illness. Then I thanked it for putting perfect creases in my trousers.

A man was strolling past a mental hospital when he suddenly remembered that he had an important meeting. Unfortunately his watch had stopped, so he had no idea whether he was late or not. Just then, he noticed a patient wandering around within the hospital fence.

Calling out to the patient, the man said: "Excuse, sir, but do you have the time?"

"One moment!" replied the patient, who immediately threw himself to the ground and pulled out a short stick. He then pushed the stick into the ground and, producing a spirit level from his pocket, assured himself that the stick was vertical. With a compass, the patient located north and, with a steel ruler, measured the precise length of the shadow cast by the stick. Pulling a slide rule from his pocket, he made a quick calculation, then packed up all his tools and turned back to the man, saying: "It is now precisely 3.56 p.m., provided today is 6 July, which I believe it is."

The man could not help but be impressed by this demonstration, and set his watch accordingly. Before leaving, he said to the patient: "That was really quite remarkable, but tell me, what do you do on a cloudy day, or at night, when the stick casts no shadow?"

The patient raised his wrist and said: "I suppose I'd just look at my watch."

Signs of Insanity

- Everyone you meet appears to have tentacles growing out of places that you wouldn't expect tentacles to be growing from.
- You're convinced that the street parking meters are really aliens gathering to invade.
- You write to your mother in Germany every week, even though she sends you mail from New Hampshire asking why you never write.
- You start fantasizing about having sex with trees.
- You wear your boxers on your head because you heard it will ward off evil dandruff spirits.
- Every commercial you hear on the radio reminds you of death.
- People stay away from you whenever they hear you howl.
- Politicians appear to talk sense.
- You start out each morning with a thirty-minute jog around the bathroom.
- You're convinced that you were Shirley MacLaine in a previous life.
- Nobody listens to you anymore, because they can't understand you through that gas mask.

- You begin to stop and consider all of the blades of grass you've stepped on as a child, and worry that their ancestors are going to one day seek revenge.
- You have deep and meaningful conversations with your toaster.
- Your father pretends you don't exist, just to play along with your little illusion.
- You become concerned that your shadow is following you.
- Every time you see a cat in the street, you wonder what it would look like in a sandwich, covered in ketchup.
- You put tennis balls in the microwave to see if they'll hatch.
- You develop an overwhelming fear of fabric softener.
- You have a blazing row with your inflatable doll, which ends with you threatening her with a sharp needle.
- Your dentist asks you why each individual tooth has your name etched on it, and you tell him it's for security reasons.
- You tend to agree with everything your mother's dead uncle tells you.
- You fear that your right leg has been taken over by dark forces.
- You like to sit in cornfields for prolonged periods of time and pretend that you're a stalk.
- When the waiter asks for your order, you ask to go into another room to tell him because "the napkins have ears".
- You despise the voices in your head, especially the one that speaks only Hindi.
- You begin to consider cannibalism as a healthy diet option.
- You see migrating flocks of ducks and only your attachment to the toaster keeps you from joining them.
- The person you always talk to is invisible to everyone but you.

The hospital psychiatrist congratulated his patient on making such good progress.

"You call this progress?" snapped the patient. "Six months ago, I was Napoleon. Now I'm nobody!"

A man went into a bookstore and asked if they had any books on paranoia. The sales assistant beckoned him closer, looked right and left, then whispered: "They're behind you."

The Queen was on a visit to a mental hospital. She talked to a male patient tending the hospital flower beds and asked him why he was there. In a calm and orderly manner, he told her his life story, adding that he had been in the institution for more than twenty years. The Queen was greatly impressed by his manner and hinted that she might be able to secure his release as he seemed completely cured and ready to resume his place in society. The man was extremely grateful and returned to his gardening as the Queen departed.

Her Majesty was just about to leave the hospital grounds when a brick hit her on the back of the head. With blood oozing from the wound, she turned groggily to see the man standing there.

He said: "You won't forget, will you?"

Mexicans

What do you call a Mexican without a lawnmower? – Unemployed.

Why did God give Mexicans noses? – So they'd have something to pick in the winter.

What's the official currency of Mexico? – Food stamps.

A US Border Patrol Agent caught an illegal alien hiding in the bushes next to the Mexican border fence. Dragging him out, the agent said: "Sorry, you know the law, you've got to go back across the border right now."

The Mexican pleaded with him. "Pleeeze, señor, I must stay in the USA. I am begging of you. For the sake of my bambinos."

The agent thought for a moment and, touched by the Mexican's plea, decided to let him stay if he could construct a sentence using three English words. The Mexican readily agreed, and the agent told him: "The three words are 'green', 'pink' and 'yellow'. Now use them in one sentence."

After no more than ten seconds' thought, the Mexican said: "Okay, is easy. The phone, it went green, green, green . . . I pink it up, and sez 'yellow'."

Why are Mexicans so short? – Because when they're young, their parents say, "When you get bigger you have to get a job."

What do you get when you cross an Eskimo and a Mexican? – A snowblower that doesn't work.

Why is the Mexican Olympic team so bad? – Because all the Mexicans who can run, jump or swim are already in the US.

You Know You're a Mexican When . . .

- You share the same social security number with all your amigos.
- You run and hide when you see the border patrol.
- The Halloween pumpkin on your front porch has more teeth than your spouse.
- You have at least thirty cousins.
- Other people tell you to stop screaming when you are really just talking.
- You're too short to go on rides in Disneyland.
- You can't imagine anyone not liking spicy food.
- You see a fence and want to hop over it.
- Your toilet paper has page numbers on it.
- Your senior prom had a daycare.
- You fart more than you breathe.

Why do Mexican kids walk around school like they own the place? – Because their dads built it and their moms clean it.

Pedro and Maria got married. Pedro was experienced in the ways of the world, but Maria was very naïve and uninformed about the birds and the bees. Pedro was a poor working man and could not afford to take time off for a honeymoon. So, that night they retired to his little shack. When Pedro was undressing Maria asked: "Oh Pedro, what is that?"

Thinking quickly, Pedro replied: "My darling Maria, I am the only man in the world with one of these." And he proceeded to show her what it was for, and Maria was happy.

The next morning, Pedro went off to work as usual. When he returned home that evening, Maria was on the front porch obviously upset about something. "Pedro, you told me that you were the only man in the world with one of those, and I saw Gonzalez the gardener changing his clothes behind the shed and he had one, too."

Thinking fast, Pedro said: "Oh, my darling Maria, Gonzalez is my very best friend. I had two of them so I gave him one. He is the only other man in the world with one of those."

The trusting Maria accepted his answer and they had sex again that night.

Pedro went off to work as usual the next morning but when he returned home, Maria was very upset, stamping her foot on the porch.

"My darling Maria, what is the matter now?"

"Pedro, you gave Gonzalez the best one!"

What's the difference between a bench and a Mexican? – A bench can support a family.

What do you call a Mexican who can swim? – A Texan.

What do you call four Mexicans in quicksand? – Cuatro Cinco.

Why were there only 5,000 Mexican soldiers at the Battle of the Alamo? – Because they only had four vans.

Middle East

Two Iraqi mothers were sitting in a Baghdad café. Then one of them reached into her bag, pulled out some family photos and said: "This is my eldest son, Mohammed. Lovely boy."

"Yes, I remember him as a baby."

"He's twenty-four. He's a martyr now, though."

"Oh, that's sad."

"And this is my second son, Ahmed. He's twenty-one."

"What a handsome young man he's become. I remember when he first started school."

"He's a martyr now, too."

"Oh, I feel for you."

"And this is my baby boy, Khalid. He's just turned eighteen."

"Ah, little Khalid. He used to come round to play at our house."

"Alas, he is also a martyr."

"Oh my . . ." said the friend wistfully. Then gazing at the photos, she sighed: "They blow up so fast, don't they?"

Did you hear about the guy who was half American, half Iraqi? – He was his own worst enemy.

What's the weather forecast for Iraq? – It will be either Sunni or Shi'ite.

A Palestinian terrorist suspect was being grilled by Israeli police. "Honest, I'm not a suicide bomber," he said. "I didn't say I wanted to blow myself up so I could sleep with seventy-two virgins. All I said was I'm dying to get laid!"

A little Palestinian girl asked her mother: "After Ali blows himself up, can I have his room?"

What do you call an honest Iranian businessman? – Asif.

It's no fun being a broody Iranian woman. Every time I said to people. "My body clock is ticking", they would hit the ground! (Shappi Khorsandi)

Why don't they teach driver's education and sex education on the same day in Saudi Arabia? – They don't want to wear out the camel.

When two families moved from Iraq to America the respective fathers had a $100 bet: in a year's time whichever family had become the more American would win.

Twelve months later, they met up again. The first father said: "I'll tell you how American I am: my son plays baseball, I go to McDonald's five times a week and I'm on my way to pick up a case of Bud for tonight. How about you?"

The second father replied: "Fuck off, towel-head!"

An Iraqi guy walked into a menswear shop in Baghdad and said: "I'd like to buy a vest."

"Certainly, sir," said the shopkeeper. "What style would you like? Bulletproof or suicide?"

A man walking through a market in Saudi Arabia saw an acquaintance getting his hand stitched back on.

The man said: "I see you won your appeal."

Did you hear about the guy in Saudi Arabia who took drugs and ended up in bed with another man's wife? – He was well and truly stoned.

What do you call a first-time offender in Saudi Arabia? – Lefty.

Two Arabian men were on an expedition across the desert, but one needed some advice when they finally reached a waterhole. "I just can't seem to get my camel to drink any water," he explained, "and it's a long way to the next waterhole and I'm worried it'll die of thirst if it doesn't drink now."

"Okay," said the other, "I'll show you what to do. Bring the camel over here and I'll hold its head in the water. Now, you put your lips around its arse and suck hard, that'll draw the water up just fine."

So the guy started sucking as hard as he could, but then suddenly he began coughing. "Oh, no," he spluttered, "the camel's head must be too deep in the water, the mud's started coming through."

An Arab guy was stopped on arrival at Los Angeles International Airport.

"Name?" said the airport official checking his documents.

"Abdul al-Rhazib."

"Sex?"

"Up to eight times a week."

"No, I mean male or female?"

"Male, female, sometimes camel."

"Holy cow!"

"Yes, cow, sheep, animals in general."

"But isn't that hostile?"

"Horse style, doggie style, any style!"

"Oh dear!"

"No, no. Deer run too fast."

A frog was sitting on the banks of the River Jordan when a scorpion approached her. "Hi," said the scorpion. "Could you do me a favour and carry me across the river on your back?"

"Are you mad?" said the frog. "You're going to sting me."

"Now why would I do that?" protested the scorpion. "If I did that, I'd drown."

Satisfied by this reasoning, the frog allowed the scorpion to jump on his back and started to swim. But about halfway across the river, the scorpion stung the frog.

"What the hell did you do that for?" shrieked the frog. "Now I will die and you will drown."

The scorpion said: "Welcome to the Middle East, bitch!"

Military

At five o'clock one winter morning, a sadistic drill sergeant with the US Marines ordered the men to undergo an immediate parade ground inspection – and they all had to be totally naked.

Shivering in the sub-zero temperatures, the men lined up in three rows as the drill sergeant, brandishing his swagger stick, began his tour of inspection. He came to a guy who wasn't standing straight, so he hit him hard across the chest with the stick.

"Did that hurt?" barked the sergeant.

"No, sir."

"Why not?"

"'Cos I'm a US Marine, sir."

Further along the line, the sergeant saw a guy fidgeting. So he whacked him hard on the butt with his stick.

"Did that hurt?" growled the sergeant.

"No, sir."

"Why not?"

"'Cos I'm a US Marine, sir."

The sergeant continued along the line until he noticed a guy with a huge erection. He immediately whacked it hard with the stick.

"Did that hurt?" snarled the sergeant.

"No, sir."

"Why not?"

"'Cos it belongs to the guy behind me, sir!"

A young soldier went into a public toilet and had to use the only available urinal, between two elderly men. He glanced to his left and saw one of the men peeing, but noticed that there were two streams.

"What the hell is that?" he asked.

"War wound," replied the old man. "I took a bullet in my dick in North Africa. They were able to save my dick but they had to leave two holes."

Then the soldier looked to his right and saw three streams! "What the hell is that?" he asked.

"War wound," came the reply. "Normandy, bullet in the dick, gave me two extra holes."

The two veterans then looked over at the young soldier in the middle and saw twelve streams!

"War wound?" they chorused.

"No, my zipper's stuck."

A husband returned home after spending ten months on a solo posting with the US Army in Alaska. He told his wife: "Honey, I want you to know that I haven't wasted my time while I've been away. I've mastered the art of mind over matter. Watch this!"

He then dropped his trousers and boxer shorts and stood before her naked. "Now watch," he said. "Dick, attention!" he barked, and his penis instantly sprang to full erection.

His wife was impressed.

Then he barked: "Dick, at ease!" and his penis immediately went soft.

"That's amazing," said his wife. "What a party piece! Hey, would you mind if I showed our neighbour Kelly?"

The husband said he had no objections, and a few minutes later Kelly – a pretty blonde wearing a short skirt and knee-high boots – called round to witness the trick. The husband could scarcely take his eyes off her long legs.

"Come on, darling," said his wife. "Show Kelly what you can do."

Gathering himself together, he barked: "Dick, attention!" and his penis stood proud.

The two women roared with laughter.

Then he ordered: "Dick, at ease!" but nothing happened. It stayed hard. "Dick, at ease!" he repeated, but still it refused to go down. Following two more fruitless attempts, the husband rushed embarrassed to the bathroom, leaving his wife to make excuses for him. After she had seen Kelly out, she went into the bathroom and found him masturbating furiously.

"What are you doing?" she asked.

He gasped: "I'm giving this son-of-a-bitch a dishonourable discharge!"

My uncle had his tongue shot off in Vietnam. He doesn't talk about it, though.

Back in 2004, an Army major asked a young man: "Son, can you tell the difference between British tanks and Iraqi tanks?"

"No, sir," replied the young man.

Shaking him by the hand, the major said: "Then welcome to the United States Army . . ."

As a show of gratitude for services to the nation, the US Army decided to give every ex-soldier a cash bonus of $1,000 for every foot between their forehead and their dick.

The first guy came along, took his pants off, they measured him and gave him $1,400.

The second guy came along, took his pants off, they measured him and gave him $1,600.

The third ex-soldier was a really old guy, a seasoned veteran from the

1960s. When he took his pants off to be measured, they saw there was nothing there.

"What happened to your penis?" they asked.

The vet mumbled darkly: "Some things stayed in Nam."

On leaving the Army, an old soldier landed a white-collar job. One day he arrived at the office to find that he had been given a new young secretary. While taking dictation, she couldn't help noticing that his fly was open. She debated whether or not she ought to say something and in the end decided to mention it to him discreetly.

"Do you know your barracks door is open?" she whispered.

The old soldier looked at her blankly but later realized what she had meant when he himself discovered that his zipper was open. Catching up with her in the corridor, he said with a grin: "By the way, Miss Daniels, when you saw my barracks door open earlier, did you see a soldier standing proudly to attention?"

"No," she replied frostily "All I saw was a disabled veteran sitting on two old duffel bags."

An Army general and a Navy admiral were sitting in a barber's shop. Both were coming to the end of their shaves when the two barbers reached for some after-shave to slap on their customers' faces.

The admiral shouted: "Don't put that stuff on me! My wife will think I've been in a whorehouse!"

The general turned to his barber and said: "You can put it on me. My wife doesn't know what the inside of a whorehouse smells like."

A young British soldier panicked during a ferocious firefight and ran for cover some distance from the action. He was crouched down nervously behind a wall when he felt a hand on his shoulder.

"What are you doing here?" asked a voice with a French accent. "Think of your regiment. Get back there and do what you're paid to do."

Pulling himself together, the young soldier said: "Yes, sorry, mate, you're right."

"Mate?!" bellowed the voice. "I am a French Army officer."

"Sorry, sir," said the young soldier. "I didn't realize I'd run back that far."

An Army major was visiting sick soldiers in hospital.

"What's your problem, soldier?" he asked.

"Chronic syphilis, sir."

"What treatment are they giving you?"

"Five minutes with a wire brush each day."

"And what's your ambition?"

"To get back to the front, sir."

Then the major moved on to the next bed.

"And what's your problem, soldier?"

"Chronic diarrhoea, sir."

"What treatment are they giving you?"

"Five minutes with a wire brush each day."

"And what's your ambition?"

"To get back to the front, sir."

Then the major moved on to the next bed.

"And what's your problem, soldier?"

"Chronic gum disease, sir."

"What treatment are they giving you?"

"Five minutes with a wire brush each day."

"And what's your ambition?"

"To get the wire brush before the other two, sir."

A general was immensely proud of his son when he joined the Marines. He told everyone how well his boy was doing and what a man he had become, and looked forward to hearing about new tales of heroism when the boy came home on leave.

Instead, when the boy arrived home, he appeared troubled. "Dad," he said, "there's something I have to tell you, and I don't think you're going to be happy about it. I had to do my first jump out of a plane and I was absolutely terrified. I was the last one to jump and when I got to the door I just froze. I couldn't do it. My drill sergeant glared at me and yelled: 'Soldier, if you don't jump out of this plane this damn instant, I'm going to stick my big, hairy cock right up your sweet little ass!'"

The father's eyes widened. "Did you jump?"

The son replied: "Only at first."

Money

A man was walking through town with his young son, who was playing with a ten-pence piece in his hand. Suddenly, the boy started choking and going blue in the face. Realizing that the boy must have swallowed the coin, the dad started panicking and shouting for help. Hearing the commotion, a smartly dressed woman asked if she could be of assistance.

"My boy's swallowed some money," the father cried, "and I'm afraid he's choking to death."

"Don't worry, sir," said the woman calmly. She then carefully took hold of the boy's testicles and started to squeeze, gently at first and then ever more firmly. After a few seconds the boy convulsed violently and coughed up the coin, which the woman deftly caught in her free hand.

"Thank you so much," said the relieved father. "I've never seen anybody do anything like that before. It was amazing. Are you a doctor?"

"No," the woman replied, "I work for Revenue & Customs."

Did you hear about the woman who earned extra money by polishing World War Two helmets? – She certainly put a smile on the face of the old soldiers at the care home.

A woman wanted to have her large lounge divided into a sitting room and a TV room by means of a partition. The joiner quoted her £700 cash for the work and she agreed. He finished the job and asked for the money, but she made an excuse about not being able to get to the bank and said she would pay him Monday.

So he called back the following Monday and said: "I am here for the partition money." But again she came up with an excuse for not paying him.

The situation went on for weeks. He kept calling for his money but she was never able to pay him until eventually, realizing that he was losing patience with her, she said: "Look, I can pay you in kind – oral, doggy whatever you like."

"Missionary will do," he said.

So she stripped off and lay on the bed. He then stuck one finger up her fanny and one up her arse and snarled: "Seven hundred quid or the partition comes out . . ."

A couple who were big spenders had always dreamed of a vacation in Hawaii but had never managed to save up enough money. Then one day they came up with an idea – each time they had sex, they would put a £20 note into a piggy bank.

After seven months of this, they reckoned there was probably enough money in the piggy bank to pay for their dream vacation, so they smashed it open. The husband was puzzled by what he found. "It's strange," he said. "Each time we had sex, I put a £20 note into the piggy bank. Yet there are £50 notes in here, too."

The wife replied: "Do you think everybody is as stingy as you are?"

A guy went to a brothel, paid the girl £200 up front and started to get undressed. She was just about to take off her red negligee when the fire alarm sounded, causing her to flee the room with the £200 in her hand. The man quickly grabbed his clothes and ran out after her.

He searched the building for her but the smoke started to get worse, and so he was forced to go outside, by which time the fire crew had arrived on the scene.

He went up to one of the firemen and said: "Have you seen a beautiful blonde in a red negligee with £200 in her hand?"

"No," said the fireman.

"Well, if you do," said the man, "screw her. It's paid for."

A wife asked her husband: "Have you ever seen a £20 note all crumpled up?"

"No," he said.

She gave a sexy little smile, reached into her cleavage and pulled out a crumpled £20 note.

Then she said: "Have you ever seen a £50 note all crumpled up?"

"No," he said.

She gave a sexy little smile, reached into her panties and pulled out a crumpled £50 note.

"Now," she said, "have you ever seen £30,000 all crumpled up?"

"No," he said, intrigued.

"Well," she said, "go and take a look in the garage."

The Sunday Times Rich List would sell a lot more copies in a recession if they called it *The Kidnappers' Bible.* (Frankie Boyle)

A young family moved into a house next door to an empty plot. One day a construction crew turned up to start building a house there. The family's five-year-old daughter naturally took an interest in all the activity going on next door and started talking with the workers. She hung around and eventually the construction crew, all of them rough diamond types, more or less adopted her as a kind of project mascot. They chatted with her, let her sit with them while they had coffee and lunch breaks, and gave her little jobs to do here and there to make her feel important. At the end of the first week they even presented her with a pay envelope containing £5.

The little girl took this home to her mother, who suggested that they take the money she had received to the bank the next day to start a savings account.

When they got to the bank, the clerk asked the little girl how she had come by her very own wage packet at such a young age.

The little girl proudly replied: "I worked all last week with a crew building a house."

"Well, you are a clever girl," said the clerk. "And will you be working on the house again this week, too?"

The little girl replied: "I will if those useless cunts at the timber yard ever deliver the fucking skirting board!"

Mothers-In-Law

A woman phoned her son-in-law and began haranguing him over the way he was treating her daughter. "You're a useless, no-good layabout," she told him, "and I don't know what my Carrie ever saw in you."

She continued in this vein for several minutes before finally pausing for a response. When none was forthcoming, she barked: "Well, have you got nothing to say for yourself?"

Eventually he drawled: "What has a one-inch dick and hangs down?"

"What?" said the mother-in-law impatiently, puzzled by the question. "I don't know."

"A bat," he said. "And what has a seven-inch dick and hangs up?"

Then he put the phone down before she could answer.

I bought my mother-in-law some crotchless knickers for her birthday. It was nothing sexual – I just wanted to give her a better grip on her broomstick.

Halfway through her mother's funeral, a wife turned to her husband and growled through clenched teeth: "When you get home, I'm going to make you pay for this!"

"What's the problem?" he said. "What have I done wrong? Is it because I'm not sharing my popcorn?"

A wife phoned her husband at work and told him: "The grandfather clock in the hall came crashing to the floor this afternoon. I don't know what caused it, but a moment earlier and it would have crushed mother."

"That's it!" exclaimed the husband. "I'm getting rid of that clock. It's always been slow."

Meeting his neighbour on the driveway, a man said: "I'm just off to visit my mother-in-law."

"Don't talk to me about mothers-in-law!" said the neighbour, polishing his car. "It was my mother-in-law who broke up my marriage."

"Why, what happened?"

"My wife caught us in bed."

Music

A man went to the doctor's. "How can I help?" asked the doctor.

"Well," explained the man sheepishly, "I was chilling out this morning listening to 'In the Air Tonight' when suddenly my iPod accidentally slipped up my arse, and now it's stuck there."

"Hmmm," smiled the doctor knowingly. "I've never heard that one before."

The man said: "It's a Phil Collins song."

Which artist had five consecutive hits in one day? – John Lennon.

What would it take to reunite the Beatles? – A gun and two bullets.

The Beatles have re-formed and brought out a new album. It's mostly drum and bass.

Between songs in a U2 concert, Bono asked the audience for complete silence. Then in the silence, he slowly started to clap his hands rhythmically and, with the audience totally under his spell, he spoke poignantly into the microphone: "Every time I clap my hands, a child in Africa dies."

At which point a voice at the back of the crowd called out: "Well, stop doing it then!"

I saw a busker with no arms, singing so badly I paid him a fiver to stop. It was just another note he couldn't hold.

A young boy was covering behind the counter of a small music shop while his father, the owner, took a toilet break. No sooner had the father gone than a female customer walked in. "Excuse me, young man," she said. "Do you happen to have 'Jingle Bells' on a seven-inch?"

"No," he replied, "but I've got dangling balls on a nine-inch."

"That's not a record, is it?" she asked.

He said: "It is for a ten-year-old!"

Somebody just gave me a shower radio. Thanks a lot. Do you really want music in the shower? I guess there's no better place to dance than a slick surface next to a glass door. (Jerry Seinfeld)

What does Björk do when she's feeling horny? – She watches pjörn.

The Rolling Stones are getting £15 million for going back on tour – and on top of that they still get their winter fuel allowance.

A guy met a famous singer in a nightclub, and they ended up getting really drunk and going back to his place.

She was all over him in the taxi, stroking and caressing his body and whispering filth into his ear, but as soon as she got through the front door she stiffened up and her attitude changed completely.

"What the fuck is that pathetic little thing?" she demanded. "How the hell do you think you're going to satisfy me with that?"

"I'm sorry, Adele," he replied. "It's the biggest fridge I could afford."

The theme for the Bond movie *Skyfall* was performed by Adele – a rare case of something beginning when the fat lady sings.

Marianne Faithfull walked into a sixties celebrity party and spotted Jim Morrison sitting quietly in a corner. She ambled over to him, undid his flies and immediately started sucking him off. She then spotted the rest of the Doors in another part of the room and in turn went round each one and sucked them off.

Just as she had finished, in walked John Lennon, so she went over to him, pulled down his flies and started to suck him off. Moments later, in came Paul, George and Ringo and she obliged each one of them, too.

Then suddenly Michael Caine burst into the room and shouted at her: "You're only supposed to blow the bloody Doors off!"

What's red and got more brains than Kurt Cobain? – The wall behind him.

George Michael was rushed to hospital with what was reported to be a Mars bar stuck up his arse. But tests later revealed it to be a careless Wispa.

When Sting dies, do you think everyone will call him Stung?

Native Americans

As part of the modernization of his tribe and its incorporation into mainstream society, a Native American chief enlisted the services of a church minister to teach him some useful words from the English language.

As they walked in the forest, the minister pointed to a tree and said to the chief: "Tree."

The chief repeated: "Tree."

A few yards further along, the minister indicated a rock and said: "Rock."

The chief repeated: "Rock."

Shortly afterwards, the minister heard a rustling sound in the bushes and spotted a couple having sex. Embarrassed, he said to the chief: "Riding a bike."

The chief looked at the couple for a moment, then raised his rifle and shot them both dead.

The minister was appalled. "We are trying to integrate your people into society. How can we do this when you have just killed two people in cold blood?"

The chief replied: "My bike."

A Native American chief was suffering from stomach pains, but was unable to pass any gas. So his squaw went to the medicine man and said: "Big chief, no fart."

So the medicine man gave her a bottle of pills and told her: "Give him three of these."

The next day, she went back to the medicine man and told him: "Big chief, no fart."

So the medicine man said: "Give him six of these pills."

The next day, she went back to the medicine man and said: "Big chief, no fart."

"Very well," said the medicine man. "There could be risk but give him the whole bottle of pills."

The next day, the squaw went back to the medicine man and said: "Big fart; no chief."

Necrophilia

A man was brought before a judge on a charge of necrophilia. The judge said: "In my twenty-five years on the bench, I've never heard such an immoral, disgusting thing. Just give me one good reason why I shouldn't lock you up and throw away the key."

The man replied: "I'll give you three good reasons. First, it's none of your damn business. Second, she was my wife. And third, I didn't know she was dead – she always acted that way in bed."

What's a necrophiliac's favourite position? – Decomposition.

What's the worst thing about going down on your grandmother? – Hitting your head on the coffin lid.

Necrophilia: it puts the "fun" into funeral.

Two necrophiliacs crept into the cemetery in the dead of night and dug up a body to have anal sex with it.

After both men had shot their load, one began to panic, asking: "What if the police come, take sperm samples and find out it was us? We need to destroy the evidence." So he shoved a straw up the corpse's arsehole and started sucking out the semen. Soon he was out of breath, so he turned to his accomplice and said: "I've had enough. You have a go now."

"No way!" said the other man. "Not with the same straw!"

I just rented the movie *Die Hard*. I was disappointed to find it was nothing to do with necrophilia.

Respect the dead: wear a condom.

I sometimes wonder if necrophiliacs are really into dead people or if they just enjoy the quiet. (Doug Stanhope)

A guy was on a first date with a girl and the conversation turned to sex. She asked him: "What's the weirdest thing you've ever done with a girl?"

He replied: "To be honest, I've only ever had sex once, so nothing that weird."

"Only once?" she said. "What was her name?"

He said: "Mary something. I couldn't make out her surname."

"Why, did you meet her in a loud club?"

"No. There was a lot of moss on the headstone."

Newfies

Two guys from Newfoundland, Jim and Bob, were standing at the men's urinals in a public lavatory when Jim glanced over and noticed that Bob's penis was twisted like a corkscrew. "My God!" said Jim. "I've never seen one like that before."

"Like what?"

"All twisted like a pig's tail."

"Well, what's yours like?"

"Straight and normal."

"Well, I thought mine was normal till I saw yours."

Jim finished what he was doing and then shook himself before putting it back in his trousers.

"What did you do that for?" asked Bob.

"Shaking off the excess drops," replied Jim. "Like normal."

"Damn!" said Bob. "And all these years I've been wringing!"

Did you hear about the Newfie who told the police he had found the mass grave of a thousand snowmen? It turned out to be a carrot field.

A Newfie walked into a store and bought a Christmas tree.

The sales clerk asked: "Will you be putting it up yourself?"

"Certainly not," said the Newfie. "It's for the living room."

A Newfie went into a hardware store and asked to buy a bath.

"Would you like one with a plug?" said the sales assistant.

The Newfie said: "Don't tell me they've gone electric!"

On a visit to Maine, a Newfie went walking in the country with his American buddy. After a couple of miles, the Newfie turned to his friend and said: "I really need to take a crap."

"There's a tree," said the friend. "Why don't you go behind that?"

The Newfie looked at the tree and said: "But I don't have any toilet paper."

"You've got a dollar, haven't you?" asked the friend. "You can wipe yourself with that."

Reluctantly the Newfie took his advice, disappeared behind the tree and did his business. Minutes later, he came back with crap all over his hands.

"What happened?" the friend asked. "Didn't you use the dollar?"

"Sure I did," said the Newfie. "But have you ever tried to wipe with three quarters, two dimes and a nickel?"

A Newfie guy was telling his friend about the Newfie girl he met last week. "She was really lovely, and we got on so well that at the end of the evening we swapped numbers."

"Sounds great!" said the friend.

"I'm not sure it was such a good idea," said the Newfie. "Now all her friends keep calling me instead of her!"

Two Newfies got married and set off on honeymoon into the Canadian wilderness. They caught a bus that was filled with bear hunters. About an hour into their journey, the bus broke down next to a nice hotel. The Newfie husband said to his bride: "There's a comfortable hotel right here. How about consummating our marriage?"

She replied: "No. I want to wait till we get to Timmins."

The repaired bus took off, but fifty miles down the road, it broke down again – this time next to a smart-looking motel.

The Newfie husband turned to his wife and said: "Look, there's a nice motel. Can we consummate our marriage?"

"No," she said. "I want to wait till we get to Timmins."

The bus was repaired and off they went. Ten miles down the road the bus broke down – this time out in the woods. However, there was a little clearing out of sight of the bus.

The Newfie bride turned to her husband and said: "I think we should go into the woods and do it."

Later when they returned the bus, the Newfie husband asked his bride: "Earlier we were next to a nice hotel and you said 'No'. Then we were by a smart motel and you said 'No'. But here we went out into the woods and did it. Why?"

She said: "I was listening to the hunters. They said if the bus broke down again, the fucking season would be over."

A young Newfie and his new bride were on their wedding night in a seafront hotel. While she climbed into bed in anticipation, he stood on the balcony, gazing at the moon, the stars and the sea.

After half an hour, she began to get impatient and asked him: "Why don't you come to bed?"

"No way," he said. "Momma told me tonight would be the most wonderful night of my life, and I ain't gonna miss a minute of it."

Two Newfies fell down a well. "It's dark down here, isn't it?" said one.

"I don't know," said the other. "I can't see a thing."

A teenage Newfie boy found a whip, a mask and some handcuffs in his mother's bedroom. "I can't believe it," he told one of his work colleagues the next day. "My mom's a superhero!"

An American, an Englishman and a Newfie were on death row at the state penitentiary. The prison governor gave them a choice of three ways to die – be shot, hung or injected with the AIDS virus.

The American said: "Shoot me in the head." The guards did, and the American fell to the floor, dead.

The Englishman said: "Hang me." The guards did, and the Englishman slumped to the floor, dead.

The Newfie said: "Give me the AIDS virus." So the guards injected him with the AIDS virus, but the Newfie just fell about laughing.

"Why are you happy?" asked the guards.

"Because you guys are so stupid," said the Newfie. "I'm wearing a condom!"

A Newfie was training to be a doctor. At medical school in Toronto, the lecturer asked the class: "Do you know what is the biggest cause of dry skin in Canada?"

The Newfie answered: "Towels."

On their first visit to the city, two Newfies went to the zoo. As they entered the big cat house, the lion let out a spine-tingling roar.

"Come on," said one Newfie nervously. "Let's get out of here."

"You go if you want," said the other, "but I'm staying for the whole movie!"

Did you hear about the Newfie who's just read the fifth book in the *Learning to Count* trilogy?

A Newfie wandered into a seedy Montreal bar that had no music, no TV and no pool table. He said to the bartender: "What do you for action around here?"

The bartender pointed to a gorilla sitting quietly in the corner. "Watch this," said the bartender. He then picked up a baseball bat from behind the bar and started hitting the gorilla ferociously about the head with the bat. The dazed gorilla staggered to its feet and gave the bartender a blow job.

"There," said the bartender, holding out the baseball bat. "Now it's your turn."

"Okay," said the Newfie, "but try not to hit me so hard."

Did you hear about the Newfie farmer who tried fish farming but had to give it up after his tractor kept getting stuck in the lake?

Two Newfies drove all the way to the Canadian mainland because they had heard about a bar that ran a competition offering free sex to any lucky winner. When they got there, they ordered some drinks and asked the bartender about it.

"Is the competition running tonight?" they asked.

"Sure," said the bartender.

"Great. How do we enter?"

"It's easy," said the bartender. "I'm thinking of a number between one and ten. If you guess right, you win free sex."

They thought for a moment and then one of them said: "Seven."

"No, sorry," said the bartender. "The number I was thinking of was four. Bad luck."

Undeterred, the pair drove all the way back to the bar the following week and asked the bartender if the free sex competition was still running.

"Yes," said the bartender.

"Okay," said one of the Newfies, "I reckon you're thinking of the number nine."

"That's real bad luck," said the bartender. "You're one out. The number was eight."

As they trudged away, cursing their misfortune, one Newfie turned to the other and said: "You know, I'm beginning to think this competition is rigged."

"It can't be," said his friend. "My wife won twice last week."

Did you hear about the Newfie who accidentally called 911 from his cell phone? – He set his house on fire because he didn't want to look stupid.

A Newfie walked into a St John's bar. The bartender said: "Hey, what are you doing here? Your best friend is up at your apartment right now screwing your wife!"

"That bastard!" the Newfie screamed, running out of the bar.

To the bartender's surprise, the Newfie returned ten minutes later. He marched up to the bar, grabbed the bartender by the lapels, and said: "I ought to fuck you up. You lied to me."

The bartender said: "What do you mean?"

The Newfie yelled: "You made me run up five flights of stairs for nothing. That wasn't my best friend. I don't even know the guy!"

A Newfie and his wife were lying in bed one night but their chances of sleep were being wrecked by their neighbours' dog barking loudly in the garden.

Eventually the Newfie said: "To hell with this!" And he stormed off.

Five minutes later, he came back up upstairs.

"What did you do?" asked his wife.

The Newfie said: "I've put the dog in our garden – let's see how they like it!"

New York

Two New Yorkers were taking a lunch break at their soon-to-be-opened store. One said: "I bet any minute some dumb tourist will walk by, put his face to the window and ask what we're selling."

Sure enough, an Englishman happened to pass by and asked the pair: "What are you selling?"

The New Yorkers replied sarcastically: "We're selling assholes."

"You're certainly doing well," smiled the Englishman. "You've only got two left!"

In New York City, muggings for Apple products are up 40 per cent. Even worse, if you have the new iPhone people camp out overnight to mug you. (Conan O'Brien)

An English tourist and her young son took a taxi in New York. As they drove through a rundown neighbourhood, the boy was fascinated by the women in short skirts and tight tops who were standing on street corners and accosting men.

"What are those ladies doing?" asked the boy.

The mother was embarrassed. "I expect they're lost and are asking for directions."

But the taxi driver interrupted. "Hey, lady, why not tell the kid the truth? They're hookers!"

"What are hookers?" asked the boy.

"They're women who sell their bodies," explained the mother, still angry at the taxi driver's insensitivity.

"Do they have children like other ladies?" asked the boy.

"Yes," said the mother icily. "Their children become New York taxi drivers."

North Korea

A North Korean travelled to England on business. He was asked: "How's life in North Korea?"

"Can't complain," he said.

Have you heard about the new American Express card that is being issued in North Korea? – You never leave home.

Last week there was a lookalike contest in North Korea. Everybody won.

Nudity

A flasher was about to board an airplane. As the pretty young flight attendant collected the boarding passes, the flasher suddenly opened his raincoat and exposed himself to her.

Without skipping a beat, she said: "I'm sorry, sir, but you have to show your ticket, not your stub."

A husband came home to find his wife naked in bed with another man.

"What are you doing?" cried the husband.

The wife turned to her lover and said: "See, I told you he was stupid."

What do you call ten naked men sitting on one another's shoulders? – A scrotum pole.

A young man moved from his parents' home into a new apartment of his own and went to the lobby to put his name on his mailbox. While he was there, an attractive young lady came out of the apartment next to the mailboxes, wearing a robe. The boy smiled at the young woman and she started a conversation with him.

As they talked, her robe slipped open, and it was obvious that she had nothing else on. The poor kid broke into a sweat trying to maintain eye contact. After a few minutes, she placed her hand on his arm and said: "Let's go to my apartment, I hear someone coming."

He followed her into her apartment. She closed the door and leaned against it, allowing her robe to fall off completely. Now completely nude, she purred at him: "What would you say is my best feature?"

Flustered and embarrassed, he finally squeaked: "It's got to be your ears."

Astounded and a little hurt, she asked: "My ears? Look at these breasts; they are full and 100 per cent natural. I work out every day and my butt is firm and solid. Look at my skin – no blemishes anywhere, so how can you possibly think that the best part of my body is my ears?"

Clearing his throat, he stammered: "Outside, when you said you heard someone coming, that was me . . ."

A guy was sunbathing naked on the beach with just his cap over his dick when a woman passed by and said: "If you were a gentleman, you'd lift your hat to a lady."

He replied: "If you weren't so fucking ugly, it would lift itself."

A couple were going to a costume party. The husband was unsure of what costume to wear. His wife was telling him to hurry up or they would be late for the party. She was walking downstairs from the bedroom, completely naked except on her feet were a big old floppy pair of boots.

"Where is your costume?" the husband asked.

"This is it," she replied.

"What kind of costume is that?" he said.

"I'm going as Puss in Boots," she explained. "Now hurry up and get your costume on."

The husband went upstairs and was back in about two minutes. He also was completely naked except he had a rose vase slid over his penis.

"What kind of costume is that?" she asked.

"I'm a fire alarm," he replied.

"A fire alarm?" she repeated.

"Yes," he said. "In case of fire break the glass, pull twice and I'll come."

A young girl hadn't been feeling well, so she went to her family doctor. The doctor ran some tests and then told her she was pregnant.

The girl said: "But I can't be! The only men I've been around are nudists from my colony and we only practise sex with our eyes."

"Well, my dear," said the doctor. "Someone in that colony must be cockeyed."

A woman climbed stark naked into the back of a taxi cab and told the driver to take her to the train station. As they went along, she noticed that he was staring at her through his rear-view mirror.

"Why are you staring at me?" she demanded.

"You're naked," he said, glancing again in the mirror. "Where is the money for your fare? How are you going to pay me?"

She immediately opened her legs, put her feet up on the front seat, grinned and said: "Does this answer your question?"

Still looking in his mirror, the taxi driver said: "Got anything smaller?"

Nuns

Three nuns died and ascended to heaven, but before they were allowed to enter, St Peter told them they each had to answer a question.

St Peter turned to the first nun and said: "What were the names of the two people in the Garden of Eden?"

"Adam and Eve," answered the first nun.

At that, the lights surrounding the pearly gates began to flash.

"You may enter," said St Peter.

Then, addressing the second nun, he asked: "What did Adam eat from the forbidden tree?"

"An apple," answered the second nun.

At that, the lights surrounding the pearly gates flashed and the second nun was allowed to enter.

Finally, St Peter turned to the third nun and asked: "What was the first thing that Eve said to Adam?"

The third nun looked puzzled and sighed: "Gosh, that's a hard one."

And the lights around the pearly gates flashed.

Two nuns were cycling along a cobbled street. One said: "I've never come this way before."

The other nun said: "It must be the cobbles."

When Queen Elizabeth gave birth, they fired a twenty-one-gun salute. When Sister Agnes at the convent gave birth, they fired a dirty old canon.

A monastery was located right next door to a convent, but the monks and the nuns were not allowed to mix or even to speak to each other.

Early one morning, a group of monks went to take a shower but after they had stripped off, they realized there was no soap. In the belief that the nuns would not yet be up, one of the monks bravely volunteered to nip next door to the convent and steal some soap from the nuns' quarters. So, stark naked, he crept into the convent and quickly found some soap in the washroom. But just as he was about to exit the building, he heard three nuns approaching the front door. He decided that his only course of action was to pose as a new statue and hope that the nuns were taken in by it.

As the nuns entered the convent, they immediately saw the naked "statue" up against the wall in the main corridor. Giggling, they walked up to it and admired it.

"This must be the new figure that the Mother Superior was talking about," said one of the nuns. She then playfully tugged on his penis, forcing the monk to drop two of the bars of soap. "Oh, look! It's a soap dispenser!" she exclaimed.

The second nun also pulled on the statue's penis and the same thing happened.

Then the third nun wanted a turn. She gave the penis an extra hard tug and shrieked: "It dispenses hand cream as well!"

Why did the Mother Superior drop dead of a heart attack? — She went to the bathroom and found the seat up.

The nuns at a small convent were delighted to hear that an anonymous donor had left his modest estate to them. Each nun had been left £50 in cash to give away as she saw fit. Sister Mary decided to give her money to the first poor person she saw.

That afternoon she saw a wretched-looking fellow leaning against a wall across the street and decided that he looked sufficiently poor to warrant her charity. So she left the convent and went to talk to him, confident that God had sent him to be a worthy recipient of her money. Approaching him, she pressed the £50 into his hand and said: "Godspeed, my good man."

As she left, the man called out to her: "What is your name?"

"Sister Mary," she replied.

The following evening, the man called at the convent and rang the bell. The Mother Superior answered the door. "I'd like to see Sister Mary," he said.

The Mother Superior explained that Sister Mary was busy in chapel but asked if she could pass on a message.

"Yes," said the man. "Give her this £550 and tell her that Godspeed came in at 10–1 in the fifth race."

Two military cops chased a fleeing draftee into a nearby convent. Spotting a nun sitting in the courtyard, he said: "Quick, sister, hide me. I don't want to be drafted and the military police are after me."

The nun lifted her skirt and told the young man to hide under it.

"You've got nice legs for a nun," he remarked from beneath the skirt.

"If you look up a little further," said the nun, "you'll find a pair of balls. You see, I don't want to be drafted either!"

Three nuns confessed to a priest that they had sinned. The first nun said: "I had impure thoughts about the bishop, Father."

The priest said solemnly: "Drink this holy water."

And she did.

The second nun said: "I let a man kiss me, Father."

The priest said solemnly: "Drink this holy water."

And she did.

The third nun burst out laughing.

"What are you laughing at?" asked the priest. "What sin have you committed that is so funny?"

She said: "I pissed in the holy water!"

The Mother Superior called two novices to her office and asked them to fetch the week's groceries from the local supermarket. As they were leaving the supermarket, they spotted a porn magazine that had been discarded in a garbage bin, so one of them hid it in her habit and smuggled it back into the convent to read later.

Later that day, the Mother Superior was doing her rounds when she hard giggling from the novices' quarters. Stepping in to investigate, she caught them with the porn magazine and told them firmly: "Go and do 500 Hail Marys, then report to me in my office. By then I will have thought up a suitable punishment for you, you wicked, wicked girls."

The girls got the Hail Marys done more quickly than the Mother Superior expected and when they went to her office they caught her pleasuring herself with a large carrot whilst reading the magazine.

"Oh, Mother, what are you doing?" they asked.

Thinking on her feet, the Mother Superior replied: "The vegetable peeler has broken, so I am having to improvise. Now as a punishment you can spend ten days in the kitchen preparing the vegetables and scrubbing the floors. Off you go."

Keen to make sure that the girls were obeying her orders, the Mother Superior went to the kitchen an hour later but was puzzled to hear groaning sounds of ecstasy coming from within. On entering, she found all the kitchen staff "peeling" different vegetables under their habits. Then in a corner she spotted the two novices, their faces bright red and sweating profusely.

"What in God's name are you two doing?" barked the Mother Superior.

"The chillies, Mother," they gasped breathlessly. "It's curry night tonight."

Two novice nuns and a Mother Superior were riding a tandem bicycle. Soon they hit a bump in the road and the young nuns giggled, at which the Mother Superior gave them a dirty look. A few minutes later, they hit another bump in the road. Again the nuns giggled and the Mother Superior expressed her disgust. When it happened for the fifth time, the Mother Superior stopped the bike, turned to the nuns and said: "Listen, if you two don't behave yourselves I'm going to put the seats back on."

A Mother Superior went into a grocery store and said: "I would like to order seventy-five bananas for the convent."

The grocer suggested: "You'll find that with such large numbers it will work out more economical if you buy a hundred."

"Oh well," said the Mother Superior, "I suppose we could always *eat* the other twenty-five."

While driving to church, an elderly priest suffered a flat tyre. A young man passing by offered to change the tyre, and the priest was happy to accept his generosity.

"I'm not a Catholic myself," admitted the young man, "but I like to help someone in their hour of need."

The young man then proceeded to change the tyre, and when he had finished he stood back to admire his handiwork. "There you go, Father," he said. "All done and dusted."

"Are the wheel nuts on tight? I wouldn't want the wheel to fall off."

"Yes, Father. They're as tight as a nun!"

"Well, in that case," said the elderly priest, "you'd better give them another couple of turns."

The Mother Superior was doing the late-night rounds of the nuns' dormitory. "Come along now, sisters," she said. "It's eleven o'clock. Candles out."

As she closed the door, she heard slurping sounds from all around the room.

A man was driving down a deserted stretch of highway when he noticed a sign out of the corner of his eye. It read: SISTERS OF ST CATHERINE's HOUSE OF PROSTITUTION 10 MILES. Thinking it must have been a figment of his imagination caused by fatigue he drove on but a few minutes later he saw another sign, which said: SISTERS OF ST CATHERINE's HOUSE OF PROSTITUTION 5 MILES. He now began to realize that the signs were genuine, so when he drove past a third sign saying: SISTERS OF ST CATHERINE's HOUSE OF PROSTITUTION NEXT RIGHT, his curiosity got the better of him and he pulled into the drive.

On the far side of the parking lot was a sombre stone building with a small sign next to the door reading: SISTERS OF ST CATHERINE's. He climbed the steps and rang the bell. The door was answered by a nun in a long black habit who asked: "What may we do for you, my son?"

He answered hesitantly: "I saw your signs along the highway and was interested in possibly doing business."

"Very well, my son," said the nun, beckoning him through the door. "Please follow me."

He was then led through a series of winding passages until he had become quite disoriented. Eventually the nun stopped at a closed door and told the man to knock on it. When he did so, the door was answered by another nun in a long habit, holding a tin cup. This nun told him: "Please place £50 in the cup, then go through the large wooden door at the end of this hallway."

So he pulled £50 from his wallet and placed it in the second nun's cup. He then trotted eagerly down the hall and slipped through the door, pulling it shut behind him. As the door locked behind him, he found himself back in the parking lot, facing another small sign: GO IN PEACE. YOU HAVE JUST BEEN SCREWED BY THE SISTERS OF ST CATHERINE's.

Nursery Rhymes

Mary had a little lamb,
It had a touch of colic.
She gave it brandy twice a day
And now it's alcoholic.

Jack and Jill went up the hill
To have some hanky-panky.
Silly Jill forgot her pill
And now there's little Franky.

Mary, Mary, quite contrary,
How does your garden grow?
"The plants are high
Since I buried my guy
Deep in the marigold row."

Mary had a little lamb.
Its fleece was white and wispy.
Then it caught Foot and Mouth Disease
And now it's black and crispy.

Jack be nimble,
Jack be quick,
Jack jumped over the candlestick.
But Jack wasn't nimble
And Jack wasn't quick,
So Jack went home with a charbroiled dick.

Humpty Dumpty sat on the bed,
Little Bo Peep was giving him head.
As he came, she started to weep,
She could tell by the taste he'd been shagging her sheep.

Mary had a little lamb,
She ate it with mint sauce,

And everywhere that Mary went
The lamb went too, of course.

Little Bo Peep has lost her sheep
And didn't know where to find them.
But a search revealed
They were in the next field
With a dirty big Welshman behind them.

The Grand Old Duke of York,
He had 10,000 men,
He marched them up to the top of the hill
Where he had them all again.

Mary, Mary, quite contrary,
How does your garden grow?
"I live in a flat,
You stupid twat,
So how the fuck should I know?"

Humpty Dumpty sat on a wall,
Humpty Dumpty had a great fall.
Got compensation paid up front,
A month off work, the lazy cunt.

Jack be nimble,
Jack be quick,
Jack jumped over the candlestick.
Dear oh dear, he should have jumped higher,
Goodness gracious, great balls of fire!

Nymphomaniacs

A woman went to the doctor and said: "Doctor, it's not fair. Everyone says I'm a nymphomaniac."

"I see," said the doctor.

"Well, are you going to do something about it?" she snapped impatiently.

"Madam," he replied, "I would be able to take better notes if you'd let go of my dick."

How do you prevent a nymphomaniac from having sex? – Marry her.

A woman went to see a psychiatrist. "Doctor," she said, "I think I might be a nymphomaniac."

"Very well," he said. "I'll see what I can do to help you. My fee is £80 per hour."

She said: "How much for all night?"

"Doctor, I need your help," said a woman in her late forties.

"What seems to be the problem?"

"My husband just doesn't satisfy me sexually. What can I do?"

"Hmm. That's a bit out of my league. Has *he* seen a doctor?"

"Yes, he has. He is perfectly okay. He just isn't enough for me. You've got to help me!"

"Well, have you considered taking a lover?"

"I have! I still don't get enough."

"Take another lover."

"I did. In fact, I have eight lovers – and I still don't get enough sex!"

"Gosh, that's an anomaly."

"Oh, Doctor! Please tell them it's an anomaly! They all keep telling me I'm a whore!"

Why does a nymphomaniac close her eyes during sex? – So she can fantasize about shopping.

A man asked his friend: "How did your date with the deaf nymphomaniac go last night?"

"Pretty good. But I need to brush up on my sign language."

"Why?"

"They kicked us out of the restaurant when I asked her if she likes the taste of gum."

Did you hear about the nymphomaniac's car? – I went from zero to sixty-nine in ten seconds.

A son asked his ninety-year-old widower father why he was marrying a young nymphomaniac whom he could never satisfy instead of a woman his own age.

The old man replied with a smile: "I'd rather have 10 per cent of a good business than 100 per cent interest in a bankrupt one."

A wealthy old man of eighty-six married a twenty-one-year-old nymphomaniac. On their wedding night, they got into bed and he held up four fingers.

Her eyes lit up. "Does that mean we're going to have sex four times?"

"No," said the old man. "It means you can take your pick."

You Know You're a Nymphomaniac If . . .

- The local hooker walks out when she sees you enter the bar.
- Your condom bill is bigger than your phone bill.
- You're divorcing your husband because he doesn't have enough male relatives.
- You read *Fifty Shades of Grey* and wondered why it's so undersexed.
- You're on first-name terms with the staff at the health clinic.
- Your boyfriend takes you to a swingers' party so he can have a rest.
- Your idea of getting dressed up does not involve more than eight ounces of clothing.
- You're being named in more than three divorce cases at once.
- You go to the pound to pick out a dog and choose the one that starts humping your leg.
- You buy K-Y jelly by the case.
- You schedule your dates with men by the hour rather than by the day.

Old People

A ninety-seven-year-old man and a ninety-six-year-old woman had formed a close relationship in an old folk's home. The highlight of their week was every Friday evening when she would jerk him off in her room. This ritual went on for fifteen months until one Friday evening he didn't show for their weekly rendezvous.

"Where were you last night?" she asked him the following morning.

"I was with another woman," he replied.

"Another woman! I guess it was someone younger. Tell me, who was it?"

"Ethel Davis."

"Ethel Davis! But she's ninety-six, the same age as me. I cater to all your needs. What's she got that I haven't?"

"Parkinson's."

Why don't old people get smear tests? – Have you ever tried to open a cheese toastie?

An old man was doing a crossword puzzle. After studying a clue for a while, he turned to his wife and asked: "What's the definition of indefinitely?"

She replied: "You know when we have sex doggie-style and your balls slap against the back of my ass?"

"Yes . . ."

"Well, I'd say when that happens you're indefinitely."

Two old men were talking about sex. One said: "I can't remember the last time I got lucky. It's been ages since I had sex. How about you?"

His friend said: "Well, I've still got what it takes to get a woman into the bedroom."

"Oh yes. What's that?"

"A stairlift."

A ninety-five-year-old man lived in a rest home but had a weekend pass to go into town. One Saturday night he went into a bar where he met a seventy-year-old woman. They started chatting and ended up going back to her apartment, where they went to bed. Five days later, he noticed he was developing a drip on his penis, so he went to see his doctor.

"Have you recently engaged in sex?" asked the doctor.

"Actually I have," said the old man.

"Can you remember the name of the woman and where she lives?"

"Yes, I can. Why?"

"Well, you'd better get over there. You're about to cum!"

Bert and Ethel were sitting at the breakfast table one morning. Out of the blue Bert said: "If I were to die suddenly, I want you to sell all my stuff immediately."

"Why would you want me to do something like that?" Ethel asked.

"Well," said Bert, "I figure that eventually you'd remarry, and I don't want some other asshole using my stuff."

Ethel looked at him and said: "What makes you think I'd marry another asshole?"

A couple in their eighties decided to consult a fertility expert to discover whether it was possible for them to have another child. The doctor said new scientific developments meant there was a chance, and he gave them a jar and asked them to return with a semen sample.

The following day they went back to the doctor's with an empty jar. "I'm sorry, Doc," said the husband. "I tried my right hand, I tried my left hand. My wife tried her right hand, my wife tried her left hand. She took her teeth out and used her mouth. But still we couldn't get the lid off the damn jar!"

This letter was sent to the school principal's office after the school had sponsored a luncheon for seniors. An elderly lady received a new radio at the lunch as a door raffle prize and was writing to say thank you:

Dear St Saviour's High School,

God bless you for the beautiful radio I won at your recent Senior Citizens luncheon. I am eighty-seven years old and live at the South Colorado Home for the Aged. All of my family has passed away so I am all alone. I want to thank you for the kindness you have shown to a forgotten old lady.

My roommate is ninety-five and has always had her own radio; but she would never let me listen to it. She said it belonged to her long dead husband, and understandably, wanted to keep it safe.

The other day her radio fell off the nightstand and broke into a dozen pieces. It was awful and she was in tears.

She asked if she could listen to mine, and I was overjoyed that I could tell her to fuck off.

Thank you for that wonderful opportunity.

God bless you all.

Sincerely,

Edna

Why is an old woman's fanny like a pork pie? – Because you have to bite through the crust and suck out all the jelly to get to the meat.

An old man woke up in the middle of the night and found, to his utter astonishment, that his pecker was as hard as a rock for the first time in two years. He shook his wife by the shoulder until she woke up and then he showed her his enormous boner. "You see that thing, woman?" he happily exclaimed. "What do you think we ought to do with it?"

With one eye open, his wife replied: "Well, now that you've got all the wrinkles out, this might be a good time to wash it."

I call my granddad Spider-Man. He doesn't have any special powers – he just finds it difficult getting out of the bath.

Two old guys, aged eighty-one and eighty-five, were sitting on their favourite park bench one morning. The eighty-five-year-old had just finished his morning jog and wasn't even short of breath. The eighty-one-year-old was amazed at his friend's stamina and asked him what he did to have so much energy.

The eighty-five-year-old said: "Well, I eat rye bread every day. It's a well-known fact that it keeps your energy level high, and that it will give you great stamina with the ladies."

So on the way home, the eighty-one-year-old stopped off at the bakery. As he was looking round, the female sales clerk asked him if he needed any assistance.

"Do you have any rye bread?" he asked.

"Yes," she said. "There's a whole shelf of it. Would you like some?"

"Sure. I'd like five loaves."

"My goodness, five loaves!" she exclaimed. "By the time you get to the fifth loaf, it'll be hard."

"I don't believe it!" he exclaimed. "Everyone knows about this stuff except me!"

A man was walking along the street when he saw an old lady approaching from the other direction. Feeling randy, he leered: "Show us your tits, love."

So she lifted up her skirt.

Henry and Mabel were sitting in the lounge of the retirement home one evening, Henry was wearing his pyjamas and dressing-gown.

Mabel glanced over and whispered: "Henry, do yourself up properly. Your willy's sticking out!"

Henry looked down and said: "Don't flatter yourself, Mabel. My willy's *hanging* out!"

My gran said to me: "Young men of today just aren't as polite and charming as they were when I was young." I had to explain: "That's because they aren't trying to fuck you now!" (Frankie Boyle)

For his seventy-fifth birthday, a husband was asked by his wife if he wanted a blow job or a hand job. Thinking that his luck was in, he replied eagerly: "I'll have the blow job, please."

"Good choice," she said. "If you put that many candles out with your hand, you'd burn your fingers!"

About to get married, a shy young man summoned the courage to ask his grandfather about sex. "How often is a married man expected to have sex?" he asked.

"Well," said the grandfather, "when you first get married, you want it all the time and maybe you'll do it several times a week. Later on, sex tapers off, down to maybe once a week. Then as you get older, it goes down to about once a month, and when you get really old, you're lucky to get it once a year, like on your anniversary."

"How about you and Grandma now?" asked the young man.

"We just have oral sex now," replied the old man.

"What's oral sex?"

"Well, she goes to bed in her bedroom, and I go to bed in my bedroom. She yells, 'Screw you!' And I yell back, 'Screw you, too!'"

A couple celebrating their fiftieth wedding anniversary decided to recapture the magic of yesteryear by booking into the same hotel where they had spent their honeymoon.

Over breakfast the wife said excitedly: "Oh, Ted, it's just like fifty years ago. My breasts feel all warm and tingly."

"So they should, Mabel. One's hanging in your porridge and the other's in your coffee!"

Why don't old ladies have Brazilians? – I don't know; it's a bit of a grey area.

A little girl was taking a shower with her grandma when she pointed down and asked: "What's that?"

"That's my beaver," replied the grandma.

The next day the girl was in the shower with her mum and again she pointed down and said: "I know what that is, Mum, it's a beaver."

"How do you know a word like that?" asked her mother, shocked.

"Grandma told me," said the little girl, "but I think hers is dead because its tongue is hanging out."

Two old men were enjoying a nice cup of tea and a biscuit. One said to the other: "I'm really starting to feel my age, George."

"What makes you think that, Bill?" asked the other. "You seem quite sprightly to me."

"Well, the other night, Moira had gone to bed early so I was flicking around the TV channels looking for something to watch and I stumbled across this adults-only channel. There was this gorgeous girl in a skimpy little French maid's outfit, pushing a vacuum cleaner around and bending over provocatively. And as her little skirt rode up, exposing her lovely little bottom with the tiny strip of black material covering her crack, all I could think was: 'We used to have a Hoover like that one.'"

A number of hotel guests were awoken one night by a furious pounding on the walls of room 214. They called the hotel manager, who let himself into the room, where he found an elderly man cursing and banging away on the wall with both fists.

"Stop that!" the manager ordered. "You're disturbing the entire hotel!"

"Damn the hotel!" yelled the old man. "It's the first erection I've had in years, and both my hands are asleep!"

An old woman was driving her husband in the country when she was pulled over by a highway patrol. The officer stepped out of his car and quizzed the old woman.

"Ma'am, did you know you were speeding?"

"What did he say?" said the woman to her husband.

The husband shouted: "He says you were speeding."

"May I see your licence?" said the officer.

"What did he say?" said the old woman.

"He wants to see your licence," shouted the husband.

She handed the officer her licence. The officer studied it carefully. "I see you're from West Virginia," he said. "I spent some time there once. I remember I had the worst sex with a woman I've ever had in my life."

"What did he say?" said the old woman.

The husband yelled: "He thinks he knows you."

Sure Signs That You're Getting Old

- You start laughing and tears run down your legs.
- All the noises you used to make during sex, you now make getting out of bed.
- Your houseplants are alive, and you can't smoke any of them.
- Having sex in a single bed is out of the question.
- 6 a.m. is when you get up, not when you go to bed.
- You and your teeth don't sleep together.
- All you want for your birthday is not to be reminded of your age.
- Getting a little action means not needing to take a laxative.
- You hear your favourite song in an elevator.
- You confuse having a clear conscience with having a bad memory.
- The end of your tie doesn't come anywhere near the top of your trousers.
- You take a cushion to football matches because the seats are uncomfortable.
- You book train tickets for the quiet carriage.
- Your reclining chair has more options than your car.
- Getting lucky means finding your car in the car park.
- You start wearing beige.
- Your health insurance company sends you a six-month calendar.
- You wake up looking like your passport picture.
- Half the stuff in your shopping trolley says, "For Fast Relief".
- People call at 9.30 p.m. and ask: "Did I wake you?"
- You look both ways before crossing a room.
- You've still got it, but nobody wants to see it.

An old couple settled down for the night. He lay on the bed but she decided to lie on the floor.

"Why are you sleeping on the floor?" he asked.

She said: "Because I want to feel something hard for a change."

An eighty-nine-year-old woman walked into the recreational room of a retirement home and, holding her clenched fist in the air, announced: "Anyone who can guess what's in my hand can fuck me tonight."

An uninterested old man called out: "An elephant."

The woman thought for a moment and said: "Near enough."

Bert agreed to fix up his widowed friend Arthur with a date. Arthur said he wanted an elegant, mature woman with a good sense of humour, and Bert said he knew just the lady. However, when Arthur met her for the first time he was horrified.

Taking Bert to one side, Arthur hissed: "She's the ugliest woman I've ever set eyes on. Her hair's falling out, she's hardly got any teeth, she's got a wooden leg and she's only got one eye!"

"There's no need to whisper," said Bert. "She's deaf, too!"

Orgasm

An Italian, a Frenchman and a Jew were boasting about how skilled they were at bringing their respective wives to orgasm.

The Italian said: "My wife screams for fifteen minutes after we have sex."

The Frenchman said: "My wife screams for thirty minutes after we have sex."

The Jew said: "The last time we had sex, I got out of bed, wiped my dick on the bedroom curtain, and my wife is still screaming!"

My wife's so ungrateful. The other day I gave her a massive orgasm and she just spat it out.

Little Johnny was sleeping in bed when his mother called out: "Rise and shine, Johnny. Time to wake up!"

Johnny shouted back: "Five more minutes, Mum!"

His mother decided to allow him the extra five minutes and started cooking breakfast.

Five minutes later, Little Johnny went downstairs into the kitchen crying his eyes out.

"What's the matter, Johnny?" asked his mother.

"I had a wet dream last night," he sobbed.

"Oh," said the mother, surprised but keeping her composure. "Well, that's nothing to cry over, is it?"

"Yes, it is," said Little Johnny. "Now whenever anyone asks me what was the first thing I said after my first orgasm, I'll have to tell them: 'Five more minutes, Mum!' "

A single girl told her psychiatrist: "I sometimes have as many as twenty consecutive orgasms during my clitoris stimulation sessions."

"That's amazing," said the normally unflappable shrink.

"Oh, I don't know," shrugged the woman, "after sixteen or so I run out of fantasies and from then on it's not much fun."

How do you know your girlfriend's having an orgasm? – My truck is parked in her driveway.

I give women two types of orgasms. Fake and none. (Adam Carolla)

A teenage girl was developing rapidly, so her mother thought it about time that she understood the facts of life.

"Emma," she began, "I think it would be nice if we had a little chat about how life is formed. As you know, a baby grows in a lady's tummy and—"

"It might be interesting to hear you tell it, Mum," interrupted the daughter, "but what I really want to know is how to fake an orgasm."

A couple who had been married for thirty-five years were lying in a hotel bed, about to go to sleep. Then through the wall they heard a young woman's voice say: "Oh, honey, you're so strong!"

The husband turned to his wife and asked: "Why don't you ever say that to me?"

"Because," she replied, "you're not strong anymore."

A few minutes later, they heard the young woman's voice again. "Oh, honey, you're so romantic!"

The husband turned to his wife. "Why don't you ever say that to me?"

"Because," she said, "you're not romantic anymore."

Ten minutes later, they heard the young woman groan: "Oh, honey, that was a fantastic orgasm! Thank you."

The husband turned to his wife. "Why don't you ever tell me when you have a fantastic orgasm?"

"Because," she said, "you're never around when I have them!"

Periods

An American schoolteacher asked her children's art class to draw on the blackboard their impressions of the most exciting thing they could think of. One boy got up and drew a long, jagged line.

"What's that?" asked the teacher.

"Lightning," said the boy. "Every time I see lightning, I get so excited I scream!"

"Very good," said the teacher.

Next, a little girl drew a wavy line with the broad side of the chalk. She explained that was her idea of thunder, which always excited her. The teacher thought that was excellent, too.

Then Little Johnny stepped to the board and made a single dot and sat down.

"What's that?" queried the teacher, a bit perplexed.

"It's a period," replied Little Johnny.

"What's so exciting about a period?"

"I don't know, Teacher," replied Little Johnny, "but my sister missed two of 'em and my whole family's excited!"

Have you heard about the new all-female delivery service? — It's called UPMS, and they deliver whenever the hell they feel like it.

What's the difference between regular blood and period blood? — You can eat period blood with a fork.

How can you tell which bottle contains the PMT medicine? — It's the one with the teeth marks.

One day, Little Jenny got her monthly bleeding for the first time. Frightened because she wasn't really sure what was happening, she decided to tell Little Johnny. He asked her to drop her panties so he could see for himself. When she did, his eyes widened in amazement.

"Listen," he said, "I'm not a doctor, but it looks to me like someone's just ripped your balls off."

What's the difference between menstrual blood and sand? — You can't gargle sand.

A guy cuddled up to his wife and whispered: "I'm in the mood for some sixty-nine. How about it?"

"Well," she said, "it's that time of the month, but if you don't care, I certainly don't."

So they went into the bedroom, and were enjoying a wild sixty-nine when they heard the doorbell ring.

"Quick! Answer the door," she hissed.

"I can't," he replied. "My face is a mess."

"It's only the mailman," she said, "but he'll have that parcel I've been waiting all week for. Just answer the door and if he says anything, tell him you were eating a jam sandwich."

So the husband hurried downstairs, opened the door and immediately apologized for his appearance. "I'm sorry about my mouth," he said, "I was eating a jam sandwich."

The mailman said: "I wasn't looking at the jam on your mouth – I was looking at the peanut butter on your forehead!"

A man and his wife were vacationing on their yacht off the coast of South Africa. After they had sailed out to sea a few miles, he asked her: "Do you want to go swimming?"

"I can't," she said. "I'm on my period."

"Damn!" he moaned. "You always take the fun out of shark fishing."

A woman was standing in an alley waiting for a friend when she was approached by a sinister-looking man brandishing a gun.

"Take off your top!" he barked.

"I can't," she said.

"Take it off!" he ordered, thrusting the gun in her face.

Shaking with fear, she pulled off her top.

"Okay, now the bra!" he demanded.

"I don't want to," she whimpered. "Please . . ."

"Do it or I'll shoot you!" he sneered.

Reluctantly she removed her bra.

"Now take off your trousers – and quick about it!" he shouted, pressing the gun into her mouth.

Terrified, she took off her trousers.

"Now your pretty little panties!" he growled triumphantly.

"You don't want me to do that," she stammered.

"Do it now!" he yelled.

So she pulled down her panties. To the gunman's horror, not only was she on her period, but she had a nasty-looking rash and maggots were crawling all over her pubic hair. He was so disgusted by the sight that he accidentally dropped his gun.

Quick as a flash, the woman picked up the gun, pointed it at him and said: "Eat me!"

Phone Sex

A man read a newspaper advertisement that said: "Dial Sexy, local rate calls." He rang the number and a woman answered: "Good evening, Dyslexia Help Line."

I had unprotected phone sex last month. Turns out I now have hearing aids.

A man said to his friend: "I've been saving a fortune lately."
  "How come?"
  "Well, instead of calling expensive sex lines, I call the Samaritans and say: 'Talk dirty or I'll kill myself!'"

I had phone sex last night. I had to get the morning-after bill.

Suffering from premature ejaculation, a man went to see a psychiatrist to see if he could find a solution to the problem. The psychiatrist made some suggestions, but the man returned the following week.
  "Oh," said the psychiatrist. "Hasn't my advice worked?"
  "Actually," said the man, "I've decided I don't want to be cured after all."
  "Why not?"
  "I just received my phone bill. I made fifteen sex-line calls last month, and they only cost me a total of £5!"

Police

A police officer knocked on the door of a man's house and said: "Excuse me, sir, have you driven your car at all this morning?"
  "No, officer," replied the man. "I've been in bed all morning."
  "I see, sir," said the officer, not convinced by the alibi. "It's just that your car was reported as having been involved in an accident, and I've just felt the hood, and it's warm, so we know you've been using it."
  The man said angrily: "Well, why don't you put your hands down your pants and touch your dick?"
  "Why?" asked the officer.
  Slamming the door in the cop's face, the man yelled: "Just because it's warm doesn't mean you've been using it!"

Two policewomen were out on the beat with a police dog on a cold winter night. One said: "I've only gone and left my knickers in the locker room back at the station, and now I'm bloody freezing!"

The other said: "Listen, Prince the sniffer dog is very well trained, let him have a whiff of your minge, and then he will go back to the station and retrieve your knickers for you."

So the dog had a sniff and off he went. Ten minutes later the dog came back . . . with the chief superintendent's glove!

What do you call a policewoman who hasn't shaved her minge for a few days? – Cuntstubble.

Driving down a country lane, a police officer spotted three parked cars all with their windows steamed up. He knocked on the window of the first car, and a half-dressed girl wound it down.

"What are you doing in there?" asked the cop.

"The tango," replied the girl.

The cop accepted her explanation and moved on to the second car. He tapped on the window and another half-dressed girl wound it down.

"What are you doing in there?" asked the cop.

"The bossa nova," replied the girl.

The cop seemed happy with her explanation, so he tapped on the window of the third car. Once again, a half-dressed girl, her hair all over the place, wound down the window.

"So what are you doing?" asked the cop. "The tango or the bossa nova?"

"Neither," said the girl. "I'm doing the boss a favour."

A Mississippi police department was staging a recruitment drive. The interviewer said to the first candidate: "Right, here's a gun with six bullets in it. All you have to do to join the force is shoot five black people and one white rabbit."

The candidate asked: "Why do you want me to shoot a white rabbit?"

"Good answer. You're in."

A woman was driving alone along a deserted road in the middle of nowhere. She came to a stop sign, but because there were no other cars about, she just slowed down a little and went straight through it. Immediately, however, she heard a siren, so she pulled over.

When the police officer walked over to her window to give her a ticket, she protested: "I know I broke the law, officer, but it doesn't really matter, does it, because there was no one around? Besides, I slowed down a bit."

The officer said: "Here, I'll show you why it matters. Get out of the car!"

She got out of the car, whereupon he pulled out his baton and started beating her violently. "No one is around," he yelled. "Now do you want me to slow down or stop?"

A woman ran into a police station and cried: "Help! I've been graped!"

"Don't you mean raped?" replied the officer.

"No, there was a bunch of them."

A policewoman was posing as a street-corner hooker as part of a vice-squad initiative. After only two nights, she had made more than a dozen arrests. Alarmed at the effect her presence was having on their trade, the genuine hookers arranged for a local evangelical preacher to visit the corner and save the poor woman's soul. Sure enough, the following night, the preacher and a group of his followers began reciting the gospel on that same street corner. Much to her annoyance, this drove away all of the undercover cop's potential arrests.

Eventually, in frustration and in an attempt to get rid of the do-gooders, she produced her badge and showed it to the preacher. "Oh, my dear," he said, shocked. "Don't they pay you enough these days to be a policewoman?"

A police detective was grilling a suspect concerning his whereabouts at the time of a vicious assault. "So you say you were out walking your dog at 9.15 p.m. on the evening of 6 February? Did you or did you not stop along the way?"

The suspect looked at him incredulously, and then asked: "Have you ever walked a fucking dog?"

The Polish

A Polish guy was having sex with a girl when he suddenly stopped mid-thrust and kept really still.

"What are you doing?" she asked.

"It's something I learned from online porn," he replied. "It's called buffering."

Why do Polish workers have see-through lids on their lunch boxes? – So they know if it's morning or afternoon.

In an attempt to rectify their nation's unwanted reputation for incompetence, a group of Poles decided to seek the advice of some eminent Americans, Germans and Japanese.

The American replied: "You must do something to earn the respect of the world. The Japanese are known for their technology and the Germans are famous for their organizational skills, while we Americans have enjoyed respect since we helped defeat the other two in the Second World War. You need to do something that will bring you international recognition."

The German added: "He's right. Why don't you find a place in the world that is in need of a bridge, but in a landscape so inhospitable and untamed that no one has ever dared build it there? And when you've built it, come back to the three of us and we will help publicize your fantastic achievement to the rest of the world."

So the Poles went off to build their bridge. They worked for six months on the design, another four months on the construction and then erected it . . . in the middle of the Sahara Desert.

When the American saw the bridge, he shook his head in despair and said: "You see, this is why you have your reputation. There is no need for a bridge in the middle of a desert. Now go and dismantle it and find a more strategic spot to erect it."

Two weeks later, the Poles returned to the group. The Japanese expert was particularly impressed. "Two weeks! You have managed to dismantle a bridge and build a new one in two weeks? That is amazing!"

"No, not exactly," replied the Poles. "You see, when we returned to the bridge, we couldn't dismantle it because there were all these Italians fishing off it!"

Two Polish guys were trapped in a dark cave. "I can't see anything," said one. "Have you got a match?"

The second guy struck the match against the wall of the cave but nothing happened. "That's odd," he said. "This match worked okay this morning."

A Polish guy went into the boss's office and handed him a pear. "What's this for?" asked the boss.

"A pay rise," replied the Pole. "My wife told me to grow it first and then ask you."

Two Polish guys were poring over their problems in a bar. One said: "I think my wife is selling drugs."

"What makes you think that?" asked his friend.

"Well, yesterday I was running late for work and the phone rang. I answered it, but before I could say anything a male voice on the line said: 'Hey, honey, is that dope gone yet?' "

Why did the Polish guy put ice in his condom? – To keep the swelling down.

When Mr Kapinski arrived home from work one afternoon, he found his neighbour waiting on the driveway. The neighbour said: "It may be none of my business, but this morning a strange man came to your house and your wife let him in. Half an hour later, I happened to glance through your living-room window, and I saw the pair of them naked having sex."

"This man," said Mr Kapinski, "was he short, about five foot five?"

"Yes, he was," said the neighbour.

"And did he have long, black, greasy hair and a scar on the left side of his face?"

"Yes, I think he did," said the neighbour.

"Don't worry," said Mr Kapinski, "that's the plumber. He'll screw anyone!"

A Polish guy thought he'd met his dream woman until he looked through her wardrobe and found a French maid's outfit, a nurse's uniform and a policewoman's uniform. He thought: "I can't go out with her – she can't even hold down a job."

A US factory that makes the Tickle Me Elmo toys – the toy that laughs when you tickle it under the arms – took on a new Polish employee. But on only the Polish guy's second day at work, the foreman complained to the human-resources manager that he was so slow, he was holding up the entire production line.

The HR manager decided to investigate for himself, and so the two men went down to the factory floor. There, they saw the Polish guy surrounded by dozens of Tickle Me Elmos while his fellow workers waited impatiently. He had a roll of plush red fabric and a huge bag of small marbles, and the HR manager and the foreman watched in amazement as he cut a piece of fabric, wrapped it around two marbles and carefully sewed the little package between each Elmo's legs.

The HR manager suddenly burst out laughing and told the Polish guy: "I'm sorry, but I think you misunderstood the instructions I gave you yesterday. Your job is to give Elmo two test tickles!"

A Polish guy had a leak in the roof over his dining room, so he called a plumber to take a look at it.

"When did you first notice the leak?" the plumber asked.

The Polish guy said: "Last night, when it took me two hours to finish my soup!"

Andrzej and Bronislaw, on a trip to the US, decided to try some of the seafood they had heard so much about back home. At the Captain's Retreat Restaurant, Andrzej ordered baked flounder and steamed lobster legs and Bronislaw asked for a huge plate of oysters. "What's this 'oh natchrel' mean?" he asked the waiter.

"That means we cook the oysters and bring them to you just as they came from the sea," the waiter replied.

Thirty minutes later, Bronislaw began experiencing horrendous stomach cramps so Andrzej called a taxi and rushed him to the emergency room of a large hospital. When the examining doctor learned Bronislaw had eaten a plate of oysters less than an hour before, he asked: "Were those oysters fresh?"

"I don't know, Doc," Bronislaw groaned. "Until today I have never seen an oyster, let alone eat one."

"Well, what colour were they when you shelled them?" the doctor asked.

Andrzej and Bronislaw looked puzzled.

"Shelled?!" they asked.

Politicians

George W. Bush woke up one December morning, opened the curtains and looked down on freshly settled snow on the lawn outside his home. To his horror and anger, he saw that someone had written in piss "George W. Bush is a Moron". He summoned the chief of police and ordered that tests be carried out on the urine to determine who was responsible.

Later that day, the chief of police reported back. "Sir," he said solemnly, "I have some bad news and some awful news."

"Okay, I can take it," said Bush. "Give it to me straight."

"Well, sir, the bad news is the urine we tested is actually your father's, and the awful news is it's your wife's handwriting."

A staunch Conservative man from the north of England married a woman who came from a Labour-supporting family. The reception was in full swing and everyone was having a great time until the groom climbed onto a table and proposed a toast, "To the Conservative Party!" Hearing this, the wife's family stormed out, and she immediately stopped talking to her new husband.

Later that night, when they got to bed in the honeymoon hotel, he tried to instigate sex with her but she pretended to be asleep and did not respond. After another two futile attempts, he gave up.

However, the wife then started to feel guilty and decided that perhaps she had been a little harsh on him. So in a tactical climbdown, she whispered: "Darling, there's a split in the Labour party and if the Conservative candidate would like to stand, there's a good chance he'll get in!"

The groom replied: "Too bloody late! The Conservative candidate has stood three times already but failed to get in, so he went independent and lost his deposit!"

Why did God give Republicans one more brain cell than a horse? — So they wouldn't shit during the parade.

Ted Kennedy: a good senator but a bad date. (Denis Leary)

A young boy told his father: "Dad, I have to write an essay for school about politics, but I don't really know what politics is. Can you help me?"

"Well," said the father, "let's take our home as an example. I am the bread-winner, so let's call me Capitalism. Your mom is the administrator of money, so let's call her the Government. We take care of your needs, so let's call you the People. We'll call the maid the Working Class and your baby brother the Future. Does that make it clearer?"

"I'm not sure, Dad," said the boy. "I guess I'll have to think about it."

That night, awakened by his brother's crying, the boy went to see what was wrong. Discovering that the baby had seriously soiled his diaper, the boy went to his parents' room and found his mother sound asleep. He then went to the maid's room where, peeking through the keyhole, he saw his father in bed with the maid. He knocked tentatively on the door but neither his father nor the maid responded. So he returned to his room and went back to sleep.

The next morning he said to his father: "Now I think I know what politics is."

"Good, son. Now explain it to me in your own words."

"Well, Dad, while Capitalism is screwing the Working Class, the Government is sound asleep, the People are being completely ignored and the Future is full of shit."

Police in London have found a bomb outside the Houses of Parliament. They've told the public not to panic as they've managed to push it inside.

What's the difference between a condom and the Houses of Parliament? – You can only get one knob in a condom.

Tony Blair was our first metrosexual Prime Minister. He had enough personality to be gay, yet caused enough atrocities to be straight. (Shazia Mirza)

Mitt Romney was rehearsing his speech for the 2012 London Olympics. He began his remarks with "Oh, oh, oh, oh, oh." Immediately his speech writer rushed over to the lectern and whispered in his ear: "Sir, those are the Olympic rings. Your speech is underneath."

On the eve of the 2012 US Presidential election a confident Mitt Romney told his wife: "This time tomorrow night you'll be sleeping with the President of the United States."

After Mitt's concession speech, he and Ann went to bed. As she was getting undressed, she asked him: "So how does this work? Is Barack coming over here or am I supposed to go over to his?"

At a news conference a journalist stood up and asked a politician: "Your assistant said publicly that you have a big penis. Would you care to comment on that?"

The politician replied: "My assistant has a big mouth."

They don't want you to vote. If they did, we wouldn't vote on a Tuesday. In November. You ever throw a party on a Tuesday? No. Because nobody would come. (Chris Rock)

Three former US Presidents were caught in a tornado, and carried off to the land of Oz, where they came before the Great Wizard.

"What brings you before the Great Wizard of Oz?" he boomed.

Jimmy Carter stepped forward timidly: "I've come for some courage."

"Consider it done," said the Grand Wizard. "Who is next?"

George Bush Sr stepped forward and said: "I was always told by the American people that I needed a heart, and while we're at it, my boy could do with a brain."

"Consider both done," said the Grand Wizard. "Who is next?"

There was a moment's silence until Bill Clinton stepped forward and asked quietly: "Is Dorothy here?"

A Democrat walked into a New York City antiques shop and after looking around for a while he spotted a lifelike bronze statue of a rat. It had no price tag but was so impressive that he decided to buy it anyway.

He took it to the shop owner and said: "How much is this bronze rat?"

The owner replied: "It's $10 for the rat and $100 for the story."

"Forget the story," said the Democrat, "I'll just take the statue."

As he walked off down the street carrying the statue, the Democrat noticed that a few real rats had started crawling out of the sewers and were following him. A little unnerved by the experience, he began to walk a bit faster, but within a couple of blocks the swarm of rats had grown to hundreds. He increased his pace, running faster and faster towards the Hudson River, now hotly pursued by thousands of squealing rats. In a panic, he ran onto the pier and hurled the bronze rat statue far out into the water. Amazingly, the thousands of real rats followed the statue into the water and were all drowned.

After catching his breath, the Democrat returned to the antiques shop and recounted the story to the shop owner who said: "Ah, you've come back for the story then?"

"No," said the Democrat. "I've come back to see if you've got any bronze statues of celebrated Republicans."

The Pope

A man was sitting next to the Pope on an airplane. The Pope was concentrating intently on a crossword puzzle, and one of the clues was clearly taxing his mind, so much so that after a few minutes he turned to his fellow passenger for help.

"Excuse me," said the Pope, "but can you think of a four-letter word ending in 'unt' that refers to a woman?"

"How about 'aunt'?" suggested the man.

"Oh, of course," said the Pope. "I don't suppose you happen to have an eraser?"

The Pope was having some work done in the Vatican. As he passed along a corridor, one of the carpenters accidentally hit his thumb with a hammer and yelled in agony: "Fucking hell!"

The Pope was horrified and told the carpenter: "My son, this is the house of God. Such profanities are not appropriate here. If you have hurt yourself in some way you should offer your prayer to our lord Jesus and he will give you relief from your suffering."

Next day as the Pope was passing, the same carpenter chopped off his fingers with a saw. "Oh, my God! Sweet Jesus help me now!" said the carpenter.

With that, the fingers levitated and miraculously reattached themselves to the poor carpenter's hand. All the blood vanished and the carpenter wiggled his fingers.

"Fucking hell!" said the Pope.

The Pope was addressing the masses in Rome and finished his sermon with the Latin phrase "*Tutti Homini*" – "Blessed be Mankind."

The sermon seemed to have been well received but the next day a women's rights group asked the Pope why he had not mentioned womankind in his conclusion. Not wishing to offend, the Pope ended his next sermon by saying, "*Tutti Homini et Tutti Femini*" – "Blessed be Mankind and Womankind."

But the following day a gay rights group took exception to the Pope's words and asked him why he had not included gays in his blessing. Eager to please, he duly amended his text, concluding his next sermon with "*Tutti Homini et Tutti Femini et Tutti Fruiti.*"

Pornography

Scientists say owls have the sharpest hearing on the planet. They've obviously never tested a man watching porn while his wife is asleep.

A male hotel guest called from his room and said to the desk clerk: "I want the porn channels disabled."

The clerk said: "You sick bastard!"

My girlfriend's a porn star. She's not going to be pleased when she finds out.

You know you're getting old when you watch a porn movie and think to yourself: "Hmm, that bed looks comfy!"

Things You Learn from Watching Porn

- Women wear high heels to bed.
- Men are never impotent.

- When going down on a woman, ten seconds is more than satisfactory.
- If a woman gets busted masturbating by a strange man, she will not scream with embarrassment, but rather insist that he fucks her.
- Women smile appreciatively when men splat them in the face with spunk.
- Women enjoy having sex with ugly, middle-aged men.
- Men always pull out.
- Women moan uncontrollably when giving a blow job.
- Women always orgasm when men do.
- A man ejaculating on a woman's butt is a satisfying result for all parties concerned.
- A blow job will always get a woman off a speeding ticket.
- People in the 1970s couldn't have sex unless there was a wild guitar solo in the background.
- Asian men don't exist.
- If you come across a guy and his girlfriend having sex in the bushes, the boyfriend won't bash seven shades of shit out of you if you shove your dick in his girlfriend's mouth.
- Nurses are forever sucking patients' dicks.
- Women never have headaches.
- Women always look pleasantly surprised when they open a man's trousers and find a dick there.
- Men don't have to beg.

I once appeared in a James Bond porn movie and the director was delighted with my performance. I came right on Q.

Little Johnny came running into his mother's house. "Mum, Mum, we're sitting in Jimmy's house watching porn."

"What?!" exclaimed his mother in horror.

"Relax, Mum," said Johnny. "It's child porn."

An out-of-work porn actor was looking for someone to represent him.

"Do you have an 8 x 10?" asked the agent?

"If I had an 8 x10," said the actor, "I wouldn't be out of work!"

Whoever said men can't multitask has obviously never seen a guy watching porn.

Pay-per-view porn: the only time when premature ejaculation is considered a good thing.

Feeling lonely and sexually frustrated, a man went online and ordered a DVD titled *Barely Bald and Legal*. When it arrived, he found it was a documentary about old tyres.

A guy got chatting to a stranger in a bar. When the conversation turned to women and porn, he said: "I saw this online porno movie once where the girl managed to gag on the guy's dick for five minutes at a time. I was so blown away by it, I decided to try it out on my wife that night, but I ended up killing her."

"No way!" said the stranger. "What happened?"

"It turned out I just had a slow internet connection."

Poverty

On his way into work one morning, a man passed a homeless guy sleeping inside a large cardboard box outside the train station. Not wanting to disturb him, the man crept over and put a Starbucks coffee cup on top of his box.

The homeless guy immediately woke up and said: "Thank you."

"No problem," smiled the man.

Then the homeless guy picked up the cup and said: "It's empty."

"I know," said the man. "It's meant to be a chimney."

I asked a pretty young homeless woman if I could take her home. She said "yes", but her smile vanished when I walked off with her cardboard box.

A homeless guy approached a man in the street and said: "Any change, mate?"

The man said, "No, you're still homeless", and walked off.

Three poor kids were sitting on a street corner wondering what it would be like to be rich. One said: "I'd like to be made of silver. Then I could break off a bit and buy that Cadillac over there."

The second boy said: "I'd like to be made of gold. Then I could break off a bit and buy a smart apartment."

The third boy said: "I'd like to be hairy."

"Hairy?" said the other two in surprise.

"Yeah, hairy. Because although my big sister only has a small patch between her legs, she says it's already bought her two new cars, a luxury penthouse apartment and a weekend away at the mayor's country ranch."

We're so broke after Christmas that I've had to get my wife to sell one of her kidneys. If things get any worse, I might have to cancel Sky Sports.

You Know You're Really Broke When . . .

- American Express calls and says, "Leave home without it."
- You clean your house hoping to find change.
- You think of a lottery ticket as an investment.
- At communion you go back for seconds.
- The Poundshop is too expensive for you.
- Dogs stop sniffing at your pockets.
- You receive care packages from Africa.
- You buy an imitation of a fake Rolex.
- Your idea of a holiday is playing Farmville.
- You have to save up to be poor.

Two elderly women were discussing the uncertain financial futures they would face when their husbands died.

One said: "My Bert has a weak heart, kidney problems and a serious lung condition, and all the medical care he has needed has eaten into our savings. When he dies and I have him buried, I'll be left virtually penniless."

The other woman said: "My Bill has a metal hip, metal plates in his skull and metal pins in his knees. We don't have any savings but when he dies and I have him cremated he'll be worth a fortune as scrap!"

I was approached in the street by a member of the Red Cross who told me that if I didn't donate £10 a month, then people in Africa would die. I can't believe the Red Cross employs such violent people.

What's the best thing about getting a blow job from a homeless woman? – You know she'll swallow.

Pregnancy

My wife's got really lazy, or as she calls it, "pregnant". (Jim Gaffigan)

Why is it that when your wife's pregnant all her female friends rub her tummy and say "congratulations", but none of them rub your dick and say "well done"?

A little girl asked her teacher: "Miss, can my mummy get pregnant?"
    "How old is she?" asked the teacher.
    "Thirty-eight," replied the girl.
    "Well, yes, your mother could get pregnant."
    Then the little girl asked: "Miss, can my sister get pregnant?"
    "How old is your sister?" asked the teacher.
    "Nineteen," replied the girl.
    "Yes, your sister could definitely get pregnant."
    Then the little girl asked: "Miss, could I get pregnant?"
    "How old are you, dear?" asked the teacher.
    "I'm seven, Miss."
    The teacher smiled: "No, you can't get pregnant."
    Hearing this, the boy sitting behind the little girl prodded her with his ruler and whispered: "See, I told you we had nothing to worry about."

During a tender and frank exchange of sentiments, a wife turned to her husband and said: "Since I got pregnant, I worry that you won't fancy me anymore and that you'll run off and leave me for someone younger and more attractive. What's your biggest fear?"
    The husband replied: "Snakes."

What do an airport and an illegal abortion have in common? – The hanger.

Interrogated by her parents, a teenage girl finally admitted that she was pregnant but couldn't say for sure who the father was.
    Her mother was furious. "Go to your room," she yelled, "and don't come out until you can give us a definite answer!"
    Two hours later, the girl came downstairs apologetically. "Mum, I think I have an idea who the father might be now."

"I should think so, too!" exclaimed the mother. "The very idea that any daughter of mine could get pregnant so young, let alone not know the father!"

"Okay," said the girl, "I think I got it narrowed down to the band or the football team."

Things Not to Say to Your Pregnant Partner

- "Oh, by the way I finished the last of the chocolate cake."
- "I'm not implying anything, but are you sure you haven't got quads in there?"
- "Looking at her, you'd never guess that supermodel in the paper had a baby. Wow! What a figure! She's a stunner!"
- "You won't need an epidural. Just relax and enjoy the moment."
- "I hope your thighs aren't going to stay that flabby forever. I can't be doing with a chubby wife."
- "I don't know why you're making such a big fuss about all this. Millions of women give birth."
- "Well, couldn't they induce labour? You know the 25th is the Cup Final."
- "I can't think what reminded me of it, but why don't we watch that documentary about the beached whale?"
- "Jim at the office passed a stone the size of a pea. Boy, that's gotta hurt!"
- "I'm jealous. Why can't men experience the joy of childbirth?"
- "Are your ankles supposed to look like that?"
- "Don't worry. This time next week it will all be over and we can get back to normal."
- "Get your own ice cream!"
- "Did I ever tell you my gran died while giving birth?"
- "Jeez, you're awfully puffy-looking today."
- "Of course I'll be there for the birth, honey. Even if it means leaving the pub five minutes early."
- "Got any milk you can spare? I can't be bothered to go to the supermarket."
- "How about we name the baby after my secretary?"
- "Hey! That rose tattoo on your hip is now the size of Madagascar!"
- "Retaining water? Yeah, like the Hoover Dam retains water!"
- "You know on the day they release you from hospital, have you decided yet what you're cooking for dinner that night?"
- "You don't have the guts to pull that trigger."

Why did the backstreet abortionist go out of business? – Her ferret died.

A woman was going to Spain on a business trip. Before leaving, she asked her husband if there was a present he wanted her to bring back.

"How about a Spanish girl?" he laughed.

The suggestion was met with stony silence.

Five days later, she returned home and he asked her whether she'd had a good trip.

"Yes, it was surprisingly enjoyable," she replied.

"And where's my present?" he smiled.

"What present?"

"The one I asked for – a Spanish girl."

"Oh, that! I did what I could; now we have to wait nine months to see if it's a girl."

A pregnant woman was waiting in line at a bank when three masked robbers burst in waving guns. As they peppered the place with gunfire, the woman ended up getting shot three times in the stomach. Happily, she pulled through, and in hospital asked the doctor whether her baby was safe.

The doctor said: "Actually, you're having triplets. And they're all fine, but each one has a bullet lodged in its stomach. But don't worry, the bullets will pass through their systems through normal metabolism."

The woman went on to give birth to two girls and a boy. Twelve years later, one of the girls said to the mother: "Mum, I've done a really weird thing. I've just passed a bullet into the toilet."

Her mother comforted her and explained about the bank robbery.

A few weeks later, the other daughter ran in with tears streaming down her face. "Mum," she cried, "I've done something really freaky!"

"Let me guess," said the mother. "You passed a bullet into the toilet?"

"Yes," replied the daughter. "How did you know?" And the mother comforted her and explained about the bank robbery.

A month later, the son announced: "Mum, I've done a very bad thing."

The mother said: "You passed a bullet into the toilet, right?"

"No, said the boy. "I was masturbating and I shot the dog!"

Abortion: unexpecting the expected.

A mother was trying to explain to her little girl how she had recently become pregnant. She explained how a baby was growing in her tummy, and how it took an egg and a sperm to make the baby. Daddy made the sperm and Mummy made the egg.

Then the little girl asked: "Mummy, if it takes a sperm and an egg to make a baby and the egg is already in your tummy, then how does the sperm get in there? Does Mummy swallow it?"

The mother said: "She does, if she wants a new evening dress."

A teenage girl tearfully told her straitlaced mother that she was pregnant. The mother was predictably angry and demanded to know who the father was.

"How should I know!" wailed the daughter. "You're the one who would never let me go steady."

What's the difference between a TV set and a pregnant girlfriend? – If you put a coat hanger in your pregnant girlfriend, you don't get a good reception.

"Honey, I'm not sure how to tell you this, but I'm pregnant."

"Jesus Christ!"

Yes, Mary and Joseph had an easy time with the naming of their first child.

A pregnant woman walked into a clothes shop, picked a dress from the rail and said to an assistant: "Is it okay to use the changing room?"

"Certainly, madam," replied the assistant.

So the pregnant woman went inside and closed the curtain. Half an hour later she still hadn't come out and the assistant started to get worried. So she went up to the curtain and asked hesitantly: "Are you all right in there?"

A voice answered: "Yes. I'm just coming out."

Then the curtain opened to reveal almost the entire changing room – the floor, walls and part of the ceiling – covered in blood and there was a dead foetus in the corner.

"Oh my God!" cried the shop assistant. "You only went in there to try on a dress!"

"Dress?" replied the woman. "I only wanted the coat hanger."

Premature Ejaculation

What's the definition of premature ejaculation? – You're squirting while she's still flirting.

A man went into a library and asked: "Has the book I ordered on premature ejaculation arrived?"

"Yes," said the librarian, "it came in sooner than expected."

Why do men get confused between hide-and-seek and sex? – In both cases after one minute they shout: "Ready or not, I'm coming!"

A young couple, on the brink of divorce, visited a marriage counsellor. The counsellor asked the wife: "What's the problem?"

She responded: "My husband suffers from premature ejaculation."

The counsellor turned to her husband and asked: "Is that true?"

The husband replied: "Well, not exactly: she's the one that suffers, not me."

A wife told her husband bluntly: "You're lousy in bed."

Aggrieved, he demanded: "How can you tell that in thirty seconds?"

They've bought out a condom now for people with premature ejaculation and they've put an anaesthetic in the lining that makes you numb and you can last for longer. Or, you can wear it inside out and you don't have to wake anybody up! (Frankie Boyle)

A guy met a girl in the pub. They chatted, got drunk and ended up at her apartment.

"Listen," he said, "I'm not very experienced and when I'm with a girl for the first time, I do suffer from a bit of premature ejaculation."

"Well, we can take it slow, babe," she smiled. "How premature?"

"Remember earlier in the pub, when you asked me about sex?"

"Yeah?"

"Then."

When I'm having sex with my wife, I like to give her about thirty seconds' warning before I'm going to come – usually when I'm taking off my socks.

A man woke his wife one morning and asked her: "Which would you prefer, sex or coffee?"

"It doesn't matter," she replied coldly. "Either way it will be instant."

Two middle-aged men were chatting in a pub. One said: "I'm getting worried about my sex life. I keep coming too soon. I just don't seem able to keep it under control."

"Don't worry about it," said his friend. "There's nothing wrong with premature ejaculation. I mean, it's sex *and* an early night."

Priests

A bartender was busy behind the bar one lunchtime when two nuns walked in. "Sisters," he said, "I'm surprised to see you here."

"Why is that?" asked one of the nuns.

"Well, to be honest," said the bartender, "we don't get many nuns in here."

The nun said: "We minister to fallen souls, and thought that this would be a good place to find them."

"Fair enough," said the bartender, and he fetched them two iced waters.

Half an hour later, the bartender was going about his duties when two rabbis walked in. "I'm really surprised to see you two here," he said.

"Why is that?" asked one of the rabbis.

"Because, to tell the truth, we don't get a lot of rabbis in this bar."

"The synagogue is closed for repairs," explained the rabbi, "and we needed somewhere quiet to debate rabbinical law."

"Fair enough," said the bartender, and he set them up with two orange juices.

Half an hour later, two Irish priests walked in. The bartender said: "Fathers, I'm really surprised to see you two in here."

One priest replied: "Why is that, my son?"

The bartender said: "Because you don't usually come in until the evening."

A retired priest was recalled to duty while the regular parish priest was off sick. During confession, he heard one of the parishioners confess to sodomy. Unable to remember the proper penance, he asked an altar boy: "What does Father O'Hagan give for sodomy?"

The boy said: "He usually gives us a candy bar and a Coke."

The worst thing about church is the standing up, then the sitting down, then the kneeling. I wish the priest would just pick a position and fuck me. (Jimmy Carr)

A priest was about to start his sermon when he noticed a young woman in the front row, wearing a tight dress with her boobs almost hanging out. He couldn't concentrate on his message to the flock, so he dismissed the service and asked to speak to the woman after everyone else had left the church.

When they were alone, the priest said sternly: "Just what do you mean, coming to church dressed like that?"

"Why, Father," the girl replied, "all of my boyfriends tell me that they can hear the angels sing when they put their heads on my breasts."

"Hmm. Well, let me check," said the priest, carefully placing his head between her breasts. After several minutes, he raised his head and said: "I can't hear any angels singing!"

"Of course not, Father," she said. "You're not plugged in yet."

A nun and a priest were crossing the desert by camel, but four days into their journey their camel suddenly dropped dead, leaving them stranded in the middle of nowhere. With no means of transport and their water supply running low, death seemed inevitable.

The priest forlornly sat on a sand dune and said to the nun: "Sister, since we're unlikely to make it out of this ghastly place alive, will you do something for me? In all my years on this earth, I've never seen a woman's breasts. Will you show me yours?"

"I suppose I could," replied the nun, "given the circumstances."

So she opened her habit and let him touch her breasts.

"Thank you, Sister," said the priest.

"You're very welcome," she replied. "Father, would you now do something for me? In all my years on this earth, I've never seen a man's penis. Would you show me yours?"

"Considering the situation in which we find ourselves I am sure the Lord would not object," said the priest.

So he lifted his robe and allowed her to stroke his penis. He quickly had a huge erection.

"Sister," he said, "do you know that if I insert my penis in the right place it can give life?"

"Is that true, Father?"

"Yes, absolutely."

"Then why don't you stick it in that camel so we can get the hell out of here?"

A priest befriended an attractive female churchgoer and invited her out for a social drink to talk about God. At the end of the evening, she asked him back to her apartment so that they could continue their stimulating conversation over a bottle of wine.

They sat down opposite each other in her lounge and began drinking and talking freely. Then suddenly the priest started praying for forgiveness for what he was about to do next, leaned forward and gave the woman a quick kiss on the lips.

"It's okay," she laughed. "It's just a kiss between friends – there is absolutely no reason for you to ask for forgiveness."

"You don't understand," said the priest. "I've slipped Rohypnol into your drink."

How is the Bible like a penis? – You get it rammed down your throat by a priest.

Two women were talking about their experiences of the Catholic Church. One said: "We had a lovely parish priest, Father Flanagan, and because of his compassion and sincerity, I have remained a committed Catholic."

"You've been lucky," said the other. "When my brother was younger, a priest bent him over the altar and took him from behind. The priest called it 'the will of God' but we call it 'the wedding we'll never forget'."

There were three priests in a railroad station, all wanting to go home to Pittsburgh. Behind the ticket counter was a girl with an amazing figure, including an enormous pair of breasts. The priests were all in embarrassing new territory, so they drew straws to determine who would get the tickets.

The first priest approached the window. "Young lady," he began, "I would like three pickets to titsburg . . ." whereupon he completely lost his composure and fled.

So the second priest went up to the window. "Young lady, I would like three tickets to Pittsburgh," he began, "and I would like the change in nipples and dimes." Realizing his slip of the tongue, he, too, fled in embarrassment.

This left the third priest to order the tickets. "Young lady, I would like three tickets to Pittsburgh, and I would like the change in nickels and dimes. And I must say," he continued, "if you insist on dressing like that, when you get to the pearly gates, St Finger is going to shake his peter at you."

What do a pint of Guinness and a Catholic priest have in common? – Black coat, white collar and you have to watch your arse if you get a dodgy one.

One morning a man came into the church on crutches. He stopped in front of the holy water, put some on both legs and then threw away his crutches.

An altar boy witnessed the scene and ran into the rectory to tell the priest what he'd just seen.

"My son, you've just witnessed a miracle!" the priest said. "Tell me, where is this man now?"

The boy said: "Flat on his arse over by the holy water."

A man went to confession and told the priest that he had recently used the F-word. The priest said: "That's three Hail Marys and watch your language."

But the man said: "I want to explain why I used the F-word."

"Very well then," sighed the priest, looking at his watch.

"You see," began the man, "I played golf on Sunday instead of going to church."

"Was that why you swore?" the priest interrupted.

"No, I was on the first tee – a par 4, 425 yards, dogleg to the left – and I hooked my drive into the trees."

"Was that when you swore?"

"No, because when I found my ball, I saw I had a clear shot to the green. But before I could play my second shot a squirrel appeared, grabbed my ball and ran up a tree with it."

"Was that when you swore?"

"No, because a buzzard flew by, caught the squirrel in its talons and flew off with it."

"So was that when you swore?"

"No, because the buzzard flew over the green and the dying squirrel let go of my ball and it landed four inches from the hole."

"Oh, no!" said the priest. "Don't tell me you missed the fucking putt!"

Fifty priests died in an accident. They all arrived at the pearly gates and found St Peter waiting for them. St Peter was looking at a clipboard with an irritated expression on his face. He announced: "To save time I'm only going to ask you all one question: Which of you has ever been involved in a homosexual relationship?"

The priests kicked the dirt and mumbled, but forty-nine of them raised their hands.

"Okay," said St Peter, "off to hell with you then – and take that deaf bastard with you!"

A priest approached a small boy in the street and said: "Could you tell me where the train station is, please?"

The boy gave him directions, and the priest said: "Thank you. If you come to my sermon tonight, I will tell you how to get to heaven."

"I don't think so," said the boy. "You don't even know how to get to the station!"

Two priests and a rabbi went for a hike one hot summer's day. After trailing through the countryside for over two hours, sweating and exhausted, they came upon a small lake. Since it was fairly secluded, they took off all their clothes and jumped in the water. Refreshed, the trio then decided to pick a few berries while letting the sun dry out their naked bodies.

As they were crossing a clearing, they spotted a group of women from their town. Instinctively the two priests covered their privates while the rabbi covered his face. After the women had gone and the men had retrieved their clothes, the priests asked the rabbi why he covered his face and not his privates.

The rabbi replied: "I don't know about you two, but in my congregation, it's my *face* they would recognize!"

A priest offered a nun a ride home in his car. She climbed into the passenger seat and crossed her legs, thereby revealing a glimpse of flesh beneath her gown.

The priest was immediately overcome with lust and slyly slid his hand up her lower leg.

"Father!" said the nun. "Remember Psalm 129."

The priest removed his hand but when he next changed gear, he seized the opportunity to slide his hand up her lower leg again.

"Father!" repeated the nun. "Remember Psalm 129."

The priest apologized. "I'm truly sorry, Sister, but the temptation was too much. I am only human after all."

Arriving at the convent, the nun sighed heavily and went on her way. When he reached his church, the priest rushed straight to look up Psalm 129. It said: "Go forth and seek, further up, you will find glory."

A priest was walking along the street when he was accosted by a Turk.

"Pictures of leetle boys?" said the Turk.

"Go away," said the priest. "I'm not interested."

But the Turk was persistent. "Go on – pictures of leetle boys?"

"I'm a man of God," said the priest. "Now will you please go away?!"

"Last chance," said the Turk. "Pictures of leetle boys?"

"Oh, okay, then," sighed the priest. "How many do you want?"

Three young priests were ready to take their final vows. The last test they had to take was a celibacy test, for which all three were required to strip naked and tie a little bell around their penis. Then a lap dancer entered the room and began wrapping her legs around the first priest.

Ting-a-ling

"Oh, Michael," said the head priest. "I'm disappointed in you. You have failed the test. Go and take a shower."

Then the lap dancer went over to the second priest and began rubbing herself up against him.

Ting-a-ling.

"Oh, Sean," said the head priest. "I'm afraid you have failed the test. Go and take a shower."

Finally, the lap dancer went over to the third priest. She pressed herself against him, whispered in his ear, stroked his groin, but got absolutely no reaction.

"Congratulations, Patrick," said the head priest. "You have passed the test. You have shown that you can resist the temptation of women. Now go and relax and take a shower with Michael and Sean."

Ting-a-ling.

Prison

A schoolteacher asked her class what their fathers did for a living. Simon said: "My dad runs the fire station."

"Very good, Simon," said the teacher. "Anyone else?"

"My dad runs the local prison," said Johnny.

"Excellent, Johnny," said the teacher. "Is he the prison governor?"

"No, he's the hardest bastard in there."

As a hooker was getting dressed after sex, she turned to her customer and asked: "Have you recently been in prison?"

"Yes," he said. "How could you tell? Is it because I wanted to take you from behind?"

"Kind of," she replied. "But it was more the way that after we finished, you ran round in front of me, bent over and said: 'Your turn now.' "

Last week, I went to visit my uncle in prison. He's been inside four times – the other six times he was receiving.

An escaped prisoner broke into a house and bound and gagged a married couple in their bedroom. While the intruder was searching for valuables downstairs, the husband managed to loosen his gag.

"Honey," he gasped, "this guy hasn't seen a woman in years. Just do what he says. If he wants sex, go along with it. Our lives depend on it."

Just then she managed to spit out her gag too. "I'm so glad you feel that way, darling," she said, "because he just told me what a lovely tight arse he thought you'd got."

Psychics and Mediums

A medium was performing on stage before a handful of people. The theatre descended into darkness, the medium entered a trance-like state and after a couple of minutes of eerie silence, he called out plaintively: "Does the name Riverside Retreat mean anything to anyone here?"

"Well, I'll be damned!" cried a woman on the front row. "That was the name of my mother's house!"

The medium said: "Well, my dear, I think I can contact her for you."

The woman said: "So can I. She's sitting next to me!"

Two fortune-tellers were chatting. "Lovely weather, we're having," said one.

"Yes," said the other. "It reminds me of the summer of 2019."

Laura visited a psychic of some local repute. In a dark and gloomy room, gazing at the tarot cards laid out before her, the tarot reader delivered the bad news: "There's no easy way to say this, so I'll just be blunt – prepare yourself to be a widow. Your husband will die a violent and horrible death this year."

Visibly shaken, Laura stared at the woman's lined face, then at the single flickering candle, then down at her hands. She took a few deep breaths to compose herself. She simply had to know. She met the tarot reader's gaze, steadied her voice, and asked: "Will I get away with it?"

Many hundreds of years ago a king went to see a fortune-teller to see what she could predict about the future. The fortune-teller told the king that one of his wives would die that year. The king didn't believe her and went away laughing.

Later that year one of the king's wives died. He remembered what the fortune-teller had told him and thought that she had caused the death of his wife. So he decided to have her burnt at the stake as a witch. First, however, he ordered her to be brought before him. He told her: "A few months ago you predicted that one of my wives would die this year, and now one of them has died. So, clever fortune-teller, tell me – when will you die?"

The fortune-teller realized that the king was planning to kill her, so she thought very carefully before answering: "I will die three days before you do, your majesty."

A woman went into a fortune-teller's booth and asked how much she charged.

"Fifty pounds for one question," said the fortune-teller.

"Fifty pounds! That's a bit expensive, isn't it?"

"Next!"

Pubic Hair

An impoverished elderly couple, Ethel and Bill, advertised for a lodger so that they could make ends meet. A young model applied and, after inspecting their modest terraced home, she decided to take the room.

"There's just one problem," said the model. "In my line of work, cleanliness is essential. I need to take a shower at least twice a day, but I can't help noticing that you don't appear to have a shower – or even a bath."

"There is a bath," said Ethel, "but it's an old tin one and we keep it out in the backyard. But we can bring that into the lounge for you. And there's no need to worry about Bill – he's off playing darts most nights."

The model decided that for such a low rent the inconvenience was acceptable and so she moved in straightaway. That night Bill went off to play darts and Ethel brought the bath into the lounge. As the model stripped off to step into the hot bath, Ethel remarked that the girl had no pubic hair.

"No," said the model. "I have to shave it for swimwear and underwear shots."

That night in bed Ethel was telling Bill about the model's shaved bush. Bill didn't believe her, but Ethel said she'd prove it to him. The following night she would leave the lounge curtains slightly open so that he could see for himself.

Bill went off to his darts as usual and Ethel prepared the bath, taking care to leave the curtains slightly open. As the model was about to step into the bath, Ethel glanced towards the curtains, gestured towards the girl's shaven hair and at the same time lifted up her own skirt which, since she wasn't wearing any knickers, revealed her hairy mound in all its glory.

In bed that night, Ethel said to Bill: "Now do you believe me?"

"Yes," said Bill, "but why did you show me yours?"

"To show you the difference," said Ethel. "But anyway, what's the problem? You've seen my pussy thousands of times."

"I know," replied Bill, "but the rest of the darts team haven't!"

Why is the rainforest often called the Brazilian rainforest? – Because deforestation will soon leave it almost completely bare, with just a thin strip of trees running up the middle of it.

A little boy went into the bathroom while his mother was taking a shower. "Mummy," he asked, "what's that between your legs?"

"That's my squirrel," she said.

Later that day, he saw his grandma in the shower. "Grandma," he asked, "what's that between your legs?"

"That's my squirrel," she said.

"Well," said the little boy, "Mummy has one, too, but hers is not as grey as yours."

Grandma replied: "That's because your mummy's squirrel hasn't cracked as many nuts as mine has."

Puerto Ricans

How many Puerto Ricans does it take to kidnap a child? – Twelve. One to do the kidnapping and eleven to write the ransom note.

How do we know there are no Puerto Ricans in heaven? – Because St Peter still has his gates.

What do you call a large group of Puerto Ricans running down a hill? – A jailbreak.

How can you tell if the kid who stole your bike is half Puerto Rican and half Polish? – He's running down the street with the bike under his arm.

Rabbis

Whenever a new Pope is elected, a little-known tradition is performed whereby the Chief Rabbi is granted an audience with His Holiness. The Chief Rabbi presents the Pope with a silver tray bearing a velvet cushion, on top of which is an ancient, shrivelled parchment envelope. The Pope responds by symbolically stretching out his arm in a gesture of courteous but firm rejection. The Chief Rabbi then retires, taking the envelope with him, and does not return until the next Pope is elected.

Upon his election in 2005, Benedict XVI was intrigued by this curious ritual, the origins of which were unknown to him. He instructed the Vatican's most eminent scholars to research it, but they were unable to shed any light on the matter. When the time came and the Chief Rabbi was shown into his presence, Pope Benedict faithfully enacted the traditional rejection but, as the Chief Rabbi turned to leave, he called him back.

"My brother," whispered the Pope, "I must confess that we Catholics are ignorant of the meaning of this ritual, performed for centuries between our two faiths. I have to ask you, what is it all about?"

The Chief Rabbi shrugged and replied: "We have no more idea than you do. The origin of the ceremony has been lost with the passage of time."

"Very well," said the Pope. "Let us retire to my private chambers and enjoy a glass of wine together, then with your agreement, we shall open the envelope and finally reveal the secret contents."

The Chief Rabbi agreed and, fortified in their resolve by the wine, they gingerly opened the ancient parchment envelope. With trembling fingers, the Chief Rabbi reached inside and extracted a folded sheet of yellowed paper.

As the Pope peered over his shoulder, the Chief Rabbi slowly opened out the paper. They both gasped with shock – it was the bill for the Last Supper.

A Jewish man asked: "Rabbi, what should I do? My son has converted to Christianity."

"I don't know," answered the rabbi. "Come back tomorrow and I'll ask advice from God."

The man came back the next day. "Sorry," said the rabbi. "I can't help you. God told me he has the same problem."

A priest, a Pentecostal preacher and a rabbi all served as chaplains to the students at a university in Georgia. They met up on a regular basis in the university coffee shop to discuss theology, both among themselves and with any passing students. One day, one of the students voiced the opinion that preaching to people wasn't that hard and that a real challenge would be to preach to a bear.

Although it initially seemed a ridiculous proposition, the three religious men gradually warmed to the idea and decided to put it into practice. They would head off into the woods separately, find a bear, preach to it and attempt to convert it.

Two weeks later, they all met up again to compare notes as to how they had fared with their respective bear conversions.

Father Kelly was first to speak. He had his arm in a sling, was on crutches and was heavily bandaged around the head. "Well," he said, "I went into the woods to find me a bear. And when I found him, I began to read to him from the Catechism. At first, that bear was not at all receptive and began slapping me around with his huge paws, but when I sprinkled him with holy water, he became as gentle as a lamb. The bishop is coming out next week to give him first communion and confirmation."

Reverend Jimmy Watson spoke next. He was in a wheelchair, with an arm and both legs in casts and he was connected to an intravenous drip. "Well, brothers," he began, "I went out and found me a bear and began to read to him from God's holy book. But that bear wanted nothing to do with me, and started snarling and growling. But let me tell you brothers, I was not prepared to let that bear reject the word of God, so I grabbed hold of him and we wrestled – my, how we wrestled – down one hill, up another and down another until we came to a creek. And when we came to that creek, brothers, I quickly pushed his head under the water and baptized his hairy soul. And just like you said, he became as gentle as a lamb. We spent the rest of the day praising Jesus."

They both turned to Rabbi Goldberg, who was lying in a hospital bed. He was in a full body cast and traction with intravenous drips and tubing connected to at least a dozen parts of his body. He was in a really bad way. Barely able to speak, the rabbi looked up plaintively at the other two and gasped: "Looking back on it, circumcision may not have been the best way to start things off . . ."

A Catholic priest and a rabbi were walking down the street one day when they spotted a pair of angelic-looking twelve-year-old boys playing football in the park. The priest turned to the rabbi, nudged him in the ribs and said: "Let's go and screw those boys."

The rabbi looked at him curiously and answered: "Out of what?"

At the end of the tax year, the Tax Office sent an inspector to audit the books of a synagogue. While he was checking the books he turned to the rabbi and said: "I notice you buy a lot of candles. What do you do with the candle drippings?"

"Good question," said the rabbi. "We save them up and send them back to the candle-makers, and every now and then they send us a free box of candles."

"Oh," replied the auditor, somewhat disappointed that his unusual question had a practical answer. But on he went, in his obnoxious way. "What about all these biscuit purchases? What do you do with the crumbs?"

"Ah, yes," replied the rabbi, realizing that the inspector was trying to trap him with an unanswerable question. "We collect them and send them back to the manufacturers, and every now and then they send us a free box of holy biscuits."

"I see," replied the auditor, seething with frustration at not being able to nail the rabbi. "Well," he went on, "what do you do with all the leftover foreskins from the circumcisions you perform?"

"Here, too, we do not waste," answered the rabbi. "What we do is save up all the foreskins and send them to the Tax Office, and about once a year they send us a complete prick."

Rednecks

A redneck boy said to his father: "Hey, Dad, I know how old I am today – I'm twelve."

"That's darn good, son," said the father.

Then the boy went into the kitchen and said to his grandma: "Hey, Grandma, know how old I am today?"

"Come closer," said Grandma. Then she unzipped his jeans, slipped her wrinkled hand into his underpants, fondled his genitals for a few seconds and said: "You're twelve."

"That's right," said the boy. "How could you tell?"

"I heard you tell your father."

How do you know if a redneck girl is old enough to marry? – Make her stand in a barrel. If her chin is over the top, she's old enough. If it isn't, cut the barrel down a bit.

What do girls from Arkansas and bears have in common? – They both suck their paws.

You Might Be a Redneck Transvestite If . . .

- You wear combat boots with a mini-dress.
- You wax your legs with turtle wax.
- You get a run in your stockings while changing a tyre on your motor-home.
- You use glitter to highlight your moustache.
- Your best silver necklace is made from beer can pull-tabs.
- You keep spare ammo in your bra.
- Your favourite leather skirt was made from the moose you shot last autumn.
- You keep a spare lipstick in your toolbox.
- You use paint thinner to remove your make-up.

A guy in Alabama saw a sign in a public toilet that read: "Please leave this toilet in the condition that you would like to find it." So he left a can of beer and a girlie magazine.

A redneck boy asked his redneck daddy: "What's sex?" Pa decided to keep his explanation simple, so he ordered Ma upstairs and told her to strip. As she lay naked on her back, Pa said to his son: "You see that hole on your ma there? You just watch yer old daddy go!" And then he proceeded to demonstrate sex.

The boy was watching with interest when his sister came in and asked him: "What are they doing?"

"Sex," replied the boy.

"What is sex?" she asked.

He said: "You see that hole on Pa there? Well, you just watch your old brother go!"

What do you call a redneck girl who keeps running away from home? – A virgin.

What does a redneck family tree look like? – A wreath.

A redneck named Bubba was tired of hearing redneck jokes dissing the name Bubba. So he went to court to change his name and appeared before a judge who asked: "Sir, why do you want to legally change your name? Are you in trouble, hiding from the law?"

"No sir, Your Honour. I'm just tired of listening to jokes about rednecks that often use that name. It's Bubba this, Bubba that, so I want my name changed."

The judge asked: "And what name do you want it changed to?"

He said: "Candy."

"Candy?" repeated the judge with raised eyebrows. "Spell it for me so that there's no confusion here."

The redneck said: "C-A-N-D-Y, Your Honour."

"Very well," said the judge, putting the name on the documents. "Your name is now legally Candy."

The redneck wasted no time in going over to tell his girlfriend. He knocked on her door and heard: "Who's there?"

He said: "It's me!"

She said: "Come on in, Bubba, the door's unlocked."

"It's not Bubba."

"Yes it is, I recognize your voice."

"It ain't Bubba no more 'cause I done legally changed it."

"What is it then?"

"Guess."

"Leroy?"

"Nope."

"Jeb?"

"Nope."

She said: "Hell, I give up, come on in."

He said: "Wait, I'll gives ya a hint. Ya holds it in ya hand and ya puts it in ya mouth."

Then the answer dawned on her. "Oh . . . come on in, Peter!"

What's the last thing a redneck stripper takes off? – Her bowling shoes.

A stranger walked into a rundown Arkansas bar and ordered a dry Martini. The bartender eyed him suspiciously and said: "You ain't from round these parts, are you?"

"No," said the stranger. "I'm from Philadelphia."

"Oh, yeah?" said the bartender. "And what exactly do you do up in Philadelphia?"

"I'm a taxidermist," replied the stranger.

"A taxidermist, huh?" said the bartender. "What's one of those?"

"I mount dead animals," explained the stranger.

"It's okay, boys," said the bartender, turning to the other customers. "He's one of us."

A young redneck girl was watching her father getting dressed in the morning. Pointing at his penis, she asked: "Daddy, when will I get one of those?"

Her father replied: "In about half an hour, when your mother goes to work."

Did you hear about the redneck who called his children Flour, Yeast and Water because they were all in-bred?

A flying saucer landed at a gas station on a lonely country road in Arkansas. The letters "UFO" were emblazoned in big letters on the side of the craft. Two bug-eyed aliens stepped out and while the gas-station manager stood paralysed with shock, his young assistant, Joe-Bob, nonchalantly filled up the tank and waved to the aliens as they took off again.

As they disappeared into the sky, the station manager turned to Joe-Bob and said: "Don't you realize what just happened?"

"Yeah," replied Joe-Bob. "So what?"

"Didn't you see those two?" persisted the manager.

"Yeah," said Joe-Bob, shrugging his shoulders. "So what?"

"But didn't you see the letters 'UFO' on the side of that vehicle?"

"Yeah. So what?"

"Don't you know what UFO stands for?"

Joe-Bob rolled his eyes. "Course I do, I've been working here three years. UFO stands for 'Unleaded Fuel Only'."

How do rednecks connect wirelessly? – Brown Tooth.

A redneck woman went to a local farm stand with her friend and asked the farmer for "the two biggest potatoes that you have".

The farmer went off to the garden and dug up two enormous potatoes. When he brought them back, the woman, struggling to hold one in each hand, said to her friend: "These here are just like my husband Jeb's balls."

The friend gasped in astonishment: "Your Jeb's balls are that big?!"

"No," said the redneck woman, "they're that dirty."

A preacher was walking down the street when he saw a young redneck kid smoking a cigarette. He said: "Son, aren't you too young to smoke?"

The boy looked up but didn't say anything.

The preacher asked: "How old are you?"

"Six."

"Six?! When did you start smoking?"

"Right after the first time I got laid."

"Right after the first time you got laid?! When was that?"

"I don't remember," said the boy. "I was drunk."

Billy-Bob and Bubba were in a bar. Billy-Bob said: "I bet you fifty bucks you can't take a sip from that spittoon over there."

Bubba promptly picked up the spittoon, put it to his lips and drank the lot.

"Hey!" said Billy-Bob, "I told you to only take a sip!"

"I couldn't help it," said Bubba. "It was all in one lump."

A redneck family had just sat down to dinner when their teenage son walked in. "Pa," he said excitedly, "I think I've found the girl I'm going to marry. And she's a virgin!"

The father immediately jumped to his feet and yelled: "Listen, boy, you ain't marryin' that girl! If she ain't good enough for her own family, she sure ain't good enough for ours!"

A young West Virginia girl asked her mother: "Ma, is it true that babies come out of the place boys put their wieners in?"

"Yep, sho' do."

"So, Ma, is that why you're missing yo' front teeth?"

Did you hear about the redneck who left his entire estate to his widow? – The only problem is she can't touch it until she turns fourteen.

On the occasion of their thirtieth wedding anniversary, Billy-Bob decided to forego a big party and instead treated Ellie-Lou to a memorable evening at home. Quietly filling the bathtub with champagne, he called her into the bathroom and they spent a sensual evening soaking in the tub by candlelight.

When they were finished, Billy-Bob decided he couldn't let all that good champagne go to waste, so he carefully poured it back into the empty bottles. However, when he was finished, he found he had nearly a half-bottle too much.

He screamed to his wife: "Ellie-Lou! You nasty bitch, why'd you piss in the tub?!"

You Might Be a Redneck Volunteer Fire Department If . . .

- Your firehouse has wheels.
- You have naked lady mud flaps on your pumper.
- You've ever let someone's house burn down because they wouldn't let you hunt on their land.
- Fire training consists of everyone standing around a fire getting drunk.
- Your department has never had two emergency vehicles pulled over for racing each other to the scene of a fire.
- On the way to an emergency call-out, you've made a detour in your pumper so that you could give your sister a lift to the shops.
- Your department's name is spelt wrong on the equipment.
- Your personnel vehicle has more lights than your house.
- You've ever taken a girl on a date in a pumper.
- Your engine had to be towed at the last Christmas Parade.
- Local TV news crews won't interview you because you embarrassed them live on air last time.
- Your pumper has been on fire more times than it's been to a fire.

How does a redneck mother know her daughter is having her period? – Her son's dick tastes funny.

A redneck walked into a truck stop with a stunned look on his face. He made his way to the counter and sat down. The waitress came over and asked: "Can I help you?"

The redneck just sat there with a blank stare on his face, then he spat and said: "Motherfucker sure can drive!"

The waitress was offended by his coarse language, so she turned on her heels and went to serve another customer instead. Ten minutes later, she thought she'd give the redneck a second chance, so she returned and asked him: "Can I help you now?"

The redneck replied by spitting and saying: "Motherfucker sure can drive!"

This time the waitress stormed off to fetch the manager. The manager went up to the redneck, grabbed him by his collar and said: "What seems to be the problem here?"

The redneck spat and said: "Motherfucker sure can drive!"

The manager told him: "Listen, buddy, this is a nice, respectable place. Maybe if you could explain who can drive and what you are talking about, I won't have to throw you out."

The redneck looked up at the manager and explained: "Well, I was in my eighteen-wheeler and I had this nineteen-year-old greenhorn kid driving. We were coming down the old mountain road, when I saw this traffic jam down right in front of us. So I told the kid, 'If you can get us out of this alive I'll suck your dick!'"

The redneck spat and added: "And that motherfucker sure can drive!"

Billy-Bob and Bubba were sitting in the back of their trailers, drinking beer and talking about life.

Billy-Bob said: "If I snuck over to your house while you were out fishing and screwed your wife, and she got pregnant, would that make us kin?"

Bubba scratched his head for a bit and then said: "I don't think so . . . but it sure would make us even."

Riddles

What's yellow and stinks of marge? – Homer's fingers.

What makes a girl go "Mmm"? – Duct tape.

What's green and eats nuts? – Syphilis.

What's the definition of skyjacking? – A hand job at 35,000 feet.

Which form enables men to have sex with women? – Chloroform.

What has a hundred balls and fucks rabbits? – A shotgun.

What's pink and hard? – A pig with a flick-knife.

Why did the baker have brown hands? – Because he kneaded a poo.

What is square and hairy? – A pubic's cube.

What's seven inches long and dangles in front of an asshole? – David Cameron's tie.

What's the difference between a bonus and a penis? – You can always rely on your wife to blow your bonus.

What can turn a fruit into a vegetable? – AIDS.

What's a condominium? – A condom for an extra small dick.

What's the fastest game at a Muslim birthday party? – Pass the parcel.

What's soft and warm when you go to bed but hard and stiff when you wake up the next morning? – Vomit.

Why does Dr Pepper come in a bottle? – Because his wife died.

What sits quietly in the corner getting smaller and smaller? – A baby with a cheese grater.

When is a pixie not a pixie? – When she's got her head down an elf's pants: then she's a goblin.

What's the difference between a pheromone and a hormone? – You can't hear a pheromone.

What's the difference between a cow and a Beatle? – The cow hasn't been milked by Heather Mills.

Why did the Seven Dwarfs use Daz? – They wanted their little things to come up Snow White.

What's black and white and shouts: "Fuck the Pope!"? – A nun who's won the lottery.

What do white onions, brown onions and a thirteen-inch dick have in common? – They all make a woman's eyes water.

Why do Indian women have a red dot on their forehead? – Because their husbands like to smoke while they have sex.

What's a muffin? – A pair of panties.

What's the best thing about being a hunchback? – You can rock yourself to sleep at night.

What's the difference between a chambermaid by day and by night? – By day, she's fair and buxom . . .

What's the smallest unit of time in the known universe? – The interval between the traffic light changing to green and the taxi driver behind you honking his horn.

What did the yellow tooth say to the white tooth? – "Is it 'cos I is plaque?"

What's long and thin, covered in skin, red in parts and goes in tarts? – Rhubarb.

How many fish are there in a pair of tights? – Five. Two eels, two soles and a little wet plaice.

Royalty

For her wedding to Prince Charles, Camilla, Duchess of Cornwall, bought new shoes, which got increasingly tight around her feet as the wedding day wore on. That night, when the festivities were finally over and the newlyweds were able to retire to their room, Camilla flopped on the bed and said: "Charles, be a dear. Take my shoes off – my feet are absolutely killing me."

Her ever-obedient Prince of Wales worked vigorously on her right shoe, but it would not budge.

"Harder!" yelled Camilla.

Charles shouted back: "I'm trying, my darling! But it's just so blooming tight!"

"Come on, my prince!" she cried. "Give it all you've got!"

At last the shoe was released from her foot, prompting Charles to let out a loud groan and Camilla to exclaim: "Ooooh, God! That feels sooo good!"

In their bedroom next door, the Queen said to Prince Philip: "See? I told you with a face like that, she would still be a virgin!"

Just then, as Charles tried to remove Camilla's left shoe, he cried: "Oh, bloody hell, darling! This one's even tighter!"

To which Prince Philip said to the Queen: "That's my boy: once a Navy man, always a Navy man!"

The Queen was showing the Archbishop of Canterbury around the royal stable, when one of the stallions farted loudly.

"Oh dear," said the Queen. "How embarrassing! I'm frightfully sorry about that."

"It's quite understandable," said the Archbishop before adding: "As a matter of fact, I thought it was the horse."

Two corgis were sitting in Clarence House following the death of the Queen Mother. One corgi turned to the other and said: "Actually, I'm glad the old girl's gone. At least we won't get blamed for pissing on the sofa anymore."

Don't you think it's quite weird for Prince Harry, getting really stoned and seeing your gran's face appearing on your money? (Frankie Boyle)

Two young students – one American, the other English – won a school prize to meet the Queen at Buckingham Palace. Their respective fathers agreed to drive them down to London, and as the big day drew nearer, both boys became really excited at the prospect of meeting the monarch. While the English boy decided to wear his best suit for the occasion, the American father advised his son to wear a University of Texas sweatshirt in order to make sure that he got noticed among the dozens of other kids who were sure to be there.

On arrival, they walked up to the palace gates and saw a sign telling them that the Queen would meet people at 11 a.m. or 2 p.m. They decided to go to the 11 a.m. session so that they could spend a bit of time in London afterwards. Sure enough, at 11 a.m. precisely the English boy, wearing his best suit, was standing in line along with all the other children, proud as punch, when the Queen appeared in view. She went straight up to the American boy, leaned over and whispered something to him, completely ignoring the English boy who was standing next to him.

After she had gone, the English boy was left in floods of tears and ran to tell his dad what had happened. "Don't worry, son," said his father. "I've got an idea.

The Queen was clearly attracted by the American lad's sweatshirt, so if we go to a tourist shop and buy you an identical sweatshirt, you can wear it and come back at two o'clock."

The English boy thought it might work, so they bought a University of Texas sweatshirt and turned up for the 2 p.m. meet and greet. Wearing his new top, the English boy stood proudly in line with the other children and, just as his father had predicted, this time the Queen went straight up to him. She then leaned over and whispered in his ear: "I thought I told you to fuck off."

The Queen is so posh that when she has an orgasm she doesn't come, she arrives.

Back in the 1970s, Jimmy Carter, Pierre Trudeau and Prince Philip, Duke of Edinburgh, were talking at a press conference. Suddenly President Carter stood up, pulled down his pants and showed off his seven-inch dick. The crowd immediately began singing "The Star-Spangled Banner".

Seeing this, Prime Minister Trudeau stood up, pulled down his pants and showed off his nine-inch dick. The crowd immediately started singing "O Canada".

Not to be outdone, Prince Philip stood up, pulled down his pants and revealed his twelve-inch dick. The crowd started singing "God Save the Queen".

The Queen and Dolly Parton die on the same day, and they both go before St Peter to find out if they'll be admitted to Heaven. Unfortunately, there's only one space left that day, so St Peter must decide which of them gets in. St Peter asks Dolly if there's some particular reason why she should go to heaven.

So she takes off her top and says: "Look at these. They're the most perfect ones God ever created, and I'm sure it will please Him to be able to see them every day for eternity."

St Peter thanks Dolly, and asks Queen Elizabeth the same question. She then drops her skirt and panties, takes a bottle of Perrier out of her purse, shakes it up and douches with it.

St Peter says: "Okay, Your Majesty, you may go in."

Dolly is outraged. She screams: "What the hell was that all about? I show you two of God's most perfect creations and I am denied admission to heaven; she performs a disgusting hygiene act and gets in! I don't get it!"

"Sorry, Dolly," says St Peter, "but a royal flush beats a pair any day."

Stamps are to rise by a staggering 30 per cent. Maybe the Post Office should try to appease public anger by at least having the Queen lower her top to expose a nipple. (Frankie Boyle)

Prince Philip and the Queen were dining in one of London's top restaurants. The waiter asked Prince Philip what he would like to order.

"We'll have two rare steaks, my good fellow," said Prince Philip.

"Does sir mean two bloody steaks?" queried the waiter.

"Yes, that's right," said Prince Philip. "Two bloody steaks!"

The Queen added: "And plenty of fucking chips!"

Sadomasochism

Did you hear about the guy who regretted subscribing to a sadomasochistic text chat service? He replied STOP, so they sent even more.

A man was sitting in a bar looking depressed when a woman approached and asked him what the problem was. He told her sorrowfully that his girlfriend had just left him, and after some pressuring, admitted that it was because he was simply too kinky for her.

"What a coincidence!" exclaimed the woman. "My boyfriend just left me because he said I was too kinky for him."

Realizing they had something in common, the two started chatting and after a few drinks she invited him back to her place. There, she left him alone in the living room and disappeared into the bedroom. Five minutes later she reappeared, dressed from head to toe in black leather and carrying chains, a whip and a ballgag, only to see the man about to leave.

"Where are you going?" she asked. "I thought you were kinky."

"I am," he replied. "I fucked your cat and just took a shit in your handbag. I'm off home now."

Forty years after attending school together, two men met up at a class reunion. They were discussing their respective wives, both of whom were childhood sweethearts, when one of the men suddenly announced: "Janey and I have never looked back since we got into S & M."

"Jane into S & M?! I don't believe it! She was always so prim and proper in school."

"Yeah, S & M, that's us. She snores while I masturbate."

In the privacy of his own home, a man put on an S & M DVD, clamped a bulldog clip to his testicles and inserted a safety pin through his foreskin. Just then the doorbell rang.

"Damn!" he thought. "Just when I've got uncomfortable!"

One of the women at the S & M club had a birthday last week. Everyone had a whip-round for her.

A man said to his drinking buddy: "You know what you suggested about spicing up my sex life? Well, last night my wife and I carried out a spot of role play. She was the teacher and I was the naughty schoolboy who needed punishing."

"And was it good?"

"Yes, but I think she went a little too far when she got my parents involved."

After reading *Fifty Shades of Grey*, a wife asked her husband to tie her tightly to the bed.

"Now what?" he asked.

"Hurt me!"

"Okay. You have saggy tits and thick ankles."

A sadist, a masochist, a murderer, a necrophile, a zoophile and a pyromaniac were all sitting on a bench in a mental institution, bored out of their minds.

"How about having sex with a sheep?" asked the zoophile.

"Let's have sex with the sheep and then torture it," said the sadist.

"Let's have sex with the sheep, torture it and then kill it," said the murderer.

"Let's have sex with the sheep, torture it, kill it and then have sex with it again," said the necrophile.

"Let's have sex with the sheep, torture it, kill it, have sex with it again and then burn it," said the pyromaniac.

Then they all turned to the masochist for his suggestion.

The masochist said: "Baaaaaa."

A man arrived home to find his wife wearing a sexy black negligee. "Tie me up," she purred," and you can do anything you want."

So he tied her up and went off to play golf.

Sailors

A young man joined the Navy and set down for his first meal on board ship. Throughout the meal, his fellow sailors emitted loud, rumbling farts, much to the amusement of everyone present. Anxious to fit in, the new boy managed to squeeze out a small, barely audible fart. The whole room immediately fell silent and everyone turned to look at him.

Slowly the huge First Mate stood up and announced in a booming voice: "All right men! The virgin's mine!"

A newly married sailor was informed by the US Navy that for the next twelve months he was going to be stationed a long way from home on a remote island in the Pacific. A few weeks after landing there, he started to miss his new wife so he wrote her a letter.

"My darling," he wrote, "it has suddenly dawned on me that we are going to be apart for a very long time. I'm already starting to miss you like crazy, and there's really not much to do around here in the evenings. Besides that, we're constantly surrounded by beautiful young native girls. Do you think if I had a hobby of some kind I could avoid being tempted by them?"

Two weeks later, his wife sent him a harmonica with a note saying: "Why don't you learn to play this to take your mind off the local girls?"

Eventually his tour of duty came to an end and he rushed home to be reunited with his wife. "Darling," he said as they embraced at the quayside, "I can't wait to get you into bed so that we can make passionate love."

Kissing him on the cheek, she said: "First, let's see you play that harmonica."

Why do sailors have tattoos on their backs? – So their shipmates will have something to read.

A sailor arrived back at his home port after a long sea voyage and headed straight for the nearest brothel. He told the Madam: "I need a woman to suck my dick."

"Sure," she said, and signalled to a gorgeous brunette.

The sailor went into a room with the girl, dropped his trousers and she started sucking away. After five minutes of frantic sucking, she came up for breath and said: "It's not getting hard, you know."

"It's not supposed to get hard," said the sailor, "just clean."

Two naval captains were sitting at the bar one night. One turned to the other and said: "You know what gets me about sailors? If you're at sea for more than a month, they get sexually frustrated and start jerking off all over the place. It makes a terrible mess on deck."

The other captain smiled knowingly before offering his advice. "Oldest trick in the book," he said. "You take the crew and divide them into two teams, then you buy a dozen barrels and put them on the ship. You tell the crew that the team which fills the most barrels wins £50."

"Well, it's a great way to keep the ship clean, but it means I'm £50 out of pocket on each voyage."

"Not so," replied the other captain. "After you get back to port, collect all the barrels and take them to the wax factory to turn the sailors' spunk into candles. You'll make a handsome profit every time."

So the captain decided to take his friend's advice. He divided the crew, bought a dozen barrels and set off to sea. Before long, the crew took to the new system and began filling barrel after barrel. When they finally reached port, the captain sold the barrels for a huge profit.

This happy arrangement went on voyage after voyage until the ship happened to return to that very first port. Coming down the gangplank, the captain was surprised to see two police officers waiting for him. They immediately slapped handcuffs on him and led him away.

"What's the meaning of this?" he demanded.

"You sick bastard," replied one of the cops. "Remember all those barrels you sold to the candle factory the last time you were here?"

"Sure," said the captain. "What about them?"

"Well, they made them into candles, sold them to the convent, and now all the nuns are pregnant!"

Schizophrenia

A charity pantomime in aid of paranoid schizophrenics descended into chaos yesterday when someone shouted: "He's behind you."

The best event at the Paralympics has to be the schizophrenic boxing.

A schizophrenic man saw a poster advertising a music night at a local pub. He thought to himself: "I've half a mind to go to that."

I'm so lazy, to have a threesome I sleep with a schizophrenic. (Stewart Francis)

Did you hear about the schizophrenic Asian? – Mahmood Swingh.

Never get into an argument with a schizophrenic and ask: "Just who do you think you are?!"

School

One day in class, a schoolteacher brought in a bag full of fruit. She said: "I'm going to reach into the bag and describe a piece of fruit, and I want you to tell me what fruit I'm talking about. Now my first fruit is round and red. So what do you think it might be?"

Little Johnny immediately raised his hand, but the teacher ignored him and chose Mary instead. "An apple, Miss," suggested Mary.

"No," said the teacher, "it's a tomato, but I like your thinking. My second fruit is small, green and hairy. What do you think it might be?"

Little Johnny raised his hand again but once more the teacher ignored him. This time she asked Melissa. "A gooseberry, Miss," said Melissa.

"Actually, Melissa, it's a kiwi fruit," said the teacher, "but I like your thinking. My third fruit is small, black and round."

Little Johnny's hand shot up. But the teacher chose Laura. "A blackberry, Miss," said Laura.

"No, Laura, it's a grape," said the teacher, "but I like your thinking."

By now Little Johnny was fed up with being repeatedly overlooked, so he shouted out: "I've got one for you, Miss. Let me put my hand in my pocket. I've got it. It's round, hard and it's got a head on it."

"Johnny, that's disgusting!" snapped the teacher.

"No, Miss," said Little Johnny, "it's a quarter, but I like your thinking."

The teacher asked her class what their parents did for a living. Little Johnny raised his hand and announced: "My mum is a substitute."

Knowing something of the family background, the teacher said: "I think you mean she's a prostitute."

"No," said Johnny. "My big sister's the prostitute, but when she doesn't feel up to it, Mum acts as a substitute."

When I went to school, sex education was mainly muttered warnings about the janitor. (Frankie Boyle)

Little Johnny went into school after being absent the previous day. "Where were you yesterday?" the teacher demanded.

"Sorry, Miss," said Johnny, "but my granddad got burnt."

"Oh, I hope it wasn't serious," said the teacher sympathetically.

"Well," said Johnny, "they sure don't fuck about at those crematoriums."

Little Johnny came home from school to find his mother waiting for him with an angry look on her face. "Your headmaster called today," she raged, "and said you'd been expelled for using the C-word. Now that wasn't clever, was it?"

"No, Mum," said Johnny. "It was cunt."

A kindergarten teacher received gifts from her students at the end of the school year. First, the florist's son handed her a beautifully wrapped gift. The teacher held the gift above her head, shook it and said: "I think it's flowers. Am I right?"

"Yes," said the boy.

The teacher's second gift was from the daughter of a sweet-shop owner. The teacher held the beautifully wrapped gift above her head, shook it and said: "I think it's a box of sweets. Am I right?"

"Yes," said the girl.

The teacher's third gift was from a boy whose father ran the local liquor store. Once again, it was beautifully wrapped. The teacher held it above her head and shook it but as she did so, it started to leak. She touched a drop of the leakage with her finger and put it on her tongue. "I think it's wine," she said. "Am I right?"

"No," said the boy.

So the teacher tasted another drop of the leakage and then said: "Is it champagne?"

"No," said the boy.

The teacher tasted another drop but unable to identify it, she finally admitted defeat. "Okay, I give up," she said. "What is it?"

The boy said: "It's a puppy."

One day, during English class, the teacher asked: "Who can tell me the meaning of the word 'indifferent'?"

There was silence until finally Little Johnny put up his hand. The teacher, hesitant to call on him because of his propensity for foul language and sexual innuendo, looked for another student to ask, but when no one else raised their hand, she said with a degree of resignation: "Yes, Johnny?"

"It means lovely, Miss."

Relieved, but a little puzzled, the teacher said: "Johnny, can you explain why you think indifferent means lovely?"

"Sure, Miss. Last night when I was in bed, I heard Mum say: 'Ooh, that's lovely.' Then Dad said: 'Yep, it's in different.'"

On the first night of a school camping trip, Little Johnny was scared and ran to the teacher's tent. "Please, Miss," he begged, "can I sleep with you tonight?"

"No," said the teacher firmly.

"But my mum lets me," pleaded Johnny.

"Oh, okay, then," said the teacher, relenting.

So Johnny jumped into the sleeping bag next to the teacher. After a few minutes, he said: "Please, Miss, can I play with your bellybutton with my finger?"

"Certainly not," replied the teacher.

"But my mum lets me," insisted Johnny.

"Oh, very well, then," sighed the teacher, desperate for a night's sleep.

Five minutes later, the teacher woke up screaming: "That's not my bellybutton!"

Little Johnny said: "It ain't my finger either!"

A young class were enjoying the first day of first grade. The teacher said: "Now that we're all grown up, we aren't going to use baby talk anymore. Instead, we're going to use grown-up words. Now who would like to start by telling us about what they did in summer vacation?"

A little girl called Jenny put up her hand and said: "This summer vacation I rode in a choo-choo."

"No, Jenny," interrupted the teacher. "We don't say 'choo-choo' anymore. We say 'train'. Remember to use grown-up words. Now who's next?"

Little Johnny raised his hand. "This summer vacation I went to Disneyland and saw Winnie the Shit."

The teacher asked the children in her class what their fathers did for a living.

"Mary, what does your father do?"

"He's a doctor, Miss."

"Thank you, Mary. And Joey, what does your father do?"

"He's an accountant, Miss."

"Thank you, Joey. Johnny, what does your father do?"

"He's dead, Miss."

"Oh, Johnny, I'm so sorry. What did he do before he died?"

"He turned purple, farted and fell on the cat, Miss."

The pretty teacher was concerned about one of her seven-year-old students. Taking him aside after class one day, she asked: "Johnny, why has your school work been so poor lately?"

"I'm in love," replied Johnny.

Holding back an urge to smile, the teacher asked: "With whom?"

"With you," he said.

"But Johnny," she said gently, "don't you see how silly that is? It's true that I would like a husband of my own someday, but I don't want a child!"

"Oh, don't worry," said the boy reassuringly, "I'll use a rubber."

For the start of the school year Little Johnny's class had a new teacher. "Good morning, class," she said, "I'm your new teacher. My name is Miss Prussy."

When the class snickered, the teacher carefully wrote her name on the chalkboard, spelling it out as she did so. "It's Prussy. P-r-u-s-s-y. Now tomorrow morning I expect all of you to remember my name. And it won't be written on the chalkboard, either."

So the next morning the teacher asked the class: "Right, which of you remembers my name?"

Only Little Johnny put up his hand.

"Thank you, Johnny," said the teacher. "So tell me, how did you remember my name?"

"Easy," replied Johnny. "I just knew that it was an everyday word but with an 'r' as the second letter."

"Well done, Johnny."

"No problem, Miss Crunt."

I once beat up the school bully with a baseball bat. Both his arms were completely broken. Which is what gave me the courage to do it. (Emo Philips)

As part of a junior-school biology lesson, the teacher drew a penis on the board and asked the children if any of them knew what it was.

Little Johnny shouted out: "My dad has two of them; a small one for weeing and a big one for cleaning the babysitter's teeth."

Trying to instil good manners into her young students, a teacher asked them the following question: "If you were on a date having dinner with a nice young lady, how would you tell her that you have to go to the toilet?"

Leroy put up his hand and answered: "Just a minute, I have to go piss, bitch."

The teacher said: "That would be terribly rude and impolite, Leroy. What about you, Jack? How would you say it?"

Jack said: "I would say, 'I am sorry, but I really need to go for a dump. I'll be right back.'"

"Well," said the teacher, "I suppose that's a little better, but it's still not very nice to say the word 'dump' at the dinner table. And you, Little Johnny, can you use your brain for once and show us your good manners? What would you say?"

Little Johnny replied: "I would say, 'Darling, may I please be excused for a moment? I have to shake hands with a very dear friend of mine, whom I hope you'll get to meet after dinner.'"

The teacher fainted.

The teacher asked Little Johnny a maths question. She said: "If I gave you £30, and you gave £5 to Becky, £5 to Mary and £5 to Susie, what would you have?"

Little Johnny answered: "An orgy."

Three boys were angry at receiving low grades from Miss Perkins, their sex education teacher. Two got Es while the third got an E minus, the lowest possible grade.

"We should get her for this," said the first boy.

"Yeah," agreed the second, "let's grab her tits."

"Yeah," interrupted the third, "and then let's kick her in the nuts."

Little Johnny had to write a two-line poem in English class. His composition was: "As I walking down the hall, I spied a cockroach on the wall."

The teacher was pleasantly surprised. She had come to expect crude poems from Little Johnny, but this one seemed harmless. She said: "Johnny, that was excellent. I would like you to repeat it, but please leave the 'cock' out of the cockroach."

So Little Johnny repeated his poem. "As I was walking down the hall, I spied a roach on the wall . . . with his cock out."

A schoolteacher asked her class of young children to name one thing they needed at home but didn't yet have.

"Alex?"

"A Nintendo Wii."

"Very good, Alex. How about you, Kevin?"

"An iPad," said Kevin.

"Oh yes, I'd like an iPad," said the teacher. "Johnny. What about you?"

Johnny remained uncharacteristically silent.

"Surely there must be something you can think of, Johnny?" suggested the teacher.

"No, nothing."

"Really, Johnny? You do surprise me."

"I know it's true for a fact," insisted Johnny. "Because last week my dad came home drunk, was sick all over the lounge carpet, and my mum said it was the last thing we needed."

The teacher asked Little Johnny to use the word "definitely" in a sentence.

Little Johnny replied: "Miss, do farts have lumps in them?"

"Of course not, Johnny."

"Then I have definitely shit my pants."

A teacher was talking to her class of eighteen-year-olds the day before an important exam. "Now, I want you all to have a good night's sleep to get ready for the exam. Is that understood?"

"But Miss," said one boy, "what if I stay up all night and have rampant sex?"

The teacher replied: "Then I would advise you to write your exam with your other hand."

It was the first day of school and the teacher was establishing the fact that she would take no nonsense from the children this year. While she was taking a head count, she was told by one boy: "My name is Billy Fuckhauer."

The teacher said: "There will be none of that kind of thing this year, Billy. Tell me your real name."

The kid said: "No, really, my name is Billy Fuckhauer. You can go across the hall and ask my brother if you don't believe me."

Tentatively the teacher went across the hall and knocked on the classroom door. There was no teacher in the classroom, so she entered the room and directly asked the class: "Do you have a Fuckhauer in here?"

"Hell no!" replied a boy in the front row. "We don't even get a cookie break!"

A first-grade teacher was having trouble with one of her students. She asked the boy: "Jason, what is the matter with you these days? Your attitude stinks."

Jason answered: "I'm too smart for first grade. My sister is in third grade, and I'm smarter than she is, so I should be in third grade too."

In an attempt to resolve the problem, the teacher took Jason along to the principal's office and while the boy waited in the outer office, she explained the situation to the principal. He told the teacher that he would give Jason a test and if he failed to answer any of the questions correctly, he would have to return to first grade and behave himself. Jason was then taken to the principal's office for the test.

"What is five times five?" asked the principal.

"Twenty-five," answered Jason.

"What is twelve minus eight?" said the principal.

"Four," replied Jason instantly.

And so it went on. Every standard third-grade question the principal asked, Jason answered correctly. Eventually the principal said to the teacher: "I think Jason can move up to third grade."

"First, let me ask him a few questions," suggested the teacher.

"Very well," agreed the principal.

"Okay, Jason," began the teacher. "What does a cow have four of that I only have two of?"

The principal looked anxious.

"Legs," answered Jason.

The teacher continued: "What does a dog do that a man steps into?"

Jason replied: "Pants."

Teacher: "What goes in hard and pink then comes out soft and sticky?"

Jason: "Bubblegum."

The principal wiped a few beads of perspiration from his brow.

Teacher: "What does a man do standing up, a woman do sitting down and a dog do on three legs?"

Jason: "Shake hands."

Teacher: "Now I am going to ask some 'What am I?' questions."

Jason: "Okay."

Teacher: "You stick your poles inside me. You tie me down to get me up. I get wet before you do."

Jason: "Tent."

Teacher: "A finger goes in me. You fiddle with me when you're bored. The best man always has me first."

The principal was now sweating profusely.

Jason: "Wedding ring."

Teacher: "I come in many sizes. When I'm not well, I drip. When you blow me, you feel good."

Jason: "Nose."

Teacher: "I have a stiff shaft. My tip penetrates. I come with a quiver."

Jason: "Arrow."

Teacher: "And finally. What word starts with an 'F' and ends in 'K' and means a lot of excitement?"

Jason: "Firetruck."

The principal breathed a huge sigh of relief and told the teacher: "Put Jason in third grade. He's obviously very smart. I got the last nine questions wrong myself."

The Scots

Two Scotsmen – Tam and Jock – were sitting in a hotel bar discussing Jock's forthcoming wedding.

"How are the preparations going?" asked Tam.

"Just fine," replied Jock. "The invitations have been printed, the flowers have been ordered, I've sorted out my best man and arranged my stag night. And I've even hired a kilt to be married in."

"A kilt?" said Tam. "You'll look very smart, I'm sure. What's the tartan?"

"Och," replied Jock, "I imagine she'll just be in white."

Why do Scottish families have double glazing? – So their children can't hear the ice-cream van.

At an auction in Glasgow, a wealthy American announced that he had lost his wallet containing £5,000 and that he would give a reward of £100 to the person who found it.

From the back of the hall a Scottish voice shouted: "I'll give £150!"

A Scotsman was farming his Highland croft when a passing American tourist asked: "How much land do you have here?"

"About two acres," replied the Scotsman.

"You know back home it takes me a day to drive around my ranch," the American boasted.

"Aye," said the Scotsman, "I once had a car like that."

Experts say 200,000 people could die from alcohol in England and Wales in the next twenty years. No figures were included for Scotland, as they currently come under "death from natural causes". (Frankie Boyle)

Two Scotsmen met up twenty-five years after their last get-together. They hugged and slapped each other's back and tears formed in their eyes as they renewed their old friendship.

"Let's have a drink like we did in the old days," the first Scot winked at his pal.

"Aye," his friend replied. "And don't forget it's your round."

Wee Jock was the only Scottish pupil in a junior class full of English children. One day the teacher announced: "Every Thursday from now on, we're going to have a general knowledge quiz. The pupil who gets the answer right can have Friday and Monday off and not come back to school until Tuesday. Right class, who can tell me which famous person said: 'Don't ask what your country can do for you, but what you can do for your country'?"

Wee Jock prided himself on his general knowledge, so he put up his hand straightaway, waving furiously in the air. But the teacher looked around the class and picked Jeremy instead. In a very English accent, Jeremy declared: "Yes, Miss, the answer is United States President J. F. Kennedy in his oft-quoted inauguration speech in 1960."

"Very good Jeremy," said the teacher. "You may stay off Friday and Monday and we will see you back in class on Tuesday."

The next Thursday came around, and Wee Jock was even more determined to get the answer right. The teacher began: "Who said: 'We will fight them on the beaches, we will fight them in the air, we will fight them at sea. But we will never surrender'?"

Wee Jock's hand shot up immediately, his arm stiff as a board, shouting, "I know. I know! Me, Miss, me, Miss!" Looking around the class, the teacher instead picked Timothy who answered in clipped English tones:

"The answer is Winston Churchill, Miss, in his memorable 1941 Battle of Britain speech."

"Very good, Timothy," said the teacher. "You may stay off Friday and Monday and come back to class on Tuesday."

The following Thursday came around and Wee Jock was hyper. He had been studying encyclopaedias all week and was ready for any question that the teacher might throw at him. The teacher began: "Who said: 'One small step for man, one giant leap for mankind'?"

Wee Jock's arm shot straight in the air. He was standing on his seat, jumping up and down, screaming: "Miss, me, Miss, meeeeee!" Instead, the teacher surveyed the room and picked Rupert who, in a plummy English accent, announced: "Yes, Miss, that was Neil Armstrong in 1969, on the occasion of the first moon landing."

"Very good, Rupert," said the teacher. "You may stay off Friday and Monday and come back into class on Tuesday."

This was too much for Wee Jock who in a fit of temper tipped over his desk and threw his chair at the wall. He started screaming: "For fuck's sake, where did all these English bastards come from?"

The teacher, looking around the class, demanded: "Who said that?"

"Sir William Wallace, Battle of Falkirk, July 1298," said Wee Jock, grabbing his coat and bag and heading for the door. "See y'all on Tuesday!"

What's the difference between a tightrope and a Scotsman? – A tightrope sometimes gives.

A young Scottish lad and lass were sitting on a heathery hill in the Scottish Highlands. They had been silent for a while, when the lass turned to him and said: "A penny for your thoughts."

The lad was a bit embarrassed, but finally he said: "If you must know, I was thinking how nice it would be if you gave me a wee kiss."

So she kissed him.

Afterwards, he once again lapsed into a pensive mood, prompting her to ask him: "What are you thinking now?"

To which the lad grumbled: "Well, I was hoping you hadn't forgotten the penny."

A Scotsman walked into an English bar. The bartender said: "I've hired a bagpipes player for tonight."

"What's the occasion?" asked the Scotsman.
The bartender said: "I want to close early."

What do you call a Scotsman holding the World Cup? — An engraver.

Jock's nephew came to him with a dilemma. "I have my choice of two women," he said, "a beautiful, penniless young girl whom I love dearly, and a rich old widow whom I can't abide."

"Follow your heart," Jock advised. "Marry the girl you love."

"Thank you, Uncle Jock," said the nephew. "That's sound advice."

"You're welcome, laddie," said Jock. "By the way, where does the widow live?"

Why are there so many beautiful women in Scandinavia? — Because the Vikings left all the ugly ones in Scotland.

Sandy became depressed and decided to end it all by hanging himself. However, his friend Donald came along in the nick of time, cut the rope and saved his life.

The next day, Sandy sent Donald a bill for the cost of the rope.

A Scotsman was walking through the centre of Glasgow with a wellington boot on his dick. He was approached by a police officer who asked him what he was doing.

The Scotsman replied: "Nothing much, just fuckin' a boot, officer."

A man went to the doctor with a large carrot wedged firmly up his arse.

"Oh, dear," smirked the doctor. "Have you been exploring your latent homosexual desires?"

"Certainly not," said the man. "Today was my first day as a door-to-door vegetable salesman in Glasgow."

As the plane lands at Glasgow Airport, passengers are reminded to set their watch back . . . twenty-five years. (Frankie Boyle)

In the Scottish Highlands, a man knocked impatiently on the door of a neighbouring farmhouse. The farmer's daughter answered the door.

"Is your father in?" asked the neighbour.

"No," he's at the Inverness farmers' market. "If it's the services of the red Ayrshire bull you want, the cost is £75."

"No, it's not that," said the neighbour.

"Well," said the daughter, "if it's the Galloway belted bull you want, the cost is £60."

"No, it's not that," said the neighbour.

"How about the small Highland bull?" continued the daughter. "The services of that bull only cost £50."

Interrupting her, the neighbour snapped: "That's not what I've come about. Your brother Alastair has made my daughter Isla pregnant. My wife and I want to know what your father intends to do about it."

"Oh, well," said the daughter. "You'll have to see my father yourself. I don't know what he charges for Alastair."

Semen

Doctor: Is your semen flow regular?
Man: It comes in snatches.

"Excuse me," said a man to the woman sitting in front of him on the bus. "You have some semen on the back of your jacket."

"It's probably yoghurt," she replied.

"No, it's definitely semen," he said. "I don't ejaculate yoghurt."

Why did the semen cross the road? – Because it was the guy's first wank in three weeks.

A girl at work was disgusted when she saw a cum stain on my work trousers. I apologized and explained that I had eaten spaghetti carbonara on my lunch break. For some reason pasta really turns me on.

What's the difference between semen and mayonnaise? – Mayonnaise doesn't hit the back of a woman's throat at 30 mph.

I came, I saw, I wiped it off and I apologized.

A man bumped into an ex-girlfriend shortly after they had split up acrimoniously. He told her: "I had sex with another woman last night, but I was still thinking of you."

"Miss me, do you?" she said with an air of superiority.

"No, it stops me from coming too quickly."

I'm a meticulous ejaculator – I always cross the tits and dot the eyes.

A man said to his wife: "I fancy kinky sex. How about I shoot my spunk in your ear?"

"No way!" said the wife. "I might go deaf."

"Well," he said, "I've been shooting my load in your mouth for the last twenty years and you're still bloody talking, aren't you?"

Sex

Complaining of feeling lethargic and listless, a guy in his sixties went to see his doctor who examined him and told him: "Your problem is that you've burnt yourself out. Your penis is worn out through all the sex you've been having over the years. I would estimate that you can only have sex another twenty times before you cause yourself serious medical damage."

The guy was devastated, and when he got home he tearfully informed his wife that he could only have sex another twenty times.

She was sympathetic and suggested: "We mustn't waste those opportunities – we should make a list."

He said: "I already made a list on my way home. Sorry, honey, your name's not on it."

A husband and wife were in the bathroom getting ready for work when the husband looked at his wife and said: "I've got to have you . . . now!" He backed her up against the bathroom door, pulled down her panties and ravaged her. He knew he was doing great because she screamed and wiggled more than she ever had before. When he finished, he started putting his clothes back on and noticed his wife was still writhing against the door.

He said: "That was the best, honey. You've never moved like that before. You didn't hurt yourself, did you?"

"No, no," she said. "I'll be okay once I can get the doorknob out of my arse."

I know I might not be the best at oral sex, but why does my wife keep rubbing my nose in it?

A girl got naked on the sofa, then pointed to the coffee table and said: "Would you rather shag me over that?"

"Sure I would," said the guy. "You're much prettier."

If oral sex is represented as a sexual position by a "69", what position is a "96"?
– Not speaking to each other.

Handy Sex Tips for Women

The following information was gained through extensive research involving men and women from all backgrounds and walks of life. It consists of the questions most frequently asked of women regarding love, sex and relationships.

Q: How do I know if I'm ready for sex?

A: Ask your boyfriend. He'll know when the time is right. When it comes to love and sex, men are much more responsible, since they're not as emotionally confused as women. It's a proven fact.

Q: Should I have sex on the first date?

A: Absolutely. There's not a moment to waste.

Q: What exactly happens during the act of sex?

A: Again, this is entirely up to the man. The important thing to remember is that you must do whatever he tells you without question. Sometimes, however, he may ask you to do certain things that may at first seem strange to you. Do them anyway.

Q: What is foreplay?

A: Nothing to worry your pretty little head about. It's not important – merely something that serves to delay the immense pleasure you'll get from having his dick thrust inside you.

Q: How long should the sex act last?

A: This is a natural and normal part of nature, so don't feel ashamed or embarrassed. After you've finished making love, he'll have a natural desire to leave you suddenly and go out with his friends to play golf. Or perhaps another activity, such as going out with his friends to the bar for the purpose of consuming large amounts of alcohol and sharing a few personal thoughts with his buddies. Don't feel left out – while he's gone you can busy yourself by doing laundry, cleaning the house or perhaps even going out to buy him an expensive gift. He'll come back when he's ready.

Q: What is afterplay?

A: After a man has finished making love, he needs to replenish his manly energy. Afterplay is simply a list of important activities for you to do after lovemaking. This includes making him a sandwich or pizza, bringing him a few beers or leaving him alone to sleep while you go out and buy him an expensive gift.

Q: Does the size of the penis matter?

A: Yes. Although many women believe that quality, not quantity, is important, studies show this is simply not true. The average erect male penis measures about three inches. Anything longer than that is extremely rare and, if by some chance your lover's sexual organ is four inches or over, you should go down on your knees and thank your lucky stars and do everything possible to please him, such as doing his laundry, cleaning his house and/or buying him an expensive gift.

Q: What about the female orgasm?

A: What about it? There's no such thing. It's a myth.

A boy's mother decided it was time to sit him down and tell him about the birds and the bees. So she told him all about how babies are created. Afterwards, he was uncharacteristically silent.

"Do you understand all the things I've told you?" asked his mother.

"Yes, I think so," said the boy.

"Any questions at all?"

"There is one thing. How are kittens and puppies made?"

"In exactly the same way as babies."

"Wow!" exclaimed the boy. "My dad will fuck anything!"

I have been in kind of a sexual dry spell lately. In the past few years I've only had sex in months that end in "arch". (Doug Benson)

Immediately after having sex in their apartment, a guy and a girl both realized they were suddenly desperate for a beer. As it was bitterly cold outside, neither wanted to venture out to the corner shop, so they devised a contest to decide who should go. Whoever could come up with the best poem would be the one to stay in bed while the loser went to fetch the beer.

They both thought for a while, then the guy said: "Okay, I got one. Two times two is four plus five is nine, I can pee in yours but you can't pee in mine."

"Okay," said the girl, eager to outdo him. "Two times two is four plus five is nine, I know the length of yours but you'll never know the depth of mine."

The guy got up.

I was sacked today for having sex in the back of my taxi with a customer. I say taxi – technically, it's a hearse.

A husband arrived home from work. "Hey, honey," he called out excitedly, "I've discovered a new position we can try to spice up our sex life."

"Really?" said his wife. "What?"

"Back to back."

"Back to back?" she queried. "How's that going to work? It's impossible. It can't be done."

"Sure it can," insisted the husband. "And I've persuaded another couple to come over and help us."

A man had an invitation to an important dance, but the problem was he didn't know how to dance. So he went to a dance studio for some lessons. The instructor told him to pretend that there was a ten-pence piece on his right shoulder and that he should touch the coin with his earlobe in time to the music. So the guy went home and practised this all week long.

The next week the instructor told him to do the same thing with his left shoulder.

The next lesson he was told to pretend that there was a fifty-pence piece on his penis and he had to flip it into the air and catch it again.

The week before the dance he had his last lesson. This time the instructor told him to pretend to bounce a £1 coin on his butt.

The night of the dance came and he met a girl. They danced and danced and the whole time he was saying: "Ten pence, ten pence, fifty pence, a pound." The girl was so impressed she asked him to make love to her the same way as he danced.

So they got back to her house and went for it. "Ten pence, ten pence, fifty pence, a pound. Ten pence, ten pence . . . oh fuck it, a pound seventy, a pound seventy, a pound seventy . . ."

A man went to see a doctor and said: "Doctor, you've got to help me. I just can't stop having sex!"

"How often do you have sex?" asked the doctor.

"Well, twice a day I have sex with my wife," said the man. "Twice a day!"

"That's by no means unusual," replied the doctor.

"But that's not all," continued the man. "Twice a day I also have sex with my secretary. Twice a day!"

"Well, I must say that is excessive," mused the doctor.

"But that's not all," added the man. "Twice a day I also have sex with a prostitute. Twice a day!"

"Well, that's definitely too much," concluded the doctor. "You've got to learn to take yourself in hand."

"I do," said the man. "Twice a day!"

Men's Hopes and Fears During Sex

Stage 1: Kissing/Light Petting

He hopes you're thinking: "Oh, I can't resist. I'm powerless before your heavy seductive aroma."

He fears you're thinking: "Yuk! Garlic breath!"

Stage 2: Undressing

He hopes you're thinking: "My God, look at the size of that!"

He fears you're thinking: "My God, look at the size of that!"

Stage 3: Foreplay/Oral Sex

He hopes you're thinking: "I could suck his beautiful manhood for hours."

He fears you're thinking: "If he doesn't warn me before he shoots his load, I'll kill him!"

Stage 4: Penetration

He hopes you're thinking: "You stallion, you're splitting me in half!"

He fears you're thinking: "Is it in yet?"

Stage 5: Her Orgasm

He hopes you're thinking: "Yes, Tom, yes!"

He fears you're thinking: "I deserve an Oscar for this performance!"

He really fears you're thinking: "Yes, Dave, yes!"

Stage 6: Postcoital Bliss

He hopes you're thinking: "Now I know what an earthquake feels like."

He fears you're thinking: "After that, I'm seriously considering becoming a lesbian."

A guy admitted to his buddy: "I've been sleeping with my girlfriend and her twin."

"Wow! How can you tell them apart?"

"Easy. Her brother has a moustache."

There was one time where I failed to perform sexually. My girlfriend said to me: "Oh don't worry, it happens to a lot of guys." Okay, there are two things wrong with that. First of all, who are these other guys? And second, if it's happening to more than one of us don't you think it could be your fault? (Jimmy Carr)

A small boy was awoken in the middle of the night by strange noises coming from his parents' room, so he decided to investigate. Peering through the door, he was shocked to see his mother and father enjoying vigorous sex.

"What are you doing?" asked the boy.

"It's okay, son," said the father, peering round from his position on top. "Your mother wants a baby, that's all."

Excited at the prospect of a new baby brother, the boy skipped happily back to his room.

The following night, the boy again heard noises from his parents' room, so he went to see what they were doing. This time he was shocked to see his mother sucking furiously on his father's dick.

"What are you doing now?" asked the boy.

"It's okay, son," said the father. "It's just a change of plan, that's all. Your mother wants a BMW instead."

A young married couple enjoyed a healthy sex life and she grew accustomed to rewarding him between the sheets for any act of generosity. But to prove that she meant more to him than just sex, one day on impulse he bought her a large bouquet of flowers.

"They're beautiful," she said before adding suspiciously: "I guess now you'll expect me to spend the weekend on my back with my legs apart?"

"Why?" he asked. "Don't we have a vase?"

I found out last night there's a fine line between yes and no. It's called the perineum.

Why Sex Is Like Riding a Bike

- You have to keep pumping if you want to get anywhere.
- It's best to wear protective head gear when entering unfamiliar territory.

- You can do it with no hands, but it's best not to try until you have plenty of experience.
- It's usually hard to control your speed the first few times you try.
- If you get a flat, try pumping it back up.
- You don't need any special clothing, but you can buy some if you're really into it.
- Do it for too long and your crotch goes numb.
- Once you learn, you never forget.
- It looks easier than it is.
- If you're with someone who is struggling to keep up, it's best to slow down and wait for them.
- Once you're over the top, you can just coast the rest of the way.
- If you fall off, you should always get straight back on.

A little boy walked in on his parents having sex and ran from the room. The father immediately jumped up and ran to calm him down.

The little boy said: "I don't like you doing that, it scares me and it sounds like Mummy is getting hurt!"

The dad assured the little boy that Mummy was not being hurt and added: "We are making you a baby brother so you will have someone to play with."

This made the little boy happy and he ran off to play.

The next day, when his dad came home, the little boy was sitting on the front porch crying his eyes out. The dad asked him what was so bad that it made him cry so hard. The little boy replied: "You know that baby brother you and Mummy were making me? Well, the milkman ate him this morning!".

How is sex like arithmetic? – Subtract clothes, add bed, divide legs and multiply.

After hearing a couple's complaints that their intimate life wasn't what it used to be, the sex counsellor suggested they vary their position. "For example," he suggested, "you might try the wheelbarrow. Lift her legs, penetrate and off you go."

The eager husband was all for trying this new idea as soon as they got home.

"Well, okay," the wife agreed hesitantly, "but on two conditions. First, if it hurts, you'll stop right away, and second, you must promise we won't go past my mother's house."

What's the best thing about owning a round bed? – You can do a lap of honour when you finish.

Three men in the pub were struggling to settle an argument about who was the best lover. Then one of them said he had a sound-measuring device and suggested that they should all take it in turns to record how loud their wives screamed during sex. The other two agreed, so a week later they all met in the pub to discuss the results.

"Well, I did the experiment," said the first guy, "and the device measured 86 decibels. Beat that!"

"No problem," said the second guy smugly. "I did the experiment and the device measured 99 decibels. Now, what do you say about that?"

"Not bad," said the third guy, "but when I did the experiment the device measured in at a whopping 125 decibels."

"One hundred and twenty-five decibels?!" said the first guy. "How on earth did you get your wife to scream that loud while you were having sex?"

"Easy," said the third guy. "She walked in while I was fucking her sister."

My ex-girlfriend said she was open to a lot of things sexually. Apparently one of those things wasn't criticism. (Daniel Sloss)

Two young men worked at adjoining desks in an open-plan office. One morning, one of them leaned over and whispered to the other: "I'm going to organize a group sex session in my apartment tonight. Do you want to come?"

"Sure. How many people will be there?"

"Three, if you bring your girlfriend."

I had sex with this girl I met in a club last night. It was inevitable it was going to happen: you could tell just by the chemistry. Rohypnol and chloroform.

A market researcher was conducting a sex survey in the neighbourhood. At one house the wife completed the survey by day but told the researcher to come back in the evening for her husband's answers.

So the researcher returned, did the survey with the husband and then compared them with the wife's answers. The researcher looked puzzled. He said: "There's something of a discrepancy here. Under 'frequency of intercourse', you said 'three times a week' but your wife said 'three times a night'."

"That's right," said the husband, "but it's only until we have paid off the mortgage on the house."

A man was lying in bed when he felt a hand reach into his boxers and start playing with his balls. It was good but he wasn't really in the mood. So he whispered: "Not tonight. I'm tired."

"Sorry, it doesn't work like that in here," said his cellmate.

Sex Organs

A man was getting ready to have sex with his girlfriend for the first time. He tried to slide his dick inside her, but he couldn't do it. He tried again, but still it wouldn't go in. Eventually he managed to force it in, but it was really uncomfortable. "I'm sorry, sweetheart," he said. "You're so tight I don't think I can bear the pain."

"Don't worry," she said tenderly. "Pull out, and I'll go to the bathroom and make things a little more comfortable."

So he climbed off and she disappeared into the bathroom. When she returned a couple of minutes later, he got back on top of her and this time was able to slide in easily.

"That's much better," he sighed. "Did you put some K-Y jelly in there?"

"No," she said. "I just peeled off the scabs."

A woman's vagina had become seriously stretched by her previous job as a hooker. Anxious to put her past behind her, she adopted a chaste lifestyle and soon found a man who wanted to marry her. Worried about how he would react to her cavernous fanny, she told him on their wedding night that as a child she had caught her private area on some barbed wire while climbing over a fence into a field, and that explained why her vagina was so big.

They then had sex for the first time. Afterwards she asked him how it had been for him.

Choosing his words carefully, he turned to her and said: "Just how far across the field were you before you noticed?"

My wife tried to be a bit sexy last night by shoving a lollipop up her fanny. I told her to be careful because she would need it to see the schoolkids across the road in the morning.

A small boy went into the kitchen one day and ran up to his mother. "Mummy, Mummy, Grandma's got a prawn between her legs!"

"Pardon, darling?" said the mother in surprise.

"Grandma's got a prawn between her legs!" the boy repeated.

"Okay, show me," said the mother, perplexed.

They both walked into the living room, where they found Grandma fast asleep with a contented look on her face. Her knickers were missing and her skirt had ridden up so that nothing was left to the imagination.

"See, Mummy? A prawn," said the little boy, pointing between his gran's splayed legs.

"No, darling, that's something special women have," said the mother, embarrassed.

"But Mummy," said the little boy, looking confused. "It tasted like a prawn."

Why did God put Woman's vagina and arsehole so close together? – So Man could turn her over and carry her home like a six-pack.

To celebrate their fortieth wedding anniversary, a couple returned to the same hotel room in which they had spent their honeymoon. The wife took off her clothes, lay down on the bed, spread her legs . . . but then the husband started to cry.

"What's the matter?" she asked.

He sobbed: "Forty years ago, I couldn't wait to eat it and now it looks like it can't wait to eat me!"

The latest club craze is to fill a woman's vagina with vodka and then suck it out with a straw. Doctors are already warning about the dangers of minge drinking.

A guy went to see a hooker who was reputed to have the world's biggest pussy. He started having sex with her but she was way too big and he was getting no satisfaction at all. So in desperation he slid his whole body inside her and tried to get off, but he accidentally fell in.

Groping around in the dark, he lit his cigarette lighter so that he could see where he was going. He was crawling around on all fours looking for the way out when he dropped his lighter. He searched everywhere but couldn't find it. Just then he bumped into another punter.

"Hey!" said the first guy. "You're lost in here too, huh? Listen, if we can find my lighter, we can walk out of here."

"Buddy," said the other guy, "if we find my car we can drive out of here!"

The Post Office released a new stamp with a picture of a clitoris on it, but they had to withdraw it because only 5 per cent of men knew how to lick it properly.

A small boy was in the bath with his mother. Pointing at her fanny, he asked: "Mum, what's that hairy thing?"

Embarrassed, she replied: "Uh, that's my sponge."

"Oh, yes, I remember," said the boy. "The babysitter's got one. I've seen her washing Dad's face with it."

How is a pussy like a grapefruit? – The best ones squirt when you eat them.

Little Johnny walked into the bathroom and saw his mum with no clothes on. He looked up at her private parts and asked: "What's that, Mum?"

Searching desperately for a reply, the mother eventually blurted out: "Uh, that's where your dad hit me with an axe."

Little Johnny yelled jubilantly: "Great shot, right in the cunt!"

A woman woke up one morning and told her husband about a dream she'd had the previous night. "I was at an auction for penises," she said. "The big ones sold for £1,000 and the tiny ones for £10."

"What about one my size?" asked the husband.

"There weren't any bids."

Understandably the husband felt crushed and decided to exact revenge. So the next morning he told his wife that he, too, had had a dream. "I was at an auction for vaginas," he said. "The really tight ones sold for £1,000 and the loose ones for £10."

"What about one like mine?" asked the wife.

"That's where they held the auction."

A guy out for a drink with his mates spotted a pretty girl and tried to chat her up by saying: "I was going to tell you a joke about my dick, but it's too long."

"What a coincidence," she replied icily. "I was going to tell you a joke about my fanny, but you'll never get it."

A friend of mine had a penis extension recently. Now his house looks really stupid. (Gary Delaney)

A man found himself sitting next to a beautiful girl on a plane. He noticed that she was reading a book on sexual statistics and saw it as an opportunity to strike up a conversation with her.

"That book looks interesting," he said.

"It is," she smiled. "I find it a fascinating subject. For instance, did you know that on average American Indians have the largest penis and that Scotsmen have the biggest-diameter penis? By the way, my name's Sally. What's yours?"

"Tonto McTavish. Pleased to meet you."

A guy picked up a girl in a noisy nightclub and took her back to his place for sex. When he pulled out his dick, she took one look at it and said: "Oh, that's small. I thought you said you had at least a foot."

"No," he explained. "I said I had athlete's foot."

What's another name for a zipper? – A penis fly trap.

A guy picked up a woman in a nightclub and took her home in a taxi. He didn't say a word throughout the journey.

Later, as they undressed, she said: "You're not the communicative type, are you?"

"No," he replied, pulling his dick from his underpants. "I do all my talking with this."

The woman looked at it disconsolately and said: "You really *don't* have much to say, do you?"

Did you hear about the man who had three dicks? – He used to fuck women left, right and centre.

A man wanted to join the Big Dick Club, so he headed down to the club to apply. The female receptionist looked at him sceptically and asked him for the size of his dick.

"Fifteen inches," he said proudly.

Hearing this, she burst out laughing before saying: "I'm sorry, sir, you don't measure up to our standards."

With tears of shame running down his face, the man made for the exit but on his way he bumped into a guy using the vending machine.

"What's up?" asked the guy, spotting the tears.

"I've just been told my dick isn't long enough for me to join the club."

"Oh, right. Well, try not to worry about it. The standards here are high. For example, do you see that bulge in my sock?"

The man nodded.

"Well, I'm just the janitor."

I've been blessed with a huge penis, though I don't understand why the priest didn't just do the sign of the cross like he did with everyone else.

A husband and wife were sitting at home watching the TV. During a commercial break he turned to her and said: "Tell me something that will make me happy and sad at the same time."

She replied: "You've got a bigger dick than all your mates."

What did one cowboy's testicle say to the other? – "Why should we hang? Dick did all the shooting!"

A sailor went to the doctor with a badly scalded penis.

"How on earth did you get that?" asked the doctor.

"It was the captain's fault," replied the sailor. "He's a right bastard, always calling emergency drills when you least expect it. This happened when he made a sudden turn to port."

"So how did that scald your penis?" the doctor inquired.

"Well," the sailor explained, "I was dipping it in his cocoa at the time."

My wife suggested I got one of those penis enlargers. So I did. She's twenty-two and her name's Kelly.

A guy picked up a girl in a club and took her back to his place. She lay on the bed expectantly while he unzipped his trousers, but she was dismayed to see that his dick was only two inches long.

"Who the hell do you think you're going to satisfy with that?" she groaned.

He smiled: "Me!"

Two ten-year-old girls got chatting after their sex education lesson at school.

"So," asked one, "do you know what a penis is, then?"

"I'm not sure," said the other. "I'll ask my dad tonight."

So the girl went home and told her dad that she'd had sex education at school but that she didn't know what a penis was. Unsure of how to explain it, he decided to drop his pants and show her for himself. "This is a penis," he told her, pointing to it.

The next day the two girls met up again.

"Did you find out what a penis is?"

"Yes, it's like a prick but much smaller!"

What's the best thing to come out of a penis when you stroke it? – The wrinkles.

Some Creative Penis Euphemisms

Anal impaler
Bacon bazooka
Beaver buster
Beef bayonet
Cherry splitter
Chimney cleaner
Cream cannon
Crotch rocket
Fun truncheon
Jive sausage
Love lance
Mayonnaise missile
One-eyed trouser snake
Passion pump
Pelvic punisher
Pennis the Menace
Perpendicular pickle
Pleasure piston

Pocket rocket
Porridge gun
Purple-headed womb broom
Russell the love muscle
Spam javelin
Sperm spitter
Spunk trumpet
Tonsil tickler
Trouser trombone
Vagina miner
Womb raider
Yoghurt slinger

A man went to the doctor and said: "It's my penis, Doc. I want you to examine it, but when you look at it you must promise not to laugh."

"Of course I won't laugh," said the doctor. "I've seen thousands of male organs over the years. Now please remove your trousers."

So the man took off his trousers. The doctor took one look at his penis and burst out laughing. "Oh my goodness!" he shrieked. "In all my years in the medical profession that is the smallest, tiniest, weeniest penis I have ever seen! I didn't know it was humanly possible to have one so minute. So tell me what the problem is."

The man said: "It's swollen."

I saw my father's penis once. But it was okay, because I was soooo young . . . and soooo drunk. (Sarah Silverman)

A little girl walked into her parents' bedroom and saw her father naked for the first time. She was immediately curious to see that he had equipment she didn't have. She asked him: "What are those round things hanging there, Daddy?"

"Sweetheart," he replied proudly, "those are God's apples of life. Without them we wouldn't be here."

None the wiser, she sought out her mother and told her what Daddy had said.

The mother asked: "And did he say anything about the dead branch they're hanging from?"

Stepping into an elevator, a small white guy found that the only other occupant was a big black dude. To break the silence, the big black dude looked down on the little white man and said: "Seven foot tall, 350 pounds, fifteen-inch dick, three-pound left ball, three-pound right ball, Turner Brown."

The little white guy immediately fainted.

The big black dude pulled the white guy up and brought him round by slapping his face. "What's wrong?" he asked.

The white guy stammered: "Excuse me, but what did you say?"

The big black dude repeated: "Seven foot tall, 350 pounds, fifteen-inch dick, three-pound left ball, three-pound right ball, my name is Turner Brown."

"Thank God!" said the little white guy. "I thought you said, 'Turn around.'"

A man walked up to a girl in a bar and said: "There are two things you should know about me. First, my dick is the length of two of the Central Bank's pens."

"And what's the second thing?" she asked.

"I'm banned from the Central Bank."

I'm going to rename my penis "Thelifeoutofme" because my wife is always willing to suck that.

I've nicknamed my penis "Elbow". It's flexible, it's hard and my mother doesn't like it on the table during dinner.

Having been shipwrecked on a desert island, a young man didn't see another human being for twenty-five years. Then suddenly one day, a beautiful young woman was washed ashore.

"How have you managed to survive all these years?" she asked, water dripping from her smooth velvety skin.

"I existed by digging for clams and eating berries," he replied.

"What did you do for love?" she purred.

"What's love?" he asked innocently.

Hearing this, she proceeded to show him, not once, not twice, but three times.

"So how do you like love?" she smiled afterwards.

"It's great," he said. "But look what you did to my clam digger!"

A girl unzipped a guy's trousers and said: "Oh dear. Your dick wouldn't make a very good clock."

"What do you mean?" he asked.

"Because," she said, "I'd struggle to get a second hand on it."

Two brothers were undergoing their physicals before joining the police. During the inspection, the doctor was surprised to see that both of the men possessed extraordinarily long penises.

"How do you account for this?" he asked the brothers.

"It's hereditary, sir," replied the older brother.

"I see,' said the doctor, writing in his file. "Your father's the reason for your elongated penises?"

"No, doctor, our mother."

"Your mother?" said the doctor in surprise. "Don't be so ridiculous! Women don't have penises!"

"I know, Doctor," replied the older brother, "but she only had one arm, and when it came to getting us out of the bathtub, she had to manage as best she could."

Shopping

A man was looking at a T-shirt in a clothing store. The young female assistant said: "Would you like to try it on?"

So he squeezed her butt and started fondling her breasts.

A young couple went Christmas shopping on Christmas Eve. Everywhere was so busy that they became separated, and the girl had to phone her boyfriend to find out where he was. Answering her call he said: "Darling, you remember that jewellery shop where you fell in love with that necklace we couldn't afford and I promised you that one day I would buy it for you?"

Filling up with emotion, she said: "Yes . . ."

"Well," he said, "I'm in the pub next door."

A man went into a department store and asked whether they had any emo Christmas lights.

"Emo Christmas lights? What are they?" asked the sales assistant.

"They're the latest thing," said the man. "They're great. They hang themselves."

My wife and I went shopping to the supermarket and as we were leaving her bag ripped open, showering the contents all over the floor. I would have helped, but not when it's her catheter.

A burly builder walked into a pharmacy but was dismayed to see there was a young woman serving at the counter.

"Uh . . . hello," he said, "I need some erm . . . God, this is embarrassing . . ."

"Don't you worry sir," she leaned in and whispered reassuringly, "I get this every day!"

He smiled back weakly.

"Condoms, is it?" she said.

"No."

"Suppositories?"

"No."

"Tampons?"

"No."

"Well, it can't be that embarrassing then, sir," she said with a smile.

"Paracetamol," he said.

"Paracetamol?" she repeated with a puzzled look. "Three pounds, please. What's so embarrassing?"

Then he pulled out his little pink purse.

A terrible explosion in a Pakistan city destroyed dozens of shops. The rescuers searched for hours in the hope of finding survivors. They were just about to give up when they heard a frail voice from beneath a pile of rubble murmur: "Don't go. We're still open."

A single woman went supermarket shopping. She bought a small yoghurt, a ready meal for one and a half-bottle of wine.

At the checkout, the male cashier said: "You're single, aren't you?"

"Yes," she said. "How can you tell?"

"Because you're really ugly."

Every town has the same two malls: the one white people go to and the one white people used to go to. (Chris Rock)

A woman went to a small-town hardware store and told the owner that she needed a new door handle.

He fetched one and asked: "You want a screw for that?"

She looked around the store and said: "No, but I'll blow you for that toaster over there!"

A man went into a pharmacy store and asked the senior sales assistant: "Do you have cotton wool balls?"

"What do you think I am?" he replied. "A fucking teddy bear?"

A woman had been planning a major shopping trip in town for weeks, and come the big day she was really ready to splash the cash. She began by finding the most perfect shoes in the first shop and a beautiful dress on sale in the second. In the third, everything had just been reduced by 40 per cent and she was eagerly scanning the racks of clothes when her mobile phone rang. It was a female doctor notifying her that her husband had just been involved in a terrible accident and was in a critical condition in the intensive-care unit. The woman told the doctor to inform her husband where she was and that she'd be there as soon as possible. As she hung up she realized she was leaving behind numerous tempting bargains, so she decided to visit a couple more stores before heading to the hospital. However, she got so carried away with the clothes on offer that she ended up shopping the rest of the morning, finishing her trip with a cup of coffee and a cream slice.

Then she remembered her husband. Feeling guilty, she dashed to the hospital. She saw the doctor in the corridor and asked about her husband's condition.

The lady doctor glared at her and shouted: "You went ahead and finished your shopping trip, didn't you? I hope you're proud of yourself! While you were out enjoying yourself for the past four hours in town, your poor husband has been languishing in intensive care!" The doctor paused for a moment, then continued: "Actually it's just as well you went ahead and finished, because it will be probably be the last shopping trip you ever take. For the rest of his life he will require round-the-clock care and you'll now be his carer."

The wife felt so guilty that she broke down and sobbed. The lady doctor then chuckled and said: "I'm just pulling your leg. He's dead. What did you buy?"

Smells

An old couple were driving along the highway when they spotted an injured skunk lying by the side of the road. The wife said: "We must stop and take it to a veterinarian."

So the husband stopped the car and they went over to inspect the wounded skunk. "Look," said the husband. "The poor thing is shivering. Why don't you wrap it in your skirt?"

"But what about the smell?" asked his wife.

"Listen," he said. "If it dies, it dies!"

What's the smelliest thing on earth? – An anchovy's fanny.

While God was distracted, Eve persuaded Adam to eat the forbidden fruit. He did so, and, realizing they were both naked, they proceeded to have sex all day long. When God learned what had happened, he took Adam to one side and gave him a stern lecture. At the end, he asked where Eve was.

"Oh," said Adam, "she's in the sea washing herself off."

"Damn!" sighed God. "How am I ever going to get the smell out of the fish?"

Sodomy

A man went into a brothel and asked: "How much for anal?"

"A hundred and fifty quid," said the hooker.

"That's a bit expensive," he said. "I think I'll leave it."

"Tight arse!" she yelled.

"Oh go on, then," he said. "You've talked me into it."

How often does a Smurf do anal? – Once in a blue moon.

A woman went to her doctor for advice. She told him that her husband had developed a liking for anal sex, but she wasn't sure it was such a good idea.

The doctor asked her: "Does it hurt you?"

"No," she said.

"Well, then," he continued, "there's no reason why you shouldn't practise anal sex if you don't mind it, so long as you take care not to get pregnant."

The woman was puzzled. "You mean you can get pregnant from anal sex?"

"Of course," smiled the doctor. "Where do you think bankers come from?"

What's grosser than gross? – Screwing someone up the arse and having the tapeworm give you head.

I was in bed with this woman and she said: "Hey, not in the ass." I said: "Hey, it's my thumb, it's my ass. If you don't like it, go in the other room." (Garry Shandling)

I just got this DVD *Hot and Horny Housewives Do Anal 3*. Do you think I'll understand what's going on if I haven't seen *1* and *2*?

A guy was having anal sex with his secretary over his office desk when his wife suddenly burst in.

The wife cried: "You can't do this to me!"

"I know," he said. "That's why I'm doing it to her."

A young man asked his date: "What do you think of anal sex?"

"Ugh!" the girl exclaimed. "Disgusting! I couldn't ever imagine letting anyone stick their dick up my back passage if I was sober."

He said: "The whisky's in the top-left cabinet."

A survey showed that 50 per cent of all newlyweds want to try anal sex – or to put it another way, 100 per cent of grooms.

Why is anal sex like Christmas? – A lot of people say it's better to give than to receive.

After being married for seven years, a wife became restless until one day she suddenly announced: "I'm bored with our sex life. It's always the same. Why don't we try the 'other hole'?"

"What?! No way!" exclaimed her husband. "And risk you getting pregnant?"

Speech Impediments

A young man went to see the doctor about his lisp. The doctor told the young man that the lisp was caused by the size of his member, which was so big it was pulling his tongue off-centre.

"Is there anything you can do about it?" asked the young man.

"Well," said the doctor, "there is an operation I could perform to shorten the length of your penis. That should cure your lisp."

So the young man agreed to the operation. Two months later, he returned to the doctor and complained that while his lisp had gone, his sex life had been ruined. "I want my penis back," he demanded.

"Thcrew you!" said the doctor.

An incurable stutterer was jailed for twelve months for burglary, but police don't expect him to finish his sentence.

A man said to a new work colleague: "Someone told me the kids at school used to call you four eyes. Why? You don't wear glasses?"

"I-I-I-I have a stutter."

A guy who had been a mute all his life was walking along the street when he bumped into his similarly afflicted friend.

The first mute signed: "Hello there, buddy, how's life?"

To which his friend said vocally: "Oh I see you're still doing all that hand-waving crap."

Stunned that his friend could actually speak, the first mute signed: "How did you learn to talk?"

His friend replied: "I went to this speech therapist who said that there was nothing physically wrong with me and gave me an intensive training course."

Frantically signing, the mute asked his friend to ring the therapist and book him an urgent appointment. The friend did just that.

So the next day, the mute went to the doctor, who, after a quick examination, said: "Right, I can get you talking if you agree to go on my intensive training course: go into the next room, drop your trousers and bend over." After the mute had followed these instructions, the therapist rushed in with a broom handle and a mallet, forcibly inserted the broom handle up the mute's arse and whacked it into place with the mallet.

The mute screamed: "AAAAAAAAaaaaaaa!!!"

"Very good," said the doctor. "Tomorrow we'll do the letter 'b'."

A group of men were working on a construction site, helping to build a twenty-storey tower block. When a guy working on the top floor accidentally kicked a brick over the side, he realized to his horror that it was about to land on the head of his boss, who was standing on the ground 100 feet below. So thinking quickly, the worker yelled at the top of his voice, "Falling brick", causing the boss to look up and step aside as the brick crashed harmlessly to the ground.

In gratitude, the boss shouted up to the worker: "That's a £100 bonus for you, son."

Another guy working on the nineteenth floor had observed the incident and, eager to earn himself a bonus, decided to kick a brick over the edge.

Unfortunately he had a bad stutter, and shouted down to the boss: "Ffffffffffff . . . fuck, he's dead!"

One of my friends has a stutter and a lot of people think that's a bad thing, but to me that's just like starting certain words with a drum roll. That's not an impediment, that's suspense. (Demetri Martin)

A wealthy playboy took a girl on a first date to an amusement park. After going on half a dozen rides, he said: "What do you want to do next?"

"Get weighed," she replied.

He thought it a strange request, but he took her to the weighing booth. After going on a few more rides, he again asked her: "What do you want to do next?"

"Get weighed," she replied.

"What again?"

"Get weighed," she repeated.

Convinced that the girl was seriously weird, the guy made an excuse to take her home early.

Her mother wasn't expecting her back so soon. "What is it, dear?" she said. "Didn't you have a nice time tonight?"

"Wousy," said the girl.

Sperm

Two sperm were having a race. One sperm said breathlessly: "All this swimming is tiring me out. How long till we reach the womb?"

"There's a long way to go yet," said the second sperm. "We've only just gone past her tonsils!"

I'm sick of people knocking on my door looking for donations. Just had a woman from the sperm bank – I really gave her a mouthful!

A young woman asked her doctor: "How many calories there are in sperm?"

"Why do you ask?" said the doctor.

"Because I'm trying to watch my weight."

"My dear," said the doctor, "if you're swallowing that much, no guy is going to care if you're a bit chubby!"

Apparently, Wi-Fi laptops can damage your sperm – but in my experience not as much as sperm can damage your Wi-Fi laptop.

Why did the sperm cross the road? – Because the student put on the wrong socks before he went for a walk.

Once upon a time there was a sperm called Stanley who lived inside a famous movie actor. Stanley was a very healthy sperm. He did push-ups and stretching routines every day while the other sperm just lazed around doing nothing. One day, one of the other sperm asked Stanley why he exercised regularly.

"Look, pal," Stanley explained, "only one sperm can get a woman pregnant, and when the right time comes, I want to be that sperm!"

A few days later, all the sperm could feel themselves getting hotter and hotter. They knew the big swim was imminent. Moments later, they were released and, sure enough, Stanley was swimming far ahead of all the others. Then suddenly Stanley stopped in his tracks, turned around and began to swim back as fast as he could. "Go back! Go back!" he hollered. "It's a blow job!"

Sports

Shortly after setting off on her round, a woman golfer ran into the clubhouse screaming in pain.

"What happened?" asked the club professional.

"I got stung by a bee," she replied.

"Where?"

"Between the first and second holes."

"Ah," said the professional. "Sounds like your stance was a little too wide."

A guy and a girl met in a bar that showed live sport on TV. As things started to get steamy between them, he said: "Let's go back to my place."

"Have you got cable?" she asked.

"No," he said, "but I have some old ropes that should do just fine."

Vince took his golf very seriously – so much so that it was jeopardizing his marriage to Eleanor because he was off playing golf seven days a week. In an attempt to save their crumbling marriage, she suggested that she should go to the course with him and take some lessons.

"Okay," he said reluctantly, "but remember, golf is a serious game. I don't want you ruining the one perfect thing in my life."

So they went to the course and Eleanor signed up to take lessons with the local pro. Meanwhile, Vince played his round and she never bothered him.

A few weeks later, a friend at the golf club asked Vince how his marriage was faring. "Things are much better," said Vince. "Since Eleanor's been taking lessons from the pro, she lets me play all the golf I want and she never gives me any hassle."

"Oh," said the friend glumly. "So I guess you don't know that she's been screwing around with the pro?"

Vince threw his clubs to the ground in a fit of rage. "I knew it wouldn't last! I knew she'd make a mockery of the game!"

What do you call a man with no arms and no legs playing basketball? – Magic Johnson.

A middle-aged couple were in the audience at the World Snooker Championships when, in the darkness, they spotted a pair of young lovers caressing each other passionately.

"I don't know whether to watch them or watch the game!" remarked the husband.

"Watch them," advised the wife. "You already know how to play snooker."

I've finally achieved my life's ambition: I've won as many Tour de France races as Lance Armstrong.

Explaining the Offside Rule in Soccer to Women

You're in a shoe shop, second in the queue for the till. Behind the shop assistant on the till is a pair of shoes which you have seen and which you must have.

The female shopper in front of you has seen them also and is eyeing them with desire. Both of you have forgotten your purses. It would be rude to push in front of the first woman if you had no money to pay for the shoes.

The shop assistant remains at the till waiting.

Your friend is trying on another pair of shoes at the back of the shop and sees your dilemma. She prepares to throw her purse to you. If she does so, you can catch the purse, then walk round the other shopper and buy the shoes! At a pinch she could throw the purse ahead of the other shopper and "whilst it is in flight" you could nip around the other shopper, catch the purse and buy the shoes!

But, you must always remember that until the purse has actually been thrown, it would be plain wrong for you to be in front of the other shopper and you would be OFFSIDE!

An elderly couple were competing in their golf club's annual seniors' tournament. On the final hole, the wife had to make a six-inch putt to tie with the leading score, but she missed and they lost out on their chance of victory.

In the car on their way home, the husband was still angry about the miss. "I can't believe you didn't hole that putt," he snapped. "It was no longer than my willy!"

"Yes, dear," she replied. "But it was much harder!"

I bought a racehorse today. I called him My Face. I don't care if he doesn't win – I just want to hear a load of posh girls shouting "Come on My Face."

A husband and wife were keen golfers but both were experiencing problems with their swing. The husband went to see the club professional, who told him: "Your grip is too tight. Loosen it so that you hold the club as you would hold your wife's breasts."

The husband followed the advice and, watched by the professional, went out to the first tee and hit the ball 280 yards straight down the middle.

So the next day his wife went in to see the professional. "You have the same problem as your husband," said the professional. "Your grip is too tight. Loosen it so that you hold the club as you would hold your husband's penis."

She followed the advice and, watched by the professional, went out to the first tee but only hit the ball a few yards along the ground.

"Okay," said the professional. "Let's try it again, but this time hold the club in your hands rather than in your mouth."

What's the hardest part of rollerblading? – Telling your parents you're gay.

Usually if someone gets caught doing drugs, it means whoever won silver wins gold. But because so many cyclists were cheating, I got a call this week to say the bike I hired when I was on holiday in Paris several years ago means I actually won the 2003 Tour de France. (Jon Richardson)

A golfer met a woman on the first tee and agreed to join her for the round. To his surprise and disappointment, she turned out to be a good player and beat him. Although he was angry at losing, he liked the woman and bought her a drink in the bar afterwards. He then offered to drive her home. She was so grateful for the lift that on the way she told him to stop the car and proceeded to give him the best blow job he'd ever had.

The next day he bumped into her again on the first tee. Once more she annoyed him by beating him at golf but again she gave him a fantastic blow job on the journey home. This continued for a week, and by the Friday he was experiencing mixed emotions. He was heartily sick of being beaten by a woman day after day but he did enjoy the blow jobs on the way home. So he arranged to take their relationship a step further and booked them into a hotel for a weekend of passion. But when he told her of his plans, she burst into tears.

"I can't," she sobbed. "I'm a transvestite."

He was livid. "You dirty lousy cheat!" he stormed. "You've been playing off the ladies' tee all week!"

The Horse Race

The Line-up:

In lane 1: Passionate Lady.
In lane 2: Bare Belly.
In lane 3: Silk Panties.
In lane 4: Conscience.
In lane 5: Jockey Shorts.
In lane 6: Clean Sheets.
In lane 7: Thighs.
In lane 8: Big Dick.
In lane 9: Heavy Bosom.
In lane 10: Merry Cherry.

AAAND THEY're OFF:

Conscience is left behind at the gate . . . Jockey Shorts and Silk Panties are off in a hurry. Heavy Bosom is being pressured and Passionate Lady is caught between Thighs, and Big Dick is in a dangerous spot . . .

AT THE HALFWAY MARK:

It's Bare Belly on top. Thighs open and Big Dick is pressed in. Heavy Bosom is being pushed hard against Clean Sheets. Passionate Lady and Thighs are working hard on Bare Belly. Bare Belly is under terrific pressure from Big Dick . . .

AT THE STRETCH:

It's Merry Cherry cracks under the strain . . . Big Dick is making a final drive . . . Big Dick moves inside and Passionate Lady is coming . . .

AT THE FINISH:

It's Big Dick giving everything he's got . . . Passionate Lady takes everything Big Dick has to offer. It looks like a dead heat but . . . Big Dick comes through with one final thrust, and wins by a head . . . Bare Belly shows and Thighs weaken . . . Heavy Bosom pulls up . . . and Clean Sheets never had a chance!

Tottenham Hotspur footballer Jermain Defoe went up to a girl in a nightclub, nuzzled her breasts and asked her if she fancied a shag. "Blimey!" she said. "You're a little forward, aren't you?"

For me, golf is a lot like a woman: if she isn't holding my wood, she should be holding an iron.

Snooker player Steve Davis pulled a groupie at a tournament and after several drinks they ended up in his hotel room. Keen to get on with shagging her idol, she stripped off and got down on all fours, presenting her arse in the air.

Never one to rush, Steve dropped his pants and started staring at the girl's body, all the while moving his head slowly from side to side, considering what to do next.

Growing impatient, the girl yelled: "Well, are you going to fuck me?!"

"Yes," replied Steve cautiously, "but I'm not sure if I should go for the easy pink or the tight brown."

At Scottish football games you're not allowed to bring food to the ground and they actually search you, when you're going in, to make sure you've not got food on you. It's nice to see we've got our fucking priorities right, isn't it? "What's this sir? A knife. I hope you weren't planning on making sandwiches." (Frankie Boyle)

After a wayward shot landed among a group of players, two golfers came to blows. One started lashing out with a six-iron, repeatedly hitting his adversary over the back with the club. Soon the police arrived to break up the fight.

"Right," said the police officer to the aggressor. "I want all the details. How many times did you hit him with that golf club?"

"Eight," he replied. "But put me down for five."

Chess: the only place where bishops will stand idly behind the little ones.

Usain Bolt went to a golf clubhouse in Georgia and asked to become a member. The secretary said: "Sorry, sir, we can't accept you here, but there's a multiracial clubhouse ten minutes down the road."
"But I'm Usain Bolt!"
"Okay, five minutes down the road."

A young man was out on a first date when he bumped into a couple of lads from his soccer team.
"Hi, skipper," they said as they walked past.
"Mm, I love a man with power," purred the young man's date, "especially the captain of a team."
"Oh, I'm not the captain," explained the young man. "I've just got a really gay run."

Steve and Rick were playing golf together, but as they stood on the first tee, Rick looked distracted.
"What's the problem?" asked Steve.
"It's that creepy new golf pro," said Rick. "I can't bear the man. He's just been trying to correct my stance."
"He's only trying to help your game."
"Yeah, but I was using the urinal at the time."

Why don't teenage boys make good goalkeepers? – They can never keep a clean sheet.

A golfer was accompanied on his round by his small white poodle. Every time the golfer hit a good drive or sank a long putt, the dog would stand on its hind legs and applaud with its two front paws.
His opponent was amazed by the animal's antics. "But what happens," he asked, "if you land in a bunker or miss a short putt?"
"The dog turns somersaults."
"How many?"
"It depends on how hard I kick him up the butt!"

I played a game of blow-football with my nephew yesterday. Sadly, he had an asthma attack halfway through. Still . . . 10–0!

Vic received a call from the coroner, who wanted to talk about his wife's recent death. Vic told him the sad story: "We were on the sixth hole, and Jackie, my wife, was standing on the ladies' tee about thirty yards ahead of the men's tee when I hit my drive. From the sound when the ball hit her head and the way she dropped like a stone, I knew instantly that she was dead. God knows where the ball ended up!"

"I see," said the coroner. "Well that explains the injury to her head but what about the ball that was wedged up her rectum?"

"Oh," explained Vic. "That was my provisional."

What is better than winning a silver medal at the Paralympics? – Not being disabled.

A man was in the pub having a quiet drink by himself when the door opened and in walked the most stunning woman he had ever laid eyes on. She was five foot nine inches tall, with stunning blue eyes, silky blonde hair, an hourglass figure barely covered by a tiny mini-skirt and a flimsy cotton top. He could see she was not wearing a bra, and her incredibly firm breasts were on show. After watching her walk in, he turned back to his beer but no sooner had he taken a sip than he noticed her pulling up another bar stool close to him and sitting down.

"Hi," she said.

"Hi," he replied, unable to believe that such a gorgeous girl would want to chat to him.

Then without further ado, she took his hand and placed it on her perfect inner thigh, rubbing it up and down. "So, does that make you feel good?" she purred. "I'll bet it does. In fact, I'll bet you've never felt this good before."

"Actually, I have," he said, correcting her. "You see, when I was eighteen, I was picked to play for the school First XV rugby team in the Public School Finals in front of a crowd of about 3,000 and I felt really good." He immediately felt rather pathetic saying that and thought she would get up and go but instead she took his hand off her thigh and put it up the front of her top. Her nipple pushed into his palm as she massaged his hand into her pert, perfect breast.

"How do you feel now?" she whispered seductively.

"Okay," he replied nervously.

Again she said: "I'll bet you do. In fact, I'll bet you've never felt this good before!"

Unbelievably, he heard himself saying: "Well, actually I have. In that game, we were down by six points with about twenty seconds left in the match. The opposition kicked the ball deep into our half of the field, where I caught it. I ran upfield, sidestepping the first few defenders, palmed off a couple of would-be tacklers, burst through four of their forwards, lofted the ball over their full-back, re-gathered and scored a try right under the posts. We were still behind by one point, but I had a simple kick at goal with which to win the match and . . ."

"Oh," she growled, clearly irritated, and pulled his hand from under her top and thrust it down the front of her skirt. His fingers immediately met what felt like a wisp of soft cotton, and she was soaking wet.

"Well, tell me this, smart ass!" she snapped. "Have you ever felt such a cunt?"

"I certainly have," he replied. "I missed the kick!"

A minister went to his local golf course in the hope of finding someone to play with. Luckily, there was a member in the professional's shop looking for a game, so they were introduced and went to the first tee.

The member asked: "What's your handicap?"

"I'm an eighteen," said the minister.

"Me, too," said the member. "Would you like to bet a pound a hole?"

The minister agreed, and when they had finished their round, they retired to the clubhouse, where the minister solemnly handed over £18. As he parted with his cash, the minister said: "I'd like you to come along to the church some time."

The member replied: "Okay. I'd like that."

Then the minister added: "And bring your mother and father. I'd like to marry them."

Strippers

Malcolm liked to work hard and play hard. When he wasn't at the office running his own company, he was usually out bowling or playing tennis. One weekend his wife decided he needed a break, so as a treat she took him to a strip club. He protested that it wasn't really his scene, but she said the change would do him good and help him unwind.

When they arrived, the club doorman greeted them. "Hi, Malcolm," he said. "How're you doing tonight?"

The wife looked surprised.

"He's just one of the guys I bowl with," explained Malcolm.

Once inside the club, they sat down and a waitress came over. "Nice to see you, Malcolm," she smiled. "Your usual bourbon on the rocks?"

The wife's eyes widened. "You must come here a lot!"

"No, no," protested Malcolm. "She's a member of the tennis club."

Moments later, a stripper came over to the table, threw her arms around Malcolm and purred: "Would you like your favourite pole dance, Malcolm?"

At this, the wife stormed out. Malcolm hurried after her and spotted her climbing into a taxi. He jumped into the back seat next to her and she began ranting and raving at him.

Fifty yards down the road, the cab driver glanced in the rear-view mirror and said: "Looks like you picked up a bitch tonight, Malcolm!"

Did you hear about the Muslim strip club? – It features full facial nudity.

Why did the man keep throwing Monopoly money at the stripper? – Because she kept putting fake tits in his face.

What do you call a 350-pound stripper? – Broke.

A fifteen-year-old boy somehow gained entry to a strip club. When his mother found out, she was understandably angry but also concerned at the possible long-term psychological effects. So she asked him gently: "Tell me honestly, Jamie, did you see anything there that you were not supposed to see?"

"Yes," replied the boy, shamefaced. "I saw Dad."

What's the difference between a stripper's boyfriend and aspirin? – Aspirin works.

What's the difference between a cocktail waitress and a stripper? – About a week.

Why do strippers always want boob jobs? – Because it's the only job they're qualified for.

Two Englishmen and a Scotsman went to a Soho strip club. They sat down at a table at the front, and soon a sexy blonde girl came over and started dancing on their table. Within a few minutes, she had taken off everything apart from her bra and panties. Then she took off her bra, and one of the Englishmen licked a

£50 note and slapped it to her left butt cheek.

The second Englishman responded by licking a £50 note and slapping it to her right butt cheek.

Finally, she removed her panties, whereupon the Scotsman whipped out his credit card, swiped the crack in her butt and disappeared with the £100.

Suicide

I called the Suicide Hotline but got put through to a call centre in Pakistan. When I told them I was suicidal, they got very excited and asked if I could drive a truck.

A depressed young woman was contemplating suicide. She went down to the New York docks with the intention of throwing herself into the water, but while she was standing at the quayside, a sailor came over and befriended her. He talked her out of killing herself and persuaded her to come to Europe, stowing away on his ship. "I know I can make you happy," he told her.

She agreed, and that night the sailor hid her in a lifeboat on his ship. Every night after that he brought her food and drink, and had sex with her till dawn. Finally, after three weeks, she was discovered by the ship's captain.

"What are you doing on board this vessel?" he demanded.

"You don't understand," she replied. "I have an arrangement with one of the sailors. He's taking me to Europe and he's screwing me."

"He sure is, lady," said the captain. "This is the Staten Island Ferry!"

A farmer's young son came down to join the family for breakfast but as he sat down at the table, his mother told him that he'd get nothing until he had been to the barn and fed the animals. The boy stormed off to the barn in a temper. He threw the chickens their corn, but as they fed, he petulantly kicked one in the leg. Next, he fed the cows and as they bent down, he angrily kicked one on the rump. Finally, he fed the pigs and as they put their snouts in the trough, he deliberately kicked one in the side. Then he marched back into the kitchen.

His mother was waiting for him. "I saw what you did!" she yelled. "You kicked a chicken, so you'll get no eggs for breakfast. You kicked a cow, so you'll get no milk. And you kicked a pig, so you'll get no bacon or sausage."

Just then the boy's father came downstairs and tripped over the family cat. Instinctively, he kicked the cat off the stairs. The boy looked at his mother and said: "Are you going to tell him or shall I?"

Did you hear about the author who committed suicide because he was suffering from writer's block? At least that's what they think – he didn't leave a note.

An Irish cop in New York was called to a disturbance in the street. A crowd had gathered to watch a young man who was threatening to jump from the roof of a ten-storey building.

The cop yelled up to the man: "Don't jump! Think of your father!"

"I haven't got a father," the man shouted back. "I'm going to jump!"

"No, don't jump!" pleaded the cop. "Think of your mother!"

"I haven't got a mother either," said the man. "I'm going to jump!"

"No, don't jump!" yelled the cop. "Think of your children!"

"I don't have any children. I'm going to jump!"

"No, please don't jump! Think of the Blessed Virgin!"

"Who?"

The cop shouted: "Jump, Protestant! You're blocking the traffic!"

A husband and wife were passengers on a plane travelling to Switzerland. Half-way through the flight, a man jumped from his seat and pulled out a gun. "This is a hijack!" he screamed. "If anyone makes a move, I'll kill them!"

The wife held her husband's hand for comfort. She looked into his eyes, smiled and then pushed him into the aisle. The hijacker immediately shot him in the head, before being wrestled to the ground by a couple of passengers.

Everyone on the plane looked at the wife in disbelief at what she had just done. She said: "Before you ask, we were on our way to the Dignitas clinic for an assisted suicide, so I did us all a favour."

After a few moments' silence, an air hostess said: "Well . . . I suppose his suffering is over now. Was he in a lot of pain?"

"Oh, no, he was fine," replied the wife. "I'm the one who's dying. I just wanted one last laugh before I go!"

A man, a woman and their three sons lived on a farm in the country. Early one morning, the farmer's wife awoke and, looking out of the window, saw that the family's only cow was lying dead in the field. Fearing that with the cow dead she would no longer be able to feed her family, the poor woman went to the barn and hanged herself.

A few minutes later, the farmer awoke. Finding both the cow and his wife dead, he saw no reason to continue living and shot himself dead.

Then the eldest son woke to find both of his parents and the cow dead. In the depths of despair, he ran to the river and decided to drown himself. When he reached the river, he found a small mermaid sitting on the bank. She said: "I've seen what has happened and know why you are so sad, but if you will have sex with me five times in a row, I will bring your parents and the cow back to life."

The son agreed to try, but after four times, he was simply unable to satisfy her again. So the mermaid drowned him in the river.

Next, the middle son woke up, and after discovering what had happened, he, too, elected to throw himself into the river. The mermaid said to him: "I have seen the tragedy that has befallen you, but if you will have sex with me ten times in a row, I will restore your family and your cow to you."

The son tried his best, but could not get beyond eight. So the mermaid drowned him in the river.

Finally, the youngest son woke up. He saw the cow dead, his parents dead and his brothers gone. Deciding that he no longer wished to live, he ran down to the river with the intention of drowning himself. When he got there, the mermaid said: "I have seen all that has happened, but if you have sex with me fifteen times in a row, I will make everything okay again."

The youngest son replied: "Is that all? Why not twenty times in a row?"

The mermaid was taken aback by the suggestion.

Then the youngest son said: "Hell, why not twenty-five times in a row, or even thirty?"

"Very well," said the mermaid, scarcely able to believe her good fortune. "If you have sex with me thirty times in a row, I will bring everybody back to perfect health."

The youngest son was just about to drop his pants when he said: "Wait! How do I know that thirty times in a row won't kill you like it did the cow?"

Did you hear about the guy who phoned the Samaritans and said that he was about to throw himself under a train? – They told him to stay on the line.

Two friends got chatting in the street. One said: "I've had a terrible time of it lately, Ellen. My sister committed suicide last month because she had run up terrible debts on her credit card."

"Oh, I'm sorry to hear that, Hannah," said the other. "A friend of mine was very depressed, too. He owed £1,000 to a loan shark, and his family were going to be thrown out onto the street the following day. He was so distraught he drove to the edge of a cliff and parked there, his head resting on the steering wheel."

"Oh, my God! What happened?"

"Luckily all the people there had a whip-round and they got him his £1,000."

"Oh, how kind!"

"Yes, it was a good job his bus was full that day.'

A middle-aged woman had been depressed for some time. One evening she turned to her insensitive boyfriend and said: "I feel like throwing myself under a bus and you're not helping."

So he gave her a timetable.

Surgery

Recovering after an operation, a patient told the surgeon: "I'm worried sick. I can't feel my legs."

"There's a perfectly simple explanation for that," said the surgeon.

"Oh, thank goodness!" sighed the patient, relieved.

"Yes," continued the surgeon. "You see the reason you can't feel your legs is because we've had to amputate both your arms."

Did you hear about the woman who had to have a canister of perfume removed from her rectum? – It was Chanel No. 2.

A man went to see a hospital consultant and said: "Doc, I don't know what's wrong with me but my testicles have turned blue!"

The consultant examined him and told him that unless he had his testicles removed, he would die.

"You can't do that to me!" cried the patient. "My life won't be worth living!"

"I'm sorry," said the consultant, "and there's no easy way to put this, but if you don't have your testicles removed within the next seventy-two hours, you'll be dead anyway."

Left with no choice, the man glumly agreed to have his balls removed.

Two weeks later, the patient returned for a post-op check and announced: "Doc, now my penis has turned blue!"

The consultant examined him and came to the conclusion that unless the penis was removed within the next seventy-two hours, the man would die.

"But, Doc," protested the man tearfully, "how will I pee?"

"Simple," said the consultant. "We'll install a plastic pipe and that will do the job."

"I don't think I can go through with this," said the man. "The thought of losing my penis is unbearable."

"Do you want to die?" demanded the consultant brusquely.

Reluctantly, the man consented to the procedure for having his penis removed.

Two weeks later, he returned for another check-up. "Doc, the pipe has turned blue! What the hell is happening to me?"

The consultant scratched his head in bewilderment. "I'm not really sure," he said. "Wait . . . do you wear jeans?"

A surgeon informed his patient: "I've got some good news and some bad news."

"What's the bad news?" asked the patient.

"We've had to amputate both your legs."

"Oh my God! What's the good news?"

"The guy in the next bed wants to buy your slippers."

A man consulted his doctor about a penile extension. The doctor suggested stitching on a baby elephant's trunk at a cost of £15,000. The man liked the sound of it and readily agreed to the procedure, but the doctor warned him that he would have to wait at least two months after the operation before having sex.

Nine weeks after undergoing the surgery, the man was having dinner with a new woman when he felt an unusual stirring in his pants and thought: "This is the night." As they chatted over dinner, his dick suddenly flew out and stole an apple off the table before retracting.

"Wow!" said the woman. "Can you do that again?"

He sighed: "My dick can, but I don't think my asshole can take another apple!"

What is the name of the painful procedure where a man has his spine and testicles removed? – Marriage.

While attending an out-of-town medical convention, a male medic started chatting to an attractive woman. He asked her to dinner, and noticed that before and after the meal she made a point of washing her hands. After emptying two bottles of wine, she invited him back to her hotel room. She slipped into the bathroom to wash her hands and then they had sex, after which she washed her hands again.

When she returned, he said: "I bet you're a surgeon."

"That's right," she said. "How did you know?"

"Because you're always washing your hands."

"And I bet you're an anaesthetist," she said.

"Yes, I am. How did you guess?"

"Because I didn't feel a thing."

Two men had a vicious knife fight, which left one in hospital, bandaged from head to toe. He couldn't even move his lips. He mumbled to the surgeon: "When will I be able to laugh again?"

"Are you crazy?" said the surgeon. "You almost died!"

"No kidding, Doc. When will I be able to laugh again?"

"I don't believe this!" said the surgeon. "You're sewn together with ten feet of thread. Why on earth do you want to know when you can laugh again?"

"Because the other guy in the fight is getting married next week and I've got his dick in my coat pocket!"

A man woke up in hospital following a major operation. "I have good news and bad news," said the doctor.

"What's the good news?" asked the man.

"We've managed to save your testicles," replied the doctor.

"Thank God! And what's the bad news?"

"They're in a bag under your pillow."

Swearing

Two brothers – one aged seven, the other aged five – were hatching a plan in their bedroom. "You know what?" said the seven-year-old. "I think it's about time we started cursing."

The five-year-old nodded his head in agreement.

The older boy went on: "When we go downstairs for breakfast, I'm going to say something with 'hell' and you say something with 'ass'. We'll see what reaction we get."

The five-year-old thought it was a great idea.

When their mother walked into the kitchen and asked the seven-year-old what he wanted for breakfast, he replied: "Aw, hell, Mom, I guess I'll have some Cheerios."

His mother gave him a resounding whack on his butt, sending him toppling from his chair. He then ran upstairs to his room in floods of tears.

Still fuming, the mother turned to the five-year-old and asked him sternly what he wanted for breakfast. "I don't know," he replied in a trembling voice, "but you can bet your fat ass it won't be Cheerios!"

A young novice nun was assigned her first job at the convent – to sweep the steps and keep the entrance clean. But she was struggling to cope with the pigeons that were crapping all over the steps as soon as she had cleaned them. Impatient, she started waving her arms at the birds and yelling: "Fuck off! Fuck off!"

Overhearing her bad language, the priest decided to have a discreet word with the Mother Superior, who promised to relay his concerns to the novice nun.

"Your language is unseemly and entirely unnecessary," the Mother Superior told her later that day. "All you have to do is say 'shoo, shoo' and swipe the pigeons with the broom and you will find they will soon fuck off by themselves."

A preacher was making his rounds to his parishioners on a bicycle when he came across a little boy trying to sell a lawnmower.

"How much do you want for the mower?" asked the preacher.

"I just want enough money to go out and buy a bike," said the little boy.

After a moment of consideration, the preacher said: "Will you take my bike in trade for it?"

The little boy asked if he could try it out first, and after riding the bike around a little while said: "Mister, you've got yourself a deal."

The preacher took the mower and began to try to crank it. He pulled on the string a few times but got no response from the mower, so he called the little boy over and said: "I can't get this mower to start."

The little boy said: "That's because you have to cuss and swear at it to get it started."

The preacher said: "I am a church minister, and I cannot cuss and swear. Indeed, I do not even remember how to cuss and swear."

The little boy said with a smile: "Just keep pullin' on that string. It'll come back to ya!"

In New York City, "fuck" isn't even a word, it's a comma. (Lewis Black)

Two car salesmen were sitting at the bar. One complained to the other: "Boy, business sucks. If I don't sell more cars this month I'm gonna lose my fucking ass!"

Just then, and too late, he noticed a beautiful blonde sitting two stools away. Immediately, he apologized for the crude language.

"That's okay," replied the blonde. "If I don't sell more ass this month, I'm gonna lose my fucking car!"

Little Johnny had a swearing problem and his father was getting sick and tired of it, so he decided to consult a psychiatrist. The shrink advised: "Since Christmas is coming up, you should ask Johnny what he wants Santa to bring him, and if Johnny swears you should leave a pile of dog shit in place of the gift."

So two days before Christmas, the father asked Johnny what he wanted. Johnny said: "I want a fucking teddy-bear sitting right fucking here beside me when I fucking wake up Christmas morning. Then when I go downstairs I want to see a fucking train going around the fucking tree, and when I go outside I want to see a fucking bike leaning up against the fucking garage."

On Christmas morning, Little Johnny woke up and rolled over into a big pile of dog shit. Confused, he walked downstairs and saw a bunch of dog shit around the Christmas tree. Scratching his head, he walked outside and saw a huge pile of dog shit by the garage. When he walked back inside with a puzzled look on his face, his dad smiled and asked: "So Johnny, what did Santa bring you this year?"

Johnny replied: "I think I got a fucking dog but I can't find the bastard!"

Tampons

A man walked into a café and asked the waitress: "What's the difference between a teabag and a tampon?"

"I don't know," said the waitress.

"In that case I'll have a coffee please, love."

Why do tampons have strings? – So you can floss after every meal.

A vampire walked into a bar and ordered a pint of blood. The bartender poured him the blood.

A few minutes later, a second vampire walked into the bar and also asked for a pint of blood. Again the bartender served the drink.

Shortly afterwards, a third vampire walked into the bar and ordered a mug of hot water.

The bartender looked puzzled. "Why do you want a mug of hot water?" he asked.

The vampire said: "I found a used tampon and I'm making tea."

What's the difference between tampons and cowboy hats? — Cowboy hats are for assholes.

Women can be volatile whilst on their periods. Have you noticed they've even got fuses on their tampons?

Tattoos

A woman was frustrated with her sex life because her husband had a massive crush on Brigitte Bardot. He was so obsessed with the French actress that his wife resorted to drastic measures in an attempt to put the spark back into their marriage. She went to a tattooist and asked for a large letter B to be tattooed on each breast. However, the tattooist pointed out that, as her breasts sagged with age, the tattoo might eventually lose its impact and so he recommended that she have a B tattooed on each buttock instead.

The woman agreed to this and had a letter B tattooed on each buttock. As soon as her husband arrived home that evening, she took off her panties, bent over and showed off the artwork.

He took one look and said: "Who the hell is Bob?"

A woman walked into a tattoo parlour and asked for a tattoo of a turkey on her left inner thigh. Beneath it she said she wanted the words "Happy Thanksgiving". And for her right inner thigh she said she wanted a tattoo of Santa Claus accompanied by the words "Merry Christmas".

"That's a most unusual request," said the tattoo artist. "Why do you want it?"

"Because," said the woman, "I'm sick to death of my husband complaining that there's nothing to eat between Thanksgiving and Christmas."

Two elderly women were in a beauty parlour getting their hair done when in walked a twenty-year-old girl wearing a low-cut top that revealed a tattoo of a rose on one breast.

One woman leaned over to the other and whispered: "Poor thing. She doesn't know it, but in fifty years she'll have a long-stemmed rose in a hanging basket!"

My girlfriend has a tattoo of a sea shell on her inner thigh. If you put your ear to it, I swear you can smell the sea.

A female punk rocker was brought in to a hospital emergency department to undergo surgery for acute appendicitis. The young woman had a green Mohican hairstyle and when she was undressed on the operating table, the theatre staff discovered that she had also dyed her pubic hair green. And above it was a tattoo reading: "Keep off the grass."

After the operation was completed, the surgeon added a small note to the dressing which read: "Sorry, had to mow the lawn."

A gay guy went to a tattoo artist and said: "I want a tattoo of a Rolls-Royce on my cock."

The tattoo artist said: "You'd be better off with a Land Rover – it won't get stuck in the shit."

A woman went into a tattoo parlour and asked the artist to tattoo a picture of Johnny Depp on her right upper thigh and Colin Farrell on her left upper thigh. The artist did so, and when he had finished he handed her a mirror so she could inspect the work.

She looked at the right thigh and said: "Wow! That's definitely Johnny Depp. Just look at those eyes." Then she examined her left thigh but complained: "That doesn't look like Colin Farrell."

The artist disagreed and suggested they settle the argument by seeking the opinion of an impartial observer. So they went to the bar next door and asked an elderly guy to identify the tattoos.

The woman raised her skirt and dropped her panties, and the old man put his face up close. "Well, ma'am," he concluded, "the one on your right thigh is definitely Johnny Depp. You can tell by the eyes and the cheekbones. The one on your left I'm not sure about – but the one in the middle is definitely Willie Nelson."

Texas

A burly Texan went to a New York clothes store to buy a new outfit for city-wear. He walked into the men's department, where a sweet young girl was serving.

"Excuse me, miss," he said. "I'm up from Texas and I want a whole new outfit, right from the tip of my hat to the soles of my shoes."

"Certainly, sir," replied the girl. "We'll start at the top. What size hat are you?"

"Eight and five-eighths," he replied.

The girl gasped: "That's really big!"

"Yeah!" he said. "We grow them big in Texas."

The girl made a note of the measurements, then asked: "And what size shirt do you wear?"

"Extra extra large," replied the Texan, "with a twenty-one-and-a-half-inch collar."

"Wow!" the girl exclaimed. "That's big!"

"Like I say, miss, we grow them big in Texas."

"How about your trousers?" asked the girl.

"A fifty-two-inch waist, forty-inch outside leg. We grow them big in Texas."

"And finally your shoes?" said the girl.

"Size seventeen," he answered. "Wide fitting. You see, we sure grow them big in Texas."

The girl began to redden. "I hope you don't mind me being personal," she said hesitantly, "but I really have to ask, how big is your . . .?"

The Texan anticipated her question. "I know what you're going to say," he replied, "and the answer is four inches."

"Four inches?!" she cried, shocked. "My boyfriend's is bigger than that!"

"That's from the ground, miss," smiled the Texan.

A Texan visitor to England asked a local man to show him the biggest building in town.

"There it is," said the Englishman. "It's quite impressive, isn't it?"

"You call that big?" scoffed the Texan. "Back in Texas we have buildings just like that but over a hundred times bigger!"

"I'm not surprised," said the Englishman. "That's the county lunatic asylum!"

A cowboy from Texas visited a brothel in Kansas City. He chose a girl, who took him upstairs to her room. As he started to undress, she remarked on how tall he was.

"I'm from Texas, ma'am," he said with a smile. "Everything from Texas is big – and I mean everything."

When he then took off his underpants, she said: "I see what you mean."

They had sex, and afterwards as he was getting dressed she said: "Was that okay?"

"Sure," he replied, without too much enthusiasm. "By the way, ma'am, what part of Texas are you from?"

Three guys – a New Yorker, a Texan and a Californian – were walking along a deserted beach when the first two came across a naked man out like a light on the sands. He was lying there with a huge erection.

The Texan, being a gentleman, took off his hat and placed it over the erect dick.

A minute or so later, the Californian appeared on the scene, walked over to the man, picked up the Texan's hat and exclaimed: "My God – what a big prick!"

To which the New Yorker replied: "Well, what else would you expect to find under a Texan's hat?"

Storming into his lawyer's office, a Texan oil millionaire demanded that divorce proceedings begin at once against his young bride.

"What's the problem?" asked the lawyer.

"I want to hit that cheatin' bitch for breach of contract," raged the oil man.

"I don't know if that will fly," said the lawyer. "I mean, your wife isn't a piece of property. You don't own her. She's not like one of your oil wells."

"I know that, but I sure as hell expect exclusive drillin' rights!"

A woman was driving along a highway in New Mexico when her car broke down. While she was looking under the hood to see what the problem was, a man surprised her by clamping his hand over her mouth, hiking up her skirt and screwing her from behind. The man then fled the scene.

When a state trooper arrived to take her statement, she told him: "I was bent over the engine when this goddamned Texan crept up behind me and started fucking me. I didn't see his face."

"If you didn't see his face, how do you know your attacker was a Texan?" asked the state trooper.

"I might not have seen him," she said, "but I could tell that he had a belt buckle that was eight inches wide and a dick that was three inches long!"

Texting

One evening a guy texted his wife: "Hi, babe, I'm at the pub with some mates. Please wash all my dirty clothes and have dinner ready for me when I get home."

A couple of minutes later, he sent her another text: "Hi, babe, I forgot to tell you that I got a pay rise, so I'm buying you a new car."

She texted back: "OMG! Really?"

"No," he replied. "I just wanted to make sure you got my first message."

Girls: if you get a message from your boyfriend saying that he wants to "kick your puppy", don't call the RSPCA. It's simply that he's not very good at predictive text.

Sitting in the pub, a young Irishman told the barman he'd just received a text from his girlfriend.

"What does it say?" asked the barman.

Reading from the phone, the young man said: "Hello birthday boy. When you get home from work, there'll be a hot bath waiting for you. When you've finished, come into the bedroom and I'll suck you dry."

"What an offer!" grinned the barman.

"I know," said the Irishman nonchalantly. "It's very kind of her, but it'll take ages. So I think I'll just use a towel."

My girlfriend said she had predictive text. So I sent her a message saying, "I'm shagging your sister." She didn't predict that.

A guy texted his boss: "What's the difference between this morning and your daughter?"

"I don't know," the boss answered.

The guy texted back: "I'm not coming in this morning."

A wife texted her husband on a cold morning: "Windows frozen."

He texted back: "Pour lukewarm water over it."

And she texted back: "Computer fucked now!"

Text: On train home. Just pulling out of Paddington. That'll make him drop his marmalade sandwich.

Therapy

A woman went to see a therapist because she was concerned about her appearance.

"Doctor," she said, "I'm so depressed because I feel so ugly. I can't get a man because I have absolutely no self-esteem. I have become convinced that nobody in the world finds me attractive. Is there anything you can do to make me feel better about myself?"

"I'm sure I can," said the therapist. "Just go and lie face down on the couch."

A man went to a therapist to say that he had a phobia about answering the phone. The therapist listened patiently to the man's fears, gave him some advice and asked him to come back in two weeks. A fortnight later the man returned as arranged.

"So how are your problems with the phone?" asked the therapist.

"I think you've cured me," said the man. "Now I answer it whether it rings or not."

A woman came home and told her husband: "Remember those headaches I've been suffering from all these years? Well, they're finally gone."

"That's great," said her husband. "How did you manage to get rid of them?"

She replied: "My friend Maria suggested I try visiting a therapist. I didn't want to tell you about it because I thought you'd laugh. But he gave me really good advice. He told me to stand in front of a mirror, stare at myself and repeat: 'I do not have a headache, I do not have a headache, I do not have a headache.' And it worked. The headaches are all gone."

"Hey, that's amazing!" said the husband. "I'm really pleased for you."

The wife continued: "I don't want to be unkind, but you haven't exactly been a tiger in the bedroom these last few years. Why don't you go to the therapist and see if he can do anything about your sex drive?"

Reluctantly, the husband agreed to try it.

After his first appointment with the therapist, the husband arrived home, tore off his clothes, picked up his wife, carried her into the bedroom, put her on the bed and ripped off her clothes, saying: "Don't move. I'll be right back."

He then went into the bathroom and when he re-emerged a few minutes later, he jumped into bed and made wild, passionate love to her, the like of which she had never experienced in their previous twenty-eight years of marriage.

Afterwards she flopped back on the bed and said: "That was fantastic!"

The husband then said: "Don't move. I'll be right back."

And again he went into the bathroom for a couple of minutes before returning to have mind-blowing sex with her that was even better than the first time.

By now her head was spinning. Whatever the therapist had said to her husband had obviously done the trick. So much so that for a third time he told her: "Don't move. I'll be right back."

This time when he dived into the bathroom, she quietly followed him. She saw him standing there in front of the mirror, repeating: "She is not my wife, she is not my wife, she is not my wife . . ."

I'm in therapy at the moment. I don't need it, obviously, but I got all these psychiatrist gift vouchers for Christmas which my family clubbed together for. What I wanted was a crossbow. (Sean Lock)

Little Johnny's next-door neighbour went to see a psychiatrist. "The other day," the woman said, "I happened to see my daughter and the little boy next door both naked, examining each other's bodies."

"Well, that's not unusual," smiled the psychiatrist. "I wouldn't worry about something as normal as that."

"But I *am* worried," insisted the woman. "I don't think it's normal at all, and neither does my daughter's husband."

A man went to a psychiatrist to seek help for his terrible addiction to cigars. The psychiatrist recommended an unusual and quite drastic form of aversion therapy. "When you go to bed tonight," he suggested, "take one of your cigars, unwrap it and stick it completely up your arsehole. Then remove it, rewrap it and place it back with all the others in such a manner that you can't tell which one it is. That way you won't dare smoke any of them, not knowing which is the treated cigar."

"Thanks, Doc, I'll try it," said the man.

And he did. But three weeks later he came back and saw the psychiatrist again.

"What?" asked the psychiatrist in disbelief. "My recommendation didn't work? It is supposed to be effective even in the most addictive of cases."

"To be fair, it kind of worked, Doc. At least I was able to transfer my addiction."

"How do you mean?"

"Well, I don't smoke cigars anymore, but now I can't go to sleep at night unless I have a cigar shoved up my arse."

Toilets

A guy lived in a remote country house with no indoor toilet, just an outhouse. The older he got, the further away the outhouse seemed to get, so that eventually he grew lazy and started peeing off the front porch. His wife was horrified and told him: "You do realize that the neighbours can you see when you're peeing off the porch?!"

He promised not to do it again but a few nights later, on a cold night, he could not face the trip to the outhouse and so he went off the porch. When he returned to bed, his wife was suspicious.

"You weren't gone long," she observed.

"No," he replied, looking guilty.

"You went off the porch again, didn't you?" she barked.

"Yes, I did."

"We talked about this, remember? How the neighbours can see you?"

"Don't worry, they won't have seen me this time. I was squatting down."

A man went into a public toilet and saw a sign which read: "Please leave this toilet in the condition that you would like to find it in."

So he left a porn magazine and a line of coke.

My wife says it's disgusting to pee in the bath. I suppose I should wait until she gets out.

A man walked into a public toilet. His arms were held awkwardly out to his sides, forearms hanging limply, fingers spread apart and his hands were shaking. He approached another man and asked: "Excuse me, but could you please unzip my fly?"

The second man was embarrassed, but felt sorry for the stranger, who appeared to be crippled. He thought how humiliating it must be to have to ask for help for something like this, so he complied, unzipping the first man's trousers.

Next, the stranger asked him to hold his penis while he peed. The second guy was even more embarrassed by this request, but reluctantly did as he was asked. Finally, the stranger finished and the second man started to put his penis back in his trousers for him.

"Oh, I can take care of that," the stranger trilled, blowing on his fingers. "I think my nails are dry now."

What's the difference between a Broadway theatre and a public toilet? – The theatre is for arts and farces.

Staggering home from the pub, a drunk was desperate for a pee so he decided to relieve himself up against a wall.

Just then, a police car pulled up, lights flashing, and a policewoman called out: "If I wasn't on my way to a burglary, I'd put you inside."

"You're not missing much," shouted the drunk. "I can never get it up after ten pints."

A man said to his wife: "Go into the bathroom and look at the size of the shit I've just done. It was so big, it made my eyes water!"

"No, thanks," she replied.

"Go on, just a quick look," he pleaded. "You won't believe it."

So she held her nose, hurried into the bathroom, looked down the toilet and then hurried out again, saying: "There's nothing down there. You must have flushed it."

"What do you mean?" he said. "It's on the scales."

I'm one of those people who like to read while having a crap . . . which is also why I'm banned from the local bookstore.

What was wrong with train toilet doors that just locked, instead of this multiple-choice system? If anything goes wrong, you'll be sitting there while the whole toilet wall slowly slides away, unveiling you like a prize on a quiz show. For 500 points, a shitting woman! (Frankie Boyle)

An American guy and a Ukrainian were standing in front of the urinals. The American pulled out a huge dick from his pants and said proudly to the Ukrainian: "Buffalo Bill!"

The Ukrainian then pulled out three enormous dicks and said: "Chernobyl!"

I went to the swimming pool last night and decided to chance a piss in the deep end. The lifeguard must have noticed because he blew his whistle so loud I nearly fell in.

A workman went into a rundown public toilet to take a dump. The toilet had two stalls separated by nothing more than a low partition, and there was another man about to step into one of them. The two men briefly acknowledged one another and then set about emptying their bowels.

The workman finished first but as he pulled up his trousers prior to flushing the toilet, some coins from his pocket fell into the toilet bowl. He looked at it, thought for a moment and then dropped a £20 note into the bowl.

The other man, who had heard the commotion, peered over the partition and said: "What did you do that for?"

The workman said: "You don't expect me to put my hand in there for sixty-five pence, do you?"

Why a Good Crap Is Better than Sex

- You never feel as if you must have sex this very minute, right now, or your body will explode.
- After a good crap, you get the chance to inspect what you've done; very few women will allow you to do this after sex.
- If you can't force one out, it doesn't matter. Nobody judges you.
- You are not considered less of a man if you can't manage another crap half an hour later.
- You are not expected to have any emotional ties with the toilet.
- You can lose more weight with one good crap than from a month of energetic sex.
- Whereas sex is sometimes accompanied by the occasional moan, a windy crap can be so musical that passers-by would swear you've got Kenny Ball and His Jazzmen in there.
- After a good crap, you don't need to ask, "Was it good for you?" You know it was!

Two flies were sitting on a toilet seat . . . until one got pissed off.

A small boy was playing with a balloon around the house, flicking it in the air with his hand. His mother told him to stop in case he broke an ornament, but he paid no attention. Finally, after incessant nagging, he stopped.

"Right," she said, "I'm just going to the shop for some groceries. I'll only be twenty minutes, so I want you to stay here and behave yourself."

As soon as she was gone, he started playing with the balloon again, flicking it from room to room until, to his dismay, it landed in the toilet bowl. He left it there and went off to play with something else.

Shortly afterwards his mother returned home in a state of high anxiety. Hurriedly dumping the groceries in the kitchen, she ran to the toilet and proceeded to unleash a torrent of diarrhoea. Relieved when it was all over, she turned to inspect the damage and couldn't believe her eyes. There in the toilet bowl was this big brown thing.

She immediately called her doctor, who could offer no obvious explanation but promised that he would come straight round. When he arrived, she led him to the toilet, where he got down on his knees and took a long, hard look at the thing. Perplexed, he took out his pen and prodded it in the hope of finding out what it might be. And POP! The balloon exploded, showering poop everywhere – all over his clothes, up the walls and on the floor.

"Doctor, are you all right?" she asked.

Wiping the poop from his eyes, he said: "Do you know, I've been a doctor for thirty-three years and this is the first time I've ever actually seen a fart!"

I like my women how I like my toilet – takes my shit, doesn't give me any shit back.

Little Johnny was in the bathroom having a pee when the toilet seat fell down on his penis. He started screaming and crying, so his mother ran upstairs to see what the problem was.

"Mummy!" he wailed. "The toilet seat fell on my penis. Will you kiss it better?"

"Honestly, Johnny," she said, "you get more and more like your father every day!"

I got in touch with my inner self today. That's the last time I buy cheap toilet paper.

A woman's first thought on discovering a skid mark in the toilet: "Yuk! That's disgusting! I must get some toilet cleaner and wipe that off."

A man's first thought on discovering a skid mark in the toilet: "Great! A challenge to see if I can wash it all away with one good piss."

What do a pussy and a warm toilet seat have in common? – They're both nice, but you always wonder who was there before you.

As a young couple walked hand in hand down a quiet country lane, the young man grew increasingly amorous, but just as he was about to make a move on his girlfriend, she announced: "Sorry, but I need a pee."

Slightly taken aback by her vulgarity, he suggested: "Why don't you go behind that hedge?"

So she disappeared behind the hedge. As he waited, he could hear the gentling rustling sound of lace panties rolling down her smooth thighs and imagined what was being exposed in the warm summer breeze. Unable to contain his lust any longer, he reached a hand through the hedge and touched her leg. He quickly moved his hand up her thigh until, to his astonishment, he found himself gripping a long, thick appendage hanging between her legs.

He shouted: "My God, Sophie! Have you changed sex?"

"No," she replied. "I've changed my mind. I'm having a shit instead."

Tourette's

A man walked into a library and asked for a book on Tourette's.

The librarian said: "Fuck off, you twat!"

The man said: "Yes, that's the one."

What's the first thing that happens when you join the Tourette's Society? – You get sworn in.

Did you hear about the man who was kicked out of a Tourette's Society meeting for using good language?

On a rare visit back to his home town, a man decided to call on his sister, who had a young son with Tourette's. It was the first time he had ever met the boy and he wasn't sure what to expect. While his sister was in the kitchen making some tea, the man and his nephew sat quietly in the living room.

Then suddenly the boy looked at his uncle and said: "Open the door, you cunt." The man felt a bit embarrassed and did not reply.

The boy said again: "Open the fucking door, you stupid cunt." The uncle now began to feel extremely awkward and did not have a clue how to respond, so he just decided to ignore the outburst and pretend that he hadn't heard it.

However, the boy became increasingly agitated and repeated: "You useless cunt, open the fucking door."

At that point, the sister came into the room and said to the man: "Don't worry, he's just trying to tell you a knock-knock joke."

What do we want? A cure for Tourette's. When do we want it? Wanker!

As part of a security check, a man was asked: "What's your name?"

"Jonathan Fucking Kennedy."

"Oh. Do you suffer from Tourette's, Jonathan?"

"No, but the vicar at the Christening did."

Specialist Cockney Rhyming Slang

Mutton Jeff – deaf
Bacon rind – blind
Canary Wharf – dwarf
Diet Pepsi – epilepsy
Birds and bees – amputees
Benny and the fucking cunting jets – Tourette's

A man was chatting up a girl in a bar when he leaned closer and said: "There's something I've wanted to tell you all evening, shit, fuck, bollocks."

"You've got Tourette's?"

"No, my wife's just walked in!"

What's the best thing about having sex with a girl who has Tourette's? – The neighbours all think you're great in bed.

A Jewish guy began dating a girl who suffered from Tourette's. His friend couldn't understand the attraction and said to him: "I can't believe you're still going out with that girl. Doesn't the fact that she has Tourette's make the relationship rather difficult?"

The Jewish guy admitted: "At first I did wonder if I had made a big mistake. But that all changed once I installed the swear box."

Transsexuals

I went to bed with two Thai girls last night. It was just like winning the lottery – we had six matching balls.

A lady walked into her doctor's office in a state of panic. "Doctor," she said. "My breasts are hairy! What can I do?"

The doctor asked: "How long does the hair grow?"

The lady replied: "From here to my balls, but that's another story!"

A boy went up to his father and asked: "Daddy, what's a transsexual?"

"Go ask your mum," he replied. "He should be able to explain it better."

What is the name of the operation where a woman changes into a man? – An addadictomy.

At the end of a hard night's sex in a Bangkok hotel room, a man was lying in bed with a girl cuddled in his arms. Suddenly, she started stroking his dick.

"Mmm," he groaned. "Are you still feeling horny?"

"No," she replied. "I just really miss mine."

Travel

Leaving a city-centre hotel, a man had just stepped out on to the street when a taxi pulled up. He got into the taxi, and the cabbie said: "Perfect timing. You're just like Jim."

"Who?" asked the passenger.

"Jim," said the cabbie. "Jim Finkel. There's a guy who did everything right. Like my coming along when you needed a cab. It would have happened like that to Jim every single time."

"Nobody's perfect," said the passenger. "I'm sure even Jim had his flaws."

"Not Jim," insisted the cabbie. "He was a one-off, a giant amongst men. He was a terrific athlete. He could have gone on the pro tour in tennis. He could play golf with the pros. He sang like an opera baritone and danced like a West End star and you should have heard him play the piano."

"He certainly sounds a special guy," conceded the passenger.

The cabbie went on: "He had a memory like a computer – could remember everybody's birthday. He knew all about wine, which foods to order and which fork to eat them with. He could fix anything. Not like me. I change a fuse and the whole neighbourhood blacks out."

"Wow, some guy, eh?" agreed the passenger.

Without skipping a beat, the cabbie continued: "He always knew the quickest way to go in traffic and avoid traffic jams, not like me: I always seem to get into them. And he knew how to treat a woman and make her feel good and never answer her back even if she was in the wrong; and his clothing was always immaculate, shoes highly polished too. Too bad he's not around anymore."

"An amazing guy," the passenger nodded. "How did you meet him?"

The cabbie said: "Well, I never actually met Jim."

"Then how do you know so much about him?"

The cabbie said: "I married his widow."

I stayed in a Turkish hotel. It overlooked the sea. Unfortunately, it also overlooked hygiene, good service and edible meals.

How do you know when the price of petrol has gone up? – London taxi drivers start taking the shortest route.

A man got in a taxi and said to the driver: "81 Ranleigh Avenue, please, mate."

The cabbie said: "Doing anything nice?"

"Well, actually, mate," said the man, "I'm going to see a woman I met on one of those adult singles sites where married people meet up for sex."

The cabbie said: "I wouldn't do that if I were you."

"Why not?"

"Because I live at 81 Ranleigh Avenue."

Ugliness

A man consulted a plastic surgeon about having some work done on his face but the medic informed him: "I'm sorry, but you're just too ugly for plastic surgery. I suggest you wear a plastic bag over your head."

"Don't you mean a paper bag?" said the man.

The surgeon shook his head. "Maybe I didn't emphasize just how ugly you are."

Ned and Bill were stranded in the desert, dying of thirst. As they staggered along beneath the blazing sun, they spotted a small shack. They knocked on the door and it was answered by the ugliest, smelliest, hairiest woman they had ever seen. Ned told the woman that they were desperate for water, and she said: "Sure you can have water – if you have sex with me."

Ned was horrified: "I would rather die in this desert," he announced, "than have sex with such a repulsive creature as you."

However, Bill valued his life and agreed to do the deed, leaving Ned waiting outside the shack.

The hideous woman dragged Bill into her private room and demanded that he make love to her. He said he would, on condition that she close her eyes. The woman shut her eyes and Bill, looking around the room, noticed a table full of corn on the cob. Thinking quickly, he fucked her with a piece of corn on the cob and threw it out of the window before she opened her eyes again.

But the woman wanted more and demanded to be pleasured a second time. Bill reluctantly agreed, provided she close her eyes again. When she had done so, he picked up another piece of corn on the cob, rammed it into her a few times and threw it out of the window before she reopened her eyes.

Finally satisfied, the woman agreed to give Bill and Ned some water. Bill shouted outside to relay the good news to his friend.

"Never mind the water," said Ned. "I want some more of that buttered corn."

Fred bumped into an old school friend who started showing off, talking about his well-paid job and expensive sports car. Then he pulled out a photo of his wife and said: "She's beautiful, isn't she?"

Fred said: "If you think she's gorgeous, you should see my girlfriend."

"Why? Is she a stunner?"

"No," said Fred. "She's an optician."

My wife has got one of those rape deterrent devices – a face like a slapped arse.

A rough, ugly woman walked into a supermarket with her bratty kids in tow. Straightaway, they ran riot, racing up and down the aisles while she yelled obscenities at them. Finally, after several complaints from shoppers, the manager went to deal with the situation.

"Good morning, madam," he said in his most charming tone. "Welcome to the store. Nice children you've got there. Are they twins?"

Wiping her nose on her sleeve, the woman answered gruffly: "Course they're not bleedin' twins. One's seven and the other's five, you dickhead! What the fuck makes you think they're twins? Do they look alike?"

"No," replied the manager. "It was just beyond my imagination to think you had been laid more than once."

A guy went on a blind date with a really ugly girl, and on seeing her for the first time declared: "Time stands still whenever I look into your eyes."

With a big goofy grin, she replied: "That's the nicest thing anyone's ever said to me."

That was when he realized what he'd meant to say was: "You have a face that could stop a clock."

A male charity collector knocked on a woman's front door and asked her if she had any old beer bottles.

She was highly indignant. "Do I look as if I drink beer?" she snapped.

The collector looked at her and said: "Okay, have you got any vinegar bottles?"

A young man came back into the office after lunch, sat down at his desk and immediately looked dejected.

"What's the matter?" asked the girl sitting at the next desk.

He said: "Somebody left a note on my desk saying, 'You're the ugliest guy I have ever seen!'"

"Don't look at me," said the girl.

"I wasn't implying it was you," he said. "I just . . ."

"No, seriously, don't look at me – you're fucking hideous."

Sam was in a bar with his buddy Al, eyeing up a couple of girls. One girl in particular had a gorgeous body and Sam couldn't keep his eyes off her until she turned around and he saw she had a face like a broken sofa. Disappointed, Sam went to the toilet for a pee, and by the time he returned to the bar the girl had gone. However, Al handed him a piece of paper containing the message: "I saw you looking at me, here's my number." And it said it was from "horse face".

A couple of days later, Sam plucked up the courage to text her. He figured that if she was able to make light of her appearance and call herself "horse face", she had to be a genuine sort of girl. So he sent her a message saying: "Hi horse face, I'd love to meet up with you."

Sadly he never received a reply. When he told his friend about this, Al looked sheepish. "Sorry, buddy," said Al, "I wrote 'horse face' on that note so you'd know it was from the ugly one!"

Three men – Mike, Wayne and Jim – were in a bar one night when they decided to wager a bet as to which of them had the ugliest wife. Mike assured the others that his wife was spectacularly ugly, so they went round to his house and recoiled in horror when she answered the door.

But Wayne was sure his wife was even uglier, so the three men called in at his house. When his wife answered the door, she was so repulsive that Mike and Jim threw up on the spot.

However, Jim insisted that his wife could beat the other two for sheer ugliness and took Mike and Wayne round to his house. He opened the door, walked into the garage and stamped on a trap door leading to the cellar.

"Is that you, honey?" called a voice from below. "Do you want me to come out?"

"Yes," said Jim.

"Should I put the bag on my head?"

"No," said Jim. "I don't want to screw you, I just want to show you off."

Dave came home from work and heard strange noises coming from the bedroom. He ran upstairs and burst in to find his best mate pumping away with Dave's rather ugly wife. He looked at the pair in utter disgust before turning to his friend. "Honestly, Terry," he said. "I have to, but you?"

Underwear

A man sat down at a bar next to an attractive woman. He glanced at her, and then casually looked at his watch.

Noticing this, the woman asked: "Is your date late?"

"No," he replied, "I recently got this state-of-the-art watch and I was just testing it."

"What's so special about it?" asked the woman.

"It uses alpha waves to talk to me telepathically."

"What's it telling you now?"

"It says you're not wearing any panties."

The woman giggled and said: "Well, it must be broken because I am wearing panties."

The man smiled, tapped his watch and said: "Damn thing's an hour fast!"

It's Probably Time to Buy New Underwear When . . .

- Dogs sniff your butt and run away yelping.
- Your boyfriend can eat you out without first having to take your panties off.
- Your underpants stand in the corner waiting for you to put them on.
- They are found to be providing a home for more than five different species of insect.
- You have to pull with both hands to get them unstuck from your butt.
- Birds suddenly fall out of trees when you walk past.
- A thick crust has formed on them.
- You are finding it increasingly difficult to sit down.
- Even when washed, they remain resolutely brown.
- People who live downwind of you start moving out.

A seedy-looking man walked into a lingerie shop. As he pawed the racks of lace panties, a female sales assistant came over and asked: "Can I help you, sir?"

"No, thanks," he said. "Just sniffing."

An Englishman, an Irishman and a Scotsman were all playing golf with their wives. As the Englishman's wife bent over to place her ball on the tee, a sudden gust of wind blew her skirt up and revealed her lack of underwear.

"Good God, woman! Why aren't you wearing any knickers?" her husband demanded.

"Well, you don't give me enough housekeeping money so I can't afford to buy any."

The Englishman immediately reached into his pocket and said: "For the sake of decency here's fifty quid. Go and buy yourself some underwear."

Next, the Irishman's wife bent over to set her ball on the tee. Her skirt also blew up to show that she wasn't wearing any panties.

"Mother of Jesus, woman!" exclaimed her husband. "You've got no knickers on! Why not?"

She replied: "I can't afford any on the money you give me."

The Irishman immediately reached into his pocket and said: "For the sake of decency here's twenty quid. Go and buy yourself some underwear!"

Lastly, the Scotsman's wife bent over on the tee. Another gust of wind took her skirt over her head to reveal that she, too, was naked underneath.

"Why are ye not wearing knickers?" her husband roared.

She explained: "You dinnae give me enough housekeepin' money tae be able tae afford any."

The Scotsman immediately reached into his pocket and said: "Well, fer the sake of decency, here's a comb, tidy yerself up a bit."

Men want the same thing from their underwear that they want from women: a little bit of support and a little bit of freedom. (Jerry Seinfeld)

Little Johnny was out in the school playground during break time. He went up to his classmate Lucy, and whispered in her ear: "I'd sure like to be in your pants right now!"

"How can you say such a thing?" she demanded angrily.

"Well, I just shat in mine!"

Vasectomy

While performing a vasectomy, the surgeon slipped and accidentally cut off one of the patient's testicles. With the patient still under anaesthetic, the surgeon decided to replace the missing testicle with an onion and hope that nobody would ever know.

A few weeks later, the patient returned for a check-up.

"How have you been?" asked the surgeon.

"Okay," replied the patient, "apart from a few side effects."

"What sort of side effects?" asked the surgeon nervously.

"Well," said the patient, "whenever I urinate, my eyes water; whenever my wife gives me a blow job she gets heartburn; and whenever I pass a hamburger stand I get an erection."

A husband went to a florist to buy half a dozen red roses for his wife's birthday. However, the guy behind the counter said: "I'm sorry, sir, this isn't a florist – it's a male clinic specializing in circumcisions and vasectomies."

The husband was mystified. "So why have you got all those flowers in the window?"

The guy behind the counter replied: "And what do you suggest we put in the window?"

A guy went to see his doctor about having a vasectomy.

"Are you sure about this?" asked the doctor. "How many children have you got?"

"I've got five teenage daughters," the man replied.

"Ah, right, now I can understand why you want the procedure."

"Yes, because if I got one of them pregnant it would be a disaster."

Harry was minutes away from having a vasectomy when his brother and sister-in-law barged in holding their newborn baby.

"Stop!" exclaimed the brother. "You can't go through with this!"

"And why not?" asked Harry.

"Don't you want to have a beautiful baby some day, like my wife and I have here?"

Harry said nothing.

The brother grew impatient. "Come on, Harry, I want a nephew. Make me an uncle."

Harry couldn't take any more of this. He gave his sister-in-law an apologetic look and asked his brother: "Are you sure you want a nephew?"

"Absolutely," said the brother.

"Well, congratulations," said Harry. "You're holding him!"

Viagra

Why do nurses give Viagra to elderly male patients in old folk's homes? – To stop them rolling out of bed.

A man was having problems getting an erection, so he went to visit his doctor, who said: "There's a new super Viagra being trialled that is ten times stronger than the standard drug. It's not widely available yet, but I do have access to some, so would you like to try it?"

"Sure," said the patient excitedly. "I'll try anything that might help cure my erection problems."

A week later, the patient bumped into the doctor in the street. "Doc, I can't thank you enough," he smiled. "I'm having incredible sex!"

"That's great," said the doctor. "I bet your wife's happy."

"Wife?" said the man. "I haven't been home yet!"

I've just bought some of that 007 Viagra. It makes you roger more.

Did you hear about the guy who accidentally took Viagra instead of Valium and ended up having forty wanks?

The reason old men use Viagra is not that they are impotent. It's that old women are so very, very ugly. (Jimmy Carr)

A man went to his doctor and asked for an urgent prescription of Viagra. The doctor said: "Very well, but remember it takes at least half an hour before it becomes effective."

"That's no good," said the man. "She'll probably have wriggled free by then."

A man was reported to the animal welfare authorities for feeding Viagra to his pet Labrador. The man is now banned from keeping any pets. And the Labrador is now a pointer.

Did you hear about the man who put Viagra in his tea? — It did nothing for his sex drive, but it stopped his biscuits from going soft.

Vibrators

A woman rang her husband at work and said excitedly: "Two packages arrived today. One's your Xbox and the other's that vibrator we ordered. I can't wait for you to get home and play with me for hours."

"You'll be lucky!" he answered. "I've only ordered one controller."

A family were driving behind a garbage truck when a dildo flew out and thumped against the windshield. Embarrassed and to spare her young son's innocence, the mother turned round and said: "Don't worry, that was an insect."

The boy replied: "I'm surprised it could get off the ground with a cock like that!"

My wife came home with a vibrator, waving it about and grinning: "I don't need you now! I don't need you now!" Guess who had to put the batteries in.

What did the banana say to the vibrator? — "I don't know why you're shaking — she's going to eat me!"

An elderly woman arrived home one night to find her daughter in bed with a vibrator. "What are you doing?" screamed the mother.

The daughter said: "Mum, I'm forty-six years old, I'm single and I haven't dated anybody in months. This is the twenty-first century. Times have changed, so give me a break!"

The mother shook her head despairingly and left the room.

The following day the father walked in on the daughter and he, too, found her with the vibrator.

"What's going on?" he demanded.

"Dad," she sighed, "I'm forty-six years old, I'm single and I haven't dated anybody in months. This is the twenty-first century. Times have changed, so give me a break!"

The father shook his head despairingly and left the room.

That night, the mother went into the kitchen and found the father sitting at the table with a beer in one hand and the vibrator in the other.

"What on earth are you doing with that?" she demanded.

"What's your problem?" he said. "Can't a guy have a beer with his son-in-law?"

A woman went into a hardware store and asked the sales assistant for two AA batteries. The assistant gestured with his fingers, said, "Come this way," and headed towards the back of the store.

"If I could come that way," she said, "I wouldn't need the batteries."

How can you tell if a woman is macho? — Her vibrator has a kick-starter.

A businessman was getting ready to go on a long work trip. Knowing his wife was always horny, he decided to get her something to keep her occupied while he was gone because he didn't relish the thought of her sleeping around. So he went to a store that sold sex toys. He thought about buying her a life-sized sex doll, but that was too close to another man for him. Then he started browsing through the vibrators, looking for something special to please his wife, and explained his needs to the old man behind the counter.

The old man scratched his head and replied: "Well, I don't really know of anything that will do the trick. We have vibrating dildos, special attachments and so on, but I don't know of anything that will keep her occupied for weeks, except . . ."

"Except what?" asked the businessman.

"Nothing, nothing," said the old man.

"Come on, tell me! I need something!" protested the businessman.

"Well," sighed the old man, "I don't usually mention this, but there is the 'voodoo dildo'."

"The voodoo dildo?" the businessman queried. "What's that?"

The old man reached under the counter and pulled out an old wooden box carved with strange symbols. He opened it and there lay a very ordinary-looking dildo.

The businessman laughed and said: "Big deal! It looks like every other dildo in this shop!"

"Wait!" said the old man. "You haven't seen what it'll do yet." He pointed to a door and said: "Voodoo dildo, the door." With that, the voodoo dildo rose out of its box, darted over to the door, and started screwing the keyhole. The whole door shook with the vibrations, and a crack developed down the middle. Before the door could split, the old man said: "Voodoo dildo, box!" The voodoo dildo stopped, floated back to the box and lay there, motionless.

Impressed, the businessman said: "I'll take it!" He took it home to his wife, told her it was a special dildo and that to use it, all she had to do was say: "Voodoo dildo, my pussy." Then he left for his trip satisfied things would be fine while he was away.

After he'd been gone a few days, the wife was unbearably horny. She thought of several people who would willingly satisfy her, but then she remembered the voodoo dildo. She lay down, placed the box between her legs, and said: "Voodoo dildo, my pussy!" The voodoo dildo shot to her crotch and started pumping. It was great, like nothing she'd ever experienced before. After three orgasms, she decided she'd had enough, and tried to pull it out, but it was stuck in her, still thrusting. She tried and tried to get it out, but nothing worked. Her husband had forgotten to tell her how to switch it off. So she decided to go to the hospital to see if they could help. She put her clothes on, got in the car and started to drive to the hospital, quivering with every thrust of the dildo. On the way, another orgasm nearly made her swerve off the road, and she was pulled over by a policeman. He asked for her licence, and then asked how much she'd had to drink. Gasping and twitching, she explained that she hadn't been drinking, but that a voodoo dildo was stuck in her pussy and wouldn't stop screwing her.

The officer looked at her for a second, and then scoffed: "Yeah, right. Voodoo dildo, my arse!"

Virginity

A young couple were both shy virgins when they married. Embarrassed about discussing sexual matters, they decided to coin a euphemism to spare their blushes. So instead of talking openly about having sex, they called it "doing the laundry".

On the first night of their honeymoon they "did the laundry'. The husband enjoyed it so much that half an hour later he asked his new bride: "Can we do the laundry again?"

"I'm sorry," she replied, "but I'm a bit tired now. Can we leave it till tomorrow?"

However, in the middle of the night she woke up and felt guilty about rejecting him. Tapping him tenderly on the shoulder, she whispered: "I'm sorry I pushed you away earlier. We can do the laundry again now if you like."

"It's okay," he said. "It was only a small load, so I did it by hand."

After dating for several months, two shy young virgins decided they were finally ready to have sex with each other. So they booked a hotel room for a dirty weekend. Their first night in bed together proved a great success, and they had sex over and over again, making up for lost time.

The next morning, the young man went into the bathroom but couldn't find a towel after showering. So he called for the girl to bring one from the bedroom. When he opened the bathroom door to her, it was the first time she had properly seen his naked body. Her eyes went up and down and, at about midway, they stopped and stared. Pointing to his small, flaccid penis, she asked coyly: "What's that?"

He said: "That's what we had so much fun with last night."

Disappointed, she asked: "Is that all we have left?"

A young man decided to lose his virginity by visiting a Nevada whorehouse. There, a girl dragged him upstairs and quickly took off her panties.

Peering between her legs, the young man asked shyly: "What's that?"

"It's my lower mouth," said the hooker.

"What do you mean, your lower mouth?"

"Well, it's like a mouth. It's got a beard, it's got lips . . ."

"Has it got a tongue in it?"

The hooker pulled him towards her and said: "Not yet!"

An old lady was proud of still being a virgin, and before she died she gave strict instructions to the funeral director regarding her headstone. She told him: "I want it to read: 'Born as a virgin, lived as a virgin, died as a virgin.'"

When she died, the funeral director relayed the old lady's instructions to the men inscribing the headstone. But they were lazy, and instead of carving out the full inscription, they just wrote: "Returned unopened."

A shy virgin was discussing her worries about her forthcoming marriage with her parish priest.

"Father," she said, "he dropped his trousers last night, and he has a thing between his legs, the like of which I've never seen before."

"Mary, that's only his penis," said the priest reassuringly.

"But, Father, there's a purple knob on the end of it."

"That's just the head of the penis, Mary."

"But then sixteen inches back from the purple knob there are two big round things. What are they, Father?"

"Well, for your sake Mary, I hope they're the cheeks of his arse!"

A devoutly religious young man was intent on marrying a virgin, but after several dates he quickly realized that all the local girls had lost their virginity by the age of sixteen. He decided the only solution was to adopt a baby girl from an orphanage, raise her until the age of five, and then send her away to a monastery for safekeeping until she was old enough to become his bride. Sure enough, after many years away, she finally reached maturity and he retrieved her from the monastery and married her.

After the wedding, they made their way back to his house and into the bedroom, where they prepared themselves for the consummation. As they lay down together in bed, he reached across for a jar of petroleum jelly.

"Why the jelly?' she asked him.

"So I don't hurt your most delicate parts during the act of lovemaking," he replied tenderly.

She said: "Why don't you just spit on your cock like the monks did?"

A girl leaned casually against a backstreet building, running her fingers through her bleached hair and smiling at the male passers-by. She wore a mini-skirt and a low-cut V-neck sweater. Finally, one of her come-hither looks paid off and she was approached by a young man.

"Hi," he said, undressing her mentally.

"Hello, handsome," she replied.

His eyes focused on her sweater and the curves it almost covered. "What's the V for?" he asked. "Veronica? Violet?"

"Uh-uh. Virgin."

"Oh, come on," he said playfully. "You're a virgin?"

"No," she winked. "It's an old sweater."

I didn't lose my virginity until I was twenty-six. Nineteen vaginally, but twenty-six what my boyfriend calls "the real way'. (Sarah Silverman)

A woman went to the doctor. She said: "Doc, what am I going to do? I've told my fiancé that I've never been with anyone before, but as soon as we have sex, he'll find out that isn't true, that I'm not a virgin. We're getting married on Saturday. Is there anything you can do to help me?"

The doctor thought for a moment. "Yes," he said, "there is an operation, but it costs £5,000."

"Five thousand pounds?!" she exclaimed in horror. "That's expensive! Is there nothing else you can do?"

The doctor thought some more. "Actually, there is another option," he said, "and it only costs £50. I can give you a quick anaesthetic and then I can sort it out here and now."

"Fifty pounds right now?" she said. "Great, I'll do that."

The night of the wedding came around, and when they had sex, the bride experienced excruciating pain and shed a little blood – all enough to convince her husband that she had indeed been a virgin.

A couple of days later, she phoned the doctor to tell him how well it went. "It's amazing!" she gushed. "What exactly did you do?"

"Simple," said the doctor. "I tied all your pubic hairs together."

An inexperienced young man, prior to his wedding, asked his father what he should do to his wife on their wedding night.

"Well," said the father, not knowing really how to say it delicately, "you take the thing you used to play with more than anything else when you were a teenager and put it where your wife wee-wees."

"Really, Dad?" the young man said.

"Believe me, son," his father responded, "you'll love it."

So on his wedding night, the young man took his baseball and threw it in the toilet.

Two sisters were still virgins at the age of eighty-three. Finally, in frustration one of them, Enid, announced:

"I'm damned if I'm going to die a virgin. So tonight I'm going out on the town and I'm not coming home until I've been laid!"

Shocked by the outburst, her sister Peggy warned: "Well, don't be too late. There are some strange people in town on a Saturday night."

All evening Peggy waited anxiously to hear the key in the door. At last – at half past one in the morning – Enid returned and headed straight to the bathroom.

A concerned Peggy called through the door: "Are you okay, Enid?"

There was no answer, so Peggy opened the door and saw Enid sitting there with her panties around her ankles, legs spread and her head stuck between her legs looking at herself.

"What is it, Enid?" cried Peggy. "What's wrong?"

Enid said: 'Peggy, it was ten inches long when it went in and five when it came out. I tell you, when I find the other half, you're going have the time of your life!"

Before going out on her first date, a virginal girl told her grandmother about it.

Her grandmother said: "Let me tell you a few things about boys. He is going to try to kiss you; you are going to like that, but don't let him do that. He is going to try to feel your breasts; you are going to like that, but don't let him do that. He is going to try to put his hand between your legs; you are going to like that, but don't let him do that. But, most importantly, he is going to try to get on top of you and have his way with you. You are going to like that, but don't let him do that. It will disgrace the family."

With that advice in mind, the granddaughter went on her date and the next day she revealed that it had gone just as the grandmother had predicted. "But Grandma, I didn't let him disgrace the family," she said. "When he tried, I turned him over, got on top of him and disgraced *his* family."

A man was left writhing in agony after being hit in the groin by a cyclist. Next day at the doctor's office, he asked: "How bad is it, Doc? Because I'm getting married next week and my fiancée is still a virgin."

The doctor said: "I'll have to put your manhood in a splint so that it will heal and keep straight. It should be okay in a couple of weeks."

The doctor then took four tongue depressors, made them into a neat little four-sided splint and wired the contraption together. The groom deliberately avoided mentioning his little mishap to his bride before their wedding day.

On their honeymoon night, his new wife opened her blouse to reveal a gorgeous pair of breasts and told him lovingly: "You'll be the first. No one has ever touched these before."

Determined to outdo her, the husband dropped his pants and said: "Well, check this out – it's still in its crate!"

An innocent girl turned to her husband in bed on their wedding night and said: "I'm really scared. I've never done this with a man before."

"Don't worry, honey," he replied. "I have."

A girl had always resisted her boyfriend's attempts to have sex before they were married. Eventually, she confessed that the reason she was still a virgin was that she was extremely flat-chested.

The boy was sympathetic. "It's not a problem," he said. "Sex isn't everything. And anyway I have a confession to make about my own body: below my waist, it's just like a baby."

"That doesn't matter," said the girl reassuringly. "Like you say, sex isn't everything."

Happy that they could be so honest with each other, they duly got married. On their wedding night, she took off all her clothes and was indeed as flat as a pancake. Then he took all his clothes off and the girl fainted.

When she came round, she gasped: "I thought you said it was just like a baby."

"It is," he said. "Eight pounds and twenty-one inches."

Virility

Don fancied himself as quite a ladies" man, so when his cruise ship went down in a storm and he found himself stranded on a desert island with six women, he couldn't believe his good fortune. The six women quickly agreed that each would spend one night a week with the only man, leaving Sundays free.

Don threw himself into the arrangement with gusto, but as the weeks stretched into months, his stamina started to wane and he began looking forward to that day of rest more and more eagerly.

One afternoon he was sitting on the beach wishing that there was another man around to share his duties when he caught sight of a guy waving from a life raft that was bobbing on the waves. Don swam out, pulled the raft to shore and cried excitedly: "You can't believe how happy I am to see you."

The newcomer eyed him up and down and cooed: "You're a sight for sore eyes, too, you gorgeous thing."

"Shit!" sighed Don. "There go my Sundays!"

A Jew, a Catholic and a Mormon gathered for an inter-faith convention. Later at the bar, the Jew started boasting about his virility, saying: "I have four sons. One more and I'll have a basketball team."

"That's nothing," said the Catholic. "I have ten sons. One more and I'll have a soccer team."

"Big deal!" snorted the Mormon. "I have seventeen wives. One more and I'll have a golf course!"

A guy and his manager went down to the docks. The manager bet every longshoreman he saw that his guy could screw and satisfy a hundred women in a row, without pausing. Bets were placed and everyone agreed that they would meet the next day.

The next day, a hundred women were lined up along the dock and the guy dropped his pants and started having sex with them. True to his word, he moved from one to the next, satisfying each one without pausing. One . . . two . . . three . . . off he went at great speed; fifty-nine . . . sixty . . . sixty-one . . . he was starting to slow down a bit; eighty-three; eighty-four . . . eighty-five . . . he was getting short of stamina, but was determined to reach his target; ninety-seven . . . ninety-eight . . . ninety-nine . . . but before he could get to the last woman he had a heart attack and died.

The manager scratched his head and said: "I don't understand it! It went perfectly at practice this morning!"

Vomit

A drunk vomited on a dog in the street. As the dog ran away yelping, the drunk said to himself: "I don't remember eating that."

Two piles of vomit were walking down the street. The first pile of vomit turned to the second and said tearfully: "I was brought up here."

I was told I had a weak stomach, but I managed to throw up further than anybody else.

Fact: you can keep puking long after you think you've finished.

Quasimodo had always longed to have sex but could never find a woman who would let him. One night in desperation he headed for the red-light district of Paris but all the hookers knocked him back, saying he was just too repulsive to have sex with. He was just about to head back to Notre Dame when he spotted a rough old whore in a shop doorway. He approached her, and she agreed to go with him, figuring that she could keep her eyes shut throughout and pretend that he was just one of her regulars.

So she led him down a dark alley, hitched up her skirt and leaned against a wall while he started banging her. She kept her eyes tightly closed until a sudden noise made her open them instinctively. As soon as she did so, she saw the grotesque creature in front of her and threw up.

"Did you just vomit?" asked Quasimodo.

"Yes," she said.

"Thank God," he said. "For a moment I thought my hump had burst."

Weddings

On their wedding night, a young woman told her new husband: "If you don't remove your socks, I am not getting into bed with you."

"No, I won't take off my socks," said the husband. "You can't make me."

"What is this?" she shrieked. "Some kind of sock perversion? Why did I have to wait until our wedding night to find out that you were kinky?"

"No, it's not a perversion," he retorted. Then with a deep sigh, he went on: "Okay, I have kept this from you all through our courting days. But here's the truth." With that, he removed his socks and she could see that the front half of one of his feet was missing. "I lost it during an accident at work," he explained. "It embarrasses me, and that's why I didn't tell you before."

Upset, she ran downstairs and phoned her mother. Sobbing down the phone, she wailed: "Terry only has a foot and a half!"

Her mother replied: "Right, young lady, you pack your bags and come straight back home. Tell Terry I'm on my way over!"

A young couple met their local church minister to discuss their forthcoming wedding. Before agreeing to conduct the service, he wanted to be sure that they were truly, madly, deeply in love.

The minister asked the young woman: "So how did you realize you were in love with John?"

She said: "When every step felt like a skip, when the birds were always singing and the sun was shining even at night."

The vicar then turned to the young man and asked: "And how did you realize you were in love with Jennifer?"

He replied: "I think it was probably when I stopped looking at porn for two days."

"Who will give the bride away?" asked the preacher.

"I could," came a voice from the back of the church, "but I'm keeping my mouth shut!"

A shy white virgin girl got married to a black guy but was rather nervous about their wedding night as she had heard that black men were much better endowed than white men. She relayed her fears to her new husband, who suggested that the best solution was for him to show her his organ bit by bit.

She lay in bed and saw three inches of him come round the door. "Are you nervous yet?" he asked.

"No, I'm okay," she replied.

Then another three inches came around the door, and he asked: "Are you still okay?"

"Yes, I'm fine," she said.

Another three inches came around the door, but she said: "I'm still not nervous."

"Okay," said her husband. "I'm coming up the stairs."

Three friends were getting married in the same hotel on the same day and, at the end of the evening, they met up to discuss the day's events over a couple of beers. One asked the other two: "As this is our wedding night, I was wondering – how many times are we expected to . . . um . . . you know . . . do it?"

Neither of the others had a definitive answer, so after another beer they decided to retire to their respective wives and planned to meet up the following morning over breakfast to compare notes regarding the wedding night action.

Just then, one of the grooms said: "Hold on, lads, we can't discuss our first night's marital activities over the breakfast table when our new wives will be sitting with us."

"You're right," agreed one of the others. "What we'll do, then, is make every piece of toast we order with our breakfast correspond with the number of times we did it. That will be our secret code."

They all decided that was an excellent idea and headed for their rooms.

The next day in the hotel dining room, the grooms were all looking a bit dishevelled, but that was nothing compared with the brides, who could barely stagger across the room.

The first groom placed his order with the waitress: "Hello, I'll have the full English breakfast with three pieces of toast please." The other two grooms smiled at him knowingly and raised a glass of fresh orange juice in a toast to his fantastic prowess.

The waitress moved to the second couple and the groom announced: "I, too, would like the full English breakfast, but could I have four pieces of toast?"

His two friends winked in admiration.

Then the waitress got to the last groom who said: "I shall also have the full English breakfast, please, yet I shall have . . . six, yes, six pieces of toast." While the other grooms stared at him in disbelief, the waitress wrote down his order and turned away, but before she could leave, the groom called after her: "And by the way, can you make two of those brown?"

What's the most difficult thing for a woman on her wedding night? – Saying "ouch!" like she means it.

A seventy-six-year-old tycoon and his twenty-year-old bride were on their way from their wedding reception to their honeymoon suite when he suddenly experienced a massive heart attack. Paramedics toiled furiously over his frail body as the ambulance sped across town.

With the tycoon's pulse remaining feeble and erratic, one of the medics turned to the young bride and suggested: "How about giving your husband a few words of encouragement? I think he could use them."

"Okay," she agreed with a shrug. Leaning towards the stretcher, she whispered: "Honey, I hope you perk up real fast. I want to have sex so bad I'm ready to jump on one of these cute guys in white."

On their wedding night, the bride and groom went up to their suite, where she stripped naked in front of him. "Darling," she said tenderly. "Will you love me always?"

"Sounds good to me!" he roared. "I'll try your arse first!"

A well-endowed man married a petite and innocent girl. He was sexually experienced and suggested making love "doggie style" on their wedding night. She didn't know what he was talking about and when he explained it, she flew into a rage and insisted they have sex using the "normal" position or not at all.

Reluctantly, he backed down, but after having sex he was unable to withdraw his penis because it was so big and she was so small. With him still wedged inextricably inside her an hour later, they found themselves in the embarrassing position of having to call an ambulance to take them to the emergency room for help. After hanging up the phone he said to her: "You know, if you had done it the way I wanted we could have walked to the emergency room."

Weight

After having sex with a fat girl, a guy said: "Here, if you want to see me again, call this number."

"Aw," she said sweetly, "men don't usually give me their numbers."

He said: "It's not mine. It's Weight Watchers."

A guy approached a fat girl in a bar and said: "You're a big girl, aren't you?"

"Tell me something I don't know," she said tearfully.

He said: "Salad tastes nice."

An obese boy went to his doctor and asked: "What's the easiest exercise I can do to lose weight?"

The doctor said: "Shake your head from side to side."

"And how often should I do that?" asked the boy.

The doctor replied: "Every time you're offered food!"

How can you tell if your girlfriend is too fat? – When she sits on your face and you can't hear the stereo.

A fat girl was dancing on a table in a nightclub when a guy walked past and said: "Amazing legs!"

She giggled and said with a smile: "Do you really think so?"

"Definitely," he replied. "Most tables would have collapsed by now."

A man walked into a shop to buy an afternoon snack. After spending a few minutes browsing the shelf behind the counter, he said to the shopkeeper: "I'll have a Kit Kat Chunky."

The shopkeeper said: "I may have put on a few pounds, but there's no need for that!"

A fat, ugly girl walked into a bar and announced: "If any of you guys can guess my weight, you can shag me."

Most people simply ignored her, but one guy in the corner shouted out: "Eighty-eight stone, you fat bitch!"

"Close enough," she replied, "you lucky bastard!"

How do you find a fat woman's pussy? – Flip through the folds until you smell shit, then go back one.

A girl in a nightclub asked a fat guy at the bar: "Have you got a pen?"

"Yes," he smiled, thinking she was coming on to him.

"Well," she said, "you'd better get back to it before the farmer notices you're missing!"

If Kate Winslet had dropped a few stone, the *Titanic* wouldn't have sunk. (Joan Rivers)

A fat girl had an accident and her mother took her to hospital. There the nurse asked the girl for her height and weight.

"Five foot seven, eight stone one pound," replied the girl quickly.

As the nurse raised her eyebrows at the information, the mother leaned over and whispered to her daughter: "Sweetheart, this is not the internet."

Who would a fat girl choose to complete her fantasy threesome? – Ben & Jerry.

A fat girl told a guy in a bar: "I want you to take me back to your place and fuck me up the arse!"

He said: "I would but I don't have any lubricant."

"Oh you won't need any, I'm very loose," she winked.

"Maybe so," he replied, "but my door frame is quite narrow."

A man told his girlfriend: "You've got a really fat arse!"

Wounded, she said: "That's below the belt."

He said: "That's the problem: not all of it is."

My girlfriend said she wanted to lose her love handles. I told her she'd look silly without any ears.

Did you hear about the guy who was so fat that his wife had to put an energy-saving light bulb in the fridge?

A large, elderly woman was waiting at the side of the road. When a young man approached, she asked him: "Can you see me across the road?"

He said: "I can see you from half a mile away."

A fat girl announced in the bar: "Last night, a guy made me come with his fingers."

The bartender said: "What were they, Cadbury's?"

A wife turned to her husband in bed and said tenderly: "You know what I think would be really romantic? When I die, I'd like to be buried in my wedding dress."

"Well," he replied, "you'd better hope you die of some kind of wasting disease, then."

A man was in a nightclub when he saw a fat girl standing at the bar. He walked up to her and said: "Fancy a dance, love?"

"Ooh, that would be nice," she replied.

"Well, off you go then," he said. "Me and my mates can't get to the bloody bar!"

How do you get a fat girl into bed? – It's a piece of cake.

Mrs Czernak, who was a little on the chubby side, was attending her regular Weight Watchers meeting. She told the woman next to her: "My husband insists I come to these meetings because he would rather make love to a woman with a trim figure."

"Well," the woman replied, "what's wrong with that?"

"He likes to do it while I'm stuck at these damn meetings!"

My wife's always moaning at me for calling her fat. She yelled: "It's not my fault. It's in my genes!"

I said: "Not all of it is."

A morbidly obese guy became stuck on the toilet during a party.

One of the guests said: "Right, we need two pounds of butter."

"Why?" said another. "To grease the seat?"

"No, to lure him out."

The government is very worried about childhood obesity. I don't know what they can do about it really except for strengthening see-saws. (Sean Lock)

A fat boy came home from school and told his mother: "I got the highest score in PE today."

"Well done," said the mother.

"By the way," added the boy, "what is BMI?"

A young man saw a fat girl in a bar. Her T-shirt said: "Watch out, I'm a maneater!"

He went over to her and said: "Excuse me love, about your T-shirt slogan . . ."

She stopped him and angrily said: "Oh let me guess, you want to know how many men I've eaten?! Well I can't help my size, you know!"

He said: "Actually, no, I wasn't going to say that at all."

"Sorry," she said, brightening. "It's just that I get defensive about my weight. So what was it you wanted to say, then?"

"That's not how you spell manatee."

A man phoned 999. "What's your emergency?" asked the operator.

"Two girls are fighting over me," he replied.

"I see," said the operator. "Well, what's the problem?"

"The fat one's winning!"

The Welsh

An American student of criminal psychology decided to do his thesis on people who sexually abuse animals, in particular men who shag sheep. So he flew to Australia, where he met a sheep farmer who confessed to having sex with some of his ewes.

"How exactly do you do it?" asked the student.

"No worries," said the Aussie. "You just grab it by the tail, hold tight and ram your dick in."

Next the student flew to New Zealand and asked a farmer there the same question.

"We do it the same way as the Aussies," said the New Zealander. "Grab it by the tail, hold on and fuck it from behind."

Finally, the student flew to Wales and asked a farmer there how he had sex with sheep.

"Well, it's a bit awkward, see," said the Welshman. "First you have to find your sheep, then you have to find a stone wall. Then you grab the sheep by the front legs, bend it back over the wall and fuck it like that."

The student was puzzled. "Why don't you fuck the sheep from behind, like they do in Australia and New Zealand?"

"Fuck it from behind?" said the Welshman in a disgusted tone. "How am I supposed to kiss it?"

Why don't Welshmen count sheep to help them get to sleep? – Because when they get to five they have to stop and have a wank.

Why don't Welshmen take their girlfriends to rugby matches? – They'd eat all the grass.

Did you hear that the price of Welsh lamb has just gone up? – It's now £6.95 an hour.

An old Welshman was talking to a newcomer to the village. After a while the old man became increasingly bitter.

"See that row of houses over there?" he said. "I built them, but do they call me Jones the builder? Do they hell! See that railway line? I laid it, but do they call me Jones the engineer? Do they hell! And see those two bridges over the river? I built those, but do they call me Jones the bridge builder? Do they hell! Years ago, I shagged one sheep . . ."

An Englishman, a Welshman and a West Indian were waiting at a hospital for their wives to give birth. There was a lot of pacing up and down before the nurse emerged and happily announced that all three were fathers of bouncing baby boys. "There's just one problem," she said. "Because all three were born at the same time, we got the tags mixed up and we don't know which baby belongs to whom. Would you as their fathers mind coming to identify them?"

The men agreed and walked into the delivery room. The Englishman immediately bent down and picked up the black baby, declaring: "This one's definitely mine."

"Excuse me," said the West Indian, preventing him from taking the baby. "I think it's fairly obvious that this is *my* son."

The Englishman took him to one side and whispered: "I see where you're coming from, pal, but one of the other two babies is Welsh and I'm not prepared to take the risk."

Widows

Two Florida widows were talking and one asked the other: "Do you ever get to feeling horny?"

"Yes," her friend replied.

"What do you do about it?"

"I usually suck on a Lifesaver."

After a moment of stunned silence her friend asked: "What beach do you go to?"

A lonely widow went on an internet dating site in search of her dream man. Her profile stated that she wanted someone who: a) won't hit me; b) won't run off and leave me; and c) must be great in bed.

For weeks she didn't receive a single reply and had almost given up hope when suddenly her doorbell rang. She answered it to find a man with no arms and no legs lying on the doormat.

"Who are you?" she asked.

"I'm your dream man," he replied.

"What makes you think that?" she asked icily.

"I've got no arms, so I can't hit you, and I've got no legs, so I can't run off and leave you."

"What makes you think you're great in bed?"

"Well," he said, "I rang the doorbell, didn't I?"

Women

What's the difference between a woman and a washing machine? – When you dump a load in the washing machine, it doesn't keep calling you for the rest of the week.

What do you show to a woman who has been driving accident-free for ten years? – Second gear.

Did you hear about the new Japanese camera? – It's so fast it can catch a woman with her mouth closed.

Never ask a woman wine-taster whether she spits or swallows.

Men lie the most, but women tell the biggest lies. A man lie is, "I was at Kevin's house!" A woman lie is like, "It's your baby!" (Chris Rock)

Why do women have two sets of lips? – One to argue, one to apologize.

A man spotted his neighbour on the front drive. "Hey, Bill, would you fancy a woman with a big fat arse the size of a tanker?"

"No, I wouldn't."

"How about a woman with breasts that sag so much they nearly hang down to her feet?"

"No, I sure wouldn't."

"Would you fancy a woman with a face so ugly you want to throw up every time you look at her?"

"Hell, no!"

"Well then, keep your filthy hands off my wife!"

What do a nine-volt battery and a woman's butthole have in common? — You know it's wrong, but you'll still end up touching it with your tongue!

Why did God create women? — To carry the semen from the bedroom to the toilet.

I don't think I'll ever meet the perfect woman. I might have to get me one of them mail-order women. You can do that: you send away to the Philippines, and they send you a wife. The only thing is, once you're on their mailing list, they keep sending you a relative a month whether you want it or not. (Adam Ferrara)

Why don't women need to learn to ski? — Because there's no snow between the bedroom and the kitchen.

A guy tried to talk his friend into going to a party. "Come on," he urged, "you never know: you might meet the woman of your dreams."

"I'm not sure," said the friend. "I don't think I want to be seen in public with that filthy slut."

What's the difference between a woman running down the street and a sewing machine? — A sewing machine only has one bobbin.

I find that women are a lot like roller coasters. They won't let me ride them because I'm too fat.

How do you give a woman freedom of speech? — Take your dick out of her mouth.

Things That Only Women Can Understand

- Cats' facial expressions.
- The need for the same style of shoes in different colours.
- Why beansprouts aren't just weeds.
- Fat clothes.
- Taking a car trip without trying to beat your best time.
- The difference between beige, off-white and eggshell.
- The need to find the nearest toilet just as your flight is called for boarding.
- Eyelash curlers.
- The inaccuracy of every bathroom scale ever made.
- Other women.

How do you blind a woman? – Put a windshield in front of her.

Why are most serial killers men? – Because women prefer to kill one man slowly over many, many years.

You know, men and women are a lot alike in certain situations. Like when they're both on fire they're exactly alike. (Dave Attell)

What's the most active muscle in a woman? – The penis.

Why are women like cartons of orange juice? – It's not the shape or size that matters or even how sweet the juice is: it's getting those tricky flaps open.

Two men were admiring a magazine photo of a famous actress. "Still," said one, "if you take away her fabulous hair, her magnificent breasts, her beautiful eyes, her gorgeous smile, her perfect cheekbones, her cute nose and her stunning figure, what are you left with?"
    The other replied: "My wife."

Women are like wine: you can only afford the cheap ones with big, ugly boxes that leak.

Why do women wear panties with flowers printed on them? – In loving memory of all the faces that have been buried there.

1 The woman goes to the store.
2 The woman fixes the salad, vegetables and dessert.
3 The woman prepares the meat for cooking, places it on a tray along with the necessary cooking utensils, and takes it to the man, who is lounging beside the grill, drinking a beer.
4 The man places the meat on the grill.
5 The woman goes inside to set the table and check the vegetables.
6 The woman comes out to tell the man that the meat is burning.
7 The man takes the meat off the grill and hands it to the woman.
8 The woman prepares the plates and brings them to the table.
9 After eating, the woman clears the table and does the dishes.
10 The man asks the woman how she enjoyed "her night off." And, upon seeing her annoyed reaction, he concludes that there's just no pleasing some women.

My ex-girlfriend's a lecturer. But then again, aren't they all? (Alistair Barrie)

Three men were discussing what part of a woman's body they liked best.
    The first said: "I like to see a woman's tits best."
    The second said: "I like to look at a woman's arse."
    The third said: "I prefer to see the top of her head."

A new study claims that you can tell a lot about a woman by the position in which she sleeps. It says women who sleep on their sides are sensitive, women who sleep on their stomachs are competent and women who sleep on their backs with their ankles behind their ears are popular.

Why can't women play ice hockey? – They have to change their pads after every period.

Why did God create Eve? – Adam demanded it as soon as he discovered he couldn't suck his own cock.

A woman said to her husband one day: "Show me your feminine side."

"Okay," he replied, and walked out the door.

When he returned fifty minutes later, she snapped: "Where have you been?" He said: "I've been parking the car."

What is six inches long and makes a man groan as soon as a woman touches it? – A gearstick.

Women can be much like volcanoes – ready to blow at any time, but probably never will.

One day, long, long ago, there lived a woman who did not nag or complain. But it was a long time ago, and it was just that one day.

She's Definitely a Keeper if You Hear Her Say . . .

- This porno scene is boring. Fast-forward to the gang bang.
- I've been complaining a lot lately. I don't blame you for ignoring me.
- I know I'm sore and my parents are in the next room, but I still want you right now!
- Why does a woman need more than two pairs of shoes anyway?
- Don't get up, I kinda like sleeping in the wetspot.
- You sure you don't mind me always dressing up in leather?
- Everybody at work is talking about that picture of my fanny you posted on Facebook. It's great. I've never been so popular.
- I love hearing stories about your ex-girlfriends. Tell me more.
- I bet it would be kinky to watch you with our babysitter.
- I hate chick flicks. Let's watch some sport instead.
- I've decided to buy myself a boob job. How big do you want 'em?
- When can your friends come round to watch us again?
- That girl is wearing the same outfit as I am. Cool! I'm going to go over and talk to her.
- The new girl in my office is a stripper. I invited her over for dinner on Saturday.
- Honey, did you leave that skid in the toilet bowl? Good one!
- I'm so happy with my new hairstyle. I don't think I'll ever change it again.
- I'll swallow it all. I love the taste.
- Are you sure you've had enough to drink?
- I've decided to stop wearing clothes around the house.
- I'd rather watch football and drink beer with you than go shopping.

- Would you like to watch me go down on my girlfriend?
- Say, let's go down to the mall so you can check out women's asses.
- I'll be out painting the house.
- I love it when you play golf on Sundays; I just wish you had time to play on Saturdays, too.
- Honey, our new neighbour is sunbathing topless again. Come and see!
- I know it's a lot tighter back there but would you please try again?
- No, no, I'll take the car to have the oil changed.
- Your mother is way better than mine.
- I signed up for yoga so that I can get my ankles behind my head for you.
- I understand fully – our anniversary comes every year. You go hunting with the guys – it's a wonderful stress reliever.
- God, if I don't get to blow you soon, I swear I'm gonna bust!

Feminism: it's fine as a hobby, but it's not going to get you a husband.

All these programmes on TV about women being domestic goddesses are just not true. I'd like to have a programme that truly represented how women approach housework. And if I did, it would be called *Fuck it, That'll Do.* (Jo Brand)

Ray, Carl and Jim were sitting in a bar talking about their favourite subject – women. In particular they talked about how they rated women from one to ten, and decided to compare their systems by rating each new woman that walked in.

The first woman that came in was a cute little redhead. She had a lovely figure and a pert arse. Ray said: "I reckon she's an eight. Carl agreed, but Jim said: "I wouldn't give her more than a one."

"Only a one?" said the others. "That's a bit harsh."

A few minutes later, a busty blonde walked in wearing a skirt so short it was little more than a belt. She had full, luscious lips. Ray said: "She's a nine in my book. Carl agreed, but Jim said: "A two at the most."

"Is that all?" said the others. "You're hard to please."

Five minutes later, a gorgeous leggy brunette walked in wearing a pair of leather trousers that stuck to her like a second skin. Every pair of male eyes in the bar turned to gawp at her beauty.

"Wow!" said Ray. "A perfect ten if ever there was one."

"Definitely a ten," agreed Carl. "My dream woman."

They turned to Jim for his rating. "Yeah, she's about a four," he said.

The others shook their heads in disbelief. "How can you say she's a four? What ratings scale are you using?"

"The Clydesdale Scale," replied Jim.

"What's the Clydesdale Scale?" they asked.

"Well," said Jim, "I just try to estimate how many Clydesdale horses it would take to pull my face off hers."

Moods of a Woman

An angel of truth and a dream of fiction,
A woman is a bundle of contradiction.
She's afraid of a wasp, will scream at a mouse,
But will tackle her boyfriend alone in the house.
She'll take him for better, she'll take him for worse,
She'll break open his head and then be his nurse.
But when he's well and can get out of bed,
She'll pick up the teapot and aim for his head.
Beautiful and keenly sighted, yet blind,
Crafty and cruel, yet simple and kind.
She'll call him a king, then make him a clown,
Raise him on a pedestal, then knock him flat down.
She'll inspire him to deeds that ennoble man
Or make him her lackey to carry her fan.
She'll run away from him and never come back
But if he runs away, then she'll be on his tracks.
Sour as vinegar, sweet as a rose,
She'll kiss you one minute, then turn up her nose.
She'll win you in leather, enchant you in silk,
She'll be stronger than brandy, milder than milk.
At times she'll be vengeful, merry and sad.
She'll hate you like poison, and love you like mad.

Moods of a Man

Horny.

Work

At the office party, a young woman told her friend: "You won't believe this, but I've just been geesed."

"You mean goosed?" said the friend.

"No, I know the difference between one finger and three!"

The police were investigating the mysterious death of a leading businessman who had jumped from the window of his twelfth-floor office. His voluptuous private secretary could offer no explanation for the action but said that her boss had been acting peculiarly ever since she started working for him a month ago.

"After my very first week on the job," she said, "I received a £50 pay rise. At the end of the second week he called me into his private office, gave me a lovely black nightie, five pairs of expensive nylon stockings and said: 'These are for a beautiful, efficient secretary.' At the end of the third week he gave me a fabulous Gucci jacket, then this afternoon, he called me into his private office again, presented me with this amazing diamond bracelet and asked me if I would consider making love to him and what it would cost. I told him that I would, and because he had been so nice to me, he could have it for £10, although I was charging all the other boys in the office £15. That's when he jumped out the window."

I fell asleep on my first night working for the Samaritans and I woke to find I had twenty-four missed calls. They can't have been important, though, because when I rang back no one answered.

A techno-geek was working late at the office when his friend dropped by to see him.

"How you doing, buddy?" asked the friend.

"Yeah, I'm good. Did you see my new secretary on the way in?"

"Yeah, she's gorgeous. How did you persuade her to work late?"

"Easy, and I'm glad you like her, because – believe it or not – she's a robot! She does everything I tell her."

"A robot?" queried the friend. "No way!"

"She's the latest model from Japan. Let me tell you how she works. If you squeeze her left boob, she takes dictation; if you squeeze her right boob, she takes a letter. And that's not all – she can have sex, too!"

"You're kidding, right?"

"No, she's something else, I tell you! Why don't you borrow her for ten minutes or so while I finish off a few things here?"

So the friend took the robot secretary into the lavatory. At first there was silence but after a couple of minutes terrible screams could be heard.

"Damn!" thought the geek. "I forgot to tell him her arse is a pencil sharpener!"

If you have a shitty job, you probably shouldn't lick your fingers at lunchtime.

A computer user rang WordPerfect Customer Support.

A voice at the other end answered: "Customer Support, how may I help you?"

The caller said: "I'm having trouble with WordPerfect."

"What sort of trouble?"

"Well, I was just typing along and all of a sudden the words went away."

"Went away?"

"They disappeared."

"Hmm. So what does your screen look like now?"

"Nothing."

"Nothing?"

"It's blank; it won't accept anything when I type."

"Are you still in WordPerfect, or did you get out?"

"How do I tell?"

"Can you see the C: prompt on the screen?"

"What's a sea-prompt?"

"Never mind. Can you move the cursor around on the screen?"

"There isn't any cursor. I told you, it won't accept anything I type."

"Does your monitor have a power indicator?"

"What's a monitor?"

"It's the thing with the screen on it that looks like a TV. Does it have a little light that tells you when it's on?"

"I don't know."

"Well, then look on the back of the monitor and find where the power cord goes into it. Can you see that?"

"Yes, I think so."

"Great. Follow the cord to the plug and tell me if it's plugged into the wall."

"Yes, it is."

"When you were behind the monitor, did you notice that there were two cables plugged into the back of it, not just one?"

"No."

"Well, there are. I need you to look back there again and find the other cable."

"Uh, okay, here it is."

"Right. Follow it for me, and tell me if it's plugged securely into the back of your computer."

"I can't reach."

"Uh huh. Well, can you see if it is?"

"No."

"Even if you maybe put your knee on something and lean over?"

"Oh, it's not because I don't have the right angle – it's because it's dark."

"Dark?"

"Yes – the office light is off, and the only light I have is coming in from the window."

"Well, turn on the office light, then."

"I can't."

"No? Why not?"

"Because there's a power outage."

"A power outage, you say? Ah . . . okay, we've got it licked now. Do you still have the boxes and manuals and packing stuff your computer came in?"

"Well, yes, I keep them in the closet."

"Good. Go get them, and unplug your system and pack it up just like it was when you got it. Then take it back to the store you bought it from."

"Really? Is it that bad?"

"Yes, I'm afraid it is."

"Well, all right then. What do I tell them?"

"Tell them you're too stupid to own a computer."

I got a job at a paperless office. Everything was great until I needed a shit.

I used to work in an eczema clinic doing exfoliations. It wasn't a great job – I was barely scraping a living. (Andrew Lawrence)

A guy went for the job of cook in a café. The boss asked: "Can you fry eggs?"

"Can I fry eggs?! I've worked in some of the top hotels in England. Give me half a dozen."

So he was given six eggs, which he immediately started to juggle. After a minute of brilliant juggling, he lobbed the eggs one by one over his shoulder towards the frying pan behind him. Each egg hit the side of the pan, cracked open and the shell fell into the bin below while the eggs slid unbroken into the frying pan.

"That's amazing," said the boss, "but it must have been a fluke."

"A fluke! Give me a dozen." The guy then proceeded to do even more elaborate juggling before repeating the spectacular finale so that there were now eighteen unbroken eggs sizzling in the frying pan.

"Well," he asked, admiring his handiwork, "do I get the job?"

"No," said the boss. "You piss about too much."

Norm had just returned to his London office after attending a week-long course in Manchester. His boss took one look at him and asked if he was sick.

"Well," said Norm, "between you and me, I met this beautiful blonde on the course. She's a sales rep who's keen to do business with us, and one thing led to another and we ended up having wild sex in her hotel room all night."

"Okay," said the boss, "that may explain your fatigue, but why are your eyes so red?"

"You see," continued Norm, "it turns out she's married and has a baby at home. She started crying with remorse, and when I thought about my own wife and kids, I started crying too."

"That's all very well," said the boss disapprovingly, "but the course finished on Friday. How come you still look so terrible?"

Norm said: "You can't sit there crying four or five times a day for four days and not look like this!"

What I don't like about office Christmas parties is looking for a job the next day. (Phyllis Diller)

I got sacked from my job as a bingo caller last week. Apparently "a meal for two with a terrible view" isn't considered an appropriate way to announce the number sixty-nine.

A middle manager got hopelessly drunk at the office Christmas party and made a fool of himself in front of his boss. His wife told him the awful truth the following morning.

"You behaved appallingly," she told him. "At one point you went up to your boss and started jabbing him in the stomach with your finger. You were really aggressive."

"Really?" said the husband, shocked.

"Yes," said the wife. "You told him exactly what you thought of him, and you probably can't remember, but he was furious."

"Well," said the husband, in a display of bravado, "it serves him right. He's an arsehole. Piss on him!"

"You did," said the wife, "and that's why he fired you."

"Well, screw him!"

"I did," said the wife, "and that's why you're back at work on Monday."

Two guys met up in a bar. "How did the job hunting go?" asked one.

The other said: "I've been offered a job, £750 a week, working for the Brittle Bone Society."

"Did you accept?"

"I snapped his hand off."

A guy in his first week in a new job called in on the Monday to say: "Sorry, I can't come in today. I'm sick." And it was the same story for the next four Mondays: each time he phoned in to say he was sick.

His boss didn't want to lose him but felt it necessary to address the situation. "You seem to have trouble getting in to work on Mondays," he said. "Is there anything we can do to help you? Do you have a problem, maybe with drink or drugs?"

"No," said the guy, "I don't do drugs and I don't drink. But my brother-in-law drinks heavily every weekend and then starts hitting my sister. So every Monday morning I go over to her place to make sure she's okay. I comfort her and, well, one thing leads to another and we end up in bed."

The boss was disgusted. "You mean you screw your own sister?"

"Hey," said the guy, "I told you I was sick."

Jim and Dave were sitting in the office chatting when a pretty girl passed them on the way to the toilet. Jim said: "I think she's really nice."

"Well, don't be shy," said Dave. "Go over and give her the old patter."

"The patter?" queried Jim, who was not as experienced with girls as his friend.

"Yes, the patter," repeated Dave.

"But I don't know any patter," said Jim. "I've never found it easy to talk to girls."

"For crying out loud," said Dave despairingly, "it's easy: all you have to say is, 'hello' and she will say, 'hello'. Then say, 'It's a nice day, isn't it?' Then she will say, 'Yes, it is.' Then you say, 'But not half as nice as you!' Then she will say, 'Oh, thank you.' Then the patter will just flow. Look, there she is now, coming back out of the toilet. Go and give it a go."

So, nervously Jim headed towards the girl, all the while re-running the patter in his head. He walked up to her and said, "Hello."

"Hello."

"It's a nice day, isn't it?"

"Yes, it is."

"But not half as nice as you!"

"Oh, thank you."

There were a few seconds of uneasy silence, eventually broken by Jim asking nonchalantly: "Been for a shit, then?"

CRAZY SH*T OLD PEOPLE SAY

Edited by Geoff Tibballs

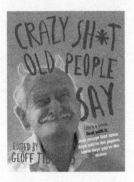

ISBN: 978-1-84901-715-2

Price: £6.99

'I have twelve CDs. I listen to eight of them. I like four of them. Why the f*ck would I need something that holds 30,000 songs?'

With old age comes grey hair, dodgy knees, a passion for *Murder, She Wrote* re-runs and an apparent God-given licence to speak one's mind without fear of retribution.

Under the guise of passing on the benefits of their experience, old people exercise their right to swear and insult. These feisty philosophers take no prisoners as they use their scalpel-like tongues to dissect modern life.

If challenged over their outrageous comments, they'll play the age card: you know the type – 'I'm eighty-six, I've fought for my country, and if I want to call you a useless f*ckwit, then I'll call you a useless f*ckwit, Vicar.'

Visit www.constablerobinson.com for more information

THE MAMMOTH BOOK OF FILTHY LIMERICKS

Edited by Glyn Rees

ISBN: 978-1-84529-682-7
Price: £7.99

The ultimate collection of X-rated and decidedly politically incorrect limericks!

This bumper new volume contains over 2,000 dirty verses, from the moderately blue to the absolutely filthy – all illustrated throughout by Gray Jolliffe, creator of the bestselling Wicked Willie cartoon character.

Here are verses so rude that even a blonde would blush, on subjects ranging from the bedroom to the bathroom and beyond. You'll find plenty of up-to-date limericks relevant to contemporary life as well as lewd old favourites on every imaginable topic, all of them guaranteed to make you laugh. Includes many newly devised limericks.

On the breast of a barmaid named Gail
Was written the price of the ale
And on her behind,
For the sake of the blind
Was the same information in Braille.

Visit www.constablerobinson.com for more information

THE MAMMOTH BOOK OF ONE LINERS

Edited by Geoff Tibballs

ISBN: 978-1-78033-8

Price: £7.99

**Over 10,000 side-splitting one liners,
covering more than 300 subjects**

This bumper collection of quick-fire jokes features a wealth of
new material alongside some old favourites. They range from
surreal observations to subtle wordplay and include what must
surely be a candidate for the world's shortest joke:
Pretentious? Moi?

I said to my doctor, 'I can't say my T's, F's or H's.'
He said, 'You can't say fairer than that.'

Never get stuck behind the Devil in a Post Office queue,
for the Devil can take many forms.

Never Moon A Werewolf

She criticized my apartment, so I knocked her flat.

Shelling shells by the sea shore, easier done than said.

Visit www.constablerobinson.com for more information

THE MAMMOTH BOOK OF TASTELESS JOKES

edited by Geoff Tibballs

ISBN: 978-1-84901-055-9

Price: £7.99

Something to offend absolutely everyone!

Thousands of off-color jokes, covering every taboo from sex and death to age and disability. No depth has been left unplumbed, no barrel unscraped, no bar left raised to bring you this epic collection of triple-X-rated jokes. There is little to no inoffensive material gathered here—a fantastic new collection of bad taste and political incorrectness. If you even think of laughing, you're a monster; if you buy it, you're beyond redemption.

My father is in a coma.
He's just living the dream.

What if God is a woman?
Not only am I going to hell, I'll never know why.

One-armed waiters.
They can take it, but they can't dish it out.

How many paranoiacs does it take to change a light bulb?
Who wants to know?

Visit www.constablerobinson.com for more information